DEVELOPMENT OF COGNITION, AFFECT, AND SOCIAL RELATIONS

The Minnesota Symposia
on Child Psychology
Volume 13

DEVELOPMENT OF COGNITION, AFFECT, AND SOCIAL RELATIONS

The Minnesota Symposia
on Child Psychology
Volume 13

EDITED BY

W. ANDREW COLLINS

University of Minnesota

LEA LAWRENCE ERLBAUM ASSOCIATES, PUBLISHERS

1980   Hillsdale, New Jersey

Lawrence Erlbaum Associates, Inc., Publishers
365 Broadway
Hillsdale, New Jersey 07642

Library of Congress Cataloging in Publication Data

Minnesota Symposium on Child Psychology, 13th, University
of Minnesota, 1978.
Development of cognition, affect, and social relations.

Papers from the conference sponsored by the Institute
of Child Development, University of Minnesota.
"The Minnesota Symposia on Child Psychology,
volume 13."
Includes bibliographical references and index.
1. Child psychology—Congresses. 2. Cognition
in children—Congresses. 3. Affect (Psychology)—Con-
gresses. 4. Social interaction—Congresses.
I. Collins, W. Andrew, 1944- II. Minnesota
University. Institute of Child Development. III. Title.
[DNLM: 1. Cognition—In infancy and childhood—
Congresses. 2.Affect—In infancy and childhood—
Congresses. 3. Social behavior—In infancy and child-
hood—Congresses. 4. Socialization—Congresses.
5. Child development—Congresses. W3 M1607 v. 13 1978/
WS105.5.S6 M622 1978d]
BF721.M545 1978   155.4   79-27560
ISBN 0-89859-023-X

Printed in the United States of America

Contents

Preface

The 13th annual Minnesota Symposium on Child Psychology was held in Minneapolis on October 26–28, 1978. As has been the tradition in this series, six developmental scholars were invited to present their work within the programmatic perspective in which it was conceived. Although in most years the contributors have been drawn from a variety of areas of developmental study, the contributors to this volume work within the area of developmental social psychology, encompassing the range of problems surrounding the development of social relations, social cognition, and affective systems.

This focus is one that has stimulated remarkable activity and diversity in recent years. The decade of the 1970s has seen a resurgence of interest in the study of emotion in both social and developmental psychology. Developmental studies of social cognition have also burgeoned, partly as an outgrowth of cognitive-developmental influences generally and partly because of increasing cognitive emphases within social psychology. Even studies of childhood social relations, which constitute a rich tradition in child psychology, have shown new vigor from the infusion of theoretical perspectives from evolutionary theory and a renewed respect for the methods and value of observational research.

By and large, however, these remarkable trends have occurred in parallel; and the choice of a focus on developmental social psychology in this volume partly reflects the need for cognitive, affective, and social-relations perspectives to be brought together into a more inclusive, coherent view of social development. Although the symposium could not be expected to achieve an integration of this sort in itself, it was hoped that the juxtaposition of chapters about current significant research on social, cognitive, and affective development might stimulate more integrative efforts in the future. Some commentaries on possibilities for integration among the six 1978 contributions are offered in Chapter 7 of this volume.

Both the value and the probable difficulty of an integrative view are apparent in the diversity of the chapters presented here. The range includes a consideration of infant emotional development, observational studies of the nature and organization of peer relations in early childhood, longitudinal research on personality constructs relevant to children's social mastery and coping, and laboratory-experimental studies of attributions and inferences about social events. There is variation not only in the domains of interest but in the methods and the ages of the participants in the research.

In Chapter 1, Robert Emde lays a foundation for the consideration of emotion in social development by proposing a *biosocial* framework for the meaning of infant facial expressions. Drawing on both psychoanalytic ego formulations and evolutionary views, he suggests that infant emotions be viewed both in terms of their relevance to the physiological, organizational, and coping states of the child and in terms of the social meanings attributed to them by caregivers. Working even more clearly within the ego psychology tradition, Jeanne Block and Jack Block (Chapter 2) describe the conceptual underpinnings and early data from their long-term longitudinal study of the personality constructs they have labeled *ego-control* and *ego-resiliency*. Like Emde's, theirs is a broad view of emotional development, in which they place affective expression and control within the framework of individual children's capacity for coping with a range of experiences. Their chapter in this volume reflects detailed consideration of the psychometric and methodological issues that surround the personality constructs they propose and, particularly, the study of their developmental stability.

In Chapter 3, by Bernard Weiner, Anna Kun, and Marijana Benesh-Weiner, the emphasis shifts from affect per se to the role of cognition in affective responses and social behavior. Elaborating the attributional perspective, to which Weiner has been a major contributor in the social-psychology literature, these collaborators propose that attribution provides a new and useful vantage point on emotional states relevant to social interaction and development. They report new data on attributions of mastery, achievement, and morality; and they argue that by incorporating an attributional perspective into the study of social development, the behavioral relevance of the child's own feelings and his perceptions of the feelings of others can be better understood. Thomas Shultz's concern in Chapter 4 is to examine in detail the nature of a fundamental social atttibution—*intentionality*. Shultz offers a historical and philosophical explication of the concept of intention, and he reports a group of new, ingenious studies of children's understanding of intentionality and their ability to use intention information in making social judgments, such as those involving morality.

By contrast to the traditional experimental approaches in the chapters on cognition, Chapters 5 and 6 on peer relations involve the observational methods that are being increasingly relied on in the study of social development. In Chapter 5, F. F. Strayer, whose research reflects his ethological perspective, describes an analysis of the social ecology of peer relations in the preschool, including both dominance and affiliative relations. He relies on observations of a number of nonverbal interactive behaviors in deriving the patterns he reports. By contrast, in Chapter 6, John Gottman's work with Jennifer Parkhurst involves the sequential analysis of conversations between young peers. Gottman observed dyads of children in their homes rather than in larger groups; and he extensively considers the methodological and analytic problems—and advantages—associated with such naturalistic data. His approach to the analysis of sequences, which is also being attempted by other investigators, represents a tool that may well be fundamental to integrative studies of social development.

Although lacunae can be identified within each of the parallel, independent research directions represented by these six chapters, striking and stimulating possibilities also become apparent in the potential interplay between them. What, for example, might be the pertinence of ego-resiliency and ego-control for the ways in which children make social attributions to themselves and others? How may the play and conversations of young peers reflect their attributional tendencies, and how may both function in achieving mastery of new situations? How may biosocial views of emotional development be related to children's dominance and affiliative tendencies in peer relations? In Chapter 7, Carroll Izard, Richard Shweder, and Willard Hartup raise additional questions and problems for the pursuit of an integrative viewpoint.

The first six chapters were initially presented during conference sessions that included not only the contributors' presentations but also discussion by a large audience from the University of Minnesota and neighboring colleges and universities. The discussion at each session was led by a roundtable of developmental and social psychologists whose interests were especially pertinent to the presentations. Many of their comments are reflected in the chapters as they appear in this volume, and their contributions are gratefully acknowledged. Those participating in roundtables were William Charlesworth, Robert Fisch, Norman Garmezy, John P. Hill, Judith Langlois, Shirley Moore, Mark Snyder, Alan Sroufe, June Tapp, and Tom Trabasso. In addition, three members of the Social Science Research Council's Committee attended the symposium sessions and participated as roundtable members. They were Carroll Izard, University of Delaware; Willard Hartup, Institute of Child Development, University of Minnesota; and Richard Shweder, University of Chicago.

The Minnesota Symposium is funded annually by PHS Grant No. 1S13 HD-10650 from the National Institute of Child Health and Human

Development to the Institute of Child Development. It is also carried out cooperatively by the faculty, staff, and students of the Institute of Child Development, whose efforts should be recognized here. Special acknowledgment is given to the Minnesota Symposium committee, composed of the following: Douglas Bolin, Judith Brady, Joyce Brady, Mary Anne Chalkley, Helen Dickison, Wayne Duncan, Virginia Eaton, Wendy Gibson, Elizabeth Haugen, Judith List, Frank Manis, and Richard Omanson. In addition, Ulrike Richardson was an efficient and enterprising assistant and secretary throughout the symposium and the preparation of this volume.

The pleasure of editing a volume such as this comes largely in the opportunity to work with talented contributors like the authors of the chapters that follow. I appreciate both their intellectual and their personal colleagueship in this enterprise.

W. ANDREW COLLINS
Minneapolis, Minnesota

1 Levels of Meaning for Infant Emotions: A Biosocial View

Robert N. Emde
University of Colorado Medical Center

I believe we stand on the threshold of a new era in our scientific understanding of the emotional life of the infant. Cross-cultural studies of adult facial expression and a renewed emphasis on analyzing patterned emotional responses (Ekman, Friesen, & Ellsworth, 1972; Izard, 1971) have given a dramatic impetus to the psychological study of emotions. At the same time, our burgeoning knowledge of the human infant as a biologically active and socially interactive being has increased our awareness of a lag in our knowledge of emotional development. We know much more about the domains of perception and cognition than we do about emotion, as several recent reviews have documented (Charlesworth & Kreutzer, 1973; Haith & Campos, 1977; Lewis & Rosenblum, 1978; Oster & Ekman, 1978; Sroufe, 1979). This lag is especially dramatic for clinicians, for whom emotional expressions are an essential orienting feature of our everyday work with patients of all ages. Even though infants cannot tell us how they feel, they have other ways of communicating emotions; and we should be able to understand more.

But a lag in knowledge does not ensure an advance, and the reader may wonder about the source of my optimism. More than anything else, such optimism stems from today's scientific climate of multidisciplinary endeavor. Kessen (1965) has documented how, earlier in this century, different theoretical approaches to child study selfconsciously fostered isolation and polemicism. In contrast, as I see it, progress today in a discipline is most often facilitated by challenges from other disciplines. Alternative points of view are sought not just for critical tests of hypotheses, but for novel ideas and for approaches found only at the boundaries between disciplines.

This essay presents a view about infant emotions that has emerged from our laboratory in recent years. It is entitled "biosocial" for simplicity (our frame of reference obviously being developmental psychology) and for emphasis of a neglected interface between biological and social aspects of emotional development. In appreciation of the high degree of organized complexity in human functioning, I argue for the usefulness of a "levels of meaning" approach for understanding infant emotional development. Although the paper highlights aspects of our own work, a special plea is made for interdisciplinary *collaborative* research efforts at a critical time in the development of our field. I conclude with some thoughts about the adaptive nature of infant emotions and their signaling functions.

THE EVOLUTION OF ORGANIZED COMPLEXITY AND VIEWING EMOTIONS

The extraordinary extent of organized complexity in human functioning is an essential background for our thinking about development. Indeed, modern biology has been characterized as the biology of organized complexity, in contrast to a biology of former times that was mainly concerned with linear and noninteractive effects. Platt (1966) has emphasized that an evolutionary perspective shows man to be the most complex entity of the universe; and, for scientists, such complexity forever ensures a large amount of indeterminacy and privacy with respect to understanding human behavior. As aspects of an individual's complex functioning, it is not surprising that human emotions elude precise or comprehensive definition.

One thing is certain: In the field of infant emotions, in the study of increasingly organized complexity, we cannot proceed from isolation. We need multiple views that tap different levels of meaning. Emotions are parts of an array of complex human systems that are in continuous interaction, that are often hierarchically arranged at different levels of organization, and that can be characterized as having varying degrees of stability or change.

In this connection, I believe there is one view about emotions that can be misleading. In this view, verbal designations of emotion states offer temporary shortcuts for description before scientific specification is possible. In one form or another, this has been put forth by Hebb (1946) and his work with chimpanzees, by Mandler (1975) in a general way, and by Bowlby (1969) and Kagan (1978) in consideration of work with human infants. An implication of this view is that emotion terms are useful *only* at an early stage of investigation, that they represent *only* global, intuitive, and inexact formulations, and that with the advance of science, designation of "emotion states" will become unnecessary. We think there is more to it (Emde &

Gaensbauer, in press). A biosocial view, incorporated by many (e.g., Chevalier-Skolnikoff, 1973; Darwin, 1872; Izard, 1977; Kaufman & Rosenblum, 1967; Tomkins, 1962, 1963) leads to the conclusion that emotional states represent complex systems of organized functioning inherent in the human person, states that are generally advantageous to the species as well as to the individual in the course of development. Evolutionary considerations seem to highlight both the complexity of emotions and their centrality in social adaptation.

Hamburg (1963) concluded that human emotions evolved because of a selective advantage in facilitating social bonds. In reviewing the course of primate evolution, he speculated that group living operated as a powerful adaptive mechanism and that, because of this, the formation of social bonds has been experienced as pleasurable and their disruption as unpleasurable. He pointed to the widespread prominence of psychophysiological changes associated with the disruption of social bonds and of instrumental behaviors that are mobilized for restoring such bonds. The research of Myers (1976) involving free-ranging and laboratory macaques provides some experimental support for the close relations between emotions and social life. Myers found that emotional and social behaviors are controlled by the same forebrain areas (prefrontal, anterotemporal, and orbitofrontal cortex), and when these regions were surgically ablated, facial expressions and vocalizations ordinarily used in emotional behavior and in social communication were unavailable for these purposes. When released from captivity, ablated animals wandered through their social groups without interacting; all indications pointed to the fact that they did not survive in what amounted to an emotionless state of aloneness.

When one looks at the evolution of primate facial expressions, one perceives a continuation of this theme: Such evolution may have occurred concomitant with the enhancement of visual capacity that brought advantageous functions of social communication for group-living species (see Andrew 1964; vanHooff, 1962; and especially the extensive review of Chevalier-Skolnikoff, 1973). Chevalier-Skolnikoff points out that in monkeys there is a shift from the prosimians to the old world monkeys and beyond—a shift marked by increasing facial expressiveness and visual function concomitant with decreasing emphasis on olfaction, touch, and sound reception. Such a shift also corresponds to a change from a nocturnal to a diurnal ecological niche and to engagement in a more complex social world.

In the evolutionary step to man, facial muscles became further differentiated in connection with speech and, as Chevalier-Skolinikoff emphasizes (1973), social communication of more subtle internal states occurs more through language than through facial expression of emotion.

Nonetheless, cross-cultural evidence that a number of discrete facial expressions, representing qualitatively separable emotional response systems, are universally recognized and expressed throughout the human species would indicate that facial expressions have continued adaptive importance (Ekman, 1971; Ekman, Friesen, & Ellsworth, 1972; Izard, 1971, 1972, 1977). Indeed, the case could be made that emotional expressions persist in the human as a univeral "language," one that is clarified and modulated by speech.

A biosocial view highlights that in human infancy, without language, emotional expressions are prominent and provide a medium of messages in the infant—caregiver system. Some messages are unequivocal and biologically necessary to the infant's survival. Crying communicates distress and gives a universal peremptory message, "come, change something"; whereas smiling communicates pleasure to caregivers and conveys, "keep it up, I like it" (Stechler & Carpenter, 1967). Further, an expression of interest reveals a readiness for learning and, for the infant, the emotion of surprise may have a basic role in facilitating the assimilation of new information (Charlesworth, 1969). Whatever specific messages such expressions as fear, anger, sadness may give in later infancy, it is certain that cognitive development increasingly alters the meaning of emotional states both before and during language development.

MEANING AND EMOTIONAL DEVELOPMENT

More than 15 years ago at a symposium on emotions, Knapp (1963) reminded participants that emotions could be viewed from three aspects—physiology, expression, and private experience. Such a scheme is useful and points out our limitations in researching emotions of preverbal infants who cannot tell us how they feel. I would now like to offer another scheme, a developmental one, that emerges from a biosocial view and emphasizes levels of meaning useful for multidisciplinary research. This scheme can be superimposed on Knapp's and has the advantage that levels of meaning apply to all aspects of behavior and serve as a guide for research questions.

The scheme has two major domains, the individual and the social. Each domain has three levels of meaning: the level of biological response, the level of organizational state, and the level of enduring trait. Further, each level of meaning has two aspects. The first is a description of patterns of behavior, and the second is a context analysis. Since contemporary researchers are interested in more than linear effects and concern themselves with interactions between levels, a context analysis explores the "boundary conditions" of phenomena, the operational principles of the system, and the especial defining conditions wherein the described patterns may or may not occur (Polanyi, 1965/1974). I now discuss the scheme, highlighting some thoughts emerging from our own research.

The Individual Domain of Meaning

At the Level of Biological Response

Sound, scientific understanding begins with a full description of species-wide behavioral patterns and how they occur. Much has been learned at this level of meaning about smiling, crying, responses to maternal separation, and other infant emotional responses (see reviews of Charlesworth & Kreutzer, 1973; Sroufe, 1979). Still, as Oster and Ekman (1978) remind us, there is much to be investigated in the area of facial-action patterns related to infant emotion. Further, patterns of posture, gaze behavior, vocalization, and temporal patterns of emotion are in need of study.

Another area hardly touched by our investigative probes relates to "spontaneous" emotional activity. In a recent study of fear, surprise, and happiness in 10–12 month-old infants, Hiatt (1978) found that control groups of infants who were not placed in emotion-eliciting situations displayed a variety of emotional activities. There was no "zero baseline" for facial expressions of emotion. In the experimental and naturalistic investigation of emotional elicitation, perhaps we ought to pay more attention to studying base rates of emotional activity. It seems to me that the human organism is primed to be emotional, that emotional activity is ongoing and fluctuates in accordance with a variety of stimulus circumstances or "incentive events," as Kagan (1978) has put it. Stimuli can be internal, from rhythmic pacemakers and internal disturbances, as well as external.

Such considerations bring us to context analysis—defining the conditions under which patterns may occur. Context analysis necessarily penetrates to other levels of meaning, forces us beyond our isolated territory of description and provides the technical basis for the replicability and generalizability of findings. First, context analysis rests on an adequate description of one's study population and the conditions under which observervations were made. Beyond this, it involves modes of sampling. I like to think that in a context analysis, one must consider the triad of *performance, competence, and relevance*. In other words, for an organized behavior, one must consider what is usual, what occurs under optimal (or special) conditions, and also what is naturalistically relevant or "ecologically valid." The field of infant developmental assessment may be illustrative. For years, there has been a focus on competence, often to the exclusion of other aspects; now, as assessment instruments are used to document more abut what is so, as opposed to what can be so, investigators are beginning to turn their attention to the other two aspects of context analysis (see Sameroff, 1978).

The importance of context analysis can also be illustrated using two examples from contemporary research on infant emotional development. There was recently a debate in the literature as the whether "stranger distress" or "stranger anxiety" exists as a regular developmental event (Rheingold & Eckerman, 1973). A context analysis settles the issue. Those investigators who emphasize a stranger's somewhat abrupt and close approach and who do longitudinal study are apt to see the phenomenon; those who emphasize a gradual warmup from a distance and who use cross-sectional study are less likely to see the phenomenon. In addition, the phenomenon is more likely to occur with mother and familiar figures absent (e.g., Campos, Emde, Gaensbauer, & Henderson, 1975), in the face of male strangers (Greenberg, Rosenberg, & Lind, 1973; Morgan & Ricciuti, 1969; Skarin, 1977), and less likely to occur in infants from multiple caregiving settings (Caldwell, 1963; Riciutti, 1974; Spiro, 1958; Stevens, 1971). The situation has been summarized by Gaensbauer, Emde, and Campos (1976), Sroufe (1977), and most recently by Horner (in press), who neatly conceptualizes the context effects as "stranger controlled" (producing the phenomenon) and "infant controlled" (not producing the phenomenon). Stranger distress clearly exists as a developmental phenomenon; if one constructs the conditions to favor its elicitation at a given age, one can demonstrate the competence for the response. On the other hand, one can construct conditions so there is not such a response; indeed, many infants may not be in situations where such a response is usual. This brings us to the third aspect of our context triad, namely, relevance. For infants in large families, there may be few such responses and none may be expected. In the case of other infants the event may mark a milestone for parents who feel that now their baby knows them and needs them in a very particular way (Bell & Harper, 1977; Emde, Gaensbauer, & Harmon, 1976).

A second example of the usefulness of context analysis comes from the current exciting work on descriptions of facial activity patterns related to infant emotion. Oster and Ekman (1978) have given us a dramatic statement about competence with respect to these expressions, telling us that all except one of the facial movement patterns distinguished by their comprehensive Facial Activity Coding System (FACS) have been seen in both fullterm and premature newborns. Indeed, now that there are species-wide patterns for emotional expression established for adults, one could imagine a search of millions of frames of film or videotapes to find such expressions in infants. But the other context questions remain: How do these expressions relate to usual behavior, and what is their relevance in the naturalistic environment of the individual baby? One would hope that programmatic research on context features of usual performance and relevance, as well as competence, will advance our knowledge and avoid the unnecessary debate and polemicism that surrounded the stranger distress "issue."

At the Level of Organizational State

Organizational state is usually considered in terms of psychophysiology (e.g., see Lewis & Rosenblum, 1978). Thus, one can think of state as referring to patterns of behavior and/or physiology which tend to repeat themselves over time and can lead to an inference about a central organizing tendency from which we can predict. Although interpretations about criteria may vary, the description of patterns that underlie inference about state in such a scheme are fairly clear (see, e.g., Hutt, Lenard, & Prechtl, 1969, and Anders, Emde, & Parmelee, 1971, for discussion of these issues with respect to the states of newborn sleep and wakefulness).

In our initial work on early emotional development, we became engrossed with matters of state. Viewing expressions at this level of meaning seemed to capture a readiness to act as well as to react; and, in work inspired by previous findings of Wolff (1959, 1966), we began to study emotional expression as aspects of state. In the infant's first two postnatal months, we found that smiling and frowning occurred as "spontaneous behaviors," as concomitants of patterns of rapid eye movement (REM) state physiology (Emde & Koenig, 1969a, b; Emde & Metcalf, 1970). REM smiling occurred more often in the premature, where it had a negative correlation with gestational age (Emde, McCartney, & Harmon, 1971); and it was found at characteristic fullterm rates in an infant whose forebrain and limbic cortex were virtually absent (Harmon & Emde 1972). In these early studies, newborn frowning was found not only linked to conditions from which we would infer distress (e.g., time since last feeding, noxious stimulation), but also linked to the rhythmically repeating internally organized REM state. Newborn smiling was most often seen as "spontaneous behavior" during the REM state and was uncommonly related to external stimulation.

This brings me to the reason I wish to consider organizational state in terms broader than the above—namely, in terms of developmental level. We found that after two postnatal months, behavior cannot easily be accounted for by internal state and endogenous rhythms. There is a shift away from endogenous control with more of life in wakefulness and less in sleep (Emde, Gaensbauer, & Harmon 1976). Further, as Dittrichova and Lapackova (1964) have observed, wakefulness becomes used in a new way. There is a developmental shift in organization.

For parents, the developmental shift is most obvious in affective development. The dramatic flowering of a baby's social smile around two months, soon to be accompanied by cooing, is well known. The newborn period of irregular smiling to external stimulation is followed by an upsurgence of smiling to stimuli in a wide variety of modalities (Emde & Harmon, 1972). REM smiling, which we have characterized as "endogenous smiling," declines during the first two postnatal months at the same time that "exogenous smiling," that form of smiling elicited from outside stimulation, increases. Such a developmental change is also concomitant with the decline of nonhunger (or endogenous) fussiness, a decline that has been documented by Brazelton (1962), Dittrichova and Lapackova (1964), and by two longitudinal studies of our own (Emde, Gaensbauer, & Harmon, 1976; Tennes, Emde, Kisley, & Metcalf, 1972).

That there is a developmental organizational state change that can be described as a biobehavioral shift from endogenous control to exogenous control is indicated by a host of changes in other sectors. These have been reviewed elsewhere (Emde, Gaensbauer, & Harmon, 1976; Emde & Robinson, 1979) and will be briefly noted here. In terms of sleep, quiet sleep increases markedly during the first two months (Parmelee, Wenner, Akiyama, Schultz, & Stern, 1967, Dittrichova, & Lapackova, 1969), there is a decrease in behavioral activity during sleep, and "behaviorally undifferentiated REM states" diminish (Emde & Metcalf, 1970). Further, the pattern of sleep onset shifts, there is an increase in the ability to sustain long periods of sleep, and there is a shift to a diurnal pattern of nighttime sleep. The interpretation that such changes reflect the maturation of forebrain inhibitory areas is bolstered by our knowledge that a variety of "transitory neurological reflexes" become inhibited during this same developmental period (see reviews in Paine, 1965; Parmelee & Michaelis, 1971; Peiper, 1963).

In the area of perception, significant scanning of the face becomes apparent around seven weeks of age when there is a prominent scanning of the eye region (Bergman, Haith, & Mann, 1971; Haith, Bergman, & Moore, 1977), a finding that corresponds to naturalistic observations of enhanced eye-to-eye contact and expressions of interest at this age. Perhaps related to this is the fact that the visual cortical evoked response undergoes rapid maturational change between 4–8 postnatal weeks (Ellingson, 1960). There also appears to be a change in organization around two months with respect to orienting and attentiveness, one illustrated by heartrate responsiveness (Graham & Jackson, 1970) and visual attention (Kagan 1970a, b).

Conditioning and habituation studies indicate different results before and after two months. Before that time, classical avoidance conditioning is difficult and operant conditioning effects are shortlived. After two months, this is not the case. The same is true with habituation, wherein almost "heroic" measures are needed before two months for a successful experiment, whereas habituation can readily be established in auditory and visual modalities after that (see Jeffrey & Cohen, 1971; Sameroff & Cavanagh, 1979).

Another developmental shift in organization occurs during the age period of 7–9 months. In social–affective development, the differential responsiveness to stranger and caregivers, with fearfulness being shown to the stranger, is prominent. A similar shift, involving both behavior and heartrate, is apparent using the stimulus conditions of the visual cliff (Campos, Hiatt,

Ramsay, Henderson, & Svejda, 1978). As was the case with social smiling and the first shift, we found that stranger fearfulness does not emerge without antecedents; certain behaviors (comparing faces and sobering to the stranger's approach) regularly precede it in development. Other changes, including those involving cognition, sleep-state organization, and heartrate organization, have been reviewed elsewhere (Emde, Gaensbauer, & Harmon, 1976).

Our longitudinal research indicates a developmental curve with respect to amounts of wakefulness during the first year. We have found an increase of wakefulness during the first two postnatal months, followed by a plateau that is then followed by a further increase in wakefulness in the two-month period immediately preceding 7–9 months. This is in turn followed by a second plateau lasting until the end of the first year. We believe such a curve can represent a model for times of developmental shift. In contrast to our previous conceptualization, we no longer think of these shifts primarily as times of rapid change. Preceding each, and roughly corresponding to the times-of-wakefulness increment, there are approximately two months of preparation during which components of new behaviors appear. These are integrated into a new emergent organization at nodal times (two months and 7–9 months) and are followed by periods of developmental consolidation. Two other investigators have recently reported a major qualitative transition in infant behavior at similar age periods. McCall (1977), in reanalyzing data from the Berkeley Growth Study, found qualitative transitions at precisely these two age points. Kagan (1977), in summarizing his research program on cognitive development, presented compelling evidence for a behavioral reorganization at the time of the second shift.

Description of patterns leading to inferences about cognitive state in infancy as they relate to emotion are extremely important at this level of meaning. They have been given programmatic attention by Decarie (1965; 1978), Kagan (1971), Campos et al. (1978) and especially by Sroufe (1979; Sroufe & Waters, 1976). Sroufe presents a scheme for relating emotional, cognitive, and social development that integrates ideas from Piaget and Sander and is consistent with the scheme advocated in this essay. In our own work, we have become particularly interested in the signalling aspects of emotional expressions and the developmental progression from biologically organized states of social signalling to psychologically organized states of cognitive-affective signalling.

In terms of context, analyzing performance, competence, and relevance for organizational state are as important as they were for the level of biological response. Descriptive patterns must be anchored according to what usually occurs, what can be shown to be available under optimal or special conditons, and what has meaning in the lives of particular infants and families. There seems to be little controversy in the current literature related to these contextual questions, perhaps because investigators are apt to stay at one mode of sampling. Patterns of response related to psychophysiology, cognition and broader aspects of developmental state are typically tested in standardized laboratory conditions or under presumed "optimal" conditions for performance. Restricting this sampling mode can be misleading, as we found when studying infant sleep-onset patterns that differed drastically in our laboratory as compared with the usual home environment (Bernstein, Emde, and Campos, 1973; Kligman, Smyrl, & Emde, 1975). Lewis, Brooks-Gunn, and Haviland (1978) have pointed out that little work has been done integrating different measurements of emotional state, and have shown the complexities which arise when one attempts to relate changes in heartrate to facial expression in individual infants. In terms of exploring the context of sampling due to biological variation, studies of emotional state in Down's syndrome infants promise to advance our knowledge of such processes in relation to the organization of both cognitive and social development (Cicchetti & Sroufe, 1978; Emde, Katz, and Thorpe, 1978).

At the Level of Enduring Trait

At the previous level of meaning, we considered emotional state as a *relatively* stable organization of emotions which appears at a biologically appropriate developmental level, and which is supplanted with further development. Such a designation of "state" reflects a basic developmental process involving change. Thus endogenously determined REM smiling gives way to exogenously determined smiling which conveys pleasure and reinforces parental approach behavior; this in turn becomes less automatic as social smiling becomes more situation- and person-specific. The process is also seen with the smile of recognitory assimilation which becomes prominent and fades when recognitory assimilation ceases to become effortful (McCall, 1972). Similarly, stranger fearfulness is over-ridden by further developmental factors along the lines of "separation–individuation" (Mahler, Pine, & Bergman, 1975). In other words, although the inference of organizational state is based on observations of repetitive patterns of behavior, these patterns shift as development proceeds. What endures is therefore at a different level of meaning.

Enduring emotional traits have to do with individual differences in response tendencies, moods, and temperament; they also lead to questions of pathology. We might assume that an "average expectable" individual would be predisposed by biology towards a basic ongoing mood of happiness with some outgoing engagement of the world. Yet it would also be true that such a person's affective response tendencies would vary within each day in characteristic dynamic modes. Many questions exist about the dynamic features of emotional traits. How do emotional traits vary with endogenous biological rhythms such as sleep-wakefulness rhythms, basic rest activity rhythms, and hormonal rhythms? Do emotion traits typify characteristic ways of responding to stress?

Thomas, Chess, Birch, Hertzig, and Korn (1963) used "mood" as one of their nine categories of behavioral functioning for looking at temperament in individual infants. With data derived from mothers' reports, they defined mood as "the amount of pleasant, joyful and friendly behavior, as contrasted with unpleasant, crying and unfriendly behavior [p. 41]." Not only did they find that most babies were regarded as "preponderantly positive in mood," but that from one period to another (from 6–27 months) the patterning of mood showed the greatest stability of their categories. In spite of these promising beginnings with respect to maternal perceptions of moods in early childhood, little research attention has been given to the direct measurement of such moods and their individual differences (see Cytryn, 1976, and Pedersen, Anderson, & Cain, 1976).

Aside from mood, it seems likely that a number of affectively related childhood traits or personality variables such as sociability, impulsivity, and perhaps even ego-control and ego-resiliency (Block & Block, this volume) would have their roots in infancy. In addition, a biosocial view might lead to the hypothesis that adaptively important affective structures having to do with learning, approach–avoidance, access to consciousness, and sociability could be recognizable as modes of behaving in infancy; these have to do with the general modulating functions of emotions and enduring individual differences in behavior might be expected.

Prediction of behavior from infancy to childhood has been poor in general, and there is compelling need for further longitudinal research to understand developmental transformations of emotional activity within individuals. Prospective studies often yield surprises that can correct limited impressions gleaned from retrospective study and from clinical populations. (For an account of some of our surprises, see the longitudinal study of infantile depression reported in Emde & Harmon, in press.)

The Social Domain

Increasingly, our research efforts have been devoted to the study of infant emotion in the social domain. Whatever else, our definition of an emotion is a social one. Further, although a baby cannot tell us how he or she feels, there is a communication of feelings to caregivers who can tell us how they feel in response to babies and who guide caregiving responses accordingly.

At the Level of Biological Response

Because they so directly communicate feelings and messages about need states, emotional expressions have been called the language of infancy. Although our longitudinal observations gave us certain convictions about regularities in caregivers' interpretations and responses to infant expressions, more systematic study was called for. Further, the adult cross-cultural work with facial expressions suggested "species-wide" messages about specific emotions and focused our attention on questions of biological response patterns involved in infant-caregiver messages. What are the species-wide messages in emotional language? Who can send and receive what? What are the universals of patterned messages between infants and caregivers? Although the research described next centers on the face, this is only a beginning. We know for example that the dynamics of endogenously and exogenously determined eye behavior are complexly organized (Haith et al., 1977) and involved in a high degree of meaningful communication with caregivers (Brazelton, 1974; Emde & Brown, 1978; Robson, 1967; Stern, 1974; Tronick, Als, Adamson, Wise, & Brazelton, 1978) and that intriguing findings have appeared suggesting early postural communication systems (Condon & Sander, 1974; Meltzoff & Moore, 1977).

Adult Judgments of Infant Facial Expressions. A previous report (Emde, Katz, & Thorpe, 1978) describes our initial studies using modifications of the Ekman and Izard forced-choice procedure for adults judging still photographs of facial expressions of infants. Not surprisingly, we found that forced judgments using categories derived from adult peak emotional expressions appeared inappropriate for the 3-month-old, whereas encouraging consistencies emerged from free-response choices. Mothers understood more and wanted to tell us more than they could in the forced-choice task. We therefore pursued two approaches for global judgment studies of infant facial expressions. One involved sorting of pictures by similarities and subsequent multidimensional scaling analysis, and another involved free responses and subsequent analysis by categorizing. In all our studies, we have used adult women experienced with children as independent judges.

The multidimensional scaling approach adapted from Shepard (1962a, b; 1974) employs 25 judges who are asked to sort stimulus cards that may either be infant pictures or verbal responses of mothers to their own infants' pictures. Judges are asked to sort these into one or more piles, putting those that seem to belong together in the same pile.

Sampling of infant facial expressions was begun in a limited fashion using 10 normal infants. Photographs were taken in standardized home sessions, beginning with infants in a wakeful state. A mother was asked to talk and play with her baby and the first five photos were taken at 30-sec intervals. The next two photos were taken with a stranger talking to the baby, and this was followed by two more photos taken during the presentation of a standard inanimate visual pattern. Next, 10 photos were taken at 30-sec intervals without any stimulus presentation. A final photo was taken during a loss-of-support stimuls (moro response). The procedure was modified at 12 months in the following manner: Four pictures were taken during maternal separation, four pictures during a stranger approach, five pictures when mother returned and greeted her infant, three more pictures when the infant was shown an inanimate object, five pictures during the infant playing peek-a-boo with mother, 10 pictures at 30-sec intervals with the infant left in an unstimulated condition, and three pictures when the infant was asleep.

One week after the taking of photographs, a visit was made to each mother and an interview conducted in order to get a mother's responses to her own baby's pictures. Interview responses were tape recorded and later transcribed. This latter procedure allowed us to do multidimensional-scaling analyses of mothers' responses, as well as of original pictures. The results of both kinds of analyses have been consistent. Similarity sortings have been done for infants' expressions at 2½ months, 3½ months, 4½ months, and 12 months of age and have involved eight different experiments each using 25 judges (Emde, Kligman, Reich, & Wade, 1978). At 2½ months, scaling solutions have been two-dimensional, with the first dimension easily characterized as "hedonic tone" and the second best characterized as "state." After 3 months, three-dimensional scaling solutions predominate. In three-dimensional solutions, hedonic tone carries the most variance, activation appears as the second dimension, and an internally oriented/externally oriented dimension is the best description for the third dimension.

These results show a striking continuity with studies of adult emotional expression. A history of similar conclusions goes back to the thinking of Spencer (1890), Wundt (1896/1971), and Freud (1915/1968) and persists through the experimental investigations of Woodworth and Schlosberg (1954) Osgood (1966), Frijda and Phillipszoon (1963), Frijda (1970), Gladstone (1962), and Abelson and Sermat (1962). As in our results, "pleasantness–unpleasantness" emerges as the major dimension, "activation" or "intensity" is the next most prominent dimension, and a third dimension is often suggested but frequently difficult to interpret. The third dimension is sometimes called "acceptance–rejection," sometimes "control," and sometimes "expressed feeling versus inner feeling."

Our free-response approach is one that also makes use of multiple judges who are asked to give responses to the same infant pictures. As in our multidimensional scaling studies, all judges have been women experienced with children. They are given a set of instructions modified from the free response technique of Izard (1971), who devised this technique for cross-cultural studies of adults. Judges are asked to record in one word or phrase "the strongest and clearest feeling that the baby is expressing." Izard found that the words used by adult subjects responding to photographs were relatively limited in number and obtained a large pool of judges to categorize such words in accordance with his scheme of fundamental emotions. We

TABLE 1.1
Free-Response Categorizing of Infant Facial Expressions

	Single Emotion Categories								Blend Categories						
	Interest	Joy	Distress	Sleepy	Anger	Fear	Disgust	Surprise	Interest/Joy	Sleepy/Joy	Interest/Fear	Distress/Anger	Joy/Distress	Interest/Surprise	Unclassifiable
3.5months (N = 70 photos)															
Study 1 (22 Raters)	21	31	5	3	1	1	—	—	3	1	—	—	1	1	2
%	30%	44%	7%	4%	1%	1%	—	—	4%	1%	—	—	1%	1%	3%
Study 2 (26 Raters)	25	26	7	5	—	—	—	—	5	1	—	—	—	—	1
%	36%	37%	10%	7%	—	—	—	—	7%	1%	—	—	1%	—	1%
Combined% (48 Raters)	33%	41%	9%	6%	1%	1%	—	—	6%	1%	—	—	1%	1%	2%
12 months (N = 70 photos)															
Study 1 (25 Raters)	24	12	9	2	1	1	1	3	4	3	2	1	—	1	6
%	34%	17%	13%	3%	1%	1%	1%	4%	6%	4%	3%	1%	—	1%	9%
Study 2 (25 Raters)	30	15	8	—	1	—	—	3	4	4	1	—	—	—	4
%	43%	21%	11%	1%	1%	1%	—	4%	6%	6%	1%	—	—	—	6%
Combined % (50 Raters)	39%	19%	12%	1%	1%	1%	1%	4%	6%	5%	2%	1%	—	1%	7%

began with Izard's accumulated lexicon of words for eight emotional categories and added a ninth, "bored-sleepy." Over 99% of our responses are categorized automatically into one of these nine categories plus a 10th of "no emotion."

Table 1.1 presents the results of free-response categorizing for the 70 infant photos samples for 3½ months and the 70 photos sampled for 12 months of age. The criterion for categorizing was agreement by more than one third of the judges. This relatively low criterion level permitted the possibility of blends with two emotions being judged beyond criterion. At the earlier age, photos meeting our one-third criterion for agreement included: interest (33%), joy (41%) distress (9%) sleepy (6%) and anger and fear (1% each). Nine percent of the pictures were blends; most of these were of interest combined with joy. At 12 months of age, 39% of pictures were classified as interest, 19% as joy, 12% as distress, 4% as surprise, 1% as sleepy and 1% each for anger, fear, and disgust. Fifteen percent of the pictures were categorized as blends; 6% were interest and joy, 5% sleepy and joy, 2% fear and interest, and 1% each for distress/anger and interest/surprise.

As the result of our experience in longitudinal study, we (Emde, Kligman, Reich, & Wade, 1978) along with Sroufe (1977) speculated that expressions of fear, surprise, and anger were prominent only in the latter half of the first year. It seemed to us that this would be consistent with an epigenetic view of these emotions that might require more experience and cognition. The free-response data are inconclusive concerning age effects. Anger and fear were judged for one picture at 3½ months, and surprise appeared as a blend with interest. However, these judgments of categories did not replicate in our second study. At 12 months, there were similar findings with respect to anger and fear; and there were more pictures that reached criterion for surprise.

Reliability of Facial Judgments.   Our two-study design (using the same pictures but with different groups of raters obtained at different times) gives us a chance to look at reliability of findings. Results are striking. At 3½ months, of the pictures categorized as a single emotion in the first study, 55 of 62 (89%) were judged beyond criterion level for the same category in the second study. At 12 months, such replication occurred for 45 of 53 (85%) of pictures categorized singly in the first study. But agreement is more dramatic when we consider the extent to which groups of judges agree that a given emotion category is present in our photographs. Correlations between Study 1 and Study 2 agreement levels on the four major categories are presented in Table 1.2. For all photos at both ages, judgment study correlations ranged from .84 to .96. Except for photos with zero values, correlations for photos ranged from .77 to .97. A somewhat surprising implication of these results is that groups of judges seemed to agree about low-signal-value emotional expressions in addition to high-signal-value expressions.

TABLE 1.2
Correlations Between Judgement Studies of Infant Photographs

	All Photos			Photos Without Zero Values	
Emotion Category	Number of Photographs	Correlation	Emotion Category	Number of Photographs	Correlation
3.5 months, set 1					
Joy	35	.94	Joy	27	.91
Interest	35	.91	Interest	27	.88
Distress	35	.91	Distress	15	.89
Sleepy	35	.86	Sleepy	13	.85
3.5 months, set 2					
Joy	35	.96	Joy	25	.94
Interest	35	.84	Interest	30	.84
Distress	35	.94	Distress	20	.92
Sleepy	35	.94	Sleepy	11	.94
12 months, set 1					
Joy	35	.96	Joy	21	.94
Interest	35	.88	Interest	30	.84
Distress	35	.92	Distress	16	.90
Sleepy	35	.91	Sleepy	14	.93
12 months, set 2					
Joy	35	.93	Joy	20	.88
Interest	35	.88	Interest	28	.82
Distress	35	.95	Distress	17	.97
Sleepy	35	.84	Sleepy	16	.77

The reliability findings about emotional messages in these pictures are encouraging and point to the robustness of their signalling features. But there are many context questions. First, are these categories of messages wholly dependent on verbal mediation? Would they appear together in similarity sortings of pictures? The answer appears to be yes. In a study in which 50 raters were randomly assigned to either a similarity sorting task or a free-response labelling task, we found a strong tendency for pictures similarly labelled in the free-response paradigm to be close together in the three-dimensional space generated from multidimensional scaling (Emde, Kligman, Reich & Wade, 1978). There are of course multiple questions that need to be answered about sampling. We sampled infants' facial expressions under special and somewhat arbitrary conditions and represented them in still photographs. "Usual performance" must be at some distance from these special conditions. One question in this area concerns the use of still photographs. Is the still photograph a meaningful unit when we know that emotional life is embedded in temporal patterns of activity? A study compared still photographs with movies. The movies contained 30-sec sequences of the infant's face and upper torso which led up to each still photograph. In three separate experimental sessions, we found that more than 75% of our photographs that met criteria for stability were judged to be in the same category using our free-response categorizing technique, regardless of whether they were presented by movies or by slides. Disagreements were explained readily by the addition of new information occurring during the 30-sec movie segment; these included discrete events such as a yawn, eye closure, and smile. It seemed to us that within the 30 sec and under the conditions of our sampling, discrete events of emotional expression were reasonably well captured by our still photographs and that such expressions seemed to be communicated in small time units that may or may not depend upon sequential coding for their interpretation.

Another question about "usual performance" had to do with the infant's "behavioral day." We had reason to believe from our prior naturalistic studies that our sampling of pictures underestimated sleep, underestimated periods around feeding, and overestimated periods with positive affective engagement. We therefore did a time-lapse video recording of an infant's face and upper torso during a continuous 12 hour period from 8 a.m. to 8 p.m. The infant was 3½ months of age, and filming was done in the home with mother and infant instructed to carry on a "typical day." Both were previously familiarized with the photographer and equipment and we subsequently established that the day of filming was typical for the baby in terms of sleep, wakefulness, and feeding when compared with records of the previous week. Further, we were able to compare amounts of wakefulness for 12 2-hr intervals of the 24 hr surrounding the filming with normative data previously collected from longitudinal studies involving 25 infants. For 11 of 12 2-hr intervals, the individual infant's sleep was within one standard deviation of our normal group means. (The single exception was from 8 to 10 p.m., when the individual infant's sleep was 1.7 standard deviations below the group mean.) After completion of filming, we sampled still photographs from our videotape at 10-min intervals throughout the 12-hr period. These photos were then judged by 25 women, as in our previous free-response catgegorizing studies. Figure 1.1 compares emotions derived from this infant with mean values derived from five infants of the same age previously sampled under our more arbitrary conditions. Comparison suggests that the previous conditions over-represented joy and under-represented sleep, and that blends were prominent in both methods of sampling. It should be mentioned that 77% of the remaining 12 unfilmed hours in the 24-hr day of our individual infant consisted of sleep; therefore, ours is undoubtedly a conservative estimate of that expression.

What about optimal performance for emotional messages? Such a question might be phrased in terms of analyzing peak emotional expressions for infants. We are engaged in a collaborative study with Izard in which he has selected still pictures representing peak emotional expressions from videotapes of his infant studies. Our free-response categorizing indicates that blends are common, even among these pictures that were selected as examples of peak emotions. We are now estimating the extent of agreement between free-response categorizing experiments, whether done in Delaware with students (Izard's judges) or in Denver with adult women experienced with

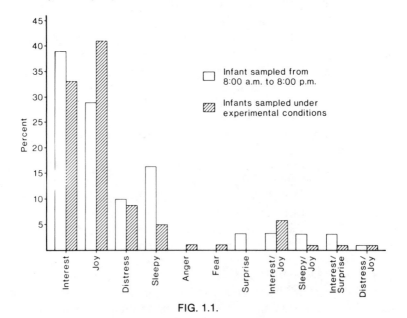

FIG. 1.1.

children. The study is ongoing, but we are already gaining increasing conviction concerning the robustness of these messages, even with diverse groups of judges and with still photographs that do not offer sequential cues related to movement and that do not offer the multiple feedback confirmation for the kinds of affective messages we experience in real life. Table 1.3 presents some data from a preliminary experiment. The table is in a similar form as Table 1.2, but with correlations between two judgment studies we have carried out for 27 photographs selected by Izard. Each of the studies uses 25 adult women as judges, and correlations are for agreement levels on major emotion categories. Fear, anger, and surprise now appear as major emotion categories in addition to joy, interest, distress, and sleepy. Correlations range from .68 to .98. As in Table 1.2 correlations are computed for all photos as well as for photos without zero percent agreement values.

Emotional Signalling. The study of deviation and individual differences are useful strategies for understanding the relevance of emotional signalling. One deviant infant group we have studied consists of those with Down's syndrome and their caregivers. We found evidence that Down's syndrome messages are noisier (Emde, Katz, & Thorpe, 1978) and are often disappointing to parents (Emde & Brown, 1978). As the result of multidimensional scaling analyses of mothers' original responses to their own Down's infants' pictures and of separate analyses of the pictures themselves, we were able to show that the noise originated in the infant signals rather than in the mothers' original interpretations of these signals. Down's syndrome emotional expressions are more ambiguous and apt to be less intense. There is a few weeks' delay in the onset of the social smile, but parental disappointment typically results from its dampened intensity. There is a bilateral upturning of the corners of the mouth, but cheeks and eyes typically do not participate. There is no brightening of the eyes, there is poor eye-to-eye contact, and there is little activation or bicycling of the arms and legs as one would expect from the normal 3–4-month-old. Individuals experiencing this sequence feel let down. Instead of rewarding a social interaction, instead of engaging and "being fun," it tends to disappoint because it violates our expectations. That there may be a general deficit in the activation of emotional expression in Down's syndrome is the subject of further study, and it is noteworthy that Cicchetti and Sroufe (1978) found a dampening of negative as well as positive expressions during the first two years of Down's syndrome develpment, a finding that could not be accounted for strictly in terms of delayed cognitive development.

Thinking about relevance and meaning leads us to the more general question of understanding "signal-operating" features as opposed to "receiver-operating" features (Green & Swets, 1966) of emotional messages

TABLE 1.3
Correlations Between Judgement Studies of Izard Infant Photographs (Set 1)

| Emotion Category | All Photos | | | Photos Without Zero Values | | |
	Number of Photographs	Correlation	Emotion Category	Number of Photographs	Correlation
Joy	27	.98	Joy	7	.98
Interest	27	.94	Interest	14	.91
Distress	27	.93	Distress	20	.88
Sleepy	27	.68	Sleepy	6	.90
Fear	27	.88	Fear	15	.83
Anger	27	.83	Anger	13	.81
Surprise	27	.97	Surprise	6	.98

between infants and caregivers. Such an understanding is crucial for any analysis of individual differences. Perhaps one could assume there is a biological potential for both species-wide expression and species-wide recognition of infant emotional expressions. If so, a masking experiment in which an ambiguous facial signal was presented to judges might result in regularities for defining receiver-operating features. This experiment has yet to be done for infant signalling. The other side of the system, that of caregiver signalling to infants and of infant receiver-operating features, is uncharted territory (Hoffman, 1978).

Our understanding of meaning will also be enriched by studying the adaptive significance of variations in infant–caregiver messages, especially when attention is given to groups "at risk" for deviant communication. As a start in this direction, we are seeking to characterize individual differences in mothers' interpretations of infant signals and also in infant signals themselves. We have developed standard sets of infant pictures at 3 and 12 months and have generated computerized normative data for an appropriate form of multidimensional scaling (INDSCAL of Carroll & Chang, 1964) and for free-response categorizing. Studies are under way with teenage mothers, parents of infants wherein there has been prolonged neonatal separation, and parents who are referred for evaluation of child abuse and child neglect. Other studies with parents of children with known psychopathology are planned.

Much work needs to be done to describe and understand individual differences with respect to infant signals. Individual features of Down's syndrome infants and other handicapped infants, because of wide intragroup variation, offer opportunities for understanding developmental consequences. In addition, autistic infants who have been hypothesized to have an early defective "sending power" with respect to emotional messages (Schopler, 1965), may offer opportunities for understanding processes involved in the pathogenesis of that disorder.

Another intriguing aspect of our understanding the context for emotional signalling has been opened up by a recent study that found a positive relationship between the frequency of predicted facial components for expression of an emotion and the independent global judgment of that emotion (Hiatt, Campos, & Emde, 1977). An ongoing study seeks to pursue these findings with several independent judgment tasks. As important as it is to study the instances of positive relationship between global judgments of emotion and predicted facial components, we are especially intrigued with findings where reliable global judgments of emotion occur in the absence of predicted components. Global judgments of emotion, even from still photographs, appear to be based on more information than we currently capture from our facial pattern analysis.

At the Level of Organizational State

In the social domain, the level of organizational state is interactional rather than internal. The description of behavioral patterns is intended to answer questions about the level of communication that has evolved between partners within an infant-caregiver system. Our own research program has barely approached the threshold of this level of meaning; but it has been discussed by others in terms of what has been negotiated (Sander, 1975), what has been transacted (Sameroff, 1975), and in terms of the characteristics of mother–infant synchrony (Brazelton, 1974; Tronick et al., 1978).

Theodore Gaensbauer, working in our infancy laboratory, has developed a program for assessing organizational states of emotional interaction in infant–caregiver pairs wherein there is documented or suspected child abuse or neglect (Gaensbauer & Sands, 1979). Robert Harmon has developed a research program for assessing similar features in the emotional interaction and play of infant–caregiver pairs in a longitudinal study of premature and full-term infants.

In terms of context analysis, one must ask the logical questions about such patterns: To what extent are the described patterns usual, to what extent are they special, and to what extent are they relevant in the life of a particular infant and his family? Questions about how these states of organization came about shade into questions at the level of enduring trait. Nonetheless, there are indications that such states involve intricate moment-to-moment reciprocal exchanges of affective expressions for their maintenance. If 1–4-month-old infants do not receive normal feedback from caregivers in face-to-face interaction, if their mothers remain still-faced for example, they may react with distress and withdrawal (Tronick et al., 1978). Of equal importance is the fact that mothers find it very uncomfortable to sit still-faced and not respond to their infants' overtures during a 3-min experimental period. An implication of this work and that of Stern (1974) is that each partner has a lot at stake in the maintenance of a continued level of organization for affective reciprocity.

At the Level of Enduring Trait

We are at the earliest phases of being able to describe and analyze enduring traits of interaction. Yet I think the prospects are for major advances. The work of Thomas, Chess, and Birch (1963, 1968) on infant temperament actually concerns parental perception of infant temperament. Following their innovative lead, a number of second-generation parental perception scales are now being developed that have advantages in terms of known psychometric properties, usefulness at different ages, and convenience for studying individual differences (Carey, 1970; Pederson, Anderson, & Cain,

1977; Rothbart, 1978). Parental perceptions are worthy of study in their own right, and it is important to realize they are not the same as infant temperament. However, I believe that Thomas et al. may have tapped a more complex *interactional* system in demonstrating their developmental continuities; perhaps they have discovered enduring interactional traits. Perhaps what has been called "infant temperament" refers to fundamental adaptational modes, to dynamic equilibria characterizing parent–infant relational systems over the course of development. Individual differences of infants are not stable in any simple way; perhaps there are relational "constants" that will give us a research handle on developmental continuities. I believe the work of Sroufe and Waters (1977) showing organizational continuities in post-separation reunion behaviors between infants and mothers at 12 and 18 months illustrates the promise of such an approach. In addition Sander (personal communication) in a 20-year followup of families originally studied in the Boston infant development study (Sander, 1962; 1964) has been most impressed by the remarkable continuity of family styles of interaction over this time span.

SOCIAL DEFINITION OF INFANT EMOTIONS AND CHALLENGES FOR UNDERSTANDING MEANING

At this point I would like to offer some thoughts about the ways we attribute emotion to infants. Broadly speaking, such a discussion belongs in the social domain of our biosocial scheme, but I offer it separately since it offers a number of challenges for understanding meaning.

Parental Attribution

We have taken the position that the best starting point for defining infant emotions is in terms of what is seen by parents, since their interpretations are likely to make a difference in an infant's life. Let us consider the example of anger. As scientists, we may choose to say that anger occurs in development when an infant shows a particular facial expression, has a particular posture, and/or demonstrates an instrumental behavior such as banging a frustrating object. But in our longitudinal studies we have encountered mothers who interpret an "angry cry" during the newborn period, a cry that is intense, prolonged, and occurs in a particular context. The context is usually one in which the mother feels her infant is expressing a need that she is unable to meet; in other words, she feels she is the cause of frustration. A common example occurs with a hungry infant who cannot be attended to immediately because mother is preparing the family meal. Still other mothers have told us that their babies do not express anger until the end of the first year when they have temper tantrums. Similar observations could be made concerning individual differences for maternal interpretations of surprise, fearfulness, and other emotions. It seemed to us that there is need for a systematic developmental study of parental attributions of emotions in their infants. We have begun such a study, surveying mothers of infants of different ages in the Denver area using both face-to-face interviews and a mail-survey approach. The initial part of this study is cross-sectional, with mothers of infants ranging in age from 1–18 months (N = 30 at each infant month). In addition to obtaining demographic information, we ask mothers if their babies have shown any of a variety of different emotions. Each mother is then asked to fill out the Differential Emotions Scale (DES) of Izard (1972) as it applies (1) to her baby, and (2) to herself. The DES lists 30 words that describe feelings, three for each of 10 emotions. Mothers are requested to indicate the frequency with which these feelings have been *expressed* (by her baby) or *experienced* (by herself) during the past week.

A factor analysis of maternal DES responses of 230 subjects (for experienced emotions) gave support to our assumption that words were understood by mothers. The factor structure originally obtained by Izard (1977) was closely duplicated, with eight clear factors emerging in our analysis. One factor combined items for anger and distress; and separate factors were obtained for joy, fear, surprise, interest, shyness, contempt, and guilt. There was no clear factor corresponding to disgust, and two of the 30 items did not load on any factor.

Although data collection is incomplete, Table 1.4 gives some preliminary findings with respect to the age of first occurrence of infant emotions. Groupings are according to infant age at the time of the survey and are for 2–4 months, 5–6 months, 7–8 months, 11–12 months and 17–18 months. All mothers felt that interest and joy were present in their infants, regardless of the baby's age. Further, there was high attribution of emotion at the early months for surprise, anger, fear, and distress. Shyness and sadness were attributed much less and, throughout the age range surveyed, disgust, contempt, and guilt were never seen as present by a majority of mothers for their infants. When comparing the onset of emotions for different infant ages, one is confronted with confounding factors resulting from differences in maternal observation time and differences in maternal memory. Mothers of older infants will have more observation time, but will have more to remember. In spite of these problems, the mean age for the first occurrence of emotions by age suggests that there are differences among emotions. The table illustrates that these differences persist even when some emotions are judged as present by a minority of mothers.

When one looks at the mean month of onset for emotions for those infants one year and over and includes only those emotions for which a majority of mothers felt their infants had exhibited them, one finds similar trends. The

TABLE 1.4
Age of First Occurrence of Infant Emotions

Emotion	Age (in months)	N	% Answering That Emotion Has Appeared	$\bar{X}$ Occurrence, if Present (in months)
Interest	2–4	37	100	1.6
	5–6	61	100	1.5
	7–8	90	100	2.0
	11–12	63	100	2.4
	17–18	59	100	2.8
Joy	2–4	37	100	1.8
	5–6	61	100	1.9
	7–8	90	100	2.0
	11–12	63	100	3.1
	17–18	59	100	2.7
Surprise	2–4	37	73	1.7
	5–6	61	95	2.3
	7–8	90	94	2.8
	11–12	63	94	4.5
	17–18	59	100	6.7
Anger	2–4	37	86	1.5
	5–6	61	93	2.6
	7–8	90	96	3.4
	11–12	63	95	5.5
	17–18	59	98	7.1
Fear	2–4	37	68	1.7
	5–6	61	74	2.8
	7–8	90	69	3.8
	11–12	63	83	6.8
	17–18	59	92	9.3
Distress	2–4	37	62	0.9
	5–6	60	77	1.3
	7–8	66	76	2.9
	11–12	63	73	4.1
	17–18	59	78	7.6
Sadness	2–4	37	38	1.9
	5–6	60	42	3.0
	7–8	90	49	4.6
	11–12	63	70	7.4
	17–18	58	55	10.1

(*continued*)

TABLE 1.4 *(contd.)*

Emotion	Age (in months)	N	% Answering That Emotion Has Appeared	$\bar{X}$ Occurrence, if Present (in months)
Shyness	2–4	37	19	2.4
	5–6	61	46	3.8
	7–8	90	64	5.1
	11–12	63	78	7.6
	17–18	59	90	10.6
Disgust	2–4	37	27	2.1
	5–6	61	34	4.1
	7–8	90	29	5.0
	11–12	63	40	7.6
	17–18	59	49	12.3
Contempt	2–4	37	11	1.3
	5–6	61	23	3.3
	7–8	89	19	4.2
	11–12	62	35	8.3
	17–18	57	32	8.5
Guilt	2–4	37	3	3.0
	5–6	61	3	4.0
	7–8	90	6	6.2
	11–12	63	32	9.0
	17–18	58	48	13.3

mean age of the first occurrence for interest is 2.6 months, for joy 2.9 months, for surprise 5.6 months, anger 6.3 months, fear 8.1 months, shyness 9.1 months, and distress 8.9 months.

It seems likely that mothers who attribute a variety of emotions early in infancy probably respond to different features of their infants' behaviors than they do at later ages. Perhaps stimulus-related features are more important early and response-related features are more important later. Analyses of correlations between maternal and infant DES scores and analyses for effects of amount of maternal experience with infants are geared to understand such age-related differences. An intriguing finding across ages is that mothers see their infants as having significantly more of most emotions than themselves. They see their infants as having more joy, interest, surprise, fear, anger, and shyness. An exception concerns distress, wherein they see themselves as having significantly more of that emotion than do their own infants.

Scientific Attribution

Up until recently, the designation of infant emotions had less to do with infants and more to do with researchers who looked for early forms of emotions in terms of one general theory or another. The difference today is not that we discount earlier ways of viewing emotions—for example, in terms of external stimulus conditions or in terms of retrospective constructions from subjective reports of adults—but that we insist on appreciating the infant *as infant* and that we are unsatisfied with single views. Single views are partial at best. In former times, it seemed as if we had to choose a psychological view, whether behavioristic or psychoanalytic, to the exclusion of a biological or social one. Today, as we integrate multiple views, we find advantages for both naturalistic relevance and scientific understanding. Further, knowing the boundary conditions of our observational field leads to a sharper picture and enhances replicability of findings.

But since the viewpoints and methods of today are so diverse, the process of scientific attribution of infant emotions is complicated. Multifaceted views lead to different terminologies. Methods of observation are various and differing populations in differing environments are under study. Under these circumstances, and when a multidisciplinary field such as this is beginning to flourish, there is a need for ensuring consistent and accurate communication. A standardized terminology with a few agreed-upon standardized techniques or "marker variables" (see Bell & Hertz, 1976) would be extremely helpful in comparing results of different investigators. Such an effort was successfully carried out for multidisciplinary sleep research both for adults (Rechtschaffen & Kales, 1968) and for newborn infants (Anders, Emde, & Parmelee, 1971). But most of all, I feel that the time is critical for collaborative studies, involving different laboratories, different techniques, and different populations. Such studies could ensure the sharing of data and methods and advance programmatic goals for the field while, at the same time, not discouraging unique approaches.

THE ADAPTIVE NATURE OF INFANT EMOTIONAL STATES

Our biosocial view highlights that infant emotional states are rooted in biology and central in biobehavioral development from the outset. Aside from evolutionary and clinical evidence that emotions facilitate social relations in general, there is also evidence for emotions being continuous factors in the lives of infants and caregivers. They provide a medium for development, with mother and infant normally establishing modes of reciprocal adjustment over constantly occurring sequences of interaction that leave both of them with a preponderance of pleasurable and positively toned expectations rather than negative ones. Early separation that denies opportunity for mutually rewarding affective reciprocity can have devastating consequences and correction of early separation can enhance affective parent-infant relations. (See reviews in Emde & Robinson, 1979;

Klaus & Kennell, 1976). Also, as has been reviewed, brief interruptions in face-to-face affective reciprocity between young infants and caregivers can lead to distress for both partners. Social smiling and enhanced eye-to-eye contact are important incentives for caregiving, and disappointment results when early smiling is dampened.

A biosocial view brings into focus that emotional states are complex. They involve aspects of appraisal and motivation with centered aspects being relations to pleasure and unpleasure—a point of view that is consistent with that of Arnold (1970). State complexity would seem to assure considerable variation and, considering this, it is all the more remarkable that evolution has wrought certain species-wide biological features. These features include the tendency for certain kinds of behavior to be experienced as pleasurable and rewarding, behavior not only related to drive satisfaction but exploratory activity and, most importantly, social interaction. The converse, that there is a tendency for certain other behaviors to be experienced as unpleasant, is equally true and is discussed further under cognitive–dynamic considerations.

We feel that soon after the neonatal period, human affective expressions can be represented in a three-dimensional space. These dimensions, especially ones of hedonic tone and activation, appear to characterize the emotional system throughout the lifespan. Since they appear to represent dimensions of biologically meaningful messages vital for adaptation and survival, we feel it is appropriate to speculate about neurophysiological underpinnings. The first two dimensions would likely involve diencephalic-reticular core brain structures, including reward and aversion systems, mediating "hedonic tone" (Olds & Olds, 1963) and the reticular activating system, mediating "activation" (Lindsley, 1951). Consistent with the early and persistent appearance of these dimensional functions is the fact that core brain structures regulate a variety of homeostatic survival systems and tend to mature early in ontogenesis (Bergstrom, 1969). The third dimension, one which has been somewhat more difficult to interpret in our studies, may represent a motivational aspect of affect, perhaps concerning regulation of incoming stimulation (see emotions as regulators of input in Pribram, 1967). On the other hand, it may also represent a general aspect of systems functioning (Fentress, 1976). Either way, its neurophysiology would be less certain, but it would not be far fetched to think of it as involving early-maturing and related core brain structures.

Discrete emotions, which could be represented as areas in our three-dimensional space, would appear to be more complex. Since they are species-wide, one would surmise that they must represent biologically meaningful messages that may reflect phylogenetically derived central nervous system "affect programs" for modes of experiencing and expressing discrete emotions (Izard, 1977). Based on our previous experience in longitudinal studies, we had thought that such expressions were not present at birth and appeared according to an epigenetic sequence. We thought such a sequence might be similar to what Redican (1975) had found in his review of facial expressions of nonhuman primates—a developmental sequence in which social cohesive expressions preceded fearful expressions which, in turn, preceded aggressive expressions. It also made sense to us that discrete expressions would require more complex organization than those regulating dimensional aspects and would necessitate feedback relationships among hypothalamic, thalamic, and autonomic nervous system regulatory centers as well as forebrain cortical areas for cognition. As such, we presumed they would be later developing.

In view of the fact that early infancy contains such a high maternal attribution of discrete emotions and also contains such a rich repertoire of facial activity patterns, we must say that the matter is not so simple. Our experimental study of fear, surprise, and happiness indicated that infants may have been judged as fearful in response to the visual cliff or the approaching stranger and yet not have facial expressions of fearfulness with predicted activity patterns (Hiatt, Campos, & Emde, 1977). Judgments can be made on bases other than what we have been studying so far. Many questions remain. What are the conditions under which a mother sees fear or anger in early infancy? To what extent are early attributions of emotion related to facial patterns of activity or other behaviors? To what extent are they related to stimulus events in the life of the baby and/or the life of the mother? Which emotional expressions make a difference in the life of the baby in terms of caregiving responses, and which are ignored?

Cognitive-Dynamic Considerations

A fascinating feature in the development of infant emotional states has to do with signalling. In early infancy, signalling is predominantly social. Crying and smiling provide appealing guides for caregiving activity. Later in infancy, with the advance of cognitive development, emotional states involve psychological signalling as well as social signalling. At approximately 7–9 months, with the attainment of stage IV of sensorimotor development (Piaget, 1936/1952), an infant's cognition reaches the point where it is more independent of action. Intentionality exists in the sense of an ability to interpose a delay between an initial perception of a goal and in terms of the capacity for circumventing detours such that we can infer the existence of means–ends relationships. As has been so nicely discussed by Sroufe (1979), anticipation beyond the motor act extends to affectivity. By 9 months, the infant laughs in anticipation of mother's return in a peek-a-boo game instead of after a completed sequence, and expresses fearfulness at moderate levels of stimulation in advance of avoidance behavior. (Also see discussion in Emde,

Gaensbauer, & Harmon, 1976). At this point it can be said that affective expression leads to behavior; it may be motivating subsequent instrumental behavior on the part of the infant instead of merely motivating subsequent instrumental behavior on the part of the caretaker. Now there is psychological signalling, and a two-phased affective response sequence that bears comparison with adult emotional responses as conceptualized by Arnold (1970). In the case of fear, such a two-phased affective sequence involves an initial phase of appraisal and a subsequent phase of expressed distress with attempts at avoidance (Emde, Gaensbauer, & Harmon, 1976).

Obviously, there are internal feedback processes before stage IV of cognitive–affective development, and internal signalling becomes more complex and subtle after stage IV. A world of questions are awaiting investigators in this area (Sroufe, 1979).

Another related area awaiting programmatic study has to do with emotional dynamics. Our biosocial view indicates emotions are ongoing processes. They are not primarily intermittent or disruptive. Rather, they vary over time and influence behavior in a variety of ways. It seems to me that emotional states in dynamic perspective operate at three levels. These include *ongoing set processes* (moods), *ongoing monitoring processes* (background activity), and *episodic salient processes* (signal affects and peak reactions).

Set processes of emotion involve everyday moods that could be said to have long time constants. They are influenced by slower acting hormones and biochemical imbalances as well as prolonged situations and psychological conflict; in short, they are influenced by relatively enduring aspects of biological and psychological structures. They operate over days and weeks and are involved in setting and resetting baseline parameters for emotional reactivity. Because of their centered relations to pleasure and unpleasure and additional relations with a wide variety of other psychological and organismic processes, moods have been considered indicators of ego functioning (Jacobson, 1957).

Ongoing monitoring processes of emotion consist of oscillating emotional activities. I postulate that a certain amount of ongoing endogenous activity of this sort keeps emotional functioning "in tune" and sets ranges for emotional responsiveness; it also accommodates to minor perturbations from either internal or external incentive events.

The first two levels of emotional–cognitive dynamics have received little attention in infancy research. Instead, most research has been concerned with the third level, that of episodic salient processes. Such processes include reactions to dramatic episodic events, which can be internal or external. Functions of episodic salient processes include mobilizing plans for action and mobilizing communications to others. A variety of anticipatory signal affects are included at this level, as well as peak emotional reactions. That some peak reactions may be maladaptive should not surprise us when we consider the inverted-U relationship that usually characterizes activation and performance. In extreme situations, and with high activation, emotions may be so intense that mobilized plans are disrupted and adaptive action (performance) declines.

As a psychoanalyst, I have a major interest in the theoretical development of affective-cognitive dynamics and a clinically useful theory of signal affect systems. Signal affects act as monitors of bodily processes and provide evaluation of where we stand in our social world. But there are not only anticipatory affects of pleasure and unpleasure and of anger, fear, and surprise as we imagine outcomes; there are also more complex combinations of affective-cognitive experience that have similar dynamic properties. These receive clinical attention in the form of "signal anxiety" and "signal depression."[1] Such anticipatory affects give us small doses of painful feelings along with relevant thoughts. Signal anxiety may have to do with uncertainties about future events and the potentiality for physical danger and helplessness. Signal depression may have to do with real or imagined disappointments and loss as well as the potentiality for a decline in self esteem. As contemporary psychoanalytic theorists have emphasized (Brenner, 1974; Emde & Robinson, 1979; Engel, 1962; Engel & Schmale, 1972; Kaufman, 1976), these complex signal affect systems are important for adaptive functioning. When solutions to problems are seen as possible, appropriate plans are mobilized; but when solutions are not perceived, pathological outcomes with defensive activity, clinical anxiety, or sustained depression may occur. It is obvious that we have much to learn about the development of signal affect systems as the infant moves from sensorimotor to representational intelligence and as meaning widens during the preschool years.

REFERENCES

Abelson, R. P., & Sermat, V. Multidimensional scaling of facial expressions. *Journal of Experimental Psychology,* 1962, *63,* 546–554.

Anders, T., Emde, R. N., & Parmelee, A. *A manual of standardized terminology, techniques, and criteria for use in scoring states of sleep and wakefulness in newborn infants.* University of California at Los Angeles Brain Information Service, NINDS Neurological Information Network, 1971.

Andrew, R. J. The displays of the primates. In J. Buettner-Janusch (Ed.), *Evolution and genetics* (Vol. 2). New York: Academic Press, 1964.

---

[1]It is interesting that Izard (1972), from his investigative stance, conceptualizes anxiety and depression as patterns of emotion that are made up of combinations of other more fundamental discrete emotions.

Arnold, M. Perennial problems in the field of emotion. In M. Arnold (Ed.), *Feelings and emotion: The Loyola Symposium.* New York: Academic Press, 1970.

Bell, R. Q., & Harper, L. V. *Child effects on adults.* Hillsdale, N.J.: Lawrence Erlbaum Associates, 1977.

Bell, R. Q., & Hertz, T. W. Toward more comparability and generalizability of developmental research. *Child Development,* 1976, *47,* 6–13.

Bergman, T., Haith, M. J., & Mann, L. *Development of eye contact and facial scanning in infants.* Paper presented at the biennial convention of the Society for Research in Child Development, Minneapolis, Minn., April 1971.

Bergstrom, R. M. Electrical parameters of the brain during ontogeny. In R. J. Robinson (Ed.), *Brain and early behavior.* New York: Academic Press, 1969.

Bernstein, P., Emde, R. N., & Campos, J. REM sleep in 4-month-old infants under home and laboratory conditions. *Psychosomatic Medicine,* 1973, *35,* 322–329.

Bowlby, J. *Attachment and loss, Volume I: Attachment.* New York: Basic Books, 1969.

Brazelton, T. B. Crying in infancy. *Pediatrics,* 1962, *29,* 579–588.

Brazelton, T. B. The origins of reciprocity: The early mother-infant interaction. In M. Lewis & L. Rosenblum (Eds.), *The effect of the infant on its caregiver.* New York: Wiley, 1974.

Brenner, C. On the nature and development of affects: A unified theory. *Psychoanalytic Quarterly,* 1974, *43,* 532–556.

Caldwell, B. Mother-infant interactions in monomatric and polymatric families. *American Journal of Orthopsychiatry,* 1963, *33,* 653–644.

Campos, J., Emde, R. N., Gaensbauer, T. J., & Henderson, C. Cardiac and behavioral inter-relationships in the reactions of infants to strangers. *Developmental Psychology,* 1975, *11,* 89–601.

Campos, J., Hiatt, S., Ramsay, D., Henderson, C., & Svejda, M. The emergence of fear on the visual cliff. In M. Lewis & L. Rosenblum (Eds.), *The development of affect.* New York: Plenum Press, 1978.

Carey, W. B. A simplified method for measuring infant temperament. *Journal of Pediatrics,* 1970, *77,* 188–194.

Carroll, J. D., & Chang, J. J. *Non-parametric multidimensional analysis of paired-comparison data.* Paper presented at joint meeting of Psychometric and Psychonomic Societies, Niagara Falls, N.Y. October, 1964.

Charlesworth, W. R. The role of surprise in cognitive development. In D. Elkind & J. H. Flavell (Eds.), *Studies in cognitive development.* New York and London: Oxford University Press, 1969.

Charlesworth, W. R., & Kreutzer, M. A. Facial expressions of infants and children. In P. Ekman (Ed.), *Darwin and facial expression.* New York: Academic Press, 1973.

Chevalier-Skolnikoff, S. Facial expression of emotion in nonhuman primates. In P. Ekman (Ed.), *Darwin and facial expression.* New York: Academic Press, 1973.

Cicchetti, D., & Sroufe, L. A. An organizational view of affect: Illustration from the study of Down's syndrome infants. In M. Lewis and L. Rosenblum (Eds.), *The development of affect.* New York: Plenum Press, 1978.

Condon, W. S., & Sander, L. W. Neonate movement is synchronized with adult speech: Interactional participation and language acquisition. *Science,* 1974, *183,* 99–101.

Cytryn, L. Methodological issues in psychiatric evaluation of infants. In E. Rexford, L. Sander, & T. Shapiro (Eds.), *Infant psychiatry: A new synthesis.* New Haven: Yale University Press, 1976.

Darwin, C. *Expression of emotion in man and animals.* London: John Murray, 1904. (Originally published, 1872.)

Decarie, T. *Intelligence and affectivity in early childhood.* New York: International University Press, 1965.

Decarie, T. Affect development and cognition in a Piagetian context. In M. Lewis & L. Rosenblum (Eds.), *The development of affect.* New York: Plenum Press, 1978.

Dittrichova, J., & Lapackova, V. Development of the waking state in young infants. *Child Development,* 1964, *35,* 365-370.

Dittrichova, J., & Lapackova, V. Development of sleep in infancy. In R. J. Robinson (Ed.), *Brain and early behavior.* London and New York: Academic Press, 1969.

Ekman, P. Universals and cultural differences in facial expressions of emotion. In J. K. Cole (Ed.), *Nebraska Symposium on Motivation.* Lincoln, Nebraska: University of Nebraska Press, 1971.

Ekman, P., Friesen, W. V., & Ellsworth, P. *Emotion in the human face.* New York: Pergamon Press, 1972.

Ellingson, R. J. Cortical electrical responses to visual stimulation in the human heart. *Electroencephalographic Clinical Neurophysiology,* 1960, *12,* 663-677.

Emde, R. N., & Brown, C. Adaptation to the birth of a Down's syndrome infant: Grieving and maternal attachment. *Journal of the American Academy of Child Psychiatry,* 1978, *17,* 299-323.

Emde, R. N., Gaensbauer, T. J., & Harmon, R. J. Emotional expression in infancy: A biobehavioral study. *Psychological Issues, A Monograph Series, Inc.* (Vol. 10). New York: International University Press, 1976.

Emde, R. N., & Gaesbauer, T. J. Modeling emotion in human infancy. In K. Immelmann, G. Barlow, M. Main, & L. Petrinovitch (Eds.), *Early development in animals and man.* West Germany: Zentrum fur interdisziplinare Forschung, University of Bielefeld, in press.

Emde, R. N., & Harmon, R. J. Endogenous and exogenous smiling systems in early infancy. *Journal of the American Academy of Child Psychiatry,* 1972, *11,* 177-200.

Emde, R. N., & Harmon, R. J. *Towards a strategy of studying mood in infants.* NIMH Workshop on the Origin and Development of Mood and Related Affective States in Infants and Young Children. Washington, D.C. November 12 and 13, 1976. In press.

Emde, R. N., Katz, E. L., & Thorpe, J. K. Emotional expression in infancy: II. Early deviations in Down's syndrome. In M. Lewis & L. Rosenblum (Eds.), *The development of affect.* New York: Plenum Press, 1978.

Emde, R. N., Kligman, D. H., Reich, J. H., & Wade, T. D. Emotional expression in infancy: I. Initial studies of social signaling and an emergent model. In M. Lewis & L. Rosenblum (Eds.), *The development of affect.* New York: Plenum Press, 1978.

Emde, R. N., & Koenig, K. L. Neonatal smiling and rapid eye movement states. *Journal of Child Psychiatry,* 1969, *8,* 57-67. (a)

Emde, R. N., & Koenig, K. L. Neonatal smiling, frowning, and rapid eye movement states.II. Sleep-cycle study. *Journal of American Academy of Child Psychiatry,* 1969, *8,* 637-656. (b)

Emde, R. N., McCartney, R. D., & Harmon, R. J. Neonatal smiling in REM states: IV. Premature study. *Child Development,*1971, *42,* 1657-1661.

Emde, R. N., & Metcalf, D. R. An electroencephalographic study of behavioral rapid eye movement states in the human newborn. *Journal of Nervous and Mental Disorders,* 1970, *150,* 376-386.

Emde, R. N., & Robinson, J. The first two months; Recent research in developmental psychobiology and the changing view of the newborn. In J. Call & J. Noshpitz (Eds.), *Basic handbook of child psychiatry* (Vol. 1). New York: Basic Books, 1979.

Engel, G. Anxiety and depression-withdrawal: The primary affects of unpleasure. *International Journal of Psycho-Analysis,* 1962, *43,* 89-97.

Engel, G., & Schmale, A. Conservation-withdrawal: A primary regulator process for organismic homeostasis. *Physiology, Emotion and Psychosomatic Illness,* CIBA Foundation Symposium 8, Amsterdam: Elsevier, 1972.

Fentress, J. C. System and mechanism in behavioral biology. In J. C. Fentress (Ed.), *Simpler networks and behavior*. Sunderland, Mass.: Sinauer Associates, 1976.

Freud, S. *Instincts and their vicissitudes. Standard Edition* (Vol. 14). London: Hogarth Press, 1968 (Originally published, 1915.)

Frijda, N. Emotion and recognition of emotion. In M. B. Arnold (Ed.), *Feelings and emotions*. New York: Academic Press, 1970.

Frijda, N., & Philipszoon, E. Dimensions of recognition of expression. *Journal of Abnormal and Social Psychology*, 1963, *66*, 45–51.

Gaensbauer, T., Emde, R., & Campos, J. "Stranger" distress: Confirmation of a developmental shift in a longitudinal sample. *Perceptual and Motor Skills*, 1976, *43*, 99–106.

Gaensbauer, T. J., & Sands, K. Distorted affective communication in abused/neglected infants and their potential impact on caretakers. *Journal of the American Academy of Psychiatry*, 1979, *18*, 236–250.

Gladstone, W. H. A multidimensional study of facial expression of emotion. *Australian Journal of Psychology*, 1962, *14*, 19–100.

Graham, F., & Jackson, J. Arousal systems and infant heart-rate responses. In H. W. Reese & L. P. Lipsitt (Eds.), *Advances in child development and behavior* (Vol. 5). New York: Academic Press, 1970.

Green, D. M., & Swets, J. A. *Signal detection theory and psychophysics*. New York: Wiley, 1966.

Greenberg, M., Rosenberg, I., & Lind, J. First mothers rooming-in with their newborns: Its impact upon the mother. *American Journal of Orthopsychiatry*, 1973, *43*,783–788.

Haith, M. M., Bergman, T., & Moore, M. J. Eye contact and face scanning in early infancy. *Science*, 1977, *198*, 853–855.

Haith, M. M., & Campos, J. J. Human infancy, In M. R. Rosenzweig & L. W. Porter (Eds.), *Annual review of psychology* (Vol. 28). Palo Alto: Annual Review Inc., 1977.

Hamburg, D. A. Emotions in the perspective of human evolution. In P. H. Knapp (Ed.), *Expression of the emotion in man*. New York: International University Press, 1963.

Harmon, R. J., & Emde, R. N. Spontaneous REM behaviors in a microcephalic infant: A clinical anatomical study. *Perceptual and Motor Skills*, 1972, *34*, 827–833.

Hebb, D. O. On the nature of fear. *Psychological Review*, 1946, *53*, 259–276.

Hiatt, S., Campos, J., & Emde, R. *Fear, suprise and happiness: The patterning of facial expression in infants*. Paper presented at the biennial Convention of the Society for Research in Child Development, New Orleans, LA, March, 1977.

Hiatt, S. *The patterning of facial expressions of fear, surprise and happiness in 10–12 month infants*. Doctoral dissertation submitted as partial fulfillment for Ph.D., University of Denver, Colorado, 1978.

Hoffman, M. L. Toward a theory of empathic arousal and development. In M. Lewis & L. Rosenblum (Eds.), *The development of affect*. New York: Plenum Press, 1978.

Horner, T. M. Two methods of studying stranger fearfulness in infants: A review. In press.

Hutt, S. J., Lenard, H. G., & Prechtl, H. F. R. Psychophysiological studies in newborn infants. In L. P. Lipsitt & H. W. Reese (Eds.), *Advances in child development and behavior*. New York, Academic Press, 1969.

Izard, C. *The face of emotion*. New York: Appleton-Century-Crofts, 1971.

Izard, C. *Patterns of emotion*. New York: Academic Press, 1972.

Izard, C. *Human emotions*. New York: Plenum Press, 1977.

Jacobson, E. Normal and pathological moods: Their nature and functions. *Psychoanalytic Study of the Child*, 1957, *12*, 73–126.

Jeffrey, W. E., & Cohen, L. B. Habituation in the human infant. In H. W. Reese (Ed.), *Advances in child development and behavior* (Vol. 6). New York: Academic Press, 1971.

Kagan, J. Attention and psychological change in the young child. *Science*, 1970, *170*, 826–832. (a)

Kagan, J. The distribution of attention in infancy. In D. H. Hamburg (Ed), *Perception and its disorders*. Baltimore: Williams and Wilkins, Research publication ARNMD (Vol. 48), 1970. (b)

Kagan, J. *Change and continuity in infancy*. New York: Wiley, 1971.

Kagan, J. *The growth of memory and the fears of infancy*. Paper presented at the biennial Convention of the Society for Research in Child Development, New Orleans, La., March, 1977.

Kagan, J. On emotion and its development: A working paper. In M. Lewis & L. Rosenblum (Eds.), *The development of affect*. New York: Plenum Press, 1978.

Kaufman, I. C., & Rosenblum, L. A. The reaction to separation in infant monkeys: Anaclitic depression and conservation withdrawal. *Psychosomatic Medicine*, 1967, *29*, 648–675.

Kaufman, I. C. Developmental considerations of anxiety and depression: Psychobiological studies in monkeys. *Psychoanalysis and Contemporary Science* (Vol. 4). New York: International University Press, 1976.

Kessen, W. *The child*. New York: Wiley, 1965.

Klaus, M. H., & Kennell, J. H. *Maternal-infant bonding*. St. Louis: C. V. Mosby, 1976.

Kligman, D., Smyrl, R., & Emde, R. A "non-intrusive" home study of infant sleep. *Psychosomatic Medicine*, 1975, *37*, 448–452.

Knapp, P. *Expression of the emotions in man*. New York: International University Press, 1963.

Lewis, M., Brooks, J., & Haviland, J. Hearts and faces: A study in the measurement of emotion. In M. Lewis & L. Rosenblum (Eds.), *The development of affect*. New York: Plenum Press, 1978.

Lewis, M., & Rosenblum, L. Introduction: Issues in affect development. In M. Lewis & L. Rosenblum (Eds.), *The development of affect*. New York: Plenum Press, 1978.

Lindsley, D. Emotion. In S. S. Stevens (Ed.), *Handbook of experimental psychology*. New York: Wiley, 1951.

Mahler, M. S., Pine, F., & Bergman, A. *The psychological birth of the human infant*. New York: Basic Books, 1975.

Mandler, G. *Mind and emotion*. New York: Wiley, 1975.

McCall, R. B. Smiling and vocalization in infants as indices of perceptual-cognitive processes. *Merrill-Palmer Quarterly*, 1972, *18*, 341–348.

McCall, R. B. *Stages in mental development during the first two years*. Paper presented at the biennial Convention of the Society for Research in Child Development, New Orleans, La., March, 1977.

Meltzoff, A. N., & Moore, M. K. Imitation of facial and manual gestures by human neonates. *Science*, 1977, *198*, 75–78.

Morgan, G., & Ricciuti, H. Infants' responses to strangers during the first year. In B. M. Foss (Ed.), *Determinants of infant behavior* (Vol. 4). London: Methuen, 1969.

Myers, R. E. *Cortical localization of emotion control*. Invited lecture of the American Psychological Association, Washington, September, 1976.

Olds, M. E., & Olds, J. Approach-avoidance analysis of rat diencephalon. *Journal of Comparative Neurology*, 1963, *120*, 259–295.

Osgood, C. Dimensionality of the semantic space for communication via facial expression. *Scandinavian Journal of Psychology*, 1966, *7*, 1–30.

Oster, H., & Ekman, P. Facial behavior in child development. In A. Collins (Ed.), *Minnesota Symposia on Child Psychology* (Vol. 11). New York: Crowell, 1978.

Paine, R. S. The contribution of developmental neurology to child psychiatry. *Journal of the American Academy of Child Psychiatry*, 1965, *4*, 353–386.

Parmelee, A., & Michaelis, R. Neurological examination of the newborn. In J. Hellmuth (Ed.), *The exceptional infant, studies in abnormalities*, (Vol. 2). New York: Brunner/Mazel, 1971.

Parmelee, A., Wenner, W., Akiyama, Y., Schultz, M., & Stern, E. Sleep states in premature infants. *Developmental Medicine and Child Neurology*, 1967, *9*, 70–77.

Pedersen, F., Anderson, B., & Cain, R. *A methodology for assessing parental perceptions of infant temperament.* Paper presented at the 4th Biennial Southeastern Conference on Human Development, April, 1976.

Pedersen, F. A., Anderson, B. J., & Cain, R. L. *An approach to understanding linkages between the parent-infant and spouse relationships.* Paper presented at the biennial Conference of the Society for Research in Child Development, New Orleans, La., March, 1977.

Peiper, A. Cerebral function in infancy and childhood. In J. Wortis (Ed.), *The international behavioral sciences series.* New York: Consultants Bureau, 1963.

Piaget, J. *The origins of intelligence in children.* (2nd ed.). New York: International University Press, 1952. (Originally published, 1936.)

Platt, J. R. *The step to man.* New York: Wiley, 1966.

Polanyi, M. On the modern mind. *Encounter,* 1965, *15,* 12–20. Reprinted in F. Schwartz (Ed.), *Psychological Issues (Vol. 8) Scientific thought and social reality. Essays by M. Polanyi.* New York: International University Press, 1974.

Pribram, K. H. Emotion: Steps toward a neuropsychological theory. In D. C. Glass (Ed.), *Neurophysiology and emotion.* New York: Rockefeller University Press and Russell Sage Foundation, 1967.

Rechtschaffen, A., & Kales, A. *A manual of standardized terminology, techniques, and scoring system for sleep stages of human subjects.* Los Angeles: University of California at Los Angeles, Brain Information Service, NINDS, Neurological Information Network, 1968.

Redican, W. K. Facial expressions in nonhuman primates. In L. Rosenblum (Ed.), *Primate behavior.* New York: Academic Press, 1975.

Rheingold, H. L., & Eckerman, C. O. Fear of the stranger: A critical examination. In H. W. Reese (Ed.), *Advances in child development and behavior* (Vol. 8). New York: Academic Press, 1973.

Ricciuti, H. Fear and the development of social attachments. In M. Lewis & L. Rosenblum, (Eds.), *The origins of fear.* New York: Wiley, 1974.

Robson, K. S. The role of eye-to-eye contact in maternal-infant attachment. *Journal of Chlid Psychology and Psychiatry,* 1967, *8,* 13–25.

Rothbart, M. Workshop presented at the International Conference on Infant Studies, Providence, R.I., March, 1978.

Sameroff, A. Transactional models in early relations. *Human Development,* 1975, *18,* 65–79.

Sameroff, A. (Ed.). Organization and stability of newborn behavior: A commentary on the Brazelton neonatal behavioral assessment scale. *Monographs of the Society for Research in Child Development,* Vol. 43 (5–6), 1978.

Sameroff, A. J., & Cavanagh, P. J. Learning in infancy: A developmental perspective. In J. Osofsky (Ed.), *Handbook of infant development.* New York: Wiley, 1979.

Sander, L. Issues in early mother-child interaction. *Journal of the American Academy of Child Psychiatry,* 1962, *1,* 141–166.

Sander, L. Adaptive relationships in early mother-child interaction. *Journal of the American Academy of Child Psychiatry,* 1964, *3,* 231–264.

Sander, L. W. Infant and caretaking environment. In E. J. Anthony (Ed.), *Explorations in child psychiatry.* New York: Plenum Press, 1975.

Schopler, E. Early infantile autism and receptor processes. *Archives of General Psychiatry,* 1965, *13,* 327–335.

Shepard, R. The analysis of proximities: Multidimensional scaling with an unknown distance function. *Psychometrika,* 1962, *27,* 125–140. (a)

Shepard, R. The analysis of proximities: Multidimensional scaling with an unknown distance function: II. *Psychometrika,* 1962, *27,* 219–246. (b)

Shepard, R. Representation of structure in similarity data: Problems and prospects. *Psychometrika,* 1974, *39,* 373–421.

Skarin, K. Cognitive and contextual determinant of stranger fear in six- and eleven-month old infants. *Child Development,* 1977, *48,* 537–544.

Spencer, H. *The principles of psychology* (Vol. 1). New York: Appleton, 1890.

Spiro, M. E. *Children of the kibbutz.* Cambridge: Harvard University Press, 1958.

Sroufe, L. A. Wariness of strangers and the study of infant development. *Child Development,* 1977, *48,* 731–746.

Sroufe, L. A. Socioemotional development. In J. Osofsky (Ed.), *Handbook of infant development.* New York: Wiley, 1979.

Sroufe, L. A., & Waters, E. The ontogenesis of smiling and laughter: A perspective on the organization of development in infancy. *Psychological Review,* 1976, *83,* 173–189.

Sroufe, L. A., & Waters, E. Attachment as an organizational construct. *Child Development,* 1977, *48,* 1184–1199.

Stechler, G., & Carpenter, G. Theoretical considerations. In J. Hellmuth (Ed.), *Exceptional infant* (Vol. 1). New York: Bruner/Mazel, 1967.

Stern, D. N. Mother and infant at play: The dyadic interaction involving facial, vocal, and gaze behaviors. In M. Lewis & L. Rosenblum (Eds.), *The effect of the infant on its caregiver.* New York: Wiley, 1974.

Stevens, A. G. Attachment behavior, separation anxiety, and stranger anxiety in polymatrically reared infants. In H. R. Schaffer (Ed.), *The origins of human social relations.* New York: Academic Press, 1971.

Tennes, K., Emde, R. N., Kisley, A. J., & Metcalf, D. R. The stimulus barrier in early infancy: An exploration of some formulations of John Benjamin. In R. R. Holt, & E. Peterfreund (Eds.), *Psychoanalysis and contemporary science.* New York: Macmillan, 1972.

Thomas, A., Chess, S., Birch, H., Hertzig, M., & Korn, S. *Behavioral individuality in early childhood.* New York: New York University Press, 1963.

Thomas, A., Chess, S., & Birch, H. G. *Temperament and behavior disorders in children.* New York: New York University Press, 1968.

Tomkins, S. S. *Affect, imagery, consciousness. The positive affects.* New York: Springer, 1962.

Tomkins, S. S. *Affect, imagery, consciousness. The negative effects.* New York: Springer, 1963.

Tronick, E., Als, H., Adamson, L., Wise, S., & Brazelton, T. B. The infant's response to entrapment between contradictory messages in face-to-face interaction. *Journal of the American Academy of Child Psychiatry,* 1978, *17,* 1–13.

vanHooff, J. Facial expression in higher primates. *Symposium of Zoological Society of London,* 1962, *8,* 97–125.

Wolff, P. Observations on newborn infants. *Psychosomatic Medicine,* 1959, *21,* 110–118.

Wolff, P. The causes, controls, and organization of behavior in the neonate. *Psychological Issues, Monograph No. 17.* New York: International University Press, 1966.

Woodworth, R. S., & Schlosberg, H. S. *Experimental psychology.* New York: Holt, 1954.

Wundt, W. Grundriss der psychologie (C. H. Judd, Translator). As quoted in Izard, 1971. (Originally published, 1896.)

2

The Role of Ego-Control and Ego-Resiliency in the Organization of Behavior

Jeanne H. Block
Jack Block
University of California, Berkeley

For what now approaches 30 years, we have been thinking about and investigating the implications of two personality parameters we have chosen to call *ego-control* and *ego-resiliency*. We began while graduate students at Stanford, many eras ago. Reasoning from the constructs as we then understood them, we sought to evaluate their behavioral relevance in a wide range of experimental situations and psychological tests—response extinction in a partial reinforcement context, norm establishment while experiencing movement in an autokinetic situation, performance in the Gottschaldt Embedded Figures Test, reactions to authority, divergent thinking, level of aspiration, reactions to stress, psychological fatigue or satiation, perceptual standards of similarity, ethnocentrism—all administered to the same group of college students. Our dissertation results (J. Block, 1950; J. H. Block, 1951; J. Block & J. H. Block, 1951; J. H. Block & J. Block, 1952) were encouraging: In diverse areas of psychology—learning, perception, interpersonal behaviors, attitudes, problem solving—the observed individual differences (often considered then to be no more than "nuisance variance") were frequently, reliably, and lawfully related to the personality constructs we had formulated. Especially powerful as a predictor was a composite variable generated by summing the behaviors of an individual over a variety of phenotypically diverse but conceptually related experimental situations (J. Block, 1950, Chapter 10).

In the intervening years at Berkeley, although interrupted often by other, pre-empting priorities, our focus on these theoretical constructs and their behavioral compass has continued. Relationships have been demonstrated, for example, between ego-control and the ability to delay gratification (J. H.

Block & Martin, 1955), to constructiveness manifested by children under conditions of frustration in a replication of the Barker, Dembo, and Lewin (1941) classical experiment (J. H. Block & Martin, 1955), to subjective certainty in the face of ambiguity (J. Block & Petersen, 1955), to similarity between self- and ideal-self-perceptions (J. Block & Thomas, 1955), and to identification and adjustment (J. Block & Turula, 1963). Ego-control and ego-resiliency have coordinated with the first two factors of standard psychological inventories (J. Block, 1965), to constellations of political–social–personal values in adulthood (J. Block, 1971), and to children's interest in and behavior with fire and other hazardous materials (J. H. Block & J. Block, 1975; J. H. Block, J. Block & W. Folkman, 1976; Kafry, 1978).

Although these studies generated useful data and extended our understandings, we came to recognize that for many of the intra-individual developmental issues with which we were concerned, a proper longitudinal study was required. Accordingly, in 1968 we initiated a longitudinal study of approximately 130 children we have since individually assessed at the ages of 3, 4, 5, 7, and most recently, at 11 years. During each of the years of assessment, every child was administered a battery of from 26 to 43 (averaging 36) widely ranging experimental procedures, requiring 10 or 11 testing sessions at ages 3 and 4, four or five sessions at ages 5 and 7, and nine sessions at age 11. In addition, we have developed extensive assessment data on the parents of these children and on parent–child interaction styles.

In the planning and implementation of our longitudinal design, we have been guided by a number of conceptual principles, theoretical choices, and methodological values. As the study starts to bear some harvest, this Symposium seems like the time and the place to bring together and to bring out the many kinds of considerations that have shaped the enterprise and, consequently, the findings beginning to emerge.

To begin, we talk of the theoretical decisions we elected to make, of how we mean the concepts of ego-control and ego-resiliency, of how we do not mean those concepts, of why we suggest these concepts may have some advantages in terms of incisiveness, power, and esthetics over a variety of related concepts. We then describe some of the measurement strategies employed and how the concepts were operationalized. The heuristic value of ego-control and ego-resiliency as an organizing rubric for the many kinds of data is then evaluated, followed by some results issuing from our study that are germane to the topic of this Symposium—social-emotional development. Finally, after bringing forward brief mention of our future research plans, we close with two suggestions—one regarding strategies of empiricism, the other regarding scope of conceptualization—that we believe can advance understanding of personality development. Our agenda is long and so we begin.

SOME THEORETICAL PERSPECTIVES

Two Meanings of Ego in
Psychoanalytic Psychology

The constructs of ego-control and ego-resiliency evolved in an attempt to integrate some of the aspects of psychoanalytic theory, especially as systematized by Fenichel (1945), with the theorizing of Lewin regarding the dynamics of motivational states in the individual (Lewin, 1935; 1936; 1938; 1951).

Psychoanalytic theory is centrally concerned with impulse, a primitive notion viewed as energizing the organism. But if the individual is to be adaptively tuned to his psychosocial ecology, impulse must be modulated and monitored, i.e., controlled. In Fenichel's (1945) terms, developmentally there must be "acquisition of tension tolerance [p. 42]." Such impulse control develops over time via the maturation and experientially derived construction of various personality structures. These personality structures, many of which have a strong cognitive component, serve to bring the individual, otherwise bent on maximizing the "pleasure principle," reluctantly under the governance of the pre-emptive "reality principle." The interrelated, sequentially organized set of personality structures, programmed to give priority to avoidance of threats to the viability of the individual but, within that overriding constraint, programmed also to gratify the individual, is what psychoanalytic theory means by the term "ego." Examples of specific "ego-functioning" structures (orientations implemented by behavioral routines) include delay of gratification, inhibition of aggression, caution in unstructured situations, "experimental action" (i.e., internal cognitive manipulation of anticipated, alternatively possible behaviors so as to foresee consequences) whenever feasible, affective constraints oriented to prevent loss of love, and so on. Common, and essential, to the functioning of each of these specific ego functions is the control of impulse. The cognitive strategems and the experienced context may vary; but in each, impulse is modulated and "ego" is served. It is this common denominator of the various specific ego structures—degree of impulse control and modulation—that we mean by *the construct of ego-control.*

These various specific ego structures (mechanisms, routines, frames) are interrelated and are invoked sequentially. The interrelations and sequencing may be effective or ineffective in maintaining the personality system of the individual within the bounds of psychological viability as the individual responds to and acts upon the flux of experience, facing different contextual demands and different contextual opportunities. Psychological viability for the individual entails a tolerable anxiety level, a tolerable mesh with situational impingements, and a tolerable level of impulse expression. The linkages of the ego structures that keep the personality system within tenable bounds or permit the finding again of psychologically tenable adaptational modes is a second broad, characteristic aspect of ego functioning, which we denote as *the construct of ego-resiliency.*

The constructs of ego-control and ego-resiliency represent abstractions, condensations, simplifications that we believe carry the essential qualities and functions of the psychoanalytic core concept of "ego." For all of the richness, insight, and seriousness of psychoanalytic theory regarding the understanding of personality functioning, it has also been imprecise, overly facile with supposed explanations, and seemingly inaccessible scientifically. The concept of ego has especially come under disparagement as being, in psychoanalytic theory, something akin to a homunculus ensconced in the pineal body. In formulating the concepts of ego-control and ego-resiliency, our intention was to respect and to encompass the phenomena that the notion of "ego" was invoked to explain (i.e., motivational control and resourceful adaptation as enduring, structural aspects of personality), but with concepts somewhat less grandiose and certainly more explicitly generative. Toward this end, Lewinian theory seemed especially apt.

In Lewin's effort to formally represent the psychological system of the individual, he posited (1) a system of needs that becomes both more differentiated and more hierarchically integrated in the course of development (cf. Werner's orthogenetic law), and (2) a sensori-motor system mediating between the internal need system and the external environment that also becomes both more differentiated and more integrated during development. Now, the very idea of differentiation (i.e., the separation or articulation of regions) within both the motivational and sensori-motor systems requires the conceptualization of boundaries and boundary-systems that can demarcate or delineate these differentiations. In his model, interposed between the need system (where motivations emanate) and the sensori-motor system (where contexts register and behaviors are forged), there was a boundary system logically positioned to have ego functions. And, in his formulation of the properties of boundaries, Lewin postulated two boundary characteristics that excited us because they could be coordinated with the two broad aspects of ego functioning we had separately conceptualized as ego-control and ego-resiliency.

Formalizing the Construct of Ego-Control

The first property of boundaries Lewin posited was *degree of permeability,* referring to the boundary's capacity to contain or to fail to contain psychological needs or tensions or forces. Lewin suggested that permeability could be assessed by the degree of communication obtaining between systems. Boundaries that were relatively permeable would permit neighboring systems to mutually influence each other. Relatively impermeable boundaries would limit the "spillage" from one system to another. Excessively impermeable boundaries would result in isolation or compartmentalization of psychological subsystems and lack of communication across systems.

The deductive or generative implications of the permeability property of boundaries are several and, stated in Lewinian terms, include:

1. Given permeability, there will be greater communication across systems.
2. Given permeability, there will be greater diffusion of tensions originating in one system to other systems.
3. Given permeability, there will be greater communication between internal systems and the external environment resulting in greater susceptibiilty to environmental demands and distractions.
4. Given permeability, there will be more direct, immediate, and untransformed manifestations of internal need states in behavior.

It seemed to us that given the behavioral implications of differences in the degree of boundary permeability, the permeability property could be coordinated with the psychoanalytic notion of impulse control. By so doing, the deductive (and when operationalized, predictive) possibilities of the Lewinian model could be brought to bear on a central aspect of ego functioning.

The construct of ego-control, then, when integrated into the Lewinian framework, relates to boundary permeability–impermeability. When dimensionalized, the underlying continuum at one end identifies what we have termed as *overcontrol:* excessive boundary impermeability resulting in the containment of impulse, delay of gratification, inhibition of action and affect, and insulation from environmental distractors. The opposite end of the continuum identifies what we have termed as *undercontrol:* excessive boundary permeability and its consequences, insufficient modulation of impulse, the inability to delay gratification, immediate and direct expression of motivations and affects, and vulnerability to environmental distractors.

Phrased in somewhat more contemporaneous terms, the concept of ego-control refers to the threshold or operating characteristic of an individual with regard to the expression or containment of impulses, feelings, and desires. Presuming the environmental context is not massively directive and compelling and registers equivalently on all of its experiencers, and presuming also that motivational impetus is constant, the ego overcontroller can be expected to have a high modal threshold for response, to be constrained and inhibited, to manifest needs and impulses relatively indirectly, to delay gratification unduly, to show minimal expression of emotion, to tend to be categorical and overly exclusive in processing information, to be perseverative, nondistractible, less exploratory, relatively conforming, with narrow and unchanging interests, to be relatively planful and organized, and to be made uneasy by and therefore avoidant of ambiguous or inconsistent situations. In contrast, the ego undercontroller can be expected to have a low modal threshold for response, to be expressive, spontaneous, to manifest needs and impulses relatively directly into behavior, to tend toward the immediate gratitification of desires, to readily manifest feelings and emotional fluctuations, to be overly inclusive in processing information, to have many but relatively short-lived enthusiasms and interests, to be distractible, more ready to explore, less conforming, relatively comfortable with or undiscerning of ambiguity and inconsistency, to manifest actions that cut across conventional categories of response in ways that are (for better or for worse) original, and to live life on an ad hoc, impromptu basis. In this conceptualization, extreme placement at either end of the ego-control continuum implies a constancy in mode of behavior that, given a varying world, can be expected to be adaptively dysfunctional.

Distinguishing Ego-Control From Other Constructs. The construct of ego-control should not be quickly and casually equated or categorized with other personality variables seemingly or even actually related to it, such as *extraversion–introversion, externalizing–internalizing, acting-out, psychopathy, reflection–impulsivity, delay of gratification, motor inhibition, activity level* (hyperkinesis versus hypokinesis), and the like. We believe that more than conceptual chauvinism prompts this suggestion. On strictly conceptual grounds, important distinctions can and must be made among a variety of personality variables commonly employed, but commonly unanalyzed, by psychologists. Extended consideration of the concepts relatable to ego-control cannot be afforded here; we are reduced to some quick observations and declarations from the armchair.

The concept of *extraversion–introversion* is generally not much more than a vaguely and variously held label and, with the exception of Eysenck's formulation (Eysenck, 1967), has not been embedded in a generative system of behavior. Even for Eysenck, the concept has had confounded and changing meaning over the years, being a blend in changing proportions of the components of *sociability* and *impulsivity* (e.g., J. Block, 1978; Guilford, 1975; Revelle, personal communication, 1976). If it is granted that an individual can be impulsive but not sociable, or sociable but not impulsive, then the inadequacy of the extraversion–introversion concept as commonly conveyed becomes apparent. Historically, the essential meaning of the term extraversion–introversion has reference to the external–internal orientation of the individual to inputs from the world: The extravert was a person perceptually oriented and highly receptive to the impingements of the outer world; the introvert was oriented and receptive to the inner world of thought and fantasy (Jung, 1923). Were the concept of extraversion–introversion to revert to its original meaning, this important distinction regarding attentional orientation would be recovered.

The concept of *externalizing–internalizing* is not so frequently invoked as is the concept of extraversion–introversion, but it also is imprecisely specified and without a position in a theoretical system. Although the dimension of externalizing–internalizing has been only informally conceputalized, it appears to be concerned with whether need tensions are discharged via external, action modes of expression or whether needs are routed internally into cognitive and visceral channels of discharge. In these terms, the externalizer need not be an undercontroller and the internalizer need not be an overcontroller, because the direction of a motivated response carries no necessary implication regarding the immediateness of, or the controls on, that motivated response. The label of externalizing–internalizing, if employed restrictedly, could usefully refer to the direction of action, allocentric or autocentric (i.e., outer or inner), taken by the individual in responding to the motivations that have gained regnancy.

The notion of *acting-out* is almost invariably misused in personological parlance. Usually, what is meant is "acting-up" and, defined in this sense, acting-out is often equated with undercontrol. However, the distinction between acting-out and undercontrol is fundamental and is well conveyed by Frosch (1977). In acting-out, as conceputalized in psychoanalytic theory, symbolic transformation of motivations are involved. Such transformations often lead to behavior that is related only in convoluted ways to the initial motivation. In undercontrol, on the other hand, motivations are directly expressed and are directly understandable through the behavior manifested. Acting-out, according to its original psychodynamic definition, does not necessarily imply undercontrol. Misunderstanding would be averted if the concept of acting-out were again reserved for behaviors derivative from symbolically-transformed motivations.

The notion of *psychopathy* is often overlapped with the notion of undercontrol. But psychopaths are not necessarily undercontrollers, as a reading of Cleckley (1964) and Smith (1978) will attest. Psychopaths can be planful and premeditated as well as shortsighted and impulsive. Perhaps the defining feature of the psychopath is a failure or inability or an absence of introspection in those contexts where more ordinary individuals have their self-percepts activated. As a result, psychopaths are unable to place themselves affectively in the situations of others and are, therefore, less constrained in the behaviors than are more empathic, introspective individuals. The undercontroller, on the other hand, is not thereby less likely (or more likely) to be introspective; the possibility of introspective undercontrollers and nonintrospective overcontrollers indicates the conceptual necessity of distinguishing between psychopathy and the construct of ego-control.

Reflection–impulsivity is a construct that, at quick glance, appears connectible to overcontrol and undercontrol. The notion of reflection–impulsivity was evolved some years ago by Kagan, Rosman, Day, Albert, and Phillips (1964) as a specific explanation for the individual differences observed in response to a "match-to-standard" task. The empirical support for this interpretation of "match-to-standard" performance has come under challenge (e.g., Achenbach & Weisz, 1975; Block, Block, & Harrington, 1974). The concept itself sometimes has been offered in a restricted form, as having no implications or generalizations beyond affecting performance in "match-to-standard" tasks (Kagan & Messer, 1975); to the extent that reflection–impulsivity is construed so narrowly, it loses relevance. Sometimes reflection–impulsivity has been applied with a broader meaning and with assorted implications (Kagan, 1966; 1967; Kagan & Kogan, 1970, p. 1315), but these implications do not derive from an explicit model and have oscillated over the years. Bothersome, too, is the commitment in the concept of reflection–impulsivity to the positive value of reflection and the negative value of impulsivity. The conceptual possibility that reflection can verge into obsessiveness and indecisiveness and that impulsivity can be linked with spontaneity and creative forms of "inaccuracy" (i.e., rejection of unimportant details, focusing instead on important general features or principles) is not recognized in the concept of reflection–impulsivity as it is in the concept of ego-control.

Delay of gratification and *motor inhibition* are single, isolated personality variables more limited in scope than the construct of ego-control, from which they may be derived but which they, in turn, cannot encompass. In the usual definition and usage of these variables, as with reflection–impulsivity, there is an unacknowledged suggestion that behavior representative of one pole of the dimension (delay of gratification or motor inhibition) is to be preferred over behavior indicative of the other pole (absence of delay of gratification or absence of motor inhibition). The conceptual possibility of excessive delay of gratification or excessive motor inhibition is not generally considered, although this recognition is incorporated in the construct of ego-control (i.e., overcontrol).

The concept of *activity level* is also not equatable with the construct of ego-control. It is probably the case that individuals can be stratified reliably with respect to their general level of activity or psychological energy, their characteristic tempo of "urges and surges." Holding the degree of ego-control constant, the individual high on activity level will *appear* more undercontrolled because there are more, and more frequent, motivations and impulses requiring expression in behavior. The child classified as hyperkinetic or hyperactive may not have an ego structure characterizable, in absolute terms, as "undercontrolling"; instead, he or she may be besieged by more impulses and motivational demands than his/her ordinary enough personality structure can modulate. The conceptual necessity of distinguishing between amount of impulse and the control of impulse requires clear separation of activity level from ego-control.

So much for this necessarily brief effort to connect and to disconnect the construct of ego-control and other concepts more or less related. Much more could, and should, be said on the issues so tersely addressed, but for now it is necessary to go on.

Antecedents of Ego-Control

Although the inborn antecedents of ego-control remain to be specified, it may be anticipated that further research will establish a significant role for genetic and constitutional factors. There are sound ethological reasons for presuming that variations in ego-control will have genetic consequence. The recent volume by Buss and Plomin (1975) on the genetic inheritance of temperament is especially pertinent. Their review and integration of the available evidence, much of it quite relevant to ego-control, is recommended to interested readers.

With respect to experiential antecedents of ego-control, abundant and increasingly clear relationships with socialization practices have been documented (J. Block, 1971). One of the developmental tasks of the young child is the learning of impulse control and the regulation of self-expression. For parents, the socialization of the child's primitive impulses is a major goal of child-rearing. Referencing the longitudinal data collected over many years at the Institute of Human Development, we found that overcontrolled adults in their mid-30s tended to come from families earlier and independently characterized as emphasizing structure, order, and conservative values. Undercontrolled adults tended to come from homes earlier and independently characterized as conflict-ridden, where the basic values of the parents were discrepant. Less emphasis was placed on socialization of the child in that parents tended to neglect their teaching roles, placed fewer demands for achievement on the child, and required less assumption by the child of personal and familial responsibilities. For a more extended discussion of the socialization antecedents of ego-control, the reader is referred to the last chapter of *Lives Through Time* (Block, 1971) and to the essay by J. H. Block (1976).

Formalizing the Construct of Ego-Resiliency

In Lewinian terms, ego-resiliency may be coordinated with a second property of boundaries posited by Lewin, the property of *elasticity*. Elasticity refers to the capacity of a boundary to change its characteristic level of permeability–impermeability depending upon impinging psychological forces and to return to its original modal level of permeability after the temporary, accommodation-requiring influence is no longer pressing. In our own conceptualization, ego-resiliency refers to the dynamic capacity of an individual to modify his/her modal level of ego-control, in either direction, as a function of the demand characteristics of the environmental context.

Degree of boundary elasticity, or ego-resiliency, has implication for the individual's adaptive or equilibrative capabilties under conditions of environmental stress, uncertainty, conflict, or disequilibrium. The selective, adaptive organizing aspects of psychoanalytic ego functioning can be subsumed under the concept of ego-resiliency. Ego-resiliency can explain dynamically both "regression in the service of the ego" (Kris, 1952) (e.g., as seen in the characteristically overcontrolled individual who is enabled to become ideationally fluid, loose, and even illogical, in certain circumstances such as "brainstorming") and what we term "progression in the service of ego" (e.g., as seen in the characteristically undercontrolled individual who becomes highly organized and even obsessive in certain circumstances, as when psychology graduate students study for their orals). The construct of ego-resiliency relates to Klein's (1954) formulation of "cognitive controls," which are concerned with the mediating, accommodating functions required to regulate drive expression in accordance with situational requirements. It appears to relate closely to the recently offered concept of "mobility" (Witkin & Goodenough, 1976), defined as the ability to use both the field-dependent and the field-independent modes of adaptation, depending on situational requirements and inner states; to the concept of "competence" (White, 1959); and to the concept of coping and coping strategies (Murphy, 1957, 1962).

Ego-resiliency, when dimensionalized, is defined at one extreme by resourceful adaptation to changing circumstances and environmental contingencies, analysis of the "goodness of fit" between situational demands and behavioral possibility, and flexible invocation of the available repertoire of problem-solving strategies (problem-solving being defined to include the social and personal domains as well as the cognitive). The opposite end of the ego-resiliency continuum (ego-brittleness) implies little adaptive flexibility, an inability to respond to the dynamic requirements of the situation, a tendency to perseverate or to become disorganized when encountering changed circumstances or when under stress, and a difficulty in recouping after traumatic experiences.

Holding the degree of ego-control constant, the ego-resilient person is resourceful before the strain set by new and yet unmastered situations, manifests more *umweg* solutions when confronted by a barrier, can maintain integrated performance while under stress, is better able to process two or more competing stimuli, is better able to resist sets or illusions, is engaged with the world but not subservient to it, and is capable of both "regressing in the service of the ego" when task requirements favor such an adaptation and, conversely, of becoming adaptively organized and even compulsive when under certain other environmental presses. With degree of ego-control held constant, the ego-unresilient (brittle) person, according to our conceptualization, is generally fixed in his/her established pattern of adaptation, has only a small adaptive margin, is stereotyped in responding to new situations, becomes immobilized, rigidly repetitive, or behaviorally diffuse when under stress, becomes anxious when confronted by competing demands, is relatively unable to resist sets or illusions, is slow to recover after stress, is disquieted by changes in either the personal psychological environment or the larger world, and cannot modify his/her preferred personal tempo in accordance with reality considerations.

Distinguishing Ego-Resiliency from Other Constructs. The construct of ego-resiliency, while related to such concepts as *intelligence, ego strength, competence, coping,* and the like, should not be viewed as the equivalent of any of them.

The concept of *intelligence* is not a unitary one; it means many different things to many different psychologists. Certainly, "intelligence" is not simply what intelligence tests measure! There is a practical or societal utility to "intelligence" tests; but there needs also to be a conceptual justification, an understanding or specification of the various cognitive capacities and processes that, when sequenced and organized, result in what is called "intelligent" behavior. The sequencing and organization of cognitive processes is obviously not unlike the sequencing and organization of ego processes from which we have abstracted the construct of ego-resiliency. The difference is that in ego-resiliency, the sequencing and organization of behavior serves broad and overarching motivational and affectual functions in addition to specific and immediate cognitive ends.

The extent to which intelligent tests, particularly of the omnibus variety (e.g., the Stanford-Binet or WPPSI), get at the crucial sequencing and organizational capacities of an individual is uncertain, arguable, and we judge, little. Omnibus intelligence tests appear to emphasize measurement of various information-processing, memorial, and cognitive elemental abilities necessary for subsequent intelligent behavior, but often do not index intelligent behavior itself. Therefore, there will be an asymmetric relation between performance on most omnibus intelligence tests and a more conceptual definition of intelligent behavior; but there will not be an equivalence.

We may further distinguish between intelligence, conceived in this grander vein, and ego-resiliency by noting that the failures of an individual in certain intelligence-requiring tasks or problems may be due not so much to cognitive or information-processing insufficiencies as they are due to orientational premises or motivational conditions within that individual. A person may be intrinsically cognitively capable, but may be made anxious by unstructured situations, or by unfamiliar adults, or in evaluative contexts, or may be intolerant of ambiguity; for these latter reasons, the person may not confront or become immersed in a cognitive problem that, if only if were faced and examined, would be found to be readily solvable. In this way, ego-resiliency or ego-brittleness can have consequential implications for effectively registered intelligence and cannot be viewed as a variable from which intelligence should be "partialled." The direction of partialling can, with justification, well be reversed. So, for this reason also, the constructs of ego-resiliency and of intelligence need to be maintained as separate.

While a popular label in personality and clinical psychology, the concept of *ego strength* has, in our view, been employed so broadly and so nonspecifically as to become little more than a jargonistic term for "adjustment." (In some versions of the concept, there arises the anomaly of excessive "ego strength"!) In our view, the original core meanings of ego strength in psychoanalysis can, when partitioned, essentially be encompassed by the constructs of ego-control and ego-resiliency.

The term *competence* has been so widely applied and so generalized since its introduction by White (1959) that it now frequently requires a modifier: We speak of "social competence" (Anderson & Messick, 1974) or "intellectual competence" or "linguistic competence," and so on. Implicit in the use of these qualifiers is the recognition that effective functioning, the core meaning of competence, is defined by criterion behaviors that are context-specific. Not only are the criteria for competence context-specific but, in a pluralistic society, definitions of competence seem to vary also as a function of cultural and subcultural values (Zigler & Trickett, 1978). The definition of competence in relativistic, context-specific terms seems to us to limit its usefulness as a theoretically generative variable (J. Block, J. H. Block, Siegelman, & von der Lippe, 1971). In contrast, ego-resiliency, conceptually defined as the ability to modify one's behavior in accordance with contextual demands, is a variable applicable across domains and across cultures.

The notion of *coping* (Murphy, 1957, 1962) is a broadly used concept, referring sometimes to intrapsychic mechanisms for modulating anxiety and sometimes to externally adaptive behaviors in the face of challenge, frustration, or stress. A broad repertoire of problem-solving or coping strategies is viewed as underlying the general capacity to cope. However, coping often is defined in ways that are not independent of behavioral outcome; that is, behaviors that "work" in negotiating difficult situations are manifestations of coping by definition, thus introducing circularity into the sense and operationalization of the construct. The construct of ego-resiliency, by contrast, is defined in formal terms that entail definite kinds of behaviors in specifiable circumstances.

The preceding discussion indicates, if only briefly, the kinds of arguments that can be advanced to distinguish ego-resiliency from other, related concepts.

Antecedents of Ego-Resiliency

The antecedents of ego-resiliency seem likely to include genetic and constitutional factors. Differences in what may be thought of as resiliency (and, given longitudinal study, may indeed prove to be resiliency) can be observed early in life in the extent and way in which the infant responds to environmental changes, can be comforted, equilibrates physiological responses, and modifies sleep–wake states (Bell, Weller, & Waldrop, 1971; Chess, Thomas, & Birch, 1959; Sander, Stechler, Julia, & Burns, 1970; Sander, Julia, Stechler, & Burns, 1972; Thomas, Chess, & Birch, 1969). At an entirely conjectural level, ego-oriented psychoanalysts have posited a rudimentary "conflict-free" ego structure with which the infant begins life (Hartmann, Kris, & Loewenstein, 1946). To the extent that a predisposition to the occurrence of societally recognized psychopathology is indicative of an absence of ego-resiliency, the evidence that has accrued for a genetic contribution to psychopathology can be interpreted as evidence as well for inborn individual differences in subsequent ego-resiliency (Rosenthal, 1970).

Experiential influences on ego-resiliency also appear to be substantial. Referencing the longitudinal data collected over many years at the Institute of Human Development, we found that individuals we would call ego-resilient tended to come from families earlier and independently characterized as having loving, patient, competent and integrated mothers, free interchange of problems and feelings, sexual compatibility of parents, agreement on values and concern with philosophical and moral issues, among other qualities. Individuals characterizable as ego-brittle tended to come from homes earlier and independently observed to be conflictful, discordant, with neurotic and anxious mothers ambivalent about their maternal role, and without intellectual or philosophical emphasis, among other qualities (Siegelman, J. Block, J. H. Block, & von der Lippe, 1970). The work of Robins (1966) is also highly pertinent. For a more extended discussion of the antecedents of ego-resiliency, the reader is referred to the last chapter of *Lives Through Time* (J. Block, 1971).

THE LONGITUDINAL STUDY

We had four major goals for our research:

1. to investigate two parameters of personality functioning, ego-control and ego-resiliency, with regard to their developmental course over the childhood years;
2. to explore the relations of ego-control, ego-resiliency, and their interaction, to cognitive functioning, affective differentiation, moral development, and interpersonal behaviors;

3. to identify parental, environmental, and experiential factors associated with differences in ego-control and ego-resiliency; and

4. to assess the predictive utility of these two constructs measured in early childhood for understanding personality characteristics, interests, achievement orientation, attitudes, and adaptations in the preadolescent and adolescent years.

The Sample

The children included in our study were drawn from the two nursery schools constituting the Harold E. Jones Child Study Center at Berkely over the three year period 1969–71. Extensive individual assessments were conducted at ages 3, 4, 5, and 7; we are currently concluding the assessment at age 11. The numbers of children participating vary by year, ranging from a high of 130 at age 4 to a low of 104 at age 7. In the 11-year-old follow-up, children from 110 families are being seen. Given the great mobility characterizing American society, the number of children lost from the study impresses us as low. Earlier analyses of subject loss showed no differential attrition as a function of socioeconomic level or ethnic origin. Following completion of the current assessment, the possible role of differential attrition will again be evaluated.

One of the participating nursery schools is a university laboratory school, administered by the University of California; the second nursery school is a parent cooperative, administered by the Berkeley Public Schools. The two schools, jointly considered, attract children from heterogeneous backgrounds with regard to education, socioeconomic level, and ethnic origin. Although the sample over-represents the middle and upper-middle class, the range of socioeconomic status (SES) is wide. Sixty-one percent of the children are white, 31% are black, and the remaining 8% represent other ethnic groups, primarily Oriental and Chicano.

Both the mothers and the fathers of the children are also included in the study. When their children were 3 years old, the parents each provided descriptions of their child-rearing orientations; when their children were 4 years old, the parents each interacted with their children in a teaching situation; when the children were 6 years old, the mothers were interviewed and completed both self-descriptive and child-descriptive adjective Q-sorts. Currently, additional parental data are being collected.

Some Orienting Principles Underlying the Research

It is important to register some of the underlying orienting and strategic principles shaping the research enterprise. Broadly put, it was out intention to apply a personality assessment model within the context of a prolonged longitudinal investigation that would begin with young children and study them over *multiple time periods* through the years.

Concern for a Broad Assessment of Personality and Cognitive Functioning. Besides our intention to study the *the same people* over *multiple time periods*, we were oriented toward the study of *multiple concepts* within each time period. In our view, longitudinal investigators have the responsibility of not being exclusively or narrowly focused on their personal theoretical concerns. Longitudinal studies are yet rare; the unique opportunity they present should be used to advance broad developmental understandings, as well as perhaps partisan theoretical emphases. In addition, then, to assessing the importance of ego-control and ego-resiliency for a wide variety of behaviors, we sought to study many additional and important aspects of psychological functioning at each age level. Table 2.1 lists the measures used at each assessment period. Various aspects of cognitive functioning—cognitive differentiation, creativity, focal attention, hypothesis–generation, memory—are represented. Additionally, cognitive-style marker variables such as field-dependence, category breadth, and reflection–impulsivity are included. Role-taking, moral reasoning, and prosocial behaviors constitute another measurement category. Affective differentiation—both recognition of affect and generation of responses to affective stimuli—is addressed by several procedures, as is the development of gender-role concepts over the childhood years. Comprehensive personality characterizations of each child provided by nursery school teachers, elementary school teachers, mothers, clinicians, and examiners complete the assessment battery.

Because we shall be traveling the longitudinal road but once and because of recognitions developed in earlier analyses of longitudinal data (J. Block, 1971), we have been oriented toward the inclusion (some might say, the overinclulsion!) of a wide variety of personality-relevant measures. Yet, inevitably, the broad net cast will still, for many psychological fish, prove inadequate. No longitudinal inquiry will provide the data base to respond to all developmental issues. We can hope only that the scope of our inquiry usefully improves understanding of developmental courses and patterns.

Concern for Measurement Using Multiple Kinds of Data. Besides study of the same sample with respect to *multiple concepts* over *multiple time periods*, we were oriented further toward the use of *multiple kinds of data*. A principle of personality assessment is to employ personality measures involving fundamentally different kinds of data, then to insist that these various kinds of measures of a given concept converge in their empirical implications.

TABLE 2.1

Significance Levels of Group Differences
on Experimental Tasks at Ages 3, 4, 5, and 7
Surrounding Ego Resiliency, Ego Control
and Ego-Resiliency/Ego-Control Conjunctions
(Specified by Independent Q-sort Descriptions of Children at Age 3')

	Age 3				Age 4				Age 5				Age 7			
Experimental Measure	Sex	UCQ	ResQ	R×C	Sex	UCQ	ResQ	R×C	Sex	UCQ	ResQ	R×C	Sex	UCQ	ResQ	R×C
Ego control indices																
Actometer[a]		.000U[b]	.01R		.03M	.000U										
Delay of gratification																
Candy train		N.S.				N.S.										
Gift delivery		.000O			.08F	.04O										
Accumulation of rewards										.008O						
DePree delay procedure													.02M			
Exploratory behavior																
Curiosity box–Play delay		.001O	.07B													
Curiosity box–Exploration	.03M	.01U														
Incidental		N.S.			.04M	.001U										
Question asking	.000M	.002U		.10BU												
Inhibition of impulse																
Competing set		.09O				.03O										
Simon Says							N.S.		.001M				.001M			
Resistance to temptation						.09U	N.S.									
Goal-setting estimates	.04M	.005U				N.S.										
Satiation time			.003B	.04BO		.07O						.06BO			N.S.	
Planfulness			.03R					.09RO			N.S.		.009F		N.S.	

Distractability	.000M				.07M		
Percept recognition–Guesses			N.S.				
Barrier intensity	.10M	.02U	N.S.		.09U	N.S.	
Motor inhibition–tempo			N.S.	N.S.	.008M		
Undercontrol experimental composite	.000U		.000U	.05B	.04M		.000U
Undercontrol Q-composite			.000U	.000U			not yet analyzed

Ego resiliency indices

Dual focus		.003R .04RO				N.S.	
Constructiveness under frustration	.01F	.01U .06R					.03RU
Premature decision making			.02O .001B				
Level of aspiration							
Achievement average		.02R	.000R				
Discrepancy average		.002B	N.S.				
Percept recognition		.06R	.07R		.09M		
PPVT, time/difficulty ratio		not yet analyzed					N.S.
Anticipating consequences							.09U .001R
Incidental learning		.06R	02RU	.04O .001R	.10R		.09U .001R
Formation of hypotheses							
Partial reinforcement			.007R .03RO	.09R			
Object sorting	.005M	.10U	.01U			.10RU	
Barrier hypothesis		N.S.	.03U .002R				
Alternative solutions, barrier		.10RU .05M	N.S.				
Digit span backwards	.009O	.000R	.007R	.04R			.03R
Motor inhibition test		.000R	.007R	.04R			
Resiliency experimental composite	.10O	.000R	.003R	.09O .003R			not yet analyzed
Resiliency Q-composite	.10O	.000R	.000R				.03R

(continued)

TABLE 2.1 (contd.)

Experimental Measure	Age3				Age 4				Age 5				Age 7			
	Sex	UCQ	ResQ	R×C	Sex	UCQ	ResQ	R×C	Sex	UCQ	ResQ	R×C	Sex	UCQ	ResQ	R×C
Cognitive abilities																
Peabody picture vocabulary			.000R										.05M	.10O	.02R	
Ravens progressive matrices					.10M		.004R				.009R	.009RU	.10M	.04U	.001R	
WPPSI picture completion			.03R			.05U										
Block Design						.02O	.003R									
Memory for sentences						.01O										
Mazes						.07O		.09RO								
Information							.10R									
Comprehension							.09R									
Similarities							.02R									
Geometric designs							.07R									
Arithmetic							N.S									
Landauer short-term memory		.06R														
Memory for narrative			.001R				.10R									.003RU
Conservation tasks											.04R	.05RU				.05RU
Convergent task composite	not yet analyzed				.02F		.000R				.002R	.03RO	not yet analyzed			
Cognitive Styles																
Reflection–impulsivity																
MFF time	.05M					N.S.				N.S.						
MFF error			.001B	.03BU			.001B		.10M	.01U		.009BU	.10M	.01O		

Field independence						
Embedded figure tests	.07R		.001F	.02R	N.S.	.07R
Rod and frame				N.S.	.000RO	.03R .02RO
Categorization-breadth						
Object sorting tasks		.07RU	.01M	N.S.	.01U	.10RU
Concept evaluation test				N.S.	N.S.	N.S.
Tinkertoy sorting			.02M	.009B	.07RU	.07RU
Composite breadth				.07B	not yet analyzed	not yet analyzed
Conceptual style						
Descriptive–analytic	.07O			N.S.	.07U	
Relational–functional	.07U			N.S.	N.S.	
Categorical	N.S.			N.S.	N.S.	
Sex role typing						.001M
Engagement–composite	.000U	.001R		not yet analyzed	not yet analyzed	not yet analyzed
Creativity						
Lowenfeld imaginativeness	N.S.		N.S.	.04F	.03U	.02F
Instances						
Unusual uses					.08R	not yet analyzed
Word association						not yet analyzed
Parallel lines						not yet analyzed
Social behaviors						
Role-taking tasks	.10F	.00R		.05F	.10B .01BU	.05U
Spatial egocentrism		.06B			.004R	
Sharing						

(continued)

TABLE 2.1 (contd.)

Experimental Measure	Age3				Age 4				Age 5				Age 7			
	Sex	UCQ	ResQ	R×C	Sex	UCQ	ResQ	R×C	Sex	UCQ	ResQ	R×C	Sex	UCQ	ResQ	R×C
Affective differentiation																
Physiognomic perception					.04F						.04R	.02RO			N.S.	
Differentiation of affect											N.S.					
Stanford locus of Control-I							N.S.		.05F		N.S.					
Moral development																
Selman moral reasoning															N.S.	
Moral behavior situations	not yet analyzed				not yet analyzed								not yet analyzed			
Conceptions of "badness"																

[a] When a particular measure was not administered at a given age, as, for example, the Actometer at ages 5 and 7, the pertinent section of the table has been left blank.

[b] Letters following the significance levels indicate the group favored in the comparison: Male vs. Female; Undercontrolled vs. Overcontrolled; Resilient vs. Brittle.

A useful basis for distinguishing among kinds of psychological data was offered by Cattell (1957, 1973) some years ago, distinctions which we subsequently have slightly modified and relabeled (J. Block, 1975; 1977). There are L (for *life*) data, O (for *observer*) data, S (for *self-reported*) data, and T (for *test*) data (the acronym, LOST can serve as a useful mnemonic).

L-data are societal, demographic, nonobserver-based, nonobstrusive, actuarial, indisputably ascertainable indicators or aspects or attributes surrounding the person, manifest in the real, natural, ongoing, everyday world. Some examples of L-data in our sample of children are gender, age, ethnicity, social class, presence of allergy, obesity, absenteeism, school grades, parental divorce, parental disagreement in child-rearing, and so on.

O-data are data derived from observers' evaluations of individuals leading more or less natural lives. Generally, these data take the form of personality ratings, checklists, Q-sorts, or diagnoses. O-data depend quintessentially on the use of an observer as an active, filtering, cumulating, weighting, configurating, integrating instrument.

S-data are data derived from the self observations of individuals regarding their behaviors, feelings, attitudes, interests, and characteristics. Self-ratings, responses to personality inventories and questionnaires, and answers to specific interview questions exemplify this kind of data.

T-data are data derived from standardized, objective, more or less artificial test or laboratory situations wherein selected, specific, readily identified or enumerated behaviors, usually but not always unbeknownst to the participating subject, are focused upon as indicators of particular personality variables.

All four of these kinds of data have their unique strengths and weaknesses. L-data are indisputably "real," but L-data often have confounded or obscure meaning. O-data are able to express the "deep structure" of behavior by permitting the integrating and contextualizing observer to recognize when a behavior has a certain significance and when it does not; but O-data can also be unreproduceable and distortion-prone. S-data are quickly gathered and are capable of generating important and nonobvious understandings of the individual; but S-data can also derive from foolish and superficial questions of little relevance to non-S behaviors. T-data are "objective," "hard" data, not dependent on what the individual being studied happens to say or how an observer makes inferences; but T-data can also be pallid, conceptually impoverished laboratory demonstrations lacking pertinence or general-izability. At this stage in the development of psychology as a science, it should now be obvious that *all* of these kinds of data can, separately and by their interrelations, help advance understanding. The wise psychologist will not willingly deprive him/herself of any of these complementary and supplementary ways of investigation.

Each of these sources of data is represented in our assessment battery. Various kinds of L-data have been noted already (e.g., illnesses, accidents, school progress, etc.); at each succeeding assessment, as the subjects have lived longer or experienced more or done more, additional L-indicators are being recorded. O-data are generated during all assessments and include observer's descriptions in nursery schools, in elementary school, observations of free play in a standardized sandbox situation, observations in a modification of Erikson's (1951) play construction situation, examiner descriptions of child functioning in structured test situations, and maternal descriptions of the child. S-data begin to be represented in the age 7 assessment and include self-descriptive adjective Q-sorts, interest expressions, patterns of free-time activities, responses in an interview, and a questionnaire. The heaviest investment in time and energy during each assessment period has gone toward T-data, including both standardized tests (e.g., the Peabody Picture Vocabulary Test, the WPPSI, the Matching Familiar Figures Test, the Rod-and-Frame Test, the Embedded Figures Test, the Concept Evaluation Test) and standardized situational or experiment-based procedures (e.g., delay of gratification (J. H. Block & Martin, 1955; DePree, 1966), motor inhibition, incidental learning, level of aspiration, sharing, signal detection, distractibility, satiation). Our study is unusual for the range of tests and procedures administered to the same sample of subjects, often over several assessment periods.

Concern for Multiple Measurement within Each Kind of Data. We aspired also to *multiple measurement within each kind of data,* so as to achieve dependability and generalizability of our measures. Within any kind of data, a behavioral datum—be it a life event, an observation, an aswer to a question, or a response in an experimental situation—can be viewed in psychometric terms as an *item* or variable of behavior. The variance of a behavioral item can be viewed as partitionable into three independent components—concept-related variance, reliable but not concept-related variance, and error variance. When error variance is large, a behavioral item is unreliable and cannot dependably relate to anything, including the concept it nominally was to represent. When reliable but not concept-related variance is present, a behavioral item will not correlate with the concept it nominally was to represent or with other measures validly representing the concept, although it may relate to other measures or to other concepts with which it inadvertently shares reliable variance. When concept-related variance is generated by behavioral item, that item can serve as an operational indicator of the concept of interest.

For various (and obvious) reasons, the proportion of concept-related variance in a behavioral item or measure is often—nay, usually—not as large as we would like. An ancient psychometric principle for improving the proportion of concept-related variance in a measure is to base that measure on an average, total, or composite of a number of concept-related behavioral items, each of which contains only a small amount of concept-related variance. By so doing, it follows from reasonable assumptions and simple algebra that the proportion of concept-related variance in the new, composite measure will be larger, the proportion of error variance will be smaller, and, unless one has been foolish or unlucky in choosing the behavioral items to be composited, the proportion of reliable but concept-unrelated variance will also be smaller.

Psychological investigators have been slow to recognize and to respond to the implications of this simple psychometric truism. Working with measures (behavioral items) swamped by error and reliable but irrelevant sources of variance, they have found disappointing relations between measures they had expected to be related. More than a little, the supposed paradigmatic failure of personality psychology, enthusiastically lamented over the last decade, can be attributed to methodological insufficiencies: A conceptual and empirical edifice cannot be built with poor tools of measurement.

In our own longitudinal investigation, to enhance the reliability and validity of our measures, the principle of compositing behavioral items has been heavily emphasized.

With respect to our O-data, Q-sorts are not based upon solitary, short-term observations of an individual; instead, the Q-sorter in effect composites his/her observations derived from seeing the subject in many different contexts and over an appreciable length of time. It may be presumed, reasonably, that error variance in the judgments rendered by an observer will tend to be reduced by this kind of compositing. The several Q-sorts available for a particular subject are then composited to form a grander composite. It may be presumed, reasonably, that reliable but irrelevant variance introduced by the idiosyncratic judgmental characteristics of the different observers will tend to be reduced by this second stage of compositing. Conceivably, for additional conceptual purposes, it can be useful to go on to further stages of compositing (e.g., compositing of Q-composites available at age 3 with those available at age 4, to form a Q-composite to best represent the child during the preschool years), and so on. Although a cumbersome approach, data-base management systems can lessen the onerousness of its implementation; we strongly believe the research consequences justify the efforts involved.

With respect to T-data, efforts were made, within logistic limits, to increase relilability by repeated but separate measurements. For example, to assess activity level, four 90-min actometer readings were taken over as many weeks and then were composited; to assess motor inhibition, three different tasks were administered and then were composited. Test procedures were evaluated psychometrically during pretesting and elongated or modified or dropped, as required, to help insure adequate reliabilities within the assessment battery.

Further with respect to T-data, in order to decrease the influence of reliable but concept-unrelated sources of variance, we sought to include, within limits, diverse situations or methods, administered by different examiners, for evaluating particularly important and broadly meaningful constructs. It may be reasonably presumed that, in the subsequently established composite, the proportion of concept-related variance will be appreciably boosted while the proportion of situational or method or examiner variance will not cumulate. For example, to study the concept of category breadth, five phenotypically different categorization tasks (behavioral items) were administered (for subsequent compositing) at age 4, two categorization tasks were given at age 5, and four at age 11. Role-taking was assessed by four different tasks at age 3 and by four tasks at age 4. Ego-control and ego-resiliency also are multiply assessed by a number of diverse T-procedures, subsequently composited, for the various ages of study. Such composite indices achieve a represenativeness and a conceptual implication going well beyond that obtainable with single measures of narrow scope and poor reliability (see also Epstein, 1979; Green, 1978; Humphreys, 1960).

Concern for Age-Appropriate Measurement of Psychological Concepts. Longitudinal investigations generally have been simply designed and have had simple intents; it has been thought useful to administer the same procedure several times and then to evaluate, usually via correlational techniques, whether individuals show "continuity" or "change." However, long-term longitudinal research that begins with young children requires a research strategy that neither depends on nor assumes the virtues of readministration of precisely the same procedures over time. At these early developmental levels, the age-appropriateness of many measures is short-lived. To evaluate important, salient aspects of psychological functioning over the childhood and adolescent years, concepts or dimensions have to be operationally indexed by procedures that are age-appropriate. The behavioral manifestation of a concept at one age may be very different from the behavioral manifestation of the same concept at a different age. The conceptual implication of a behavior at one age may be very different from the conceptual implication of the same behavior at another age. Because of the changing relations between genotype and phenotype (i.e., behavioral expression) as a function of development, the search for homotypic similarities across age is often not only futile, it is wrong. As Bell et al. (1971) and Waters and Sroufe (1977) have emphasized, developmental psychologists must seek age-appropriate expressions of underlying abilities and personality characteristics. Many failures to find evidence for developmental coherence probably reflect nothing more than a neglect of the necessity of age-appropriate measurement of concepts.

Recognition of this inescapable problem requires the adoption of a measurement strategy that does not depend upon the repetitive application of the same but perhaps meaning-changed procedures to exemplify a concept. Perhaps the only alternative is to use a conceptual domain-sampling approach. The conceptual domain-sampling strategy requires multiple but diverse indicators of a concept, the concept then being represented by some average or total or composite of the multiple indicators. The presumption is that the concept entails a domain of indicators and that composites based upon a good sample of indicators can be expected to be reliable and valid measures of the concept. It also follows that two samples of indicators of a concept need not overlap; the only requirement is that samples decently represent the conceptual domain. It is well known that two intelligence scales, composed of entirely different but intelligence-related items, will correlate highly, even if the two sets of intelligence-sampling items are administered at two widely-separated times. Similarly, it should be possible to develop nonoverlapping sets of experiment-based, concept-related, age-appropriate measures that, when composited, correlate from one age to another. The design of our assessment battery sought to follow this psychometric strategy, insofar as feasible, so as to respond to the measurement problem posed by the ever-changing developmental status of children.

Operationalizing the Constructs of Ego-Control and Ego-Resiliency

In our earlier discussion of ego-control and ego-resiliency, a number of behavioral manifestations of these two concepts were cited. These conceptually a priori expectations shaped the choice of tests and experimental situations to be included in the assessment battery to index ego-control and ego-resiliency at each age level.

The Experiment-Based Index of Ego-Control. Measures included in the assessment battery that, on an a priori conceptual basis, were expected to relate to ego-control are presented in Table 2.2. These measures included actometer readings, a Curiosity Box (after Banta, 1970), level of aspiration, delay of gratification, barrier behaviors, satiation, yielding to contextual "pull," planfulness, guessing behaviors, and measures of preferred tempo in the motor inhibition task. Scores on those measures administered within any given year were standardized to give equal weighting to each procedure and then composited to provide an experiment-based index of ego-control at each assessment period.

The Experiment-Based Index of Ego-Resiliency. Measures included in the assessment battery that, on a conceptual a priori basis, were expected to relate to ego-resiliency are also indicated in Table 2.2. These measures included the ability to change preferred tempo under instruction as reflected by three motor inhibition tasks, incidental learning, the ability to process two

TABLE 2.2
Components, Selected on an a priori Conceptual Basis, of the Experiment-Based Composites of Ego-Control and Ego-Resiliency at Ages 3, 4, 5, and 7

Age 3	Age 4	Age 5	Age 7
Ego-undercontrol			
Actometer scores, composited over four readings	Actometer scores, composited over four readings		
Delay-of-gratification score (reflected)	Delay-of-gratification score (reflected)	Delay-of-gratification score (reflected)	Delay-of-gratification score (reflected)
Barrier tasks, intensity scores, composited over barrier door and block tower tasks	Barrier tasks, intensity scores, composited over barrier drawer and block box tasks	Barrier puzzle tasks, intensity score	
Satiation + cosatiation trials (reflected)	Satiation + cosatiation trials (reflected)	Satiation + cosatiation trials (reflected)	Satiation trials (reflected)
Percept recognition, mean trial first guess offered (reflected)	Percept recognition, mean trial first guess offered (reflected)		
Competing set—contextual errors	Competing set—contextual errors		
Motor inhibition—mean time, standard condition, two trials on each of three tasks (reflected)	Motor inhibition—mean time, standard condition, two trials on each of three tasks (reflected)	Motor inhibition—mean time, standard condition, two trials on each of three tasks (reflected)	Simon says—errors
Level of aspiration, mean estimate over four trials	Level of aspiration, mean estimate over four trials		
Lowenfeld Mosaic test—planfulness (reflected)		Lowenfeld Mosaic Test—planfulness (reflected)	Lowenfeld Mosaic Test planfulness (reflected)
Curiosity Box—initiation time (reflected)			
Concept evaluation test-yes score	Concept evaluation test-yes score	Concept evaluation test-yes score	

Ego-resiliency

Barrier tasks—number of alternative solutions, composited over barrier door and block tower tasks	Barrier tasks—number of alternative solutions, composited over barrier drawer and block box tasks	Barrier tasks—number of alternative solutions, in puzzle task	Peabody Picture Vocabulary Test, time/difficulty correlation
Motor inhibition—Regression-adjusted scores in slow condition, composited over three tasks	Motor inhibition—Regression-adjusted scores in slow condition, composited over three tasks	Motor inhibition—Regression-adjusted scores in slow condition, composited over two tasks	Digit span backwards, total score
Dual focus—regression-adjusted score		Dual focus—regression-adjusted score	Spatial visualization, correct, non-egocentric responses
Level of aspiration—discrepancy score (reflected)	Level of aspiration—discrepancy score (reflected)		Rod and frame test, accuracy score
Distractability—power score	Distractability—power score		
Percept recognition—mean trial of correct recognition (reflected)	Percept recognition—mean trial of correct recognition (reflected)		
Incidental learning—total recall		Incidental learning—total recall	
Sigel object sorting task—mean number of objects in scorable categories	Sigel object sorting task—number of objects in scorable categories	Unstructured object sorting, number of objects in scorable categories	Physiognomic perception test, weighted maturity score
	Concept evaluation test—consistency of standards score	Concept evaluation test—consistency of standards score	Concept evaluation test—consistency of standards score
	Alternative hypotheses task—trial at which criterion for recognition of pattern change achieved (reflected)		Partial reinforcement, trials to extinction (reflected)
		Anticipation of consequences—total	Anticipation of consequences—total score

sorts of information simultaneously as reflected in a dual focus task, the ability to profit from feedback as manifested in successive estimates in a level-of-aspiration task, the ability to perceive communalities among diverse stimuli, recognition of change in environmental contingencies using a partial reinforcement paradigm, repetition of a series of digits in backward order, the ability to generate alternative solutions, evaluation of intra-individual consistency in the application of one's own standards for similarity as reflected in McReynolds Concept Evaluation Test (McReynolds, 1954), the ability to work under conditions of distractability, and resourcefulness under frustration. Again, scores on those measures administered within any given year were standardized to give equal weighting to each procedure and then composited to provide an experiment-based index of ego-resiliency at each assesment period.

In operationalizing the constructs of ego-control and ego-resiliency, diverse measures were employed, each presumed to contribute concept-related variance to the composite indices subsequently derived which were then expected to have greater generalizability and implicativeness. It should be recognized that these two experiment-based composites have not benefitted from the homogeneity improvements expectable when traditional item analysis or measure-purification procedures are applied. Our conceptual expectations were not always subsequently empirically justified by the data obtained; we know, after the fact, that our composites can be improved appreciably. By evaluating now the measures in the composites, those measures that were unreliable or undiscriminating could be identified and dropped; other measures, previously omitted, that proved discriminating could be incorporated in a revised composite. These recognitions can be used to improve the validity of the composites in subsequent studies—but not in this one. Because the experiment-based ego-control and ego-resiliency scores have not been subjected to psychometric refinement, the relationship surrounding these composites should be viewed as lower bounds on what can be obtained in succeeding, and benefitting, studies employing this kind of index.

The Observer-Based Indices of Ego-Control and Ego-Resiliency. In addition to the experiment-based indices of ego-control and ego-resilience, a second, entirely independent method was used to objectify these concepts. Comprehensive personality descriptions of each child were provided by their nursery and elementary school teachers. The teachers had the opportunity to observe each child, on a day-to-day basis, in a variety of settings, for several months prior to completing the personality descriptions. They were trained to use the California Child Q-Set (J. H. Block & J. Block, 1969), consisting of 100 personality-relevant items adapted from the adult form of the California Q-Set (J. Block, 1961), to describe each child in their class using a forced-choice format. Three independently formulated Q-sort descriptions were obtained for each child at age 3 and were composited to provide an overall formulation of the child's functioning as viewed by his or her teachers. The same procedures were followed at age 4 with, typically, three completely different teachers providing their impressions of each child, again using the CC Q-set. At ages 7 and currently at 11, CC Q-sort descriptions of each child again are obtained from their elementary school teachers (and teacher-aides when possible). Eleven different teachers were involved in Q-sorting at age 3; nine teachers, none of whom overlapped with earlier or later observers, contributed to the Q-sort composites at age 4; and at age 7, the last assessment for which data are complete, a total of 67 different teachers were involved because of the number of different schools and classes to which children had been assigned.

The estimated internal consistency reliabilities of the Q-items, based on intraclass correlations among the observers, averaged .65 at both ages 3 and 4. At age 7, each child was typically described by only one teacher and therefore item reliabilities cannot be inferred.

Having achieved reliable personality descriptions of each child, the Q-data were used to generate indices of ego-control and of ego-resiliency. Separately, criterion definitions of ego-control and of ego-resiliency had been provided by three clinical psychologists who used the CC Q-set to describe a hypothetical ego-undercontrolling child and, separately, a hypothetical ego-resilient child. The criterion-definers showed high levels of agreement, the reliabilities of the composited undercontrol and ego-resilient criterion definitions being .91 and .90, respectively. Having established highly consensual criterion definitions of the ego-control and ego-resiliency constructs, the *actual* composite Q-description of each child in the 3-year-old group was then correlated with the criterion definition of undercontrol and, separately, with the criterion definition of ego-resiliency. The resulting correlations index the similarity between the personality of the child as seen by his or her nursery school teachers and the criterion definitions. A high correspondence between the CC Q-description of a child and the criterion definition, say, of ego-resiliency can be taken to mean the child is resilient. These two indices serve as scores and are referred to as the Teacher-Based Q Undercontrol and Ego-Resiliency Indices. At age 4 and at age 7, the same procedures were followed again to derive Teacher-Based Q Undercontrol and Ego-Resiliency Index scores. The procedure will be repeated again at age 11.

Construct Validity of Ego-Control and Ego-Resiliency

We present four kinds of evidence in support of the construct validity of the ego-control and ego-resiliency concepts: the behavioral implications of the experiment-based indices of ego-control and ego-resiliency; the convergent–discriminant validity of the concepts, as assessed from the experiment-based indices and the observer-based indices for the two sexes over four ages; some evidence regarding the generalizability of these concepts and findings to studies of other samples by other investigators; and some evidence for a correspondence of our concepts, as measured via O- and T-data in samples of children, with coordinate concepts, as measured via S-data in samples of adults.

Behavioral Implications of the Ego-Control and Ego-Resiliency Experiment-Based Indices. As one way to evaluate the construct validity of the concepts of ego-control and ego-resiliency, the experiment-based ego-control and ego-resiliency scores were related to the teacher-based CC Q-descriptions. The CCQ-items describing the children at age 3 that were significantly correlated with the independently derived experiment-based undercontrol composite at age 3 were identified. Similarly, the CC Q-items describing the children at age 4 that were significantly correlated with the independently derived experiment-based undercontrol composite at age 4 were identified. The items in the *intersection* of these two sets of results, i.e., those CC Q-items significantly correlated with the experiment-based composites at both age 3 and age 4, are presented in Table 2.3, Part A. Table 2.3, Part B includes the CC Q-items jointly and significantly correlated with the experiment-based ego-resiliency composites at both ages 3 and 4.

Thirty-four of the 100 CC Q-items were significantly correlated ($p < .05$) with the experiment-based ego-control indices at both ages 3 and 4, of which 21 are not significantly related to the ego-resiliency construct. Children scoring in the undercontrolled direction on the two experiment-based ego-control composites developed one year apart are described at both ages 3 and 4 by separate sets of nursery-school teachers who had no knowledge of the performances of the children in the assessment situations as more active, assertive, aggressive, competitive, outgoing, attention-seeking, extrapunitive, overreactive to frustration, jealous, exploiting, and as less compliant, orderly, yielding, and private than children scoring in the overcontrolled direction on the experiment-based ego-control indices. These stringently discerned and highly differential personality characteristics are strongly consistent with the conceptual meaning of undercontrol and overcontrol.

Thirty-three CC Q-items were significantly correlated ($p < .05$) with the experiment-based ego-resiliency indices at both ages 3 and 4, of which 20 are not significantly correlated with the ego-control construct. Children scoring high on the two experiment-based ego-resiliency indices developed one year apart were described at both ages 3 and 4 by separate sets of nursery-school teachers who had no knowledge of the performances of the children in the assessment situations as more empathic, able to cope with stress, bright, appropriate in expressions of emotion, self-accepting, novelty-seeking,

TABLE 2.3A
CC Q-Items Significantly Correlated at
Both Age 3 and Age 4 with the
Experiment-Based Ego-Undercontrol Index at Age 4

| | Correlations | |
| | Age 3 (N = 118) | Age 4 (N = 128) |
CC Q-Item		
Considerate of other children	−.30 a[a]	−.32 a
Helpful and cooperative	−.24 a	−.24 a
Keeps thoughts to self	−.40 a	−.18 b
Transfers blame to others	.29 a	.33 a
Characteristically stretches limits	.27 a	.36 a
Concerned with moral issues	−.19 b	−.32 a
Takes advantage of others	.33 a	.35 a
Tries to be the center of attention	.31 a	.23 a
Uses and responds to reason	−.24 a	−.42 a
Is physically active	.43 a	.30 a
Is vital, energetic, lively	.44 a	.27 a
Is restless and fidgety	.35 a	.34 a
Likes to compete	.31 a	.27 a
When in conflict, tends to give in	−.32 a	−.20 b
Has high standards of performance for self	−.21 b	−.21 b
Is physically cautious	−.32 a	−.27 b
Has rapid mood shifts	.26 a	.21 b
Is afraid of being deprived	.19 b	.32 a
Is jealous and envious	.19 b	.34 a
Tends to dramatize or exaggerate mishaps	.22 b	.22 b
Is neat and orderly	−.19 b	−.19 b
Is obedient and compliant	−.28 a	−.26 a
Has a rapid personal tempo	.43 a	.34 a
Is unable to delay gratification	.30 a	.43 a
Is attentive, able to concentrate	−.38 a	−.32 a
Is planful, thinks ahead	−.33 a	−.38 a
Is dependable	−.28 a	−.31 a
Teases other children	.27 a	.22 b
Is self-assertive	.33 a	.25 a
Is aggressive	.40 a	.32 a
Likes to be alone, enjoys solitary activities	−.36 a	−.28 a
Overreacts to minor frustrations	.30 a	.35 a
Is shy and reserved	−.41 a	−.30 a
Is reflective	−.45 a	−.42 a

[a]The letter a signifies significance at or beyond the .01 level; the letter b at the .05 level. Items significantly correlated at only one age level are not included.

TABLE 2.3B
CC Q-Items Significantly Correlated at
Both Age 3 and Age 4 with the
Experiment-Based Ego-Resiliency Index at Age 4

CC Q-Item	*Correlations*	
	Age 3 *(N = 118)*	*Age 4* (N = 128)
Considerate of other children	.26 a[a]	.25 a
Reverts to immature behavior under stress	−.40 a	−.27 a
Concerned with moral issues	.32 a	.23 a
Prefers nonverbal methods of communication	−.24 b	−.21 b
Helpful and cooperative	.20 b	.28 a
Characteristically tries to stretch limits	−.24 b	−.23 b
Open and straightforward	.22 b	.18 b
Uses and responds to reason	.44 a	.43 a
Shows recognition of others' feelings; empathic	.24 a	.25 a
Restless and fidgety	−.29 a	−.26 a
Curious and exploring; seeks new experiences	.26 a	.27 a
Tends to go to pieces under stress	−.28 a	−.22 b
Has high performance standards for self	.38 a	.40 a
Seeks reassurance about his/her worth	−.21 b	−.26 b
Shows specific behavioral mannerisms	−.31 a	−.19 b
Has bodily symptoms as a function of conflict or tension	−.23 b	−.19 b
Is afraid of being deprived	−.29 a	−.25 a
Unable to delay gratification	−.39 a	−.27 a
Attentive and able to concentrate	.49 a	.44 a
Planful, thinks ahead	.43 a	.31 a
Appears bright	.46 a	.34 a
Is verbally fluent	.43 a	.25 a
Is dependable	.27 a	.34 a
Appears to feel unworthy; thinks of self as "bad"	−.22 b	−.34 a
Tends to be suspicious, distrusting	−.19 b	−.21 b
Tends to imitate those admired	−.31 a	−.23 b
Is self-reliant	.29 a	.33 a
Is competent, skillful	.45 a	.37 a
Emotional reactions are inappropriate	−.21 b	−.39 a
Tends to be sulky, whiny	−.28 a	−.20 b
Is creative in perception, thoughts, work or play	.36 a	.25 a
Is reflective	.37 a	.28 a
Is easily victimized, scapegoated	−.20 b	−.18 b

[a]The letter a signifies significance at or beyond the .01 level; the letter b at the .05 level. Items significantly correlated at only one age level are not included.

fluent, self-reliant, competent, creative, and as less anxious, conflicted, suspicious, sulky, imitative, and seeking of reassurance. These rigorously obtained and highly differential personality characterisitcs are strongly consistent with the conceptual meaning of ego-resiliency.

Convergent-discriminant Validity of the Ego-Control and Ego-Resiliency Indices. The two different and independent methods (experiment-based indices and teacher-based Q-indices) used to objectify the two concepts, ego-control and ego-resiliency, at three time periods and for both sexes can be placed within the convergent–discriminant validation matrix framework formalized by Campbell and Fiske (1959). The data, uncorrected for attentuation, are presented in Table 2.4A. This table contains a great deal of information, and some explanation is in order. The convergent validities are represented in the upper-left-hand and the lower-right-hand quadrants for ego-control and ego-resiliency, respectively, for boys and for girls. Within these quadrants, the correlations enclosed within the squares indicate the cross-time correlations for each of the two alternative methods of assessment. For the reader's convenience, the many correlations in Table 2.4A are arranged in summary form in Table 2.4B.

We suggest that these findings are, overall, rather substantial by current standards, although improvement is needed. There is appreciable convergent–discriminant validity for both the ego-control and the ego-resiliency concepts at several ages, both in the sample of girls and in the sample of boys. The concepts of ego-control and ego-resiliency, as expected, prove to be relatively independent.

Validity Generalization of the Ego-Control and Ego-Resiliency Concepts. While the evidence for both construct and convergent–discriminant validity is reasonably robust within our own study, the methods employed and the findings must generalize beyond the particularities of our longitudinal study if they are to merit serious consideration. Just as reliable scores indexing ego-control and ego-resiliency must be developed that are not dependent upon one or two possible domain-misrepresenting measures, relationships must be developed that are not dependent upon the specific sample of children that happen to have been studied. As a first test of these aspirations, a "mini" study of the network of findings surrounding the ego-control and ego-resiliency constructs was conducted using a cross-sectional approach with a sample of children differing in their demographic characteristics from our own sample (Schiller, 1978). Schiller's sample consisted of 90 3-, 4-, and 5-year-old children (mean age = 51 months) from upper-lower-class and lower-middle-class backgrounds who were attending eight different nursery schools in the San Francisco Bay area. Following the general design of the longitudinal study, Schiller administered a subset of

TABLE 2.4A
Ego-Control and Ego-Resiliency
Convergent-Discriminant Validation Matrix*

| | | Undercontrol | | | | | | Resiliency | | | | | | |
| | | Teacher-based Q-sort Composites | | | Composite of Experimental Scores | | | Teacher-based Q-sort Composites | | | Composite of Experimental Scores | | | |
Measure	Age	3	4	7	3	4	5	3	4	7	3	4	5	7
Undercontrol														
Teacher-based Q-sort composites	3	—	82[a]	57[a]	47[a]	39[a]	12	-25	-04	05	-15	11	-28	-03
	4	70[a]	—	50[a]	36[c]	43[b]	18	-33[c]	-16	-02	-08	-07	-28[c]	-26[c]
	7	47[b]	56[a]	—	45[b]	42[b]	33[c]	21	-02	16	14	-17	-26	-07
Composite experiment-based scores	3	52[a]	34[c]	31[c]	—	55[a]	25	01	-04	-04	-07	-26	-14	-21
	4	49[a]	40[a]	34[b]	43[b]	—	27[c]	-33[c]	-13	-04	-28	-27[c]	-19	-28[c]
	5	02	-01	34[c]	08	22	—	00	-03	10	-07	-20	-03	-14

Resiliency

Teacher-based	3	05	-13	02	-04	-18	01	—	65^a	33^c	45^a	30^c	44^b	34^b
Q-sort	4	-14	-30^c	-18	-36^b	-42^a	-15	69^a	—	47^a	52^a	34^b	29^c	42^b
composites	7	-02	-03	-03	00	-21	07	19	38^b	—	21	35^b	24	25^c
Composite	3	-24	-18	-23	-15	08	-30	38^b	33^c	18	—	19	50^a	46^b
Experiment-	4	-14	-27^c	-02	-23	-20	-11	41^b	52^a	29^c	41^b	—	17	44^a
based	5	-06	-04	-12	-05	-24	-23	23	38^b	49^a	43^b	18	—	62^a
scores	7	-03	-11	-15	-19	-37^b	-47^a	37^b	53^a	49^a	14	52^a	51^a	—

*Decimals are omitted. *Above* the diagonal are entered the correlations for *boys*; those *below* the diagonal are the correlations for girls. p values are: a, < .001; b, < .01; c, < .05. All corrections are *uncorrected* for attentuation.

TABLE 2.4B
Summary of Ego-Control and Ego-Resiliency
Convergent–Discriminant Validation Matrix

	Average Correlation[a] Within Method Across Years (CC Q experimental composites)	Average Correlation Between Methods Across Years (CC Q vs. experimental composites)	Average Correlation Between Constructs Across Years (Ego-control vs. ego-resiliency)
Ego-control			
Girls	.43	.31	−.15
Boys	.53	.35	−.11
Ego-resiliency			
Girls	.40	.39	−.15
Boys	.44	.35	−.11

[a]The average correlations were obtained using r to z transformation.

tests and experimental procedures to index ego-control and ego-resiliency. Her measures of ego-control included scores derived from the Curiosity Box, level-of-aspiration procedure, Motor Inhibition Test, and the Lowenfeld Mosaic Test (Lowenfeld, 1954). To experimentally index ego-resiliency, Schiller used the level-of-aspiration procedure, the Motor Inhibition Test, a different measure of the ability to formulate alternatives solutions (the Preschool Interpersonal Problem-solving Test of Shure and Spivack, 1974), two measures of role-taking ability, and a measure of pro-social behavior (Rutherford & Mussen, 1968). For each variable within each set of measures, scores were standardized before being composited into experiment-based indices of ego-control and ego-resiliency.

To obtain an external and independent criterion of ego-control and ego-resiliency, Schiller developed teacher-based Q-sort criterion scores of ego-control and ego-resiliency by having nursery school teachers use a subset of 54 CC Q-items to describe each child. Two teachers contributed their descriptions of a child and, because of the number of nursery schools represented, many different teachers were involved in the Q-sorting process. The composited teacher-based descriptions are, therefore, somewhat less reliable than those obtained in our longitudinal study. Further, by virtue of the lesser number of assessment procedures forming the experiment-based ego-control and ego-resiliency indices, they, too, may be less reliable than our own. Despite these attenuating factors, however, Schiller's results correspond well with those issuing from our longitudinal study. Table 2.5 presents the CC Q-correlates of the experiment-based ego-control and ego-resiliency indices obtained by Schiller using the abridged set of CC Q-items as well as the comparable correlations obtained in the present study.

TABLE 2.5
Correlations of CC Q-Items
with Experiment-Based Indices of Ego-Undercontrol
and Ego-Resiliency in Two Studies:
A Replication[a]

	Ego-Undercontrol		Ego-Resiliency	
	Block (N = 128)	Schiller (N = 82)	Block (N = 128)	Schiller (N = 82)
Is considerate	−.32**	−.28**	.25**	−.04
Gets along well with others	−.20*	−.28**	.22*	−.05
Is admired and sought out	−.11	−.03	.12	−.01
Is helpful, cooperative	−.24**	−.18*	.28**	−.07
Seeks physical contact	.08	.01	−.04	.08
Develops genuine relationships	−.07	−.22*	.05	.02
Regresses under stress	.25**	.07	−.27**	−.24**
Characteristically pushes limits	.36***	.36***	−.23*	−.04
Is eager to please	−.07	−.13	.07	−.09
Transfers blame to others	.33**	.27**	−.23*	−.08
Expresses negative feelings directly	.02	.12	.04	−.07
Is fearful and anxious	.03	.22*	−.21*	−.23*
Tends to brood and worry	−.06	.07	−.16	−.13
Uses and responds to reason	−.42***	−.09	.43***	.14
Is vital, energetic, lively	.27**	.12*	.11	.03
Arouses liking in adults	−.19*	−.24**	.19*	.09
Cries easily	.29**	−.07	−.14	−.11
Tends to lend, give, share	−.30**	−.17*	.28	−.06
Is restless and fidgety	.34**	.42***	−.26**	−.13
Is inhibited and constricted	−.12	−.05	−.08	−.12
Is resourceful	−.05	−.09	.16	.07
Likes to compete	.27**	.24**	−.03	.29**
Is curious, exploring	−.03	−.06	.27**	−.03
Is persistent	.01	−.14	.17	−.01
Tends to yield in conflict	−.20*	−.08	.00	−.01
Can recoup after stress	−.22	−.25**	.19*	.00
Goes to pieces under stress	.22*	.04	−.22*	−.03
Has high performance standards	−.21*	−.06	.40***	.19*
Seeks reassurance	.13	.24**	−.26**	−.24**
Tends to be indecisive	−.13	−.01	−.05	−.13
Has rapid shifts in mood	.21*	.06	−.24**	−.06
Is afraid of being deprived	.32**	.17	−.25**	−.11
Is jealous and envious	.34**	.13	−.27**	.18*
Tends to exaggerate mishaps	.22*	.02	−.16	.00
Is neat and orderly	−.19*	−.22*	.03	.22*
Becomes anxious in unstructured situations	−.03	.04	−.11	−.14
Is obedient and compliant	−.26**	−.09	.15	.10
Is attentive, able to concentrate	−.32**	−.36***	.44***	.15
Is unable to delay gratification	.43***	.31**	−.27**	−.22*

(continued)

TABLE 2.5 (contd.)

	Ego-Undercontrol		Ego-Resiliency	
	Block (N = 128)	Schiller (N = 82)	Block (N = 128)	Schiller (N = 82)
Is planful, thinks ahead	-.38***	-.25**	.31**	.23*
Is verbally fluent	-.19*	.00	.25**	.24**
Becomes strongly involved	-.09	-.03	.15	.12
Is dependable	-.31**	-.30**	.34**	.07
Is easily offended	.23*	.24**	-.12	-.02
Teases other children	.22*	.21*	-.08	.01
Is self-assertive	.25**	.03	-.06	-.03
Seeks to be independent	-.08	-.11	.18*	.00
Is aggressive	.32**	.31**	-.17	-.10
Is self-reliant	-.13	-.14	.33**	.00
Is competent, skillful	-.17	-.19*	.37***	.26**
Is stubborn	.15	.03	-.11	-.16
Tends to be sulky, whiny	.26**	.11	-.20*	-.12
Overreacts to frustration	.35***	.13	-.16	-.17
Is creative	-.21*	-.07	.25**	.19*

[a]*: $p < .05$; **: $p < .01$; ***: $p < .001$.
[b]In the Schiller (1978) study, two persons independently completed a subset of 54 Q-items from the CC Q. In the Block study, three nursery school teachers independently completed the full 100-item CC Q. In the Schiller study, the experimentally derived indices of ego resiliency and ego undercontrol were based upon five and four experimental measures, respectively. In the Block study, the experimentally derived indices of ego resiliency and ego undercontrol were based upon eight and nine experimental procedures, respectively.

A recent follow-up study of infants and toddlers by Gove and Arend (1979) provides further evidence for the validity of the ego-resiliency and ego-control concepts. Construct validity is reflected by the appreciable correlations between their experiment-based composites for ego-resiliency and ego-control (based on subsets of four and six tasks, respectively) and their teacher-derived Q-sort indices of the two constructs (correlations of .48 and .35 for ego-resiliency and ego-control, respectively; $N = 26$, $p < .01$ and .05, one-tailed tests). Measures of ego-control did not correlate with measures of ego-resiliency, indicating discriminant validity.

Construct validity is reflected, also, in the relationships found between the behaviors of 18-month old toddlers in the Stange Situation (Ainsworth & Wittig, 1969), and their behavior at 2 years of age in a problem-solving situation (Matas, Arend, & Sroufe, 1978), with ego-resiliency and ego-control measured at ages 4 and 5. Toddlers who were evaluated as securely attached at 18 months (active initiation of contact or interaction following separation from the caregiver, ability to derive comfort from the caregiver when distressed, use of the caregiver as a base to support exploration) or evaluated as competent in a problem-solving task at 2 years (manifesting enthusiasm, persistence, effective use of adult support) scored higher on both experiment-based and teacher-derived Q-sort indices of ego-resiliency at ages 4 to 5 than children assessed as less secure or less competent in the earlier studies. Infants whose insecure attachment was manifested by avoidance of the caregiver upon reunion, as predicted, scored higher on the Q-based index of overcontrol. Infants whose insecure attachment was manifested by crying and an inability to settle upon reunion tended to score higher on undercontrol at ages 4 to 5. Securely attached infants later were moderate on ego-control, as predicted. The experiment-based battery to measure ego-control did not yield significant results with regard to earlier attachment or earlier assessed competence.

Thus, the nomological network of findings across data domains and across ages and gender now has received some extension across samples and investigators.

Extension of the Concepts of Ego-Control and Ego-Resiliency to S-Data and to Adults. It is of considerable interest to note that the concepts of ego-control and ego-resiliency not only maintain stability of psychological meaning across the O- and T-data domains and across ages 3 and 4, but correspond well with the S- and O-data defining these constructs in adults as well (J. Block, 1965, Chapter 8). Observer descriptions expressed via the California Q-Set (J. Block, 1961), from which the children's CC Q-set was derived, were available on several samples of adults scoring high and scoring low on the first two, and fundamental, factors of the MMPI (S-data).

Individuals scoring at one extreme of the first factor of the MMPI were described independently, via the O-data of the California Q-set, as significantly more responsible, bright, productive, compassionate, likeable, verbally fluent, adept in coping with stress, self-accepting, and as less self-defeating, anxious, vulnerable, and distrustful than individuals scoring at the other end of the dimension. Because of the tenor of these results, we earlier suggested this MMPI factor be labeled, "ego-resiliency." The correspondence of these findings with the differently obtained results surrounding the concept of ego-resiliency in our study of children is most compelling. Clearly, there are important equivalences between children identified as ego-resilient by observer-based and test-derived data and the adults identified as ego-resilient by self-report data.

Individuals scoring at one extreme of the second factor of the MMPI were described independently, via the O-data of the California Q-set, as being significantly more undercontrolled, rebellious, extrapunitive, inconsistent, manipulative, overreactive to frustration, talkative, and as more likely to test limits. Individuals scoring at the other end of the dimension were independently characterized as significantly more overcontrolled, conforming, submissive, slow, unvarying, and moralistic. The results, by their coherence, suggested that the MMPI factor might be labeled "ego-control." The congruence of the behavoral correlates of this S-data dimension with those surrounding the concept of ego-control in our study of children is striking. Clearly, there is an impressive similarity between the children identified as under- or as overcontrolled by our O- and T-data and those adults identified as under- or as overcontrolled by S-data.

To summarize these several validational efforts to evaluate the usefulness and generality of the ego-control and ego-resiliency concepts, we suggest that we have been able to demonstrate the presence in behavior, for both sexes, over time, across different samples of different ages, and across methods of experimentation, observation, and self-report, of two context-responsive personality subsystems that separately and in conjunction appear to have consequentiality.

Some Empirical Ramifications of Ego-Control and Ego-Resiliency

Having shown that the constructs of ego-control and ego-resiliency can be operationalized in several ways that then display generally attractive convergent and discriminant validity across domains of measurement, gender, appreciable lengths of time, and additional subject samples differing in age, and different investigators, we turn now to consider the import and ramifications of ego-control and ego-resiliency with regard to concepts and measures extending well beyond these initial definitional and validational concerns.

The Structure and Logic of the Data Presentation. There are various ways of organizing our findings for presentation and various considerations to which we must attend. Four our purposes here, we have chosen to explore the implications of ego-control and ego-resiliency that override the possible influence of gender, even though our male and female subjects differ often both with respect to level of ego-control and the behavioral quality of their manifestations of ego-control. On another occasion, we expect to consider closely the differential developmental progression of the sexes with regard to ego-functioning. For now,however, to stringently evaluate the functional relevance of ego-control and ego-resiliency, we have elected to assess the envelopmental power of the constructs *after statistically controlling for the effects of gender.* The easy way to achieve this analytical intention is via hierarchical multiple regression analysis, the logic and attractions of which are well conveyed by Cohen and Cohen (1975).

In our many multiple regression analyses of the implications of ego-control and ego-resiliency vis-à-vis our host of "dependent" variables, the variable of gender has always been introduced first, prior to the introduction of the ego-control and ego-resiliency variables. By so doing, insofar as gender is confounded the ego-control and ego-resiliency variables subsequently entered into the multiple regression equation, the role of gender is controlled or "partialled out" in a way logically identical to analysis of covariance. The independent variables, ego-control and ego-resiliency, are then entered into the multiple-regression analysis to evaluate their respective explanatory power for the dependent measure. Finally, the possibility of a significant interaction of ego-control and ego-resiliency with the dependent measure is evaluated by forming a "product variable" from the ego-control and ego-resiliency measures, then entering this constructed variable into the multiple-regression analysis to identify the additional variance contributed by this measure over and beyond the variance already encompassed by ego-control and ego-resiliency (Cohen, 1978).

As the primary measures of ego-control and ego-resililency to be entered as independent variables into this analytical structure, we chose to employ the indices of ego-control and ego-resiliency generated from the earlier described Q-sort composites characterizing the children at the age of 3 years. Two considerations contributed to this decision: We wished to use ego-control and ego-resiliency measures from the earliest possible time, which meant indices available from the assessment at age 3; and we wanted to use the indices in which we had the greatest faith, which, for us, meant the Q-based indices.

It will be remembered that these Q-descriptions were contributed by three nursery-school teachers, each of whom had observed each child for 3 hours each day, 5 days a week, for several months before offering their independent Q-characterizations. These observers did not "score" the children with respect to our ego variables; rather, they described the children in the terms made available by the Q-language, using the forced-distribution method to bring their language scalings into a commensurate frame of reference. After compositing these comparably offered personality descriptions, these composites were referenced against criterion-definitions of ego-control and ego-resiliency, as described earlier, to generate "scores" for each child.

In our view, the extensive observational base for these descriptions, the methodological advantages of the Q-sort method, the multiplicity and independence of the observers, and the "removed" nature of the derivation of the ego-control and ego-resiliency "scores"—all these considerations taken together—provide us with the best available (and in absolute terms, quite good) measures of ego-control and ego-resiliency. Around these measures, we orient the subsequent multiple regression analyses and reference the strengths and weaknesses, validity and invalidity of other, and later, measures, especially those in the experimental or T-domain.

Relations Between O-Indices of Ego-Control and Ego-Resiliency at Age 3 and T-Data at Ages 3, 4, 5, and 7.   Table 2.1 presented the currently available experimental or T-domain findings accruing from our several analytical decisions. The extensity of experimental procedures, applied over so long a period to the same subject sample, makes this table unprecedented in developmental psychology.

Some further explanation is helpful for a proper reading and perspective on the reported relationships. Measures have been grouped into various a priori categories; in a number of instances, however, the assignment of a particular measure to a particular category should be understood as arbitrary. Generally, for diverse and usually supportable reasons, particular procedures were administered during only one or two of the four assessment years: Certain procedures appropriate at one or two age levels were deemed inappropriate at earlier or later times; certain procedures were intrinsically unrepeatable, for memorial reasons; certain procedures, after employment, were thought to be weak or weaker than later available procedures; logistical problems when the children entered the public school system restricted testing time and precluded continued use of certain procedures; and, we were sometimes unwise. Also, because of our strategic emphasis on the compositing of concept-relevant experimental measures or "items," a logic that presumes the essential interchangeability of items, we did not feel tied to the usual (and, as we have already noted, sometimes misguided) preoccupation of longitudinal studies, i.e., the application, repeatedly over the years, of seemingly same procedures to the studied sample. When a measure was not administered at a given age, the pertinent section of Table 2.1 has been left blank. Non-significant relationships and measures not yet analyzed are also noted. Where an independent variable explains significant incremental variance, the probability level and the direction of relationship are indicated. The reader may wish to know that at age 3, ego-control and ego-resiliency are essentially unrelated, correlating –.10. Additionally, at this age level, both are essentially independent of sex (correlations of .07 and –.02 for ego-control and ego-resiliency, respectively). The Peabody Picture Vocabulary Test, considered by some to be a general-purpose intelligence measure, was administered at age 3; it correlates –.01 and .37, respectively, with ego-control and ego-resiliency.

To provide a context for viewing the results presented in Table 2.1, the percentage of the total number of multiple-regression analyses yielding significant ($p < .05$) results for ego-control, ego-resiliency, and/or their interaction at each age level will be indicated. At age 3, 51% of the multiple-regression analyses issued significant results involving at least one of three independent variables; at age 4, the percentage is 44%; at age 5, the comparable percentage is 50%; and at age 7, 46% of the analyses were significant. These percentages, which are high absolutely, become more impressive when it is recognized that all of these analyses are independent; that the dependent variables derive from the generally less tractable experimental or T-data domain; that 11 nursery-school teachers contributed to the CC *Q*-descriptions of the children at 3, from which the independent variables for ego-control and ego-resiliency were derived; that 15 different examiners were involved in collecting the experiment-based dependent data; and that the effects of sex have been partialled out prior to testing for the effects of ego-control and ego-resiliency. The results of these analyses demonstrate that the two dimensions of ego functioning with which we are concerned, ego-control and ego-resiliency, can be measured reliably at age 3 and account for significant amounts of variance in both the personality and cognitive realms, both contemporaneously and across a time span of 4 years.

Examining the effects of sex, we find a trend toward increasing sex differences from the preschool years to age 7. The percentage of multiple-regression analyses showing significant sex effects is about the same during the preschool years (16% at age 3; 13% at age 4; and 14% at age 5) but increases markedly to 29% at age 7. This pattern accords well with the evidence for increasing sex differentiation with age noted by J. H. Block (1976) when she categorized the studies cited by Maccoby and Jacklin (1974) according to the age of the subjects.

Not only do sex differences emerge in greater frequency by the age of 7; we find sex effects also in the *pattern* of psychological correlates surrounding particular dimensions. In particular, ego-control in 7-year-olds appears to be manifested quite differently in boys and girls. As a result, the formula for our a priori conceptual, experiment-based ego-control index, which we applied equally to the two sexes, has issued results which do not support our anticipations. Because the analyses were conducted only days before this writing, we have not yet properly explored the reasons for, and implications of, these findings. It seems reasonable to ascribe this disappointment in part to the relative brevity of the assessment conducted at age 7, (only 4 hours). But the experiment-based ego-resiliency composite at age 7 has fared well in both sexes, and so this explanation is not sufficient. We believe the major reason for the breakdown of the ego-control experiment-based composite at age 7 lies in our deficient understanding of the demand quality of the procedures employed, given the diverging developmental progression of the sexes. During the preschool years, our subjects were more children than they were boys and girls; by age 7, however, they need to be recognized as boys and as girls and not viewed, conglomerately, simply as children. Given this belated insight, we expect that we will have to develop separate experiment-based indices of ego-control for males and for females much in the way that different scoring templates already are used for the two sexes when scoring for ego-control in psychological inventories (J. Block, 1965).

Although much should be said about the voluminous T-domain results reported in Table 2.1, only those findings most pertinent to social and affective development are now mentioned. We then go on to a richer and more germane source of information about the social-affective realm, additional and later observer data. It should be noted, however, that among the many undiscussed findings in Table 2.1 some dramatic coherencies across time can be observed, and also some dismaying failures. Of especial interest are some empirical indications that ego-control as tempered by ego-resiliency influences attention-deployment strategies, memory, and ease of memorial access. A full and critical evaluation of the salience of ego-control and ego-resiliency as organizing rubrics for behavior in different domains over time is being delayed until data from the comprehensive assessment now underway of the subjects at age 11 become available.

One consequential aspect of the self-concept is the nature of the premises developed by the child about the self–world relationship. Some children face the world with confidence and the expectation that their behaviors can produce effects in the world (Baumrind, 1973; J. H. Block, J. Block, & Harrington, 1975; Piaget, 1954; Rotter, 1966; White, 1959), while other children approach the world tentatively, anticipating that their efforts may go unheeded (J. H. Block, J. Block, & Harrington, 1975; Harrington, J. H. Block, & J Block, 1978; Hunt, 1961). Our T-data suggest that early undercontrol relates to confidence in goal setting (level of aspiration), to active engagement with the experimental tasks presented (engagement composite), to inquisitive, exploratory orientation (Curiosity Box, incidental curiosity), and to active, intense efforts directed at overcoming barriers (barrier tasks). One aspect of the self-concept—and the most salient component of the self-concept in preschoolers, according to Keller, Ford, and Meacham (1978)—relates to action schemata. The set of T-findings surrounding the effects of early undercontrol emphasizes action, engagement, boldness, and assuredness that may, or may not, generally be contextually appropriate.

Role-taking ability has been shown to be importantly related to prosocial behaviors—altruism, empathy, sharing, caring (Krebs & Sturrup, 1974; Rubin & Schneider, 1973; Selman, 1971). We find that ego-resiliency as it is manifested at age 3 predicts role-taking ability as reflected by performance on a set of Flavell's role-taking tasks (Flavell, 1968) and spatial non-egocentrism as reflected by performance on an adaptation of Piaget and Inhelder's "three-mountain" problem (Piaget & Inhelder, 1956). Early ego-resiliency also is found to relate to sharing behavior in an experimental situation designed to elicit altruism (Rutherford & Mussen, 1968) and to field independence-dependence (as measured by the Embedded Figures Test and by the Rod-and-Frame Test), a dimension previously shown to have implications in the social domain (Witkin & Goodenough, 1977).

Looking at the T-data in the difficult-to-sample affective domain, ego-resiliency assessed at age 3 relates only to scores on the Physiognomic Perception Test at age 5. The Physiognomic Perception Test (Ehrman, 1951) measures the consensually referenced accuracy of the subject in matching a word to one of four line drawings (e.g., the word, "anger," vis-à-vis a circle, a line rising from left to right, a square, and a jagged line, this last being the alternative that norms designate as correct).

The T-procedures bearing on the social-affective domain, although of interest, are few in number and lacking in direct pertinence. This should not be surprising since, by their very nature, T-assessment procedures trade off both the richness and the complexity of social experience for the affectively sparser, but also eminently manageable, scores derivable from standardized tests. To gain understanding of social-affective development, it seems likely psychology will have to rely primarily on observer-based data, to which we now turn.

Relations betweeen O-Indices of Ego-Control and Ego-Resiliency at Age 3 and O-Data at Ages 4 and 7. Following the multiple-regression logic earlier described, it is possible to evaluate the consequentiality of ego-control and ego-resiliency, as assessed when the children were 3 years old by the Undercontrol and Ego-Resiliency Q-Composites, for the social and affective behaviors characterizing these children at ages 4 and 7, as extensively described in these later years by entirely independent sets of teachers' Q-descriptions.

In the interests of data reduction and to simplify the reporting task, the 100 items in the CC Q-set have been grouped, according to both empirical and conceptual criteria, into 40 homogeneous mini-scales or "superitems," so as to lessen (albeit at some cost) the redundancy among our Q-items. Table 2.6 reports the results surrounding the superitems at ages 4 and 7, the superitems being classified into large, somewhat arbitrary categories: ego-control, ego-resiliency, orientations on self and the world, social behaviors, social stimulus value, and behavioral symptoms. The relations in Table 2.6 demonstrate the time-spanning power of the ego-control and ego-resiliency indices developed at age 3 in predicting important aspects of ego, social, and cognitive functioning at ages 4 and 7. At age 4, one year after the initial assessment, ego-control and/or ego-resiliency accounted for significant ($p < .05$) portions of the variance of 90% (36 of 40) of the superitems. Four years after their initial assessment, these two variables measured at age 3 account for significant portions of the variance in 47.5% (19 of 40) of the CC Q-superitems at age 7. The number and, as we shall see, the nature of these relations across time strike us as compelling.

Early-measured ego-control relates to the CC Q-superitems assessed at age 4 and age 7 that we have grouped as related to ego-control in many and conceptually required ways. Children with high scores on the undercontrol index at age 3 were described independently one and, often, 4 years later as: energetic, curious, restless, expressive of impulse, and as less constricted, less

TABLE 2.6
Observation-Based Findings at Ages 4 and 7
Surrounding Ego-Control and Ego-Resiliency
as Specified by Independent Q-Sort Descriptions
of the Children at Age 3[a]

California Child Q-Sort "Superitems"	Age 4								Age 7							
	Sex		UCQ₃		ResQ₃		R×UC		Sex		UCQ₃		ResQ₃		R×UC	
	Raw r	MRSig	Raw r	MRSig	Raw r	MRSig	Raw r	MRSig	Raw r	MRSig	Raw r	MRSig	Raw r	MRSig	Raw r	MRSig
Ego-control																
Inhibited, constricted			-.63	.000O	-.12	.005B					-.37	.000O	-.27	.006B		
Compliant			-.58	.000O	.28	.04R					-.53	.000O				
Energetic, active			.57	.000U	.09	.03R					.49	.000U	.16	.06R		
Curious, exploring	.22	.04M	.16	.01U	.50	.000R							.18	.09R		
Restless, fidgety	.20	.06M	.35	.007U	-.32	.007B			.35	.002M	.33	.001U			.08	.07BU
Undercontrolling of impulse			.62	.000U	-.39	.001B					.37	.001U				
Calm, relaxed			-.44	.000O	.44	.000R					-.27	.01O	.21	.07R		
Ego-resiliency																
Worrying, anxious			-.14	.03O	-.40	.000B							-.32	.009B		
Recoups, resilient			.14	.01U	.48	.000R							.25	.03R		
Externalizing vulnerability			.35	.001U	-.51	.000B									.28	.10BU

84

	(1)	(2)	(3)	(4)	(5)	(6)
Brittle, fragile margin of integration					.23 .07U	
Intolerant of ambiguity		.37 .002U	-.49 .000B			-.26 .02B
Verbal facility		-.23 .003O	-.39 .000B .42 .000R			.28 .01R
Rigid repetition under stress		-.12 .04O	-.43 .000B			
Withdraws under stress		-.41 .000O	-.15 .02B			
Orientations on self and world			.47 .000R			not significant
Autonomy striving			.54 .000R	.43 .10RU	.23 .03U	.20 .06R
Likes to compete	.26 .01M	.48 .000U		.19 .09M	.24 .02U	
Likes to play alone	.31 .003M	-.40 .000O			-.30 .02O	
Fantasy orientation	.20 .06M	-.15 .05O	-.34 .002B	.30 .01M		not significant
Negative self-image			-.27 .009B			not significant
Negative evaluation of others			not significant			
Imitates those admired	-.24 .03F			-.24 .05F		-.21 .10B
Behaves in sex-typed ways		not significant				-.20 .09B
Admits negative feelings		not significant				.20 0.8BU

(continued)

TABLE 2.6 (contd.)

California Child Q-Sort "Superitems"	Age 4				Age 7			
	Sex Raw$_r$ MRSig	UCQ₃ Raw$_r$ MRSig	ResQ₃ Raw$_r$ MRSig	R×UC Raw$_r$ MRSig	Sex Raw$_r$ MRSig	UCQ₃ Raw$_r$ MRSig	ResQ₃ Raw$_r$ MRSig	R×UC Raw$_r$ MRSig
Social behaviors								
Empathic		-.41 .001O	.51 .000R			-.30 .008O		
Interpersonal reserve		-.57 .000O	-.08 .04B			-.38 .000O	-.18 .06B	
Interpersonal relatedness			.25 .009R			not significant		
Straightforward, open			.34 .003R					-.24 .07RO
Protective of others			.26 .01R			not significant		
Teases		.25 .04U			.21 .09M	.21 .05U		
Manipulative		.44 .000U	-.27 .04B					
Seeks physical contact		.19 .06U				.21 .07U		

86

Social Stimulus Value						
Interesting, arresting	.28 .003U		.21 .01R			.39 .000R
Popular with peers			.35 .001R		not significant	
Scapegoated by peers			.21 .03RO			
Attractive	-.24 .02F	-.34 .001O	.33 .001R	-.32 .01O		.31 .005R
Behavioral Symptoms						
Bodily symptoms			-.38 .000B		not significant	
Behavioral mannerisms		-.12 .08O	-.30 .002B			-.18 .10B
Inappropriate affect	.22 .04M	-.05 .04O	-.55 .000B		not significant	

[a]The reader should note that, in a few multiple regression analyses, an independent variable explains significant incremental variance even though the direct correlation of the independent variable with the dependent variable is clearly not significant. This seeming discrepancy can result as a function of suppressor effects not recognized by the direct correlation.

compliant, and less relaxed. Clearly, these personality characteristics embody the core meaning of the construct of ego-control and testify to its long-term social and affective implications.

Similar support for the implicativeness of early-measured ego-resiliency is provided by the CC Q-superitems assessed at ages 4 and 7 that we have classified as relevant to ego-resiliency. Children with high scores on the ego-resiliency index at age 3 were described independently at age 4 as: able to recoup after stress, verbally fluent, less anxious, less brittle, less intolerant of ambiguity, and as less likely to externalize or to become rigidly repetitive or to withdraw under stress. At age 7, the number of relationships is fewer and the correlations of lesser significance; nevertheless, these data continue to underscore the importance and the essential progressive continuity of ego-resiliency.

Before continuing with Table 2.6, we detour briefly to present some perspective on the reciprocal implications of ego-control and ego-resiliency gained by considering a subset of the CCQ-findings. Some of the CC Q-superitems significantly related at age 4 to ego-control at age 3 are also related to ego-resiliency as measured at age 3; other CC Q-superitems significantly related to ego-control are not related to ego-resiliency, and vice versa. By attending only to the CC Q-superitems *conjointly* related to ego-control and ego-resiliency, classifying these items according to the particular pattern of ego-control and ego-resiliency relationships manifested, vivid psychological portrait emerges of the individuals representing each of these patterns. Table 2.7 presents, in four quadrants, the CC Q-superitems at age 4 that were significant ($p < .05$) functions of *both* earlier (age 3 ego-control and also earlier ego-resiliency. The quadrants are identified as: Resilient Undercontrol, Resilient Overcontrol, Brittle Undercontrol, and Brittle Overcontrol.

While the correlation betweeen ego-control and ego-resiliency as measured at age 3 is of zero order ($r = -.10$), the position of an individual child in this two-dimensional psychological space has strong implications for manifestly different patterns of interpersonal functioning. For the undercontrolling child, the presence of ego-resiliency tends to temper the expression of impulse without suppressing spontaneity, engagement, and enthusiasm. For the undercontrolling child with little ego-resiliency, however, impulse is unmodulated and we see a restless, externalizing, impulsive, easily disrupted child, a syndrome that fits more than a little the description of the hyperactive child (Whalen & Henker, 1976).

For the overcontrolling child, the presence of ego-resiliency results in a high degree of socialization that fits and feels well, a relative absence of anxiety and intimidation in reacting to and acting on the world. The overcontrolling child with little ego-resiliency appears victimized, immobilized, anxious, overwhelmed by a world apprehended as threatening and unpredictable. There is appreciable evidence of psychopathology in the Brittle

TABLE 2.7
CC Q-Items Significantly Associated with the Four Ego-control/Ego-resiliency Conjunctions

Resilient Undercontroller	*Resilient Overcontroller*
Energetic, active	Compliant
Curious, exploring	Calm, relaxed
Recoups, resilient	Empathic
Interesting, arresting	

Brittle Undercontroller	*Brittle Overcontroller*
Restless, fidgety	Inhibited, constricted
Undercontrolling of impulse	Worrying, anxious
Externalizing, vulnerable	Intolerant of ambiguity
Brittle, narrow margin of integration	Rigidly repetitive under stress
Manipulative	Interpersonally reserved
	Withdraws under stress
	Manifests inappropriate affect
	Manifests behavioral mannerisms

Overcontroller, as evidenced by behavioral mannerisms, inappropriate affect, and immobilization when confronted by stress.

Thus, within the individual, the reciprocal interactions of ego-control and ego-resiliency have much consequence for the nature of the perceptual and behavioral premises established, the development of character structure, and the quality of functioning in the interpersonal world.

Returning now to further consideration of Table 2.6, it may be observed that, with respect to the CC *Q*-superitems reflecting orientations toward the self and the world, children who were ego-resilient at age 3 were seen as task oriented and as emphasizing of autonomy and independence at age 4, while less resilient children were seen as critical and devaluing of both self and others. Undercontrol at age 3 relates to an emphasis on and pleasure derived from competition, a manifestation of engagement and desire for active mastery also seen in the T-data as salient components of undercontrol. Children who were described at 3 as overcontrolling were seen as enjoying solitary play and as oriented toward fantasy at age 4, manifestations of reserve and psychological "distancing."

The CC*Q*-superitems in the realm of social behaviors also are substantially influenced by early ego-control and ego-resiliency. In general, positive patterns of social interaction (e.g., empathy, protectiveness, relatedness, directness) are associated with early ego-resiliency, while negative interpersonal behaviors (e.g., teasing, manipulativeness) are associated with early undercontrol.

Ego-resiliency as assessed as age 3 has significance for the later-evaluated social stimulus value of 4-year-olds and, to a lesser extent, 7-year-olds. Early ego-resiliency is associated with positive social stimulus value: with being seen as popular, interesting, and physically attractive at age 4. The ability to modify behavior in response to the demand qualities of a situation, a hallmark of ego-resiliency, benefits social interactions where differentiated responsiveness to moods, interests, needs, and sensitivities of others is a necessary condition for communication and relatedness. It is not surprising that the more resourceful, responsive, resilient children evoke positive evaluations and reactions from both adults and peers. Negative reactions in the form of scapegoating and victimization, on the other hand, are elicited by overcontrolling children. One might conjecture that these negative, aggressive behaviors represent extreme attempts by their peers to evoke responses from these inhibited, shy, constrained children.

In summarizing the results from the O-data domain, abundant evidence for behavioral coherencies with regard to ego-control and ego-resiliency across time were found. We also find evidence for the implicativeness of these concepts for interpersonal behaviors, for social evocativeness, for patterns of pesonal adaptations, and for psychopatholoy. Not surprisingly, the relationships with the measures of ego-control and ego-resiliency achieved at age 3 are both more robust and more numerous at age 4 than at age 7. Several factors may contribute to this observation. First, the *Q*-sorts at age 4 are more reliable, since three teachers typically contributed to the CC *Q*-composites at that age, whereas at age 7, typically only one teacher described each child. A second attentuating factor is that nine teachers were involved in *Q*-sorting when the children were 4-year-olds, while 67 teachers contributed *Q*-sort descriptions of the children at age 7. Third, the elementary-school teachers necessarily developed their knowledge of the children in a more restricted context than that available to nursery school teachers who see the children at work, at rest, at play, alone, and with peers. Fourth, and perhaps most critical, children are active, developing creatures; new information, new experiences, and new efforts to integrate information and experiences serve to modify earlier-established orientations on the world and to transform behaviors. Seven-year-olds simply have had more developmental time than 4-year-olds and, for this reason alone, will have evolved further from the way they were at age 3.

Relations between O-Indices of Ego-Control and Ego-Resiliency at Age 3 and S-Data at Age 7. The final sets of data to be presented derive from data in the S-domain, scores obtained from self-descriptions provided by the children at age 7, and the preferences expressed by them for television programs classified into several broad categories.

The children were given a 19-item set of descriptive phrases and asked to "describe the child in this picture," the picture being a color Polaroid picture of the subject placed on a stand to encourage detached evaluation and thus benefit discrimination. The children were instructed to place the cards in one of five clearly labeled categories ranging from "Very Much Like the Boy/Girl in This Picture" to "Not At All Like the Boy/Girl in This Picture." Because of the age of the children, an unforced distribution was used. Following completion of the self-description, the child was asked to use the cards once again to describe the child in the picture in the way his/her classmates would describe him/her. The adjectives selected for the task were pretested for vocabulary level and, as an additional check on understandings, the child was asked to read aloud each word and to indicate any adjectives that had unclear meaning. The adjectives were familiar to and comprehended by the children.

The results of multiple-regression analyses, completed according to the format described earlier, are presented in Table 2.8.

It is of interest to note that children appear to respond in a more discriminating way when describing themselves according to their construals of their classmates' perceptions of them than when under the self-descriptive instructions. Asking children to consider their classmates' impressions of them requires greater objectivity and appears to have resulted in more candid responses.

Results of these analyses indicate that children judged as undercontrolled at age 3 say their peers would describe tham at age 7 as lazy, less neat, less obedient—adjectives clearly connecting with the conceptual definition of undercontrol. Early-evaluated ego-resiliency does not produce significant results except when conjoined with ego-control. Resilient, overcontrolled children say they are shy, while brittle undercontrolling children indicate their

TABLE 2.8

Self-descriptive Items at Age 7 Significantly Associated with Ego-Control and Ego-Resiliency as Specified by Independent Q-Sort Descriptions of the Children at Age 3

Self-Descriptive Q-Items	Age 7			
	Sex	UCQ$_3$	ResQ$_3$	R×UC
My classmates say I am helpful	.04F[a]			
My classmates say I am shy	.04F			
My classmates say I worry	.002M			
My classmates say I get mad easily	.03M			
My classmates say I obey	.04F	0.1O		
My classmates say I am neat		0.5O		
I am lazy		.007U		
My classmates say I am lazy		.000U		
I am shy				.03RO
My classmates say I like to be the best				.02BU

[a]Letters following the significance levels indicate the group favored in the comparison: Male vs. Female; Undercontrolled vs. Overcontrolled; Resilient vs. Brittle.

classmates think they like to be the best. The adjective self-descriptions are also sex-differentiating. Girls describe themselves in the peer condition as significantly more helpful, shy, and obedient, while boys in the same condition say these are more worried and more easily angered. These results are attenuated to some degree by our inability to use the forced-choice Q-sort format with children at this age. It is likely that greater discrimination would have resulted if effects due to the operation of response sets could have been lessened.

Early ego-control and ego-resiliency are found to be associated with the television-program preferences of boys and girls at age 7. Children were asked to indicate their favorite television program, and the nominated programs were subsequently grouped into one of nine categories: family situation comedies, educational television, cartoons, children's programs (non-cartoon), game shows, aggressive shows (crime shows and westerns), sports, cultural programs (ballet, music, dramatic theatre), and miscellaneous. The multiple regression analysis strategy earlier-described was applied to the televison preference data. Preference for family situation shows was expressed by girls ($p < .007$) and by children seen as both resilient and undercontrolling (ER × EC) at age three ($p < .004$). Aggressive television programs were preferred by boys ($p < .003$) and by children seen as brittle and undercontrolling (ER × EC) at age three ($p < .05$). Cartoon shows (typically Saturday morning cartoon programs) were preferred by children described as brittle and nonresilient at age 3 ($p < .001$). These data are of considerable interest because they suggest that television programs have a differential "pull," depending upon the personality characteristics of the child. Children "at risk" for watching TV programs in which violence and aggression are featured (crime shows and westerns) are those children who, it might be argued, are most likely to be influenced by the programs content.

The findings in the S-domain deriving from self-descriptive adjective Q-sorts not only fit well with the results of analyses in the O-domain; they also provide additional support for our conceptualizations of ego-control and ego-resiliency and attest again to the salience of these dimensions over time.

GOING FURTHER

The present report, it should be remembered, is an interim and selective accounting of our longitudinal journey; the study continues, and our effort to make sense of our data continues. There is no need now for a discursive discussion. As we have gone along, we have communicated our scientific (and personal) beliefs, preferences, goals, understanding, and puzzlements. Our results have been conveyed and commented upon. We expect this report to be superceded as progress is made on three major analytical themes now being pursued.

Shortly, we will be involved in evaluating the data from the assessment being completed at the preadolescent age of 11 years. (In addition, we are planning for the assessment to be conducted at age 14, when the children are well into adolescence). The host of assessment data soon to be available will abruptly double the length of time spanned by our longitudinal study, from 4 years (age 3 to age 7) to 8 years (from age 3 to age 11). The kind of analyses reported here will be extended to new data, further to evaluate the consequentiality, direct and via transformation, of early character structure for later personality, social behavior, and cognitive status. The measures being administered at age 11 are listed in Table 2.9.

A second analytical focus will be on systematically relating the extensive L-, O-, and S-data available regarding the parents to the qualities of their children as evaluated concomitantly and years later. These data already have received some attention, and relationships have begun to emerge that we judge to be exciting and of great implication.

Our third analytical preoccupation, now underway, is an attempt to better understand personality differences and personality similarities by better understanding the psychological demand qualities of the situations in which these differences and similarities are observed. Just as one can scale or order individuals with respect to various personality dimensions, one can scale or order situations with respect to various facets of their "evocativeness." A Q-set has been developed and is being applied to describe situations as they would (or should) register on a hypothetical normative individual. By using this Q-set to characterize each of the many experimental situations encountered by our subjects in the course of longitudinal study, we expect to be able to then order the situations experienced with regard to various "presses" and "pulls." Subsequently, it may be feasible to perceive, more abstractly and more functionally than before, the nature of the situations that differentially influence the behavior of individuals varying with respect to pesonality. We are especially keen on the possibility this approach may have for offering a conceptual understanding of the kinds of situations differentially responded to by the sexes.

Plans for future analyses, however, are not the note on which we shall end this long essay. Instead, and at the risk of seeming presumptuous, we wish to suggest two guiding recognitions that the study of personality development might well adopt in its empirical and conceptual future.

There has been disappointment with the empirical results regarding personality development accruing in the scientific literature. Relationships have been weak and inconsistent; lawfulness has been hard to find. In response to these failures of expectation, some psychologists have become disillusioned about the scientific possibilities of the field. Others have sought a larger principle that could underlie the erratic empirical accomplishments to date and have converted the observation of poor lawfulness from one time to another to an assertion of a conceptual viewpoint: There is little implication

TABLE 2.9
Procedures Included in the
Assessment Battery for 11-Year-Olds

Experimental Measures (T-Data)

Alternate uses
Alternative hypotheses (partial
  reinforcement)
Associative drift
Children's embedded figures test
Circles test (Torrance)
Curiosity box
Delay of gratification (DePree)
FASP (embedded figures test)
Gough perceptual acuity test
Incidental learning
Interpersonal problem solving test
  (Shure & Spivack)
Kogan metaphoric triads test
Level of aspiration (pursuit rotor)
Lowenfeld mosaic test
Matching familiar figures test
  (two forms)
McReynolds concept evaluation test

Motor inhibition tasks (Draw-A-Line,
  yellow Brick Road)
Number distraction test (Santostefano)
Object sorting test
Peabody picture vocabulary test
Pettigrew category width test
Phenomenology of emotions (Block)
Physiognomic perception test (Ehrman)
Play configurations (Erikson)
Ravens progressive matrices
Rod and frame test
Signal detection task
Similes test
Stanford memory test (Landauer)
Stroop color–word test
Susceptibility to associative priming
Wechsler intelligence scale for children

Self-Report Measures (S-Data)	*Observer-Derived (O-Data)*
Activities checklist	Behavior ratings (completed by each *E*)
Adjective self-descriptive *Q*-sort	California Child *Q*-sort (completed by
Interview	elementary school teachers)
Kelly rep test	Adjective Q-sort description (completed
	by mother and father independently)
	Environmental Q-sort (completed
	by home interviewer)

Parent Data

Loevinger sentence completion test
Rest defining issues test
Child-rearing practices report Q-sort
Adjective *Q*-sort descriptions of self
  and of child
Maternal Interview

of character structure at one stage for character structure at a later stage, because situations and environmental contexts change with time. By simply assuming behavior to be largely and directly a function of the operative situational context, a quite sufficient explanation of the observed absence of lawfulness is claimed.

As is now well recognized, this "reconciling" explanation is logically flawed because it depends upon often unrecognized and often unexamined assumptions (e.g., J. Block, 1975, 1977; Epstein, 1979). Positive assertions predicated only on failures to reject the null hypothesis are difficult to justify seriously. All one needs to do to fail to reject the null hypothesis is to execute research of poor quality and to evaluate research badly. Studies lacking in statistical power, using measures that are invalid or unreliable, and evaluated naively will continue to provide "evidence" for "personality inconsistency." A better examination of the nature and basis of the developmental "discontinuities" that doubtless will be found to exist must first await research that brings to a sufficient point of precision and accuracy the specification of the psychological qualities being studied in individuals over time and over context. The road to improving the quality of our empiricism is long and difficult, but there is good reason to believe psychology can go much further than yet it has. In making this progress, we anticipate that ancient methodological principles, some of which have been incorporated in our longitudinal study, will prove worthwhile.

In the last 15 years or so, the field of developmental psychology has been dominated by issues of cognitive development. The journals record this general emphasis; due homage especially should be paid Piaget for his important contribution to the recognitions won. But, for all the importance and even centrality of cognitive psychology for the understanding of many aspects of behavior, it should also be realized that cognitive psychology, as generally conceived and generally studied, deals with only a small portion of the mental lives, the experience, and the consequently forged behaviors of individuals. The psychological world of the individual is surprisingly seldom occupied by the purely cognitive problems with which psychologists have been prone to concern themselves. Cognition in everyday life is not oriented around such problems as pouring water into containers of different shape or the factors influencing the swing of a pendulum. Paradigmatic and essential to study though such cognitive problems are, they are problems without a social or interpersonal context, placed before an individual presumed to function without passions and without highly personal, often behaviorally preempting affect-optimizing criteria.

Thus, psychological thinking about how cognitive structures are created and transformed has derived primarily from consideration of how children interact with the physical world. In the version of the physical world provided to the child, the child observes a "reality" that is impressively orderly and follows clearly inferable rules. The child can test the nature of this reality by actions, actions that elicit direct, immediate, unequivocal feedback from the world. Further, and for entirely useful reasons, the cognitive problems employed are selected to be distant from the central motivational system of the child so that the "cool" process of cognitive structural development can be perceived most purely, without the intrusive influence of "hot" motivations.

But children live in an interpersonal world as well, a world which, depending on time, place, and person, can be far more central, psychologically, than the physical world. And, they must construct intake, output, and integrational structures for dealing with this interpersonal world. The social world is complex and perhaps ultimately fractious, behaving in ways only fuzzily comprehensible. Efforts by the child to test the nature of the interpersonal reality by acting upon it have erratic or dim results; social feedback is often indirect, delayed (sometimes forever in the interpersonal sphere), and equivocal, permitting only the uneasiness of uncertain inference instead of the pleasure of certain deduction afforded by the physical world. Because there is little or no feedback on the basis of which to build cognitive structures for dealing with the social world, the child must evolve and apply not-so-cognitive structures functional enough or sufficient for the predication of behavior. In doing so, the principles that come into play to govern such structures, construed in the absence of unmistakeable, unambiguous feedback, are principles that are less than rational. They include the forms of irrationality called "primary process modes of thought" (Freud, 1900/1953), the "cognitive illusions" observed by Tversky and Kahneman (e.g., 1974), and attributional errors in social judgment (e.g., Jones, Kanouse, Kelley, Nisbett, Valins & Weiner, 1972), among others.

"Irrational" modes of perception, action, and cognition are due, at least in part, to intrinsic information-processing limitations of the human mind. But also, these intrinsic limitations develop the possibility for individuals to be influenced by strong motivations, pervading fears, and prevailing aspirations. The extent to which and way in which reigning passions will affect development of the not-so-cognitive structures can be expected to be a joint function of the efficacy of the reality-testing available to the developing child and the motivational stresses being endured.

The processes underlying the development of not-so-cognitive structures (premises, orientations, attitudes on the world, deutero-learnings, scripts, and so forth) are, of course, the processes underlying the development of personality or ego structures. Conceived in these terms, the timeliness of extended study of character development becomes apparent; there is promise of a fruitful integration of cognitive and personality psychology. In that integration, reasoning from the relationships reported earlier, we anticipate that concepts very much akin to ego-control and ego-resiliency will be found useful.

ACKNOWLEDGMENTS

The research reported is being supported by a National Institute of Mental Health Research Grant MH 16080 to Jack and Jeanne H. Block and by a National Institute of Mental Health Research Scientist Award to Jeanne H. Block. The ordering of the authors' names is immaterial; they could as well be reversed. As with other "projects" we have parented and nutured, we both have contributed, differently but equally. We wish to express our appreciation to the children and their families who continue to participate in our longitudinal study. Much has been asked of them; they have responded with a grace and enthusiasm that we find affirming. We are grateful to the teachers, both at the Harold E. Jones Child Study Center and in the cooperating Bay Area elementary schools who have devoted many hours to completing the Q-sort descriptions upon which our analysis depend heavily. The administrative staff in these schools also have facilitated our research efforts in many ways for which we are thankful. We are deeply appreciative of the research staff, Myrna Walton, Jolinda Taylor, Judy Casaroli, Mark Haarz, Joy Moore, Mimi Rosenn, Rachel Melkman, Suzie Schmookler, Tammy Socher, Jon Feshbach, Elaine Simpson, Marjorie Hayes, Jackie Heumann, and Betty Goodman, whose diligence, sensitivity, and committment during the process of data collection were essential to the success of our research venture. In addition to participating in data collection, Drs. Anna von der Lippe and Ellen Siegelman importantly contributed to the development of the assessment battery for the 3-year-olds. Finally, we wish to thank our colleague, Professor David Harrington, for the many responsibilities he assumed on this project over the years, participating in data collection, supervising the scoring and coding of the data, managing the complex data bank, and for his many psychological perceptions.

REFERENCES

Achenback, T. M., & Weisz, J. R. Impulsivity-reflectivity and cognitive development in preschoolers: A longitudinal analysis of development and trait variance. *Developmental Psychology*, 1975, *11*, 413–414.

Ainsworth, M. D. S., & Wittig, B. A. Attachment and exploratory behavior in one-year-olds in a strange situation. In B. M. Foss (Ed.), *Determinents of infant behavior* IV. London: Methuen, 1969.

Anderson, S., & Messick, S. Social competency in young children. *Developmental Psychology*, 1974, *10*, 282–293.

Banta, T. J. Tests for the evaluation of early childhood education: The Cincinnati Autonomy Test Battery (CATB). In J. Hellmuth (Ed.), *Cognitive studyies* (Vol. 1). New York: Brunner/Mazel, 1970.

Barker, R. G., Dembo, T., & Lewin, K. Frustration and regression: An experiment with young children. *University of Iowa, Studies in Child Welfare*, 1941, *18*, 1–314.

Baumrind, D. The development of instrumental competence through socialization. In A. D. Pick (Ed.), *Minnesota symposium on child psychology* (Vol. 7). Minneapolis: University of Minnesota Press, 1973.

Bell, R. Q., Weller, G. M., & Waldrop, M. F. Newborn and preschooler: Organization of behavior and relations between periods. *Monographs of The Society for Research in Child Development*, 1971, *36*, 1–2 (Whole No. 142).

Block, J. *An experimental investigation of the construct of ego-control.* Unpublished doctoral dissertation, Stanford University, 1950.

Block, J. *The Q-sort method in personality assessment and psychiatric research.* Springfield, Ill.: C. C. Thomas, 1961.

Block, J. *The challenge of response sets.* New York: Appleton-Century-Crofts, 1965.

Block, J. *Lives through time.* Berkeley, Calif.: Bancroft Books, 1971.

Block, J. *Recognizing the coherence of personality.* Unpublished manuscript, University of California, Berkeley, 1975.

Block, J. Advancing the science of personality: Paradigmatic shift or improving the quality of research? In D. Magnusson and N. S. Endler (Eds.), *Psychology at the crossroads: Current issues in interactional psychology.* Hillsdale, N.J.: Lawrence Erlbaum Associates, 1977.

Block, J. Review of H. J. Eysenck & S. B. G. Eysenck, *The Eysenck Personality Questionnaire.* In O. Buros (Ed.), *The eighth mental measurement yearbook.* Highland Park, N.J.: Gryphon, 1978.

Block, J., & Block, J. H. An investigation of the relationship between intolerance of ambiguity and egocentrism. *Journal of Personality,* 1951, *19,* 303–311.

Block, J., Block, J. H., & Harrington, D. M. Some misgivings about the Matching Familiar Figures Test as a measure of reflection–impulsivity. *Developmental Psychology,* 1974, *10,* 611–632.

Block, J., Block, J. H., Siegelman, E., & von der Lippe, A. Optimal psychological adjustment: Response to Miller's and Brofenbrenner's discussions. *Journal of Consulting and Clinical Psychology,* 1971, *36,* 325–328.

Block, J., & Petersen, P. Some personality correlates of confidence, caution, and speed in a decision situation. *Journal of Abnormal and Social Psychology,* 1955, *51,* 34–41.

Block, J., & Thomas, H. Is satisfaction with self a measure of adjustment? *Journal of Abnormal and Social Psychology,* 1955, *51,* 254–259.

Block, J., & Turula, E. Identification, ego-control and adjustment. *Child Development,* 1963, *34,* 945–953.

Block, J. H. *An experimental study of a topological representation of ego structure.* Unpublished doctoral dissertation, Stanford University, 1951.

Block, J. H. *Familial and environmental factors associated with the development of affective disorders in young children.* Paper presented at the National Institute of Mental Health Conference on Mood and Related Affective States. Washington D.C., November, 1976. (a)

Block, J. H. Issues, problems, and pitfalls in assessing sex differences: A critical review of the *Psychology of sex differences. Merrill-Palmer Quarterly,* 1976, *22,* 283–308. (b)

Block, J. H., & Block, J. An interpersonal experiment on reaction to authority. *Human Relations,* 1952, *5,* 91–98.

Block, J. H., & Block, J. *The California Child Q-Set.* Institute of Human Development, University of California, Berkeley, 1969. (In mimeo)

Block, J. H., & Block, J. *Fire and young children: A study of attitudes, behaviors, and maternal teaching strategies.* Technical Report for Pacific Southwest Forest and Range Experimental Station, Forest Service, U.S. Department of Agriculture, 1975.

Block, J. H., Block, J., & Folkman, W. *Fire and children: Learning survival skills.* U.S. Department of Agriculture Forest Service Research Paper, PSW-119, 1976.

Block, J. H., Block, J., & Harrington, D. *Sex-role and instrumental behavior: A developmental study.*   Paper presented at the meeting of The Society for Research in Child Development, Denver, April, 1975.

Block, J. H., & Martin, B. Predicting the behavior of children under frustration. *Journal of Abnormal and Social Psychology,* 1955, *51,* 281–285.

Buss, A. H., & Plomin, R. *A temperament theory of personality.* New York: Wiley, 1975.

Campbell, D. T., & Fiske, D. W. Convergent and discriminant validation by the multitrait-multimethod matrix. *Psychological Bulletin,* 1959, *56,* 81–105.

Cattell, R. B. *Personality and motivation structure and measurement.* New York: World Book Company, 1957.

Cattell, R. B. *Personality and mood by questionnaire.* San Francisco: Jossey-Bass, 1973.

Chess, S., Thomas, A., & Birch, H. Characteristics of the individual child's behavioral reponse to the environment. *American Journal of Orthopsychiatry,* 1959, *29,* 791-802.

Cleckley, H. M. *The mask of sanity* (4th ed.). St. Louis: C. V. Mosby Co., 1964.

Cohen, J. Partialed products *are* interactions; partialed powers *are* curve components. *Psychological Bulletin,* 1978, *85,* 858-866.

Cohen, J., & Cohen, P. *Applied multiple regression/correlation analysis for the behavioral sciences.* Hillsdale, N.J.: Lawrence Erlbaum, Associates, 1975.

DePree, S. *Time perspective, frustration-failure and delay of gratification in middle-class and lower-class children from organized and disorganized families.* Unpublished doctoral dissertation, University of Minnesota, 1966.

Ehrman, D. M. *A preliminary investigation of a new research method.* Unpublished doctoral dissertation, Stanford University, 1951.

Epstein, S. The stability of behavior: I. On predicting most of the people much of the time. *Journal of Personality and Social Psychology,* 1979, in press.

Erikson, E. H. Sex differences in the play configurations of preadolescents. *American Journal of Orthopsychiatry,* 1951, *21,* 667-692.

Eysenck, H. J. *The biological basis of personality.* Springfield, Ill.: C. C. Thomas, 1967.

Fenichel, O. *The psychoanalytic theory of neurosis.* New York: Norton, 1945.

Flavell, J. H. *The development of role-taking and communication skills in children.* New York: Wiley, 1968.

Freud, S. *The interpretation of dreams.* In *The standard edition of the complete works of Sigmund Freud.* Vols. 4-5, 1953. London: Hogarth Press, 1953. (Originally published 1900)

Frosch, J. The relation between acting out and disorders of impulse control. *Psychiatry,* 1977, *40,* 295-314.

Gove, F., & Arend, R. *Competence in preschool and kindergarten predicted from infancy.* Paper presented at the biennial meeting of the Society for Research in Child Development, San Francisco, March, 1979.

Green, B. F. In defense of measurement. *American Psychologist,* 1978, *33,* 664-670.

Guilford, J. P. Factors and factors of personality. *Psychological Bulletin,* 1975, *82,* 802-814.

Harrington, D., Block, J. H., & Block, J. Intolerance of ambiguity in preschool children: Psychometric considerations, behavioral manifestations, and parental correlates. *Developmental Psychology,* 1978, *14,* 242-256.

Hartmann, H., Kris, E., & Loewenstein, R. M. Comments on the formation of psychic structure. *The Psychoanalytic Study of the Child,* 1946, *2,* 11-38.

Humphreys, L. G. Notes on the multitrait-multimethod matrix. *Psychological Bulletin,* 1960, *57,* 86-88.

Hunt, J. McV. *Intelligence and experience.* New York: Ronald Press, 1961.

Jones, E. E., Kanouse, D. E., Kelley, H. H., Nisbett, R. E., Valins, S., & Weiner, B. *Attribution: Perceiving the causes of behavior.* Morristown, N.J.: General Learning Press, 1972.

Jung, C. G. *Psychological types.* New York: Pantheon, 1923.

Kafry, D. Fire survival skills: Who plays with matches? Technical Report for Pacific Southwest Forest and Range Service, U.S. Department of Agriculture, 1978.

Kagan, J. Body build and conceptual impulsivity in children. *Journal of Personality,* 1966, *34,* 118-128.

Kagan, J. Biological aspects of inhibition systems. *American Journal of Disadvantaged Children,* 1967, *114,* 507-512.

Kagan, J., & Kogan, N. Individual variation in cognitive processes. In P. Mussen (Ed.), *Carmichael's manual of child psychology* (3rd ed., Vol. 1). New York: Wiley, 1970.

Kagan, J., & Messer, S. B. A reply to "Some misgivings about the Matching Familiar Figures Test as a measurement of reflection–impulsivity." *Developmental Psychology,* 1975, *11,* 244–248.

Kagan, J., Rosman, B. L., Day, D., Albert, J., & Phillips, W. Information processing in the child: Significance of analytic and reflective attitudes. *Psychological Monographs,* 1964, *78,* No. 1. (1, Whole No. 578)

Keller, A., Ford, L. H., & Meacham, J. A. Dimensions of self-concept in preschool children. *Developmental Psychology,* 1978, *14,* 483–489.

Klein, G. S. Need and regulation. In M. R. Jones (Ed.), *Nebraska Symposium on Motivation* (Vol. 2). Lincoln: University of Nebraska Press, 1954.

Krebs, D., & Sturrup, B. *Altruism, egocentricity, and behavioral consistency in children.* Paper presented at the meeting of the American Psychological Association, New Orleans, September, 1974.

Kris, E. *Psychoanalytic explorations in art.* New York: International Universities Press, 1952.

Lewin, K. *A dynamic theory of personality.* New York: McGraw-Hill, 1935.

Lewin, K. *Principles of topological psychology.* New York: McGraw-Hill, 1936.

Lewin, K. *The conceptual representation and the measurement of psychological forces.* Durham, N.C.: Duke University Press, 1938.

Lewin, K. *Field theory in social science.* New York: Harper, 1951.

Lowenfeld, M. *The Lowenfeld Mosaic Test.* London: Newman Neame, 1954.

Maccoby, E., & Jacklin, C. *The psychology of sex differences.* Stanford, Calif.: Stanford University Press, 1974.

Matas, L., Arend, R., & Sroufe, A. Continuity of adaptation in the second year: The relationship between quality of attachment and later competence. *Child Development,* 1978, *49,* 547–556.

McReynolds, P. The Rorschach concept evaluation technique. *Journal of Projective Techniques,* 1954, *18,* 60–74.

Murphy, L. B. A longitudinal study of children's coping methods and styles. *Proceedings of the Fifteenth International Congress of Psychology,* Brussels, 1957, 433–436.

Murphy, L. B. *The widening world of childhood: Paths toward mastery.* New York: Basic Books, 1962.

Piaget, J. *The construction of reality in the child.* New York: Basic Books, 1954.

Piaget, J., & Inhelder, B. *The child's conception of space.* London: Routledge and Kegan Paul, 1956.

Revelle, W. Personal communication, December 16, 1976.

Robins, L. N. *Deviant children grown up.* Baltimore: Williams & Wilkins, 1966.

Rosenthal, D. *Genetic theory and abnormal behavior.* New York: McGraw-Hill, 1970.

Rotter, J. B. Generalized expectancies for internal versus external control of reinforcement. *Psychological Monographs,* 1966, *80,* No. 1. (Whole No. 609)

Rubin, K. H., & Schneider, F. W. The relationship between moral judgment, egocentrism, and altruistic behavior. *Child Development,* 1973, *44,* 661–665.

Rutherford, E., & Mussen, P. H. Generosity in nursery school boys. *Child Development,* 1968, *39,* 755–765.

Sander, L., Julia, H., Stechler, G., & Burns, P. Continuous 24-hour interactional monitoring of infants reared in two caretaking environments. *Psychosomatic Medicine,* 1972, *34,* 270–282.

Sander, L., Stechler, G., Julia, H., & Burns, P. Early mother-infant interaction and 24-hour patterns of activity and sleep. *Journal of American Academy of Child Psychiatry,* 1970, *9,* 103–123.

Schiller, J. *Child care arrangements and ego functioning: The effects of stability and entry age on young children.* Unpublished doctoral dissertation, University of California, Berkeley, 1978.

Shure, M., & Spivak, G. *The Preschool Interpersonal Problem-solving Test.* Philadelphia: Department of Mental Health Sciences, Hahnemann Community Mental Health/Mental Retardation Center, 1974.

Siegelman, E., Block, J., Block, J. H., & von der Lippe, A. Antecedents of optimal psychological adjustment. *Journal of Consulting and Clinical Psychology,* 1970, *35,* 283–289.

Smith, R. J. *The psychopath in society.* New York: Academic Press, 1978.

Thomas, A., Chess, S., & Birch, N. G. *Temperament and behavior disorders in children.* New York: New York University Press, 1969.

Tversky, A., & Kahneman, D. Judgment under uncertainty: Heuristics and biases. *Science, 185,* September 27, 1974.

Waters, E., & Sroufe, A. The stability of individual differences in attachment. In A. Sroufe (Chair), *The organization of development and the problem of continuity in adaptation.* Symposium presented at the meeting of The Society for Research in Child Development, New Orleans, 1977.

Whalen, C. K., & Henker, B. Psychostimulants and children: A review and analysis. *Psychological Bulletin,* 1976, *83,* 1113–1130.

White, R. W. Motivation reconsidered: The concept of competence. *Psychological Review,* 1959, *66,* 297–333.

Witkin, H. A., & Goodenough, D. R. *Field dependence revisited* (ETS RB-76-39). Princeton, N.J.: Educational Testing Service, 1976.

Witkin, H. A., & Goodenough, D. R. Field dependence and interpersonal behavior. *Psychological Bulletin,* 1977, *84,* 661–689.

Zigler, E., & Trickett, P. K. IQ, social competence, and evaluation of early childhood intervention programs. *American Psychologist,* 1978, *33,* 789–798.

3

The Development of Mastery, Emotions, and Morality from an Attributional Perspective

Bernard Weiner
University of California, Los Angeles

Anna Kun
University of California, Santa Barbara

Marijana Benesh-Weiner
University of California, Los Angeles

Attribution theory is now entering its second decade as the dominant paradigm in social psychology. Its predecessor, dissonance theory, was replaced for a number of reasons, the primary one being the greater range of phenomena to which an attributional analysis could be applied. This theoretical robustness is demonstrated in extensions of attribution theory beyond the confines of social psychology. For example, personality psychologists are examining the degree to which traits are part of the implicit psychology of observers and merely are imposed or attributed by perceivers, rather than being integral to individuals. Clinical psychologists are exploring the attributional components of psychotherapy: the causes to which patients' ascribe their problems, the functional role of attributions in depression and neurosis, and the client's acceptance of self-responsibility. And motivational psychologists are assessing the behavioral consequences of perceived causality, including the relation between causal ascriptions and traditional motivational indicators such as choice and persistence.

There is no unified body of knowledge that neatly fits into one specific attribution theory, and there are many types of attribution theorists and theories. Nevertheless, there are some central problems that guide the thoughts of all investigators in this field (e.g., Heider, 1958; Kelley, 1967; Weiner, 1974). Attribution theorists are concerned with perceptions of causality, or the perceived reasons why a particular event has occurred. Three general programs of research germane to this paper have emerged from the analysis of perceived causality. First, general laws have been developed that relate antecedent information and cognitive structures to causal inferences. Second, the perceived causes of behavior have been specified, with particular consideration given to a distinction between internal or personal causality versus external or environmental causality. And third, causal inferences have been found to be associated with expectancy, affect, and observed behavior. For example, assume that one's toes are stepped on while riding the subway. Attribution theorists ask:

a. What information is available enabling the person to reach a causal inference (e.g., the clenched fist of the agressor, the observation that other people's toes are being stepped upon, the observaton that only people standing near the door are stepped on)?

b. What are the conceivable causes of the event (e.g., an intentional aggressive act, an accident, a result of standing too near the door)?

c. What are the consequences of the causal ascription (e.g., expecting to be stepped on or not again; feelings of anger or sympathy; hitting the aggressor, deriding the transportation system, or moving away from the door)?

ATTRIBUTION THEORY AND DEVELOPMENTAL PSYCHOLOGY

The links in the attribution sequence presented in the prior paragraph are likely to be influenced by the cognitive maturity of the actor. Young children have limited information processing capacities and consequently may reach different causal inferences than adults; cognitive maturity may influence the number and kind of conceived causes; and the functional significance or the behavioral consequences of causal attributions may shift with developmental change. Thus, an attributional approach is quite amenable to issues in developmental psychology.

To date, developmentalists with an interest in attribution have studied causal cognitions chiefly as part of a broader interest in the growth of knowledge (Weiner & Kun, in press). In this paper, we move away from the focus on intellective functioning and consider aspects of motivational and emotional development from the attributional perspective. That is, we are primarily concerned with the last stage in the temporal sequence described above, the consequences of causal perceptions.

Consequences of causal attribution are illustrated here by examining three topics: mastery, achievement-related affects, and moral judgments. Mastery and affect represent impoverished research areas within developmental psychology, while the more recent data in the moral domain are forcing a reconsideration of the popular stage analysis. Themes from both under- and over-researched areas were selected for this paper to illustrate the potential fruitfulness of the attributional approach for developmental psychology.

MASTERY

Attribution theorists assume that the basic motivational principle guiding human conduct is the desire to understand and to affect the environment (Heider, 1958; Kelley, 1967). This is quite similar to what other psychologists have called "mastery." For example, White (1959), the most cited source in the mastery field, states that mastery, or striving for competence, includes behavior which "promote[s] an effective...interaction with the environment...and is continued...because it satisfies an intrinsic need to deal with the environment [pp. 317–318]." This construct has been invoked to account for a variety of phenomena, including exploration, curiosity, and play behavior (see Harter, 1978).

How does one "know" that mastery has been attained? If attributional principles are applied to answer this question, then the concept of covariation is called upon. According to attribution theorists, covariation information is the foundation of the attribution process. It is assumed "that condition will be held responsible for an effect which is present when the effect is present and which is absent when the effect is absent [Heider, 1958, p. 152]." Extending this definition to mastery, we suggest that covariation of perceived effort expenditure with a desired outcome provides sufficient evidence of personal control. That is, perceived effort–outcome covariation produces *feelings of mastery*.

Prior research (Weiner, 1974; Weiner, Russell, & Lerman, 1978) has demonstrated that causal attributions of a desired outcome to the self (effort and/or ability) augment certain positive emotions, such as feelings of pride, confidence, and general self-esteem. These feelings are presumed to increase the likelihood of future mastery-oriented activities. Hence, an attributional depiction of mastery behaviors is as follows:

effort-outcome covariation   mastery activities
           \   ∕
causal ascriptions to the self → increase in esteem-related affects
(feelings of mastery)

Note that in this analysis, emotion, rather than the acquisition of competence, is central to the mastery process (see Harter, 1978; White, 1959).

Once mastery or management of the environment in a particular situation is established, the affective consequences of goal attainment diminish. We suggest this is mediated by an attributional shift from the self to the ease of the environmental task which, in turn, dampens affective reactions to goal attainment. New goals are then established, thus altering the direction of behavior. This proposed sequence is analogous to the upward shifts following success that are observed in level-of-aspiration research (e.g., Lewin, Dembo, Festinger, & Sears, 1944).

An investigation by Nuttin (1973) nicely illustrates the *information-causal ascription-affect-behavior* sequence that we have proposed. Nuttin distinguishes *causality pleasure*, or the positive affect that is gained when one personally causes an event, from *stimulus pleasure*, which is the positive affect associated with the event per se. To demonstrate causality pleasure and to separate this state from stimulus pleasure, Nuttin placed a few 5-year-olds in an experimental room containing two "machines." Both machines had colored lights and movable handles. For one machine (A), the onset of the lights was preprogrammed by the experimenter; but for the other machine (B), the lights went on or off when the handle was moved beyond a designated point. In short, although both machines stimulated the viewer perceptually and included motoric responses, the children were the producers or the causes of the stimulation only with machine B. Participants were free to spend their time with either machine; and the experimenters recorded various indexes of choice and preference, including the time spent with each machine and verbal reports of liking. Both the observational and the self-report data confirmed that the children strongly preferred machine B over machine A.

Applying our attributional analysis to these data, we suggest that on the basis of the observed covariation between their own actions and the onset of the lights in machine B, the children inferred that they were personally responsible for the stimulation from that machine. Self-attribution of the outcome (mastery) augmented certain positive affective states, which increased the desire for repeated commerce with machine B. Thus, the information-causal attribution-affect-behavior sequence is captured within the Nuttin paradigm. Research with very young infants by Watson (1966, 1967) may be interpreted similarly, although the requisite inferences about the cognitive abilities of an infant may be questionable.

Nuttin's (1973) experiment was sufficiently provocative and consistent with our way of thinking to warrant the initiation of a series of similar studies. In our research, children of different ages were studied, and the effects of a gain in mastery were also examined. We additionally had hoped to report on the consequences of a loss of mastery, but that must remain for future research.

An Experimental Investigation of Mastery

In the first study, preschool boys and girls (N = 23; mean age = 5.1 years) and boys and girls in lower elementary school (N = 17; mean age = 8.2 years) were brought individually into an experimental room containing two slide projectors in distinctive booths. The booths were separated by a partition.

One of the projectors was preprogrammed to present slides at an average rate of one every 3 sec. This speed had been found in pilot studies to be the average rate of response when the projector flashed slides contingently. The second exposed identical stimuli, but it had to be activated by the children. Activation was accomplished by pressing a red button on the table holding the projector. An identical button was on the table holding the preprogrammed projector, but it had no instrumental function. The slides were redundant and relatively devoid of intrinsic interest, protraying either colors or letters. The stimuli were selected to be uninteresting so that the causality pleasure would not be masked by the stimulus pleasure. (See Kun, Garfield, & Sipowicz, in press, for a more detailed description of the experimental room, equipment, etc.)

The first step in the procedure was to introduce the child to both of the projectors. The experimenter went into both booths with the child. In each booth, the experimenter placed the child's finger on the button adjacent to the projector and pushed the button ten times. After this demonstration, the child was taken to the center of the room and then was allowed to play freely with the two machines for the next five minutes. The time spent in the booths and the number of button presses were recorded. After five minutes had elapsed, the child was taken into an adjoining play room for a 10-min rest interval and then brought back into the experimental setting for three more minutes. Following this, some questions were asked regarding the perceptions of the contingencies.

Guided by Nuttin, we expected that children would prefer the contingent to the noncontingent projection. Furthermore, inasmuch as older children are better information processors and attributors than younger children, the developmental hypothesis was that older children would experience causality pleasure (interest) sooner and display earlier preference for the contingent projector than the younger children.

Figure 3.1 shows the amount of time spent at the contingent minus the noncontingent projectors for the younger and older children during the first (prior to the play break) and the second time intervals. For both age groups at both times there is a preference for the contingent projection. However, there is a significant age X session interaction, with the relative preference for the contingent projection reversing among the two age groups across the two sessions. To our surprise, the preference for contingency is markedly more evident in the younger than the older children in the second time interval. Perhaps this indicates greater pride or pleasure taken in accomplishment among the younger children, since the instrumental response is not likely to be very challenging, difficult, or novel for the older children.

Our initial hypothesis was that the older children would be better able to process covariation information and thus would have an earlier preference for the contingent projection. The data shown in Figure 3.1 provide, at best, suggestive support for this belief. However, the self-report data indicate that

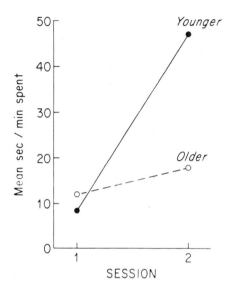

FIG. 3.1. Mean seconds per minute spent at the contingent minus the noncontingent projectors.

even this finding may be more complex than it appears. Both age groups perceived the contingent projector as equally controllable. However, the younger children expressed the belief that more control was possible over the noncontingent projector than did the older children. Thus, the younger children initially may have persisted at the noncontingent booth because of the continued attempt to *gain* control. Because a distinction between the desire to be in a situation that one is controlling, and the desire to gain control, was not incorporated into the present investigation, a second experiment was conducted to examine the motivational properties of a gain in control.

Effects of Gain of Control

In this study of 19 preschool (mean age = 5.6 years) and 19 lower-elementary (mean age = 7.7 years) children, the procedure from the previous experiment was followed with one important alteration: When the experimenter re-entered the experimental room for the second session, she once more explained how the slide projector worked. During this demonstration, the noncontingent projector was made contingent, with eight demonstration trials at a random 50% contingency rate followed by six more trials with total contingency. Both machines then remained 100% contingent.

Figure 3.2 shows the average amount of time per minute at the contingent minus the noncontingent projectors during the initial 5-minute interval, as well as the relative time spent for each minute during the second 3-minute session. First, Fig. 3.2 indicates that there is a clear preference for the contingent over the noncontingent projector in the initial time interval. In

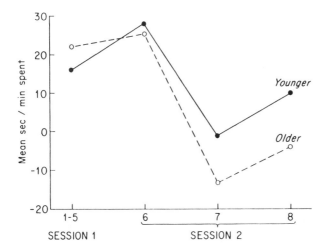

FIG. 3.2. Mean seconds per minute spent at the contingent minus the noncontingent projectors during Session 1 and for each minute during Session 2. Prior to Session 2 the noncontingent projector was made contingent.

addition, the figure reveals that in Session Two there is a change in the relative preference for the noncontingent-to-contingent projector so that it equals that of the contingent-contingent projector. Clearly, then, contingency is the cause of the differential initial preferences. However, contrary to our thinking, the preference for the projector associated with a gain of control did not *exceed* that of the continuously controllable projector. No developmental trends were found in these data, possibly because the age disparity between the two groups of children in the present study (2.1 years) was less than in the previous experiment (3.1 years).

There are a number of post hoc explanations for the failure of the gain-of-control hypothesis. We think it is premature to give up the idea that a gain of control particularly engenders positive affect. It may be that a different experimental paradigm is needed in which the gain of control is exhibited with a response that is not already mastered in a virtually identical situation. Or perhaps the gain was too quick and we should have employed schedules permitting a gradual increment in the response-outcome covariation. These are guides for future research.

In these two experiments, we have examined mastery behavior from an attributional viewpoint and have introduced an experimental paradigm that is based upon the definition of mastery as the perception of effort-outcome covariation. In addition, we have stressed that positive affect accompanies self-ascriptions for desired events and may motivate further attempts to master the environment. We hope that these are heuristic ideas that might breathe some experimental life into a highly important and much discussed area, but one in which our thinking has been little advanced in recent years.

ACHIEVEMENT-RELATED AFFECT

The attributional interpretation of mastery assumed that positive affect is augmented given ascription of goal attainment to effort expenditure; that is, there is a direct linkage between attribution and emotion. We now turn to a fuller discussion of the union of cognition and affect.

In research with adults, two distinct literatures support the belief that perceived causality influences emotional reactions. One body of research has primarily focused on fear reactions, utilizing a misattribution paradigm in which internal arousal or fear is falsely ascribed to the stimulus situation or to a placebo pill (e.g., Nisbett & Schachter, 1966; Schachter & Singer, 1962). A second research direction, more germane to our present interests, concerns the emotional consequences of perceived causality in achievement-related contexts. It is intuitively reasonable to believe that there is an association between causal ascriptions for achievement outcomes and our feelings about these accomplishments. For example, one is not likely to experience pride in success when receiving an "A" from a teacher who gives only that grade, or when defeating a tennis player who loses all his or her other matches. In these instances, the cause of the success (the ease of the task) is external to the actor. On the other hand, an "A" from a teacher who gives few high grades, or a victory over a highly rated tennis player, typically generates a great deal of positive emotion. In these instances the causes of success are likely to be perceived as the high ability and/ or great effort expenditure of the actor. (For a more detailed discussion of the attribution-emotion linkage see Weiner, 1977.)

Recently, Weiner, Russell, and Lerman (1978) suggested that particular causal attributions are uniquely associated with specific emotional reactions. They tested this hypothesis by compiling a dictionary list of about 250 words that described potential affective reactions to academic success and failure. Adult participants were given one of 11 causes of success or failure (ability, short- or long-term effort, task difficulty, luck, mood, intrinsic interest, own personality, others' personality, others' motivation, and fatigue) embedded in a brief story concerning good or bad test performance. They were then asked to report the intensity of the listed emotions that they thought would be experienced in this situation. The methodological limitations or advantages of this procedure have been discussed elsewhere (see Weiner et al., 1978); but it should be noted that the basic findings have been replicated using a less reactive procedure (see Weiner, Russell, & Lerman, 1979).

There were a number of general findings of interest. First, there was a set of "outcome-dependent, attributionally-independent" emotions that represented positive or negative reactions to success and failure, regardless of the "why" of the outcome. For example, given success outcomes, the affect words *pleased, happy, satisfied, good,* and so on were chosen as highly likely to be experienced, independent of the attribution for the success. Similarly, a number of outcome-linked emotions were chosen for failure, including *uncheerful, displeasure,* and *upset.* These positive and negative emotions also were expected to be the most intensely experienced reactions.

But for both success and failure, many affect words were discriminably related to specific attributions. Table 3.1 shows the causal attributions for success and failure that were linked with a distinguishing emotion. The table includes many associations that our intuitions readily verify: Success due to perceived high ability leads to feelings of *confidence and competence; gratitude* is experienced if we attribute success to others; luck ascriptions generate feelings of *surprise;* and so on. It certainly is the case that often the truth is not new. One unexpected finding shown in Table 3.1 that thus far has not been fully replicated is that stable and unstable effort ascriptions generate opposite degrees of subsequent arousal. This is of interest because of its suggestion that arousal is a product of cognitions, rather than preceding and inducing emotions and thought.

Table 3.1 also shows that failure-related emotions of *incompetence, guilt, resignation, and aggression* are perceived to follow from different perceived reasons for failure (respectively, ability, effort, personality and others). It is of interest to note that at times causal attributions for success and failure yield opposing reactions, as would be anticipated given diametric outcomes (*competence* versus *incompetence,* given ability attributions; *gratitude* versus *aggression,* given attributions to others). At times, however, the same affect is associated with both positive and negative outcomes for a given attribution (*surprise,* when attributions are to luck); and for still other ascriptions, such as immediate or long-term effort, the affects that accompany success (respectively, *activation* or *relaxation*) are unrelated to the failure-linked affects (*guilt* and *shame*).

TABLE 3.1
Attributions and Dominant Discriminating Affects
for Success and Failure[a]

Attributions	Success	Failure
Ability	Competence Confidence	Incompetence
Unstable effort	Activation Augmentation	Guilt Shame
Stable effort	Relaxation	Guilt & shame
Personality	Self-enhancement	Resignation
Others	Gratitude	Aggression
Luck	Surprise	Surprise

[a]Based on Weiner et al., 1978.

It was evident, however, that the intensity of the emotions that were perceived to be linked with causal attributions were less strong than the intensity of the reported outcome-united emotions. This suggested to us that labeling or cognitive activity and differentiation reduces emotional reactivity to an event. Cognitions give rise to the richness of human affective life, but at the same time they might inhibit our "gut-level" and more vivid feelings. It has been said that the romantic hates the intellectual.

In addition to linkages of emotion with outcome and attributions, there apparently is a third stage in the cognition–emotion process among adults. Attributions for success and failure are classified into causal dimensions, including locus and stability. Further affective experiences then follow as a consequence of the fact that some ascriptions have implications for how one views oneself and what will happen in the future. Thus, causal dimensions are linked with esteem-related emotions and goal expectations. We suspect that these dimension-tied affects have greater longevity and long-run importance than the outcome- or attribution-linked emotions.

In achievement-related contexts, the adult actor therefore might progress through the cognition–emotion steps in these scenarios:

a. "I just received a 'D' on the exam. That is a very low grade." (This generates feelings of being unhappy, frustrated, and upset.) "I received this grade because I did not try hard enough"(followed by feelings of guilt and/or shame). "There is really something lacking in me and it is likely to remain constant" (ensued by low self-esteem or lack of worth and hopelessness).

b. "I just received an 'A' on this exam. That is a very high grade" (generating happiness). "I received this grade because I worked very hard during the entire school year" (producing contentment and relaxation). "I really do have some positive qualities that will persist in the future"(followed by high self-esteem, feelings of self-worth, and optimism).

These conclusions, based on research with adults, suggested a number of developmental questions about emotion. Up to now, there has been a dearth of developmental research concerning affects, with the few investigations centered upon facial expressions, fear, attachment, and other biologically-based emotions (see, for example, Lewis & Rosenblum, 1978). There are a number of reasons for the void in the study of the higher-order, more distinctly human emotions. First, the study of these types of affect was hampered by theoretical emphases. Initially, barriers were imposed by the behaviorists' insistence on observables; then with the advent of Piaget and centering of attention upon intellective functioning, affects were again shunted aside. Second, those who have worked in this area are aware of the methodological difficulties; it takes great frustration tolerance and, perhaps, a bent toward self-destruction to pursue the study of experiential states.

Since we had both the above qualities, we have plunged into the development of emotions, although it is unclear whether we are studying feelings or *thoughts about feelings*. We actually view these as intertwined phenomena and expect that, at times, one implies the other.

Our first goal was to see if we could trace the attribution-affect bonds that are so clear in adults' minds. That is, we wanted to explore how the development of causal thinking relates to (and, we thought, precedes) the growth of certain aspects of emotional life. We also hoped to begin to explore the entire cognition-emotion sequence that we believe characterizes the achievement domain for adults. Perhaps children only react with the high-intensity outcome-linked affects prior to the growth of cognitive differentiation and attributional understanding. Perhaps among the very young causal dimensionalization is not possible, so that esteem-related affects and feelings of optimism and pessimism are not evident. And perhaps causal dimensions also show a developmental progression; for example, locus may come before stability and therefore emotions related to self-esteem may antedate temporal-related affects such as hopelessness. We only begin to tackle some of these questions in the research to be reported next.

An Experimental Study of Achievement-Related Affect

The initial approach to these issues involved 188 children and 188 adults. The children were grouped into two developmental levels, mean ages 6.4 years and 10.4 years. The experiment had three distinct parts: assessment of causal concepts, assessment of emotional understanding, and testing the perceived relation between causes and emotions. Thus, we began with what might be considered a miniature attribution and affect I.Q. test, and then measured the perceived cause-affect association.

Four causes were examined—ability, effort, luck, and other persons—each of which was paired with two question stems containing known antecedents of that particular attribution. For example, a question in which ability was specified as the correct answer was:

Tommy adds numbers very fast and always gets the right answer.
Yesterday Tommy added numbers together very quickly and got the right answer. Why was this?

  a. Tommy had good luck.
  b. Tommy tried very hard to add the numbers correctly.
  c. Tommy is good at arithmetic. ["Good at" was the label we used to connote high ability.]
  d. Someone helped Tommy add the numbers correctly.

In this example, consistency of behavior was the ability cue. The relation between consistency and ability inferences has been clearly established in research with adult subjects (Frieze & Weiner, 1971).

An effort stem was:

> George played his lesson on the piano for two hours every day. Later he played this lesson perfectly. Why was this?

In this example persistence of behavior is the cue for an effort ascription.

Participants answered eight causal attribution questions for either success or failure. Each of the four attributions was the correct answer for two of the questions.

The emotion items had a similar format. The four emotions examined were: *sure of himself, proud* (which among adults is linked with both short- and long-term effort), *surprised,* and *thankful.* A typical question was:

> Timmy wanted to do something very special for his friend. How do you think that Timmy felt?
> a. sure of himself
> b. proud
> c. thankful
> d. surprised

Pictures of the facial expression and bodily posture that accompany these emotions also were shown as each alternative was stated. In one experimental condition, only the four attribution-linked affects were available as responses. In a second condition, the choice was among five affects, one outcome-linked emotion (*happy* or *sad*) along with the four attribution-linked emotions.

In the final linkage phase of the experiment, the attribution was given and the emotion was again assessed with either four or five alternatives. Items representing the causes were given in two story themes, one academic and one involving an athletic accomplishment. For example,

> Peter did not know how to spell any of the words on the list. When it was his turn, he guessed at the spelling word and spelled it right. Peter knew that the reason he did well was because of good luck. How do you think that he felt?

To summarize, the subjects were given 24 success-related or 24 failure-related multiple-choice questions (8 causes + 8 emotions + 8 linkages). There initially were choices among four attributions, and then participants had to select between the same four or five emotions in both the affect and linkage phases of the study.

Before presenting the results of this study, a word about methodology is in order. Since we relied on verbal responding in this procedure, we were aware of a number of potential methodological problems. With regard to the independent variable, there is the difficulty that children may not understand some of the words we used to describe a situation. We therefore repeatedly reminded the children to ask questions when they did not understand something being read to them. In regard to the dependent variable, children made choices between four (or five) words. In this case they were explicitly asked, prior to their choice, whether they knew the words. Also, the various verbal labels were written on cards to help the children keep the alternatives in mind. Since the older participants could read better than the younger children, all the participants were required to say the word aloud as they pointed to a particular card representing their answer. But, despite these precautions, it is still likely that overall age differences may be less revealing than interactions between particular responses and age.

In the second and third parts of the investigation, when the verbal choices concerned emotion words, pictures accompanied the written words. While the use of pictures reduced reliance on reading and memory, pictures do not solve all our problems. Some emotions, such as anger, were quite easy for us to depict and for participants to identify; while others, such as shame, were more problematic. Indeed, a visual approach may be less satisfactory than a verbal approach since different affective states are not equally well represented by a set of pictures.

Differences in the relative complexity of the various emotion concepts also create problems for testing the understanding of the various emotions. Some emotions, such as anger, are unidimensional in the sense that all behaviors ensuing from them may be conceptualized as directed toward the removal or destruction of the cause of the emotional state. On the other hand, emotions like shame may generate behaviors that serve a more diffuse set of goals. Consequently, our use of only a small subset of behavioral consequences to identify an emotion may test the understanding of some emotions more adequately than others.

Another problem with the verbal method is that children might not know the adult's word for a particular emotional situation, even though they have their own idiosyncratic representation for that emotional situation. When such cases were detected in our pilot work, appropriate substitutions were made when possible (e.g., the word *thankful* rather than *grateful*).

In sum, our procedure is open to many of the criticisms that have been levelled against Piagetian research in which verbal criteria are used to assess childrens' understanding of concepts. However, there does seem to be an essential difference between using verbal techniques to study complex emotions as opposed to logico-mathematical concepts. The development of a vocabulary of emotions may be an integral part of the development of these emotions, while no analog exists in everyday language for the logical constructs examined in the Piagetian research.

Only a few of the many findings from this study can be presented here. Indeed, we are less interested in conveying specific findings than in outlining a general research approach. Let us begin with the data on attributions and then progress to the results on emotions and the linkages.

Attributions. As would be anticipated, there were marked developmental trends for all attributions, particularly between the two groups of children. Figure 3.3 shows the mean correct responses in the success and failure conditions for the two younger age groups. A score of 2 is perfect, while a score of 1 indicates a correct response to one of the two attribution-related questions. The scores of adults are not included for they approximate 100%, a finding which merely replicates the pilot data used to select the questions.

Figure 3.3 indicates that for success, "others" is far the most readily understood cause. This is not merely because children have a propensity to give "others" as a response, regardless of the question asked. A discrimination index composed of the mean correct response minus the mean incorrect use of the response also far exceeds the remaining causes for the "other" attribution. Help from others also is correctly identified as the causal attribution for success more often than hindrance from others is for failure. However, this is significant only for the younger age group; "others" is the only attribution for which there is a significant age X outcome interaction.

Another unanticipated finding is that lack of effort is the most correctly identified cause for failure. In addition, it also is greater than the correct response of high effort as a cause of success. More specifically, if Joey did not practice the piano lack of effect was perceived as the cause of failure. But

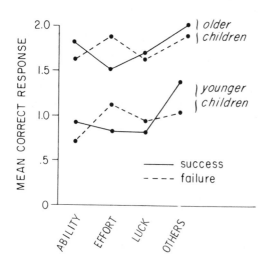

FIG. 3.3.   Mean correct attributional identification among the two youngest developmental groups. A score of 1 indicates 50% correct; 2 indicates 100% correct responses.

when he did practice a great deal, it was not as strongly evident to the participants that effort was the reason for his success.

The predominance of the correct ascriptions to "others" for success and lack of effort for failure were highly significant, whether comparisons were across outcomes within the attribution or between attributions within an outcome. This seems to be a reversal of a hedonic-bias hypothesis, which might suggest most salience for internal causes for success and for external reasons for failure. The data further indicate that causes having an intentional or a purposive character, whether internal or external, are understood earlier than noncontrollable causes such as ability and luck.

Emotions. The mean correct emotion responses for the four success-related and the four failure-related affects appear in Fig. 3.4. Note that *surprise* is included among both outcome groupings. Looking at the condition in which *happy* and *sad* were not possible responses, it is evident from Fig. 3.4 that the developmental effect is sizable. Adults and older children perform almost perfectly, while the younger children's mean correct response is only 1.2, compared to a possible score of 2.

The younger children's data indicate that the most well-understood affects are *surprise, anger,* and then *shame* ("ashamed"). These are the only emotion words included in this experiment that have been identified as fundamental human emotions by theorists such as Ekman (1972) and Izard (1977). The data offer some support for the primacy hypothesis.

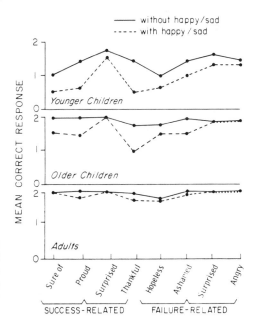

FIG. 3.4. Mean correct affective identification as a function of developmental level and the availability or unavailability of the outcome-linked affects (happy or sad).

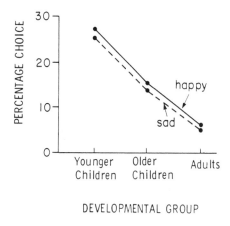

FIG. 3.5. Mean intrusions (percentage choice) of outcome-contingent affects (happy or sad) as a function of developmental level.

Further analyses confirmed that the best comprehended emotions were *surprise* and *anger*. For each developmental level, Fig. 3.4 shows the correct responses in the two conditions respectively with and without the inclusion of outcome-linked affects (*happy* or *sad*) as available alternative responses. The outcome-linked affects are least likely to be the selected response when the so-called fundamental emotions are designated as correct. This is evident in the data from both groups of children.

Turning to the outcome-linked affects alone, Fig. 3.5 gives the percentage of responses of *happy* and *sad* for the three developmental groups. The outcome-linked affects are increasingly less likely to be chosen by each older age group. Hence, it is not merely that errors decrease with maturity, but rather a particular kind of affective identification is shifting; namely, the participants are becoming more discriminating. One might speculate that the intensity of their actual emotional responses also decreases because of a shift away from the outcome-linked to the attribution-linked affects.

Linkages.   Figure 3.6 shows the "correct" emotional identification in the success and failure conditions, given information about the linked causal attribution. Among younger children, the identification of *thankful,* given success due to the help of others, was especially prevalent. On the other hand, *surprise,* given failure due to bad luck, was selected relatively less by both children and adults (*angry* often was the response selected).

Again, marked age differences appeared. The availability of the outcome-linked affect particularly altered the responses of the younger age groups. However, the influence of *happy/sad* interacts with the particular affect, as well as with developmental level. For example, Fig. 3.7 shows the percentage difference between the "correct" affective response for failure when *sad* was not an alternative response and when it was. Among the adults, the difference approximates zero for all the affects; the outcome-linked affect did not alter

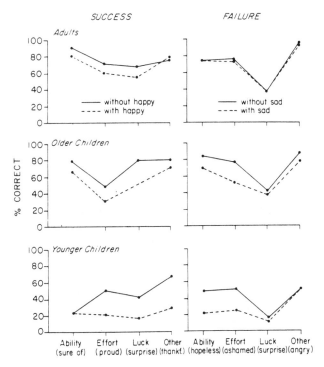

FIG. 3.6. Mean percentage correct affective identification given the causal attributions as a function of developmental level.

FIG. 3.7. Mean percentage difference correct in the failure condition when the outcome-linked affect (sad) is and is not available as a response, as a function of developmental level and the specific attribution–affect linkage tested.

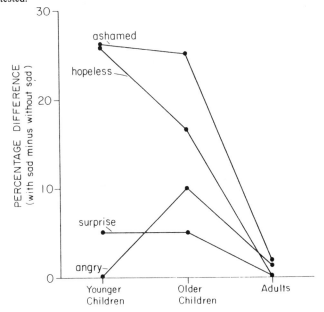

the response pattern. Among the younger age groups, failure due to a lack of ability and a lack of effort often did elicit the emotion of *sad* (displacing *hopeless* and *ashamed*); while failure due to bad luck and interference from others did not result in similar displacement of *anger* and *surprise*. It is interesting to note that ability and effort, to which *hopeless* and *ashamed* are linked, are the internal causes, while *surprise* and *anger* are associated with causes external to the actor.

Does this mean that the emotions of surprise and anger are identified or learned in the same way by the children? As previously indicated, they both have been classified among the fundamental emotions. However, there appear to be some very central differences between these affects, when examined from an attributional viewpoint. There is much greater correct selection of surprise in Phase 2 of this experiment (affective identification) than in Phase 3 (linkage identification). This means that children know what surprise is, but do not realize that one "should" feel suprised when the outcome is due to bad luck. Affective understanding comes before causal knowledge, which is contrary to our expectation that thoughts determine feelings. That is, understanding of luck probably comes later than the comprehension of surprise. This pattern is not evident with regard to anger: Causal information is an effective cue for the identification of anger. It may be that, in this case, the causal information is a sufficient rather than a necessary cue.

Even further, in the success condition the ascription of a positive outcome to others enhances the identification of the affect of *thankfulness* (compare Fig. 3.4 and 3.6), and this may be necessary rather than just sufficient information. It seems likely that among certain affects, particularly those represented phylogenetically, emotional experience does not necessitate any cognitive work, while for other affects there must be antecedent cognitive activity.

To summarize, we have examined the development of the understanding of affects that are known to be linked with particular causal ascriptions. Although we are just initiating work in this area, it is clear that there are systematic and understandable developmental trends. It is time to turn to the relation of attributions to the development of complex affective patterns that do not seem to be biologically rooted.

MORAL EVALUATION

There are few areas as extensively researched in child development as moral judgment and evaluation. The reasons for this productivity are many, including the ascendance of Piagetian psychology and its concern with mental life, the appeal of the Piaget-Kohlberg stage analysis, and the ease of manipulating intent and outcome information in an experimental design. For some time, a number of empirical generalizations derived from the Piagetian conceptual analysis were fairly well accepted. They included the following:

1. Moral evaluations are a function of two types of information, intent and outcome, interacting with the cognitive maturity of the judge.
2. Young children base moral evaluations on the objective consequences of an act and do not make use of intent information.
3. Adults base moral evaluations on the subjective intent of an action and discard outcome information.

Attribution theorists offer an alternative to the less complex Piagetian stage analysis (see Benesh-Weiner, 1978; Heider, 1958; Shaw & Sulzer, 1964) by proposing that moral evaluation is one application of a general process that occurs in other motivational domains as well (e.g., achievement). In this section, we examine the implications of an attributional analysis for the interpretation of previous moral-judgment research findings.

Attribution of personal responsibility for an event or "outcome" is one precursor of an evaluation of someone; consequently, information establishing personal responsibility indirectly influences moral and achievement evaluation. Attribution of personal responsibility is a complex judgment, drawing on such information as the actor's behaviors and exertions, ability, intent, the uniqueness of that intent, the difficulty of the task attempted, the presence of "chance" factors, and the extremity of an outcome (see Kelley, 1973; Shaw & Sulzer, 1964). Furthermore, moral responsibility is not, of course, an all-or-none decision. Rather, the contribution that personal as opposed to environmental factors make to causing an event may vary markedly. A person can be held more or less responsible for an outcome inasmuch as factors such as ability, intention, exertion, task difficulty, and even outcome vary in magnitude.

While moral evaluation may follow from the assignment of moral responsibility; and (2) an evaluation of the actor's behavior. For example, judgment process may be distinguished: (1) an assignment of moral responsibility; and (2) an evaluation of the actor's behavior. for example, John might say, "I intend to hit Joe," while Bill could reveal, "I intend to kill Joe." In both cases there may be equal responsibility, but differential evaluation, because of the different outcomes. Similarly, evaluations could be different when John or Bill bear different degrees of responsibility for the *same* event.

In the attributional view, a variety of models for dealing with causal problems may co-exist in both children and adults (see Kelley, 1973). Because of this, less stress is placed by attribution theorists on the contrasts between the thinking of children and adults. Differences in the patterns of evaluation are conceived as quantitative rather than qualitiative. For instance, evaluations of children and adults may differ because of disparate weighting of similar kinds of information rather than because of contrasting cognitive approaches.

These general ideas influenced a series of investigations examining the determinants of both moral and achievement judgments (Benesh-Weiner, 1978). The results of this research, as well as data from other recent investigations (Buchanan & Thompson, 1973; Chandler, Greenspan, & Barenboim, 1973; Farnill, 1974; Gottlieb, Taylor, & Ruderman, 1977; Parsons, Ruble, Klosson, Feldman, & Rholes, 1976; Surber, 1977), seriously challenge the three generalizations about the moral judgment literature listed earlier in this section.

Effects of Varying Task Difficulty on Moral Evaluation

In both moral and achievement situations, intent and outcome influence interpersonal evaluation; but Weiner and Peter (1973) have also distinguished different evaluation processes in these two motivational domains, suggesting that achievement evaluations are part of a reward-oriented outcome system, whereas moral evaluations are part of a punishment-oriented intent system. In other words, they suggested that achievement actions generally beget more reward than punishment; on the whole, praise is given for success more readily than blame is given for failure. On the other hand, morally relevant behavior generally results in more punishment than reward, with negative intent producing more blame than the praise given for positive intent.

Another factor in evaluations in both achievement and moral-judgment situations is task difficulty, an external causal factor, that has been shown to play an important role in influencing perceived causality (see Heider, 1958; Parsons, 1974). In the literature on moral evaluation, the task typically undertaken (or avoided) is "easy." For example, the scenarios used for judgments often involve helping a lost child get home (when one knows the way), straightening a room, or not breaking a window. These are actions that all individuals can accomplish readily; the environmental barriers preventing a moral behavior are minimal. "Helping" or good intent in these situations is not noteworthy and can be readily ascribed to external factors (the ease of the task); in addition, most people in these situations probably would have good intent. While many moral acts in everyday life are indeed relatively simple, other actions require difficult sacrifices, such as foregoing one's own desires and needs to care for someone else. In these instances, where the task is difficult, good intentions are more likely to be seen as internal to the actor and will be approved or "rewarded."

A wider range of task difficulty levels could greatly alter the empirical generalizations that have been drawn from previous studies. For example, reward is greater given success at a difficult rather than an easy task (Atkinson, 1964). Thus, if the moral tasks in moral-judgment scenarios are easy, rewards for positive outcomes would probably be minimal. On the other hand, tasks in achieving studies (e.g., completing a puzzle) involve performance judged against some standard of excellence (see Atkinson, 1964) and, by definition, are relatively demanding. Hence, reward for success in the achievement domain would be enhanced. In short, the differential reward observed in the achievement and the moral domains and the characterization of achievement as a reward system and morality as a punishment system could be the result of inadequate sampling of tasks. Attribution theory calls attention to this bias by stressing the additional factor of task difficulty as a determinant of perceived responsibility and evaluation.

Participants in this experiment were 118 13–14-year-old males and females. Each subject judged 16 stories (two levels of intent X two levels of outcome X two levels of task difficulty X two motivational domains). Task difficulty in the achievement domain was varied by having the story actor perform a test that many (or few) others could pass. In the moral domain, the relatively easy task was caring for a cheerful but ill mother, while the more difficult task was caring for a mother "hard to get along with." Thus, for example, subjects judged stories such as:

1. George wants to get into his community college. The entrance exam is not very difficult. 90% of the students who take the exam pass, and then are admitted. George works and prepares himself. He passes the exam for the community college. [Positive intent, positive outcome, easy task, achievement domain.]

2. Joe's mother is sick and he has to stay with her to see that her needs are taken care of. Now that she is sick, Joe's mother has become a very difficult woman, hard to get along with. Joe does not want to help her; secretly he wants to put her in a nursing home. She finds his presence irritating. She gets worse. [Negative intent, negative outcome, difficult task, moral domain.]

The actors in the story were rewarded or punished on a scale from +10 to –10 (see Benesh-Weiner, 1978, for a more detailed presentation of the procedure).

Table 3.2 shows the evaluative judgments as a function of task difficulty and motivational domain. The table clearly shows that difficult tasks are more highly rewarded than easy tasks in both motivational domains, while the overall level of reward between the two domains is quite similar.

It has been suggested that prior research has confounded task difficulty and motivational domain. If this is the case, it appears that disparate evaluations in judging moral or achievement situations may have been ascribed incorrectly to motivational domain, rather than to the unnoticed task difficulty variable.

TABLE 3.2
Mean Evaluation for Easy and Hard
Moral and Achievement Tasks[a]

Task Difficulty	Moral	Achievement
Easy	1.7	1.5
Hard	3.2	2.6

[a]From Benesh-Weiner (1978).

TABLE 3.3
Mean Evaluation as a Function of
Motivational Domain, Task Difficulty and Intent[a]

| | Moral | | | Achievement | | |
Intent	Hard	Easy	Difference	Hard	Easy	Difference
Positive	6.7	6.4	0.3	6.7	5.0	1.7
Negative	-0.4	-3.1	2.7	-1.5	-2.0	0.5

[a]From Benesh-Weiner (1978).

The interaction between the subjective factor of intent (effort), task difficulty, and the motivational domain is shown in Table 3.3. First, it is evident that there is a highly significant effect when comparing positive with negative intent or effort. Of greater interest in the present context is the finding that, in the moral domain, punishment for negative intent is augmented when the task is perceived as easy, whereas in the achievement domain reward for high effort is enhanced when performance is at a difficult task. In other words, when something moral is easy, then one really "ought" to intend to do it, while if it is difficult to achieve a goal, then high effort is especially noteworthy. Thus, prior selection of easy moral tasks and difficult achievement tasks may heighten the use of intent information in moral evaluation when intents are negative and effort information in achievement evaluation when effort is expended. Furthermore, when both the moral and the achievement tasks are easy, the importance of intent in moral evaluation relative to effort in achievement evaluation may be exaggerated. It is obvious that adequate experimental designs must provide for sampling across intent and difficulty levels.

An important difference between achievement and moral evaluation reported by Weiner and Peter (1973) was replicated in these data; namely, outcome appears to be more heavily weighted as an evaluative determinant in achievement than in moral contexts. Thus, success in spite of a lack of effort is rewarded in achievement settings, whereas a favorable outcome in spite of negative intent is punished in the moral domain.

In summary, evaluations are products of the interacting factors of motivational domain, intent, outcome, and task difficulty. Judgments are multidetermined, rather than linked exclusively to one category of information. These results are consistent with the complexity that attribution theorists expect from mental events. The factors manipulated in the present study are a small but important subset of the many determinants of moral and achievement judgments.

Effects of Varying Outcome Extremity on Moral Evaluation

In the study just reported, adolescents were the only age group sampled. A related investigation is now reported in which judgments were made by 6- and 7-year-old children, as well as college students (ages 18–24). We were concerned with the judgmental similarities between these two populations as much as with their disparities.

The focus in this study was the use of outcome and extremity-of-outcome information in the moral evaluations of both children and adults. Although it is now widely recognized that children's moral evaluations are multidimensional and will be affected by intent, outcome, and extremity of outcome information (Armsby, 1971; Buchanan & Thompson, 1973; Farnill, 1974; Hebble, 1971), it has been less widely recognized that adults use outcome information in their moral evaluations. Attribution theorists expect, however, that in some situations information about the outcome of a person's acts will affect moral evaluation, even when the actor apparently does not intend the outcome. For instance, a person may be held responsible for a harmful outcome on the grounds that he or she "should have known better," that is, should have known the consequences of that action, even though there was no actual intent to harm. Or a person may be held responsible to some degree for outcomes with which he or she is associated in any way when that outcome has extreme effects (see Shaw & Reitan, 1969; Shaw & Sulzer, 1964). However, from an adult's point of view, most outcomes represented in the moral-evaluation literature are not compellingly important or extreme in their effects on others. For instance, one or seven cups may be broken, or someone gets home in time (or is late) for dinner.

In the present experiments, two story themes were used in which extremity of outcome, as well as intent and direction of outcome, were varied. Sixteen judgments were made by each participant (two levels of intent X two levels of outcome X two levels of extremity X two story themes). The two story themes involved a lost child or the vigilance or negligence of a baby sitter. Two scenarios were:

1. A little boy is lost and comes up to Tom and asks Tom to help him get home. Tom knows the way and wants to help. He tells the boy the way to the house; the boy gets home. [Positive intent, positive outcome, mild extremity

of outcome. The extreme outcome given this theme is "His parents are thrilled and happy to have him back because he has been lost for two nights."]

2. Tom is a baby sitter. Tom does not like children and does not like being with them. Tom does not try very hard to see that they are happy and cared for. One day a man tries to rob the house and kidnap the children. Tom is in the kitchen. So the man is able to kidnap the children. [Negative intent, negative outcome, severe extremity of outcome. The mild outcome given this theme involves the children's candy being stolen by another child.] Judgments ranged from +10 to –10, with children tested individually and assigning "happy" or "sad" faces to the story actor (see Benesh-Weiner, 1978, for additional procedural details).

The results indicate that adults did not neglect outcome information; in fact, it is a highly significant factor in their judgments. Additional research reported in Benesh-Weiner (1978) indicates that adults use outcome information in their evaluations across a wide variety of morally-relevant scenerios. Further, outcome information has a relatively greater impact on adults' evaluations when the outcomes are extreme. Of course children also used outcome information and made greater use of this information in their evaluations than did adults, giving both more reward for positive outcomes and more punishment for negative outcomes than adults. In short, children and adults apparently use outcome information in quantitatively, rather than qualitatively, different ways.

Extremity of outcome influenced the moral judgments of children and adults in a similar manner. Table 3.4 indicates that extremely positive outcomes result is greater reward than mildly positive outcomes. Even more evident is the fact that extremely negative outcomes augmented assigned punishment. For example, when the children are kidnapped as opposed to losing candy, the baby sitter is especially punished, independent of intent. There is no difference between children and adults in the extent to which extremity information increased reward or punishment. These findings were replicated using a different experimental design, but it is still not clear whether one is held more *responsible* for extreme rather than mild outcomes,

TABLE 3.4
Mean Evaluation as a Function of
Extremity and Outcome[a]

Extremity	Outcome	
	Positive	Negative
Mild	1.0	–1.8
Extreme	1.7	–3.2

[a]From Benesh-Weiner, 1978.

or whether moral *evaluation* is influenced by this information, while personal responsibility is unaffected.

It *is* clear that children make use of intent information. Indeed, in our research children reward positive intent and punish negative intent to as great an extent as do the adults. Although this at first seems inconsistent with other moral-judgment literature, recent studies, as well as a close inspection of the prior research (Surber, 1977; see review in Benesh-Weiner, 1978), show that developmental trends in the use of intent are quite weak after the age of 6 or 7. Most of the intent-linked judgment variance as a function of maturity occurs between the ages of 4 and 6; and even this variance may be accounted for by the sequence of information presentation, rather than being due to the presence or absence of the concept of intentionality (see Feldman, Klosson, Parsons, Rholes, & Ruble, 1976; Parsons et al., 1976).

To summarize, the attributional approach to judgment and evaluation points to the complexity of the process, broadening consideration of the information that may be used to include the type of motivational domain, the difficulty of the task, and the extremity of the outcome, among others. In addition, the attributional approach lends itself to a consideration of the similarities as well as the differences in the decision processes of children and adults; in many cases, similarities are striking and differences are more apparent than real. We believe that a new conceptualization for moral judgment is needed and that attribution theory may be able to contribute to this theoretical foundation.

CONCLUSION

We have been trying to convey a few simple messages in this brief cafeteria excursion into the disparate fields of mastery, emotions, and achievement and moral evaluation. First, we believe that attribution theory provides a common framework with which to examine a variety of psychological issues. The general approach is first to identify the information cues that are used to infer causality and/or responsibility. These cues include effort–outcome covariation (as in the mastery experiments), past success history (as in the emotions study), and the difficulty of the task and extremity of the outcome (as in the achievement and moral judgment research). Then the perceived cause of the event is specified. The causes range from the internal factors of ability and effort to the external factors of luck, task ease and difficulty, and help or hindrance from others. The inferred cause influences feelings of control and mastery, the quality and the intensity of inferred and actual affective experience, and judgments or evaluations of others. Thus, causal inferences guide our motivational, emotional, and social lives.

As noted previously, there was a time when developmental psychology was mired in the sterility of behaviorism; this changed with the insights of Piaget concerning the richness of intellective functioning. We think it is now time to address ourselves to the problems of psychodynamics: feelings of responsibility and control, affective lives, emotional understanding, the development of achievement strivings, interpersonal concerns, and so on. We also believe that attribution theory can aid in this very difficult struggle.

ACKNOWLEDGMENTS

This chapter was written while the first author was supported by Grant MH 25687-04 from the National Institute of Health. Reprint requests should be sent to Bernard Weiner, Department of Psychology, University of California, Los Angeles, California 90024.

REFERENCES

Armsby, R. E. A reexamination of the development of moral judgments in children. *Child Development,* 1971, *42,* 1248–1251.

Atkinson, J. W. *An introduction to motivation.* Princeton, N.J.: Van Nostrand, 1964.

Benesh-Weiner, M. *Moral evaluation: Simple or complex process?* Unpublished doctoral dissertation, University of California, Los Angeles, 1978.

Buchanan, G., & Thompson, S. A quantitative methodology to examine the development of moral judgments. *Child Development,* 1973, *44,* 186–189.

Chandler, M. J., Greenspan, S., & Barenboim, C. Judgments of intentionality in response to videotaped and verbally presented moral dilemmas: The medium is the message. *Chlid Development,* 1973, *44,* 315–320.

Ekman, P. (Ed.), *Darwin and facial expression: A century of research in review.* New York: Academic Press, 1972.

Farnill, D. The effects of social-judgment set on chlidren's use of intent information. *Journal of Personality,* 1974, *42,* 276–289.

Feldman, N. S., Klosson, E. C., Parsons, J. E., Rholes, W. S., & Ruble, D. N. Order of information presentation and children's moral judgments. *Child Development,* 1976, *47,* 556–559.

Frieze, I., & Weiner, B. Cue utilization and attributional judgments for success and failure. *Journal of Personality,* 1971, *39,* 591–606.

Gottlieb, D. E., Taylor, S. E., & Ruderman, A. Cognitive bases of children's moral judgments. *Developmental Psychology,* 1977, *13,* 547–556.

Harter, S. Effectance motivation reconsidered: Toward a developmental model. *Human Development,* 1978, *21,* 34–64.

Hebble, P. W. The development of elementary school children's judgment of intent. *Child Development,* 1971, *42,* 1203–1215.

Heider, F. *The psychology of interpersonal relations.* New York: Wiley, 1958.

Izard, C. E. *Human emotions.* New York: Plenum, 1977.

Kelley, H. H. Attribution theory in social psychology. In D. Levine (Ed.), *Nebraska symposium on motivation.* Lincoln: University of Nebraska Press, 1967.

Kelley, H. H. The process of causal attribution. *American Psychologist,* 1973, *28,* 107–128.

Kun, A., Garfield, T., & Sipowicz, C. Causality pleasure in young children: An experimental study of effectance motivation. *Developmental Psychology,* in press.

Lewin, K., Dembo, T., Festinger, L., & Sears, P. S. Level of aspiration. In J. McV. Hunt (Ed.), *Personality and the behavioral disorders.* Vol. I. New Yorker: Ronald Press, 1944.

Lewis, M., & Rosenblum, L. A. (Eds.), *The development of affect.* New York: Plenum, 1978.

Nisbett, R. E., & Schachter, S. Cognitive manipulation of pain. *Journal of Experimental Social Psychology,* 1966, *2,* 227–236.

Nuttin, J. R. Pleasure and reward in motivation and learning. In D. Berlyne (Ed.), *Pleasure, reward, preference.* New York: Academic Press, 1973.

Parsons, J. E. *Causal attribution and the role of situational cues in the development of children's evaluative judgments.* Unpublished doctoral dissertation, University of California, Los Angeles, 1974.

Parsons, J. E., Ruble, D. N., Klosson, E. C., Feldman, N. S., & Rholes, W. S. Order effects on children's moral and achievement judgments. *Developmental Psychology,* 1976, *12,* 357–358.

Schachter, S., & Singer, J. E. Cognitive, social, and physiological determinants of emotional state. *Psychological Review,* 1962, *69,* 379–399.

Shaw, M. E., & Reitan, H. Attribution of responsibility as a basis for sanctioning behavior. *British Journal of Social and Clinical Psychology,* 1969, *8,* 217–226.

Shaw, M. E., & Sulzer, J. An empirical test of Heider's levels of attribution of responsibility. *Journal of Abnormal and Social Psychology,* 1964, *69,* 39–46.

Surber, C. F. Developmental processes in social influence: Averaging of intent and consequences in moral judgment. *Developmental Psychology,* 1977, *13,* 654–665.

Watson, J. S. The development and generalization of "contingency awareness" in early infancy: Some hypotheses. *Merrill-Palmer Quarterly,* 1966, *12,* 123–135.

Watson, J. S. Memory and "contingency analysis" in infant learning. *Merrill-Palmer Quarterly,* 1967, *12,* 55–76.

Weiner, B. (Ed.), *Achievement motivation and attribution theory.* Morristown, N.J.: General Learning Press, 1974.

Weiner, B. Attribution and affect: Comments on Sohn's critique. *Journal of Educational Psychology,* 1977, *69,* 506–511.

Weiner, B., & Kun, A. The development of causal attributions and the growth of achievement and social motivation. In S. Feldman & D. Bush (Eds.), *Cognitive development and social development.* Hillsdale, N.J.: Lawrence Erlbaum Associates, in press.

Weiner, B., & Peter, N. A cognitive–developmental analysis of achievement and moral judgments. *Developmental Psychology,* 1973, *9,* 290–309.

Weiner, B., Russell, D., & Lerman, D. Affective consequences of causal ascriptions. In J. H. Harvey, W. J. Ickes, & R. F. Kidd (Eds.), *New directions in attribution research, Vol. 2.* Hillsdale, N.J.: Lawrence Erlbaum Associates, 1978.

Weiner, B., Russell, D., & Lerman, D. The cognition–emotion process in achievement-related contexts. *Journal of Personality and Social Psychology,* 1979, *37,* 1211–1220.

White, R. W. Motivation reconsidered: The concept of competence. *Psychological Review,* 1959, *66,* 297–333.

4 Development of The Concept of Intention

Thomas R. Shultz
McGill University

ANALYSIS OF THE CONCEPT OF INTENTION

Any treatment of the development of the concept of intention in children could reasonably be expected to benefit from a careful definition of intention. The difficulties encountered by psychologists who have attempted to study the development of a concept or ability without a precise and widely agreed upon specification of the object of their analyses are well known. Examples from developmental studies of syntax (e.g., Chomsky, 1959; Bever, 1968), propositional logic (Braine, 1978; Falmagne, 1975), and number (Brainerd, 1976; Macnamara, 1975) come readily to mind. In order to avoid similar problems, I will attempt at the outset to specify what I mean by the concept of intention. Defining intention is not especially easy to do, of course, perhaps because it is one of those semantically primitive notions which, although essential to the definition of many other terms, cannot itself be reduced to any more fundamental dimensions of meaning (cf. Meiland, 1970). At the outset, however, following conventional English usage, I consider *intention* to refer to a mental state that guides and organizes behavior. It is essentially a determination to act in a certain way or to bring about a certain state of affairs.

It is perhaps important to draw a distinction between this interpretation and that favored by phenomenologists such as Brentano and Husserl (Aquila, 1977; Brentano, 1960; Gurwitsch, 1969–70), who consider intention to be essentially synonymous with mental awareness or mental conception. Their definition is, for present purposes, both too broad and too narrow. It is too broad because it encompasses virtually all conscious mental activity—

131

hearing, seeing, meaning, feeling, remembering, etc.—too narrow in that it is restricted to mental states of which the person is explicitly aware. Psychologists have long doubted that people are actually aware of most or even many of their mental processes, and there is indeed some recent evidence for this general lack of awareness (Nisbett & Wilson, 1977).

Our own definition of intention as a determination to act is more consistent with the old psychological concepts of will (James, 1890) or purpose (Tolman, 1932). It has much in common as well with more contemporary psychological concepts such as plans (Miller, Galanter & Pribram, 1960; Schmidt, 1976), rules (Harré & Secord, 1972), voluntary actions (Bindra, 1976), choices (Irwin, 1971), scripts (Schank & Abelson, 1977), and procedures (Klahr & Wallace, 1976). It should be clear from even these few selected citations that the concept of intention has long played a crucial role in psychological explanations of human behavior. This is no less true of philosophical analysis, of which it has been asserted that "no theory of the mind can be adequate unless it provides a satisfactory account of intention [Meiland, 1970, p. 1]." The purpose of the research reported here is to determine whether young children, somewhat like philosphers and psychologists but in their own intuitive way, come to understand behavior in terms of the concept of intention.

An Aspect of Causal Reasoning?

The emphasis on the explanatory function of intention raises the question of its relation to other forms of explanation, such as causal attribution. Could intentionality be considered as a particular kind of causal factor, perhaps even a crucial factor in the causal explanation of human behavior? This was indeed the avenue by which I approached the problem of the development of the concept. With a number of research colleagues, I have been exploring over the last few years the child's developing conception of causation—how the child comes to explain behavioral and physical events by attributing them to their respective causes. One thing that has become abundantly clear in the physical or nonbehavioral realm is that empiricist notions of causation do not correspond to the fundamental character of the child's causal inferences (Shultz, 1979). Empiricist principles such as regularity of succession, temporal contiguity, spatial contiguity, and covariation, although useful in understanding many cause–effect situations, are clearly not the fundamental basis for the child's understanding of causation. We have found that young children, like many contemporary philosophers of science, instead construe causation in terms of a generative mechanism, wherein the causal event actually produces the effect event.

We soon began to wonder whether there was some analogous conception in the child's causal explanation of behavior. Is there something that generates or produces human behavior, and does the young child have any intuitive ideas about such production? We suspected that something like intention might be the crucial concept and, indeed, found a good deal of support for this within philosophy of social science. We found there a systematic view of people as agents who direct and control their behaviors and the idea that for the most part people act in accordance with their own self-generated rules and plans. This sort of analysis can be traced back to the writings of Aristotle and Aquinas and was well developed by a number of 19th century philosophers such as Kant. It has been further elaborated by several contemporary philosophers such as Hampshire (1965), Harré and Secord (1972), T. Mischel (1969), Peters (1958), C. Taylor (1964), and R. Taylor (1966). None of these writers deny that a physical–mechanistic framework may sometimes be appropriate for explaining behavior. After all, things do happen to people that may not be part of their regular, ongoing, self-determined pattern of actions. People do make mistakes, have accidents, and emit reflexes, and are occasionaly buffeted about like inanimate objects. But all of these philosophers do insist that most of human behavior, and virtually all of what we consider to be socially important behavior, consists of that which people as agents have made happen for various reasons or purposes. We are all active agents in much of our social life. And our intentions, rules, and plans can well be considered to be the efficient (in the sense of Aristotle, as in Wallace, 1972), productive causes of our own actions.

It is interesting that this notion of agency has recently been extended to explaining physical changes in the inanimate world. Harré and Madden (1975) discuss two general metaphors for causal explanation. One is the familiar paradigm of colliding billiard balls which has so heavily influenced conceptual analyses of causation since Newton. This metaphor would lead us to suppose that all effects are produced by an active external cause that impresses itself on an otherwise passive and inert effect. Such a metaphor is prevalent even in contemporary psychology, classical conditioning perhaps being the clearest example. The other metaphor concerns a man who, after sitting in his lawn chair on a pleasant summer afternoon, suddenly jumps up, retrieves his lawn mower, and starts to mow his grass in a systematic and efficient fashion. Any successful causal explanation of his behavior would presumably emphasize concepts such as agency, intention, or plan. And in that sense, the second metaphor is presumably much more appropriate to social science than is the first metaphor. Moreover, Harré and Madden (1975) proceed to demonstrate the applicability of the second metaphor to a number of purely physical phenomena involving inanimate objects. The explosion of a stick of dynamite, the workings of a powerful magnet, and various chemical reactions are all considered as examples requiring reference to intrinsic states such as agency rather than to exclusively external stimulation. Whatever one may think of Harré and Madden's extension of agency to the physical realm, it is clear that many philosophers consider it to be an essential component of the causal explanation of human behavior. Even this proposal has proved to be controversial, however, and will be discussed more extensively later when we examine whether young children consider intentions to be causes of behavior.

Intention and Moral Responsibility

Psychological study of the development of the concept of intention has so far focused almost exclusively on the use of intention information in making moral judgments about the actions of another person. This work has been stimulated largely by Piaget's (1932) early and highly influential book, *The Moral Judgment of the Child*. But the idea that intention was important in determining moral and legal responsibility was formulated as early as 1789 by Jeremy Bentham. This notion was adopted and elaborated by a number of subsequent moral and legal philosophers including Austin (1873) and Hampshire and Hart (1958) and has come to serve as one of the cornerstones of Anglo-American jurisprudence (e.g., Williams, 1953). Generally, it is claimed that, if an action is not intentional, then the agent of that action is not morally responsible for it (but see D'Arcy, 1963, for a critique and revision of this view). The concept of intention has, in this sense, been considered indispensable in making a legal determination of *mens rea* (Williams, 1953; see Leahy, 1977, for a psychological investigation of the child's developing notion of *mens rea*). Piaget (1932) initiated the study of the psychological development of this idea by telling young children pairs of stories in which a well-intentioned act leading to considerable damage is contrasted with an ill-intentioned act leading to negligible damage. For example:

A. There was a little boy called Julian. His father had gone out and Julian thought it would be fun to play with his father's ink-pot. First he played with the pen and then he made a little blot on the table cloth. B. A little boy who was called Augustus once noticed that his father's ink-pot was empty. One day that his father was away he thought of filling the ink-pot so as to help his father, and so that he should find it full when he came home. But while he was opening the ink-bottle he made a big blot on the table cloth. Are these two children equally guilty (or as the young Genevese say, "la même chose villain")? Which of the two is naughtiest (sic), and why [Piaget, 1932, pp. 122–123]?

Piaget found that children above 8 or 9 years of age responded that the former child, Julian, is naughtier because he acted with a bad intention, whereas children below 8 or 9 years considered that the latter child, Augustus, is naughtier because he made a bigger ink-blot. In the 40 years following the publication of Piaget's book on moral judgment, this basic shift from a concern with objective outcomes to subjective intentions has been replicated many times in a variety of different cultures (see Hoffman, 1970, and Simpson, 1974, for comprehensive reviews).

Until quite recently, the common inference drawn from such data was that children below 8 or 9 years of age are either not aware of intentions or, if they are aware of them, do not see their relevance to issues of moral responsibility (cf. Hoffman, 1970). However, contemporary researchers have discovered a number of methodological flaws in Piaget's original technique and, in correcting and exploiting these flaws, have demonstrated the use of intention in moral judgments by children as young as 5 or 6 years. Recent investigations of this issue have in fact made it one of the liveliest and most sophisticated areas in the study of social cognition. One of the problems with Piaget's initial stories was that they varied information on both consequences and intentions simultaneously: The child with the good intention does more damage than the child with the bad intention. It has been shown in four recent experiments that, when amount of damage is held constant, and only intentionality is varied, even young children judge intentional damage to be more culpable than unintentional damage (Berg-Cross, 1975; Chandler, Greenspan & Barenboim, 1973; Elkind & Dabek, 1977; Gutkin, 1972). Still other researchers have noted that Piaget's stories invariably presented the intention information before the consequence information. It was speculated that younger children might be focusing only on the more recent information, thereby ignoring the intentionality of the protagonist. Again, at least four different experiments have found evidence that this does interfere with the young child's use of intention information (Austin, Ruble & Trabasso, 1977; Feldman, Klosson, Parsons, Rholes & Ruble, 1976; Gottlieb, Taylor & Ruderman, 1977; Nummedal & Bass, 1976). Children as young as 5 or 6 years of age do use intention information when it is presented at the end of the story. Other methodological difficulties concern the hypothetical nature of verbal stories, as opposed to real behavior, and the additional problems inherent in reasoning about someone else, as opposed to oneself. In our own research, we have found these factors to have important influences on the use of causal inference schemes by young children (Shultz & Butkowsky, 1977; Wells & Shultz, 1978). Chandler et al. (1973) reported that presenting the moral situations on film produced more effective use of intention information than was typical of hypothetical stories. And Keasey (1977) found that 6- and 7-year-olds made greater use of intention information when judging their own behavior than when judging another child's behavior. Piaget (1932, p. 183) himself had suggested that the young child may be more likely to employ intentionality in judging his own behavior than in judging someone else's behavior and had even presented some evidence for it (pp. 125–126). And finally, an experiment by Bearison and Isaacs (1975) suggests that when young children fail to use intentions in moral judgments, this may represent more of a "production deficiency" than a "mediation deficiency." They found that, although 6-year-olds did not spontaneously infer the protagonist's intention, they were indeed capable of doing so when prompted; and at that point intention information did mediate their moral judgments.

The role of intention in forming moral judgments is clearly an interesting topic, either from a theoretical or a practical point of view. However, it is certainly not the only way to study the concept of intention and probably not the most direct way. It is clear that researchers in this area have been primarily interested in moral judgment and only secondarily interested in intention. Few of them even ask the child explicitly about the intentions of the protagonist; it has been much more typical for the researcher to merely infer whether children were using intention information from the pattern of their moral judgments alone. Although I will return to some observations on the relation between intention and moral judgment at the close, my primary purpose here is to examine the child's developing notion of intention per se. As we will see, there are many interesting aspects of knowledge of intention, quite independent of its role in other sorts of judgments.

Other Indications of the Child's Knowledge of Intention

Psychological studies of the child's developing knowledge of intention outside of the moral judgment context are extremely rare. However, a few studies do suggest the pervasiveness and importance of the intention concept in the minds of young children. Berndt and Berndt (1975) had 5-, 8-, and 11-year-olds judge whether the consequence of an actor's behavior, portrayed either in a story or on film, was intended or not. They found that children of all ages tested judged intentional actions correctly, but that 5-year-olds incorrectly inferred that accidents were also intended. Perhaps this indicates a general tendency for young children to see all actions of others as intentional. A study by Whiteman, Brook, and Gordon (1974) found that 6–12-year-olds' perceptions of intentionality varied as a function of both the instrumentality and the consequentiality of the action. The more instrumental the action was in producing a desired consequence and the greater the desirability of that consequence, the more likely the child was to infer that the action was intentional.

There is also evidence from the literature on early language learning that very young children seem to have intention on their mind a good deal of the time. For example, Brown (1973) has found that, at about 2 years of age, children begin to modify the generic verb in several different ways. One of their primary modifications is to combine the verb with what Brown terms semi-auxiliaries or catenatives such as *gonna, wanna,* and *hafta.* According to Brown, these catenatives express intentionality. The child uses them to name actions which he or she is just about to perform as in *I wanna go* or *I gonna run.* Such expressions seem to refer to the immediate future, conveying a fairly explicit formulation of the child's own intentional state. Of course, there is much more involved in thinking about intention than simply knowing that you have one, but it is interesting that children as young as 2 years are sufficiently aware of their own intentions that they can and do state them so clearly. Also revealing in this respect is the apparent early and pervasive use of the agentive case by children just beginning to speak (Bloom, Lightbown, & Hood, 1975; Bowerman, 1976; Brown, 1973; Slobin, 1970). The agentive case, of course, expresses the notion of an animate being initiating some action as in *dog run* or *Mommy read*. Although it is not entirely clear from the use of this case exactly what children assume about the intentional states of such agents, it is clear that they do have a firm notion of agency, i.e., that animate individuals perform their own actions.

Further evidence of early understanding of agency has emerged from Watson and Fischer's (1977) recent study of elicited pretending. They found that 2-year-olds could treat an object as if it had a will of its own, making it initiate and control simple actions such as eating, washing, and sleeping. Of course, the concepts of agency and intentionality are not precisely identical. Intentionality could perhaps be regarded as a more advanced and more refined analysis of how agents generate their own behavior. In this sense, a notion of intention presupposes knowledge of agency, but the reverse would not necessarily hold. One could possess knowledge of agency without having a concept of intention.

Our own research focuses on several aspects of the child's developing knowledge of intention that have not as yet received much attention in the psychological literature. This research is discussed under seven different headings: (1) distinguishing intended actions from mistakes, (2) distinguishing intended actions from elicited reflexes and passive movements, (3) intentions as causes, (4) conditional versus nonconditional intentions, (5) intending an act versus intending a consequence, (6) recursive awareness of intention, and (7) naturalistic observations on the use of intention in moral judgments.

INTENTIONAL VERSUS MISTAKEN BEHAVIOR

Intentional behavior, as specified earlier, is done with a determination to act in a particular way or to bring about a particular state of affairs. In the case of mistaken behavior, an intentional state of mind may also be present, but there is mismatch between that intentional state and the behavior. In other words, the resulting behavior is something different than was intended. The child's awareness of this distinction was assessed by presenting a number of items in which an action could be performed either by intention or by mistake and then asking the child in each case whether the action had been done on purpose. Children were asked to make such judgments both with respect to their own behavior and with respect to the behavior of others. A number of philosophers (Anscombe, 1957; Hampshire & Hart, 1958) have suggested that, although we appear to have a direct subjective awareness of our own intentions, we are able to know the intentions of others only indirectly by virtue of inference based on objective evidence. Thus, it may well be predicted that the child's understanding of intentionality in others derives principally from knowledge of his or her own mental states and their relation to his or her own behavior. This would presumably account for the findings of Keasey (1977) that young children employ intentions more in judging their own behavior than in judging the behavior of someone else.

In our experiment, children were tested in triads of three children from the same age level. In each triad, one child (A) generated data first as an agent judging his own behavior and then later as an experienced observer judging the behavior of a second child (B). A third child (C) generated data as an inexperienced observer judging the behavior of that second child (B). Child C then proceeded to serve in the next triad as the non-data-generating agent (role B in the first triad) for two additional children. We expected that agents might know more about intentional states than would observers and that experienced observers (i.e., observers who had just served as an agent engaging in the same behaviors) might know more about the intentional states of an agent than would observers who probably never engaged in these precise behaviors.

The participants were 17 children at each of three ages: 3, 5, and 7 years. Eight children from each age group were randomly assigned to the role of inexperienced observer. Another eight children at that age level served in both the agent and experienced observer roles. One child from each age group served as agent for the two observers in the first triad tested with that age group, and hence generated no data at all.

The procedure was as follows: four items, each of which contained an intentional behavior and an analogous behavior that was contrived to constitute a mistake, were used for each of the three assessed roles. In the intentional form of the so-called *pointing* item, a shiny penny and a dull penny were placed on the desk in front of the agent. The agent was asked to notice where each penny was, to close his or her eyes, and to pick up the shiny penny. When the agent had picked up the shiny penny (as all did), the examiner acknowledged this, and then directed a question about the intentional state of the agent to either the agent or the observer, depending on which role was being assessed: "Did you (s/he) mean to pick up the shiny penny?" In the mistaken form of the pointing item, everything was done as before except that the agent wore a set of prism glasses that laterally distorted his or her field of vision. After the glasses were removed, the agent discovered that he or she had picked up the dull penny by mistake. Again, a question about the intentional state of the agent was posed: "Did you (s/he) mean to pick up the dull penny?"

In the intentional form of the *verbal repetition* item, the agent was asked to repeat the sentence *She lives in a house.* In the mistake form, the agent was asked to repeat several times consecutively the "tongue twister" *She sells sea shells by the sea shore,* during which mistakes inevitably resulted. After each of these productions, the intentional question was posed: "Did you (s/he) mean to say it like that?"

For the so-called *finger lifting* item, the agent was instructed to clasp his or her hands together and then to lift the finger that the examiner pointed to (one of the two index fingers). This was the intentional form. In the mistake form, the agent had to clasp his or her hands with the wrists crossed so that the right hand was now on the left side and the left hand on the right side. Again the examiner pointed to a finger (one of the ring fingers) which the child was supposed to lift. As before, the intentional form always produced a correct response, whereas the mistake form produced an error. After each response, the intention question was posed: "Did you (s/he) mean to lift that finger?"

In the intentional form of the *hand movement* item, the agent was asked to rhythmically and repeatedly tap his or her head with one hand and his or her stomach with the other hand at the same time. After acknowledging the two simultaneous tapping motions, the examiner asked, "Did you (s/he) mean to do that?" In the mistake form, incompatible repetitive movements were used to produce mistaken action. Here the agent was asked to rub the stomach with a large circular motion while tapping the head at the same time. The examiner identified the outcome, e.g., "You are making circles on your head and your stomach," and asked, "Did you (s/he) mean to do that?"

For each triad, the three roles were always assessed in the same order: (1) an agent (child A) judging his or her own behavior; (2) an inexperienced observer (child C) judging the behavior of an agent (child B); and (3) an experienced observer (child A) judging the behavior of an agent (Child B). Children not serving as an agent or an observer in a particular assessment were asked to sit in the hall outside until it was their turn to participate. When children were tested in pairs, as in sessions (2) and (3), the agent was cautioned not to give any hints to the observer as the examiner wanted to find out how much the observer knew about what the agent was doing. There were 24 possible orders of the four items and each of them was used once within each age group (eight triads × three roles). Within each item, the order of the intentional and mistaken forms was randomly determined for each separate time that item was used. Responses to the intention questions were recorded verbatim and later coded as 0 for a negative response, meaning, "No, I (s/he) didn't mean to do it," and 1 for a positive response, meaning, "Yes, I (s/he) did mean to do it."

These scores were summed across the four intentional items and across the four mistaken items that each child received. Thus each child generated two intentionality scores, one for the intentional items and one for the mistaken items, and each of these scores could range from 0 (reflecting judgments of the absence of intention) to 4 (reflecting judgments of the presence of intention). These scores were subjected to an analysis of variance in which age served as a between triads factor and role and form of item served as within triads factors. Because of the fact that one child played two roles within each triad, the assumption of homogeneity of covariances was in doubt. Conservative degrees of freedom were used, in accord with Winer's (1962) recommendation for such situations. The analysis yielded only a sizeable main effect for form of item, $F(1, 21) = 34.50$, $p < .001$, reflecting greater inference of intention in the intentional items ($\bar{x} = 3.17$) than in the mistaken items ($\bar{x} = 1.49$). This form effect held for all three age levels and all three roles, as there were no other significant main or interactive effects. It was apparent that children between 3 and 7 years of age could accurately distinguish intentional from mistaken actions emitted either by themselves or by someone else. Furthermore, they could correctly assess the intentionality of another child's actions even when they themselves had not previously performed those same actions.

INTENTIONAL VERSUS REFLEXIVE OR PASSIVE BEHAVIOR

A very similar study was conducted on the distinction between intentional behaviors and those produced reflexively, or through passive movements. A number of philosophers (Harré & Secord, 1972; C. Taylor, 1964; R. Taylor, 1966) have emphasized this distinction in their analysis of intention, maintaining that reflexes and passive movements occur without the presence of a relevant intentional state. In our study, behaviors were selected that could occur either spontaneously (i.e., intentionally) or through passive movement or reflex (i.e., unintentionally). As in the first study, children were tested in triads to determine whether knowledge of intentional states would be more accurate in judging one's own actions than in judging the actions of someone else and to determine whether previous experience in generating the behaviors would facilitate understanding of their intentional characteristics when observing them in others.

The participants were 25 French-speaking children from each of three age groups: 3–4, 5–6, and 7–8 years. Twelve children from each age group were randomly assigned to the role of inexperienced observer. Another 12 children at that age level served in both the agent and experienced observer roles. One child from each age group served as agent for the two observers in the first triad tested with that age group, thus generating no data for the study.

The procedure was introduced to the children in the same way that it was done in the first study, except that all testing was conducted in French, in which to do something intentionally or *on purpose* is expressed as *faire exprès*. Two behavior items, one reflex and one passive movement, were employed. Each of these items was used in three different forms: (a) elicited, (b) elicited with instructions to inhibit, and (c) intentional. The instructions-to-inhibit form was always presented after the elicited form, but whether the intentional form followed or preceded the elicited forms was randomly determined in each instance. The reflex used was the standard femoral or knee-jerk reflex. For all three forms of this item, the child–agent was asked to sit on the edge of a table, cross the right leg over the left one, and relax. The reflex was elicited with the examiner tapping the side of his hand against the child's knee. In another form, the examiner also asked the child to intend *not* to move his or her leg. In the intentional form of this item, the examiner sat on the table, demonstrated an intentional leg movement himself, and asked the child if he or she was able to do this. In each case, the examiner asked whether the child moved his or her leg on purpose.

In the elicited form of the passive-movement item, the examiner held the child's arms down at his side while instructing the child to try to get rid of the examiner's arms by pushing upward. After about 10 sec, the examiner would release the child's arms, which elicited a slow involuntary upward movement of the arms. This was repeated in the second form where the examiner instructed the child to try not to move his arms when they were released. In the intentional form of this item, the examiner raised his own arms up from his side and asked the child if he or she was able to do this. In each instance the examiner inquired whether the child had moved his or her arms on purpose.

The order of the different roles in each triad was the same as in the first study: (1) agent, (2) inexperienced observer, and (3) experienced observer. Also, as in the first study, children not being tested waited in the hall and agents were cautioned against giving any hints to the observer. Order of administration of the two behavioral items was randomly determined in each instance. Responses to the intention questions were recorded verbatim and later coded as –1 for a negative response, meaning essentially, "No, I (s/he) didn't do it on purpose," and +1 for a positive response, meaning essentially, "Yes, I (s/he) did do it on purpose." Responses of "I don't know" and lack of responses were scored as 0.

In the analysis of variance for these scores, age served as as between-triads factor, and role, item, and form of item served as within-triads factors. As in the first study, conservative degrees of freedom were employed because it was questionable to assume homogeneity of covariances. The analysis yielded a large main effect of form of item, $F(1, 33) = 58.11, p < .001$, and a smaller age × form of item interaction, $F(2, 33) = 7.98, p < .01$. The Tukey (a) technique (Winer, 1962) was used to compare means for the main effect, and it was found that the scores for the intentional form ($\bar{x} = .213$) were significantly ($p < .01$) higher than those for the elicited ($\bar{x} = -.546$) and elicited with instructions to inhibit ($\bar{x} = -.681$) forms. Means reflecting the age × form of item interaction are presented in Table 4.1. These means were compared using Cicchetti's (1972) extension of Tukey's procedure to interactions. It was revealed that scores in the intentional form exceeded scores on the two elicited forms only for the 5–6 and 7–8-year-olds, but not for the 3–4-year-olds. Thus, children between 5 and 8 years of age clearly perceived more intentionality in intentional movements than in reflexive or

TABLE 4.1
Mean Intention Scores in the Study on
Reflexive and Passive Movements

	Form of Item				
Age	Intentional		Elicited		Elicited with Instructions to Inhibit
3–4	−.125	ns[a]	−.347	ns	−.389
5–6	.305	s	−.542	ns	−.861
7–8	.458	s	−.750	ns	−.792

[a]The symbol s between two means indicates that these means differ at $p < .01$. The symbol ns indicates that the two means are not significantly different.

passive movements. The same trend was evident for 3–4-year-olds, but it did not reach an acceptable level of statistical significance. The absence of any main or interactive effects of role indicated that children could make these distinctions just as accurately when observing someone else's behavior as when judging their own behavior and that previous experience in generating the behaviors did not facilitate their perception of intentionality in others. Although instructions for the agent to inhibit the elicited behavior appeared to heighten somewhat the impression of nonintentionality, this difference too failed to reach statistical significance at any age level. However children are able to make these distinctions between elicited and intentional behaviors, they do not appear to be relying on self-observation or on instructions suggesting that the agent is trying to inhibit the behavior.

INTENTIONS AS CAUSES OF BEHAVIOR

The question of whether intentions are causes of behavior has generated a great deal of controversy within the literature on philosophy of science. Many philosophers of the 18th and 19th centuries had no difficulty whatsoever in conceiving of intentions as legitimate causes. Bentham (1789/1948), for example, defined a voluntary action as one that follows and is caused by an act of the will. And John Stuart Mill (in D'Arcy, 1963) argued that a volition is "simply a cause: our will causes our body actions in the same sense . . . in which cold causes ice and a spark causes an explosion of gun powder [p. 98]." Later, Wittgenstein (in D'Arcy, 1963) argued against this view of intention or will as a cause of voluntary actions. He claimed that because intentions do not exist in the material sense, having no extent in space and no mass, they could not possibly cause anything. Wittgenstein's comments inspired a number of 20th century philosophers who then wrote rather elaborate attacks on the notion that intentions could be causes (e.g., Anscombe, 1957; Meldon, 1961).

Besides the "immaterial" sort of objection, it has also been argued that causes must be logically independent of effects and that this does not hold for intentions, because intentions cannot even be described without reference to the intended behavior (Meldon, 1961; Von Wright, 1971). In other words, intentions are merely descriptions of or rationalizations for actions, and, as such, cannot cause actions. This objection would appear to be contradicted by the results of our first two studies, wherein children functioning either as agents or as observers drew clear psychological distinctions between actions and intentions. They expressed the knowledge that, although the action turned out one way, the intention behind it was something else all together. A number of these objections to considering intention as cause have been critically examined by Davidson (1963) and Mackie (1974). Many such objections turn out, under close scrutiny, to be based on rather outdated notions of causation and, as well, reveal a lack of psychological sophistication.

However, this controversy is resolved within philosophy of science, the question of concern here is whether young children regard intentions as causes. Perhaps the most direct approach to this issue would be to ask children *why* questions about behavior, e.g., "Why did you point to the shiny penny?" or "Why did he move his leg?," and to note the incidence of answers referring to some intentional state. The sorts of answers children provide to *why* questions could, of course, be influenced by a number of factors, situational and otherwise. Also, there is the issue of how many intentional attributions will be required to conclude that intentions are being considered as causes—50%, 75%, 90%? This becomes a fairly arbitrary decision with little statistical precision.

A somewhat less direct, but perhaps more interesting, approach would be to see whether children assimilate information about intentions into their causal schemes just as they do with other sorts of causal information. One of the most heavily studied causal schemes in recent years has been the so-called scheme for multiple sufficient causes, first proposed by Harold Kelley (1972, 1973). This scheme specifies that any of two or more possible causes is sufficient to produce an effect. Given that the effect has occurred and that one possible cause is absent, the scheme implies the presence of another possible cause. And given that the effect has occurred in the presence of one possible cause, the scheme leads to a relatively uncertain or indeterminate implication regarding the presence of another possible cause. Initial developmental studies from our own laboratory (Shultz, Butkowsky, Pearce, & Shanfield, 1975) and by Smith (1975) and Karniol and Ross (1976) suggested that this scheme was not within the grasp of children below about 8 or 9 years of age. However, more recent experiments indicate that some of the deficiencies young children exhibit with respect to the scheme for multiple sufficient causes consist of performance, rather than competence, problems. We have found that 4- and 5-year-olds can use this scheme more effectively in explaining human behavior if (a) the behavior is presented as real, as opposed to hypothetical (Shultz & Butowsky, 1977; Wells & Shultz, 1978); (b) the behavior is the child's own rather than someone else's (Wells & Shultz, 1978); and (c) use of the scheme is inferred from the child's spontaneous behavior instead of from a conscious judgment (Wells & Shultz, 1978). Furthermore, we have found that even 3-year-olds reveal some competence with the scheme when it is applied to a simple physical phenomenon (activation of a light by either one of a pair of switches) as opposed to social behavior (Bindra, Clarke, & Shultz, 1980).

With respect to the assimilation of intentional information to this causal scheme, it is of interest to note that our study on reflexes and passive movements appear to provide an appropriate and natural context for the application of the scheme. In this study, we provided the child with information on the presence or absence of an external cause for the observed behavioral effect and asked about the presence or absence of a relevant intentional state. For example, the agent's leg is seen to move either with or without a tap from the hand of the experimenter. For such a case, the scheme for multiple sufficient causes predicts the presence of another possible cause in the nonelicited or intentional condition but not in the elicited conditions. As reported earlier, the obtained inference data from the intentional question corresponded to this predicted pattern for all age groups and significantly so for the 5–6 and 7–8-year-olds. When there was no sufficient external cause present, intention was inferred to be present; but when there was a sufficient external cause present, intention was more likely to be seen as absent. These data, of course, were responses to a direct question about the presence or absence of the internal, intentional state of the agent ("Did you (s/he) do it on purpose?"); and they are merely being redescribed here in terms of the scheme for multiple sufficient causes.

A more open-ended causal question was also asked just before the intentional question, e.g., "What made your (his/her) leg (arms) move?" Responses were coded as +1 if they referred to some internal, intentional cause, e.g., "Because I tried;" -1 if they referred to some external cause, e.g., "Because of your hand;" and 0 if they expressed a lack of knowledge or were otherwise ambiguous with respect to the internal/external dichotomy. In the analysis of variance, age served as a between-triads factor and role, item, and form of item served as within-triads factors. As before, conservative degrees of freedom were applied to within-triads tests. There were significant main effects for both item, $F(1, 33) = 31.83$, $p < .001$, and form of item $F(1, 33) = 7.82$, $p < .01$, as well as an item × form of item interaction, $F(1, 33) = 16.44$, $p < .001$. The mean causality scores are presented in Table 4.2 as a function of item and form of item. Cicchetti's (1972) techniuqe for multiple comparisons indicated that for the knee-jerk item, attributed causes were less internal in the two elicited forms than in the nonelicited, intentional form, a pattern predicted by the scheme for multiple sufficient causes. No such effect

TABLE 4.2
Mean Causality Scores in the
Study on Reflexive and Passive Movements

| | Form of Item | | | | |
| | | | | | Elicited with Instructions to |
Item	Intentional		Elicited		Inhibit
Knee-jerk	-.259	s^a	-.750	ns	-.815
Arm-lifting	-.250	ns	-.037	ns	-.194

[a]The symbol s between two means indicates that these means differ at $p < .01$. The symbol ns indicates that the two means are not significantly different.

was evident for the arm-lifting item, however, perhaps because the presence of a specific external cause was more difficult to discern. After all, the agent's arms began to rise only after the experimenter took his hands away.

In any case, it may be concluded that young children treat information about intentions just as they treat information about other causal factors. That is, intentional information is readily assimilated to the scheme for multiple sufficient causes. This was particularly true for 5-6- and 7-8-year-olds when asked a specific question about intention and for all ages from 3-8 years when asked a more open-ended causal question about the knee-jerk phenomenon.

CONDITIONAL VERSUS NONCONDITIONAL INTENTIONS

One of the major problems involved in thinking about whether intentions cause behavior concerns the difference between conditional and nonconditional intentions. In a conditional intention, some circumstance or condition is included as part of what is intended (Meiland, 1970). An agent intends to do X if circumstances C are present, but not if they are not. An intention may be considered nonconditional if the agent's complete intention is to do X, regardless of the fulfillment of any particular condition. For example, I may intend to go to the beach on a given day only if it is sunny or, alternatively, I may intend to go regardless of the weather conditions. The former would constitute a conditional intention and the latter a nonconditional intention. It would seem that only nonconditional intentions could be truly causal in the sense of being both necessary and sufficient for a certain behavioral effect (see Mackie, 1974; Nagel, 1961; and Von Wright, 1971, for analyses of causation in terms of conditionship). A conditional intention may be necessary, but is certainly not sufficient, for the production of an intentional behavior. It is not sufficient because the specified condition must also be satisfied in order for the behavior to emerge. It is perhaps worth noting in this connection that the specified condition for an intention may be conditional with respect to time alone, as when I intend to go to the beach only on the condition that it is the afternoon.

The prevalence of such conditions for intentions may give behavioral observers (including psychologists) the impression that so-called intentional behavior is actually elicited by external stimulation. The observer notes that when an external change has registered upon the agent, the agent behaves in a certain fashion. And this, naturally enough, leads the observer to conclude that the behavior is externally caused. To return to our earlier example, one might well conclude that sunshine causes people to go to the beach. Such explanatory paradigms have been with us since the beginnings of scientific psychology and are still very much with us today. A good example would be William James' (1890) "ideomotor" theory of voluntary action that has been elaborated and extended by a number of contemporary psychologists (e.g., Bindra, 1976; Greenwald, 1970; Kimble & Perlmuter, 1970). One of the basic features of this approach is the assumption that external stimulation controls the activation of both voluntary and involuntary movements. Voluntary actions are said to differ from involuntary or innate responses only to the extent that the former are produced through learned, rather than innate, neural paths.

The basic problem with such explanatory paradigms from the standpoint of intentionality is that they fail to make certain distinctions: between intentional and nonintentional behaviors, and between conditional and nonconditional intentions. Moreover, such paradigms engender a view of the human organism as basically more passive and reactive than seems reasonable. Our central purpose here, though, is not to criticize the various psychological theories of voluntary behavior, but rather to examine the young child's concept of conditional intention.

For this purpose, we set up some situations in which the child was behaving according to a conditional intention. On some occasions, the child executed the intended behavior when the appropriate conditions were satisfied, whereas on other occasions, he or she was led to execute the intended behavior when appropriate conditions were not satisfied. The former responses may be termed commissions and the latter commissive errors. Following each response, the child was asked whether or not the action was intended. If the child could successfully identify commissive errors as unintentional and correct commissions as intentional, this would constitute evidence that he or she knows that actions can be conditionally intended. For both commissive errors and correct commissions, the same intended behavior is executed. But only in the latter case are the appropriate conditions satisfied. That is, to recognize a commissive error as unintentional requires the knowledge that the intention was conditional as opposed to nonconditional.

Without this knowledge, both commissive errors and correct commissions would presumably be considered as intended.

To examine notions of conditionality, two different procedures were administered to each child in a group of 12 boys and 12 girls between the ages of 3.0 and 3.9 years (mean age = 3.5). The first was a card game in which the child and the examiner as players were each provided with one-half of a standard deck of cards. The child and the examiner each turned over a card at the same time. If the two exposed cards matched in color, the first player to slap his or her hand down on the table would win the pair of cards. If the two newly exposed cards did not match in color, play would continue until the colors did match and one of the players could then win all of the exposed cards by slapping his or her hand on the table before the other player. In this procedure, the intended action was slapping one's hand down on the table. The appropriate condition for this intended act was that the two cards just exposed matched in color. A correct commission consisted of the child slapping his or her hand on the table when the colors matched. A commissive error consisted of the child slapping his or her hand on the table when the colors did not match. The examiner managed to elicit two responses of each type from every child by controlling the speed of the game. Speeding up her own responses would tend to elicit commissive errors on the part of the child, whereas slowing down her own responses would encourage correct commissions on the part of the child. The examiner also made an attempt to mix the order of these two types of responses. After each of the two responses of each type, the examiner asked if the child's action had been intentional: "Did you mean to slap your hand down?"

The second procedure consisted of a word game in which the child was induced to give an intended verbal response once when the appropriate conditions were satisfied and once when they were not satisfied. To elicit the commissive error, the examiner asked the child to repeat the word *shop* five times in succession as quickly as possible. Then the child was asked, "When you come to a green light, what do you do?" Most people in this situation, concentrating very hard on not allowing the previous repetitions of *shop* to confuse their response, carefully articulate the response "stop." This can be considered as an intended response, but as one emitted under the wrong conditions since the traffic signal in the question was described as green and not red. When this mistake occurred, the examiner asked, "You *stop* when you get to a green light?" Then, when the child realized his or her mistake, the examiner asked, "Did you mean to say "*stop?*" To elicit the correct commission, the examiner asked the child to repeat the word car five times in succession as quickly as possible. The child was then asked, "When you come to a green light, what do you do?" This tended to receive answers such as "I go," "I walk," or "I cross," and was followed by the intentional question, "Did you mean to say *go?*"or whatever it was that the child answered. One-half of the children of each sex received the commissive error item first and the correct commission item second, while the other half received the opposite order.

The results for both procedures were so uniform as not to require statistical analysis. During the card-game procedure, every child maintained that their two correct commissions were intended and that their two commissive errors were not intended. The same pattern held in the word game procedure with two exceptions. The manipulation failed to take in the case of one boy who responded "go" to the shop–stop item. And one girl responded with "stop" to both items and failed to realize either of her mistakes. With these two exceptions, recognition of commissive errors as unintended and correct commissions as intended was perfect. Children as young as 3 years do seem to know the difference between their own conditional and nonconditional intentions and to be able to identify their own mistakes with respect to conditional intentions.

INTENDING AN ACT VERSUS INTENDING A CONSEQUENCE

A number of the classical writers on intention such as Jeremy Bentham (1789/1948) and John Austin (1873) have pointed out that intention may focus on the act, or on the consequence of the act, or on both. This distinction poses a number of interesting possibilities: Both the act and its consequence may be intended, neither may be intended, or one but not the other may be intended. In other words, there can be concordance between act and consequence with respect to intention, or there can be discordance. Examples of concordance are quite common and of no special interest, but cases of discordance are probably quite rare and undoubtedly of greater theoretical interest in terms of distinguishing intending an act from intending a consequence. For example, a young girl may intend to touch her baby brother's eye, but not actually intend the consequence of hurting him and making him cry. Or conversely, she may intend the consequence of making him cry, and yet, because of the constant presence of the mother, not be able to perform any action to bring about that consequence. Nonetheless, her intended consequence might well come about without any such intended action on her part, as when the baby cries from some other cause.

The main focus of the present study was to examine the child's developing knowledge of this distinction between intending an act and intending a consequence. Within the same study, it was also possible to examine whether the child could distinguish an intended from an unintended action and an intended from an unintended consequence. The same triad procedure used in our first two studies was employed here to determine whether children develop these kinds of intentional knowledge first with respect to their own behavior and then later extend it to the behavior of others. A further purpose of the study was to test Meiland's (1970) proposal that one cannot intend something that one knows to be logically impossible.

The participants were 25 children drawn from each of three age levels: 5–6, 7–8, and 9–10 years. Twelve children from each age group were randomly assigned to the role of inexperienced observer and another 12 children from that age group served in both the agent and experienced observer roles. One child from each age level served as agent for the two observers in the first triad tested with that age level, thus not generating any data.

In the procedure, the child serving as agent played a simple *choose-and-match game* against a gumball machine that dispensed red or green gum balls. The object of the game for the agent was to choose either a red or a green gum ball, trying to match it with the color of the gum ball to be dispensed by the machine. On each trial, the agent selected either a red or a green ball from a small transparent cup and placed that ball in the tray of the machine. The machine contained several hundred gum balls, roughly half of which were red and half green. After the agent made his or her play, the examiner turned the crank of the machine to dispense a gum gall. If the colors matched, the agent won the two gum balls; if the colors did not match, the machine won both balls.

The action involved in this game was the choosing of which color ball to play, and it could be done intentionally by the agent or not intentionally with the examiner contravening the agent's choice, insisting that the opposite color be played. Similarly, the consequence could either be intended (winning) or not intended (losing). The various possibilities are listed in Table 4.3. An intentional question was posed after each act: "Did you (s/he) mean to play the red (green) one?" and after each consequence: "Did you (s/he) mean to win (lose)?" The sequence of wins and losses, of course, varied randomly. Interventions by the examiner in the agent's choice occurred on a predetermined random schedule, and the game continued until there were at least two instances of each of the four possible outcomes listed in Table 4.3. As in the first two studies, the order of the different roles in each triad was invariably agent, inexperienced observer, and experienced observer.

TABLE 4.3
Schematic Design of the Study on
Intending Act Versus Consequence

	Consequence	
Act Determined By	*Win*	*Loss*
Child	1. Act intended, consequence intended	2. Act intended, consequence not intended
Examiner	3. Act not intended, consequence intended	4. Act not intended, consequence not intended

In order to test the hypothesis that one cannot be considered to intend something that is logically impossible, the last agent in each triad was given four additional trials in which he or she could play only yellow or blue gum balls. Since the machine obviously contained only red and green balls, the consequence of winning became logically impossible. Nonetheless, after each act on these four trials, the child was asked, "Do you mean to win?" to determine whether the child considered logical impossibility to preclude intentionality.

Responses to intention questions in the triad procedures were coded as 1 if they were positive (indicating intentionality) and as 0 if they were negative (indicating a lack of intentionality). These scores were summed across the two repetitions and subjected to an analysis of variance in which age served as a between-triads factor and role, determiner of action, consequence, and focus of question (act versus consequence) served as within-triads factors. In the interest of clarity and simplicity, only a series of planned comparisons assessing each of the principal theoretical predictions are presented here. Each planned comparison was computed as a single degree of freedom regression variance that was tested against the appropriate error variance from the overall analysis (Winer, 1962).

The hypothesis that children could distinguish intending an act from intending a consequence was assessed by contrasting the means for act versus consequence in those two cells where they are discordant with respect to intention, namely Cells 2 and 3 of Table 3. In Cell 2, where the act was intended and the consequence was not, the intention score for act ($\bar{x} = 1.75$) was significantly higher than for consequence ($\bar{x} = 0.46$), $F(1, 33) = 376.99$, $p < .001$. In Cell 3, where the consequence was intended and the act was not, the intention score for act ($\bar{x} = 0.75$) was significantly less than that for consequence ($\bar{x} = 1.61$), $F(1, 33) = 168.71$, $p < .001$. These tests were done separately for each age level and were found to be significant ($p < .001$) in every case. Thus, the hypothesis that children from 5–10 years of age can distinguish intending an act from intending a consequence of the act is supported.

The hypothesis that children could distinguish intended from not-intended actions in this situation was tested by contrasting the means for child versus examiner as determiner of action for questions that focused on actions only. The mean intention score was found to be significantly higher when the child determined the act ($\bar{x} = 1.77$) than when the examiner determined the act ($\bar{x} = 0.79$), $F(1, 33) = 333.36$, $p < .001$. This test was repeated for each age level separately and was found to be significant ($p < .05$) in each case. Apparently, then, children of these ages know the difference between intended and not-intended actions.

The hypothesis that children could distinguish intended from not-intended consequences was assessed by contrasting the means for win versus loss for questions that focused on consequences only. Intention scores were significantly higher in the case of intended consequences or wins ($\bar{x}$ = 1.70) than in the case of not intended consequences or losses ($\bar{x}$ = 0.46), $F(1, 33)$ = 214.69, $p < .001$. This effect was also found to be significant ($p < .001$) at each of the three age levels, supporting the hypothesis that children of these ages can distinguish intended from not intended consequences.

The hypothesis that one does not intend the logically impossible was evaluated in a separate analysis of variance performed on the answers to the intention question posed during that procedure. These scores were coded as +1 for a positive response, –1 for a negative response, and 0 for an uncertain or ambiguous response, and summed over the four trials. Age level was the only factor in this analysis and was found to be significant, $F(2, 33)$ = 12.16, $p < .001$. The mean intention scores were 2.42 for the 5–6-year-olds, –0.75 for the 7–8-year-olds, and –3.00 for the 9–10-year-olds. These means were compared using Tukey's (a) procedure (Winer, 1962), and it was revealed that the 5–6-year-olds had significantly higher intention scores than did the 7–8-year-olds ($p < .05$) and the 9–10-year-olds ($p < .01$). Dunnett's (1955) procedure for comparing all treatment means with a control mean was modified to compare each of these three means to the theoretical mean of 0. It was found that the 5–6-year-olds scored significantly greater than 0 and the 9–10-year-olds scored significantly below 0 ($p < .01$). Thus, it appears that 5–6-year-olds do intend what should appear to be logically impossible and the 9–10-year-olds indicated that the logically impossible cannot be intended. The 7–8-year-olds appear to be in a transitional period in this respect.

In summary, there was good evidence that children between 5 and 10 years of age can distinguish intending an act from intending a consequence and can distinguish intended from not intended acts and consequences. There appears to be a developmental trend with respect to the hypothesis that one cannot intend the logically impossible. This hypothesis was contradicted by the 5–6-year-olds and supported by the 9–10-year-olds. The effects of role were minimal throughout, indicating that children of these ages know as much about intending the acts and consequences of others as they do about intending their own acts and consequences.

RECURSIVE AWARENESS OF INTENTION

All of the studies presented so far have focused on the child's developing awareness of intention in him- or herself or in others. And the obtained evidence suggests fairly accurate knowledge of intentional states even in children as young as 3 years of age. But this is a sort of elementary, first-level awareness that does not adequately describe everything that people know about the concept of intention. In addition to being aware that agents have intentions that guide and control behavior, people eventually become aware that other agents with whom they interact share this knowledge. In other words, a person comes to realize that others are aware of intentions, too, perhaps in some cases that person's own intentional states. As Schmidt (1976) has pointed out, this kind of recursive awareness of intention makes possible strategic acts, acts that are performed in order to disguise one's own intentions or to lead others to misinterpret one's intentions. It is likely that this recursive awareness of intention makes social interaction truly interactive in the sense that agents are at that point fully aware of their fundamental similarity to other agents and fully aware that social knowledge can be reciprocal.

Although recursive knowledge of intention has not received explicit attention from child developmental researchers, there have been a few studies investigating analogous phenomena in role-taking (Devries, 1970; Flavell, 1968; Gratch, 1964). Interestingly, the only psychological investigation to focus explicitly on recursive awareness of intention was done with chimpanzees. Premack (1976) set up a procedure whereby a chimpanzee was shown which of two containers was baited with a desired food. Then the chimp was separated from the containers by a mesh partition, and a trainer came in and stood by the containers, not knowing which one had the food. In this situation, chimpanzees were quite successful through grunting and gesturing in communicating to the trainer which container had the food. In one case, a so-called "good" trainer, who was dressed in a particular way, would then retrieve the food from the container selected by the chimp and give it to the chimp. In another case, a so-called "bad" trainer, again distinctively dressed, would retrieve the food from the container selected by the chimp and keep it for himself. Premack's experimental question was this: Would the chimp disguise its intentions and thereby deceive the bad trainer by selecting the empty container? Although Premack describes such a skill as "first-level intentionality," it is in our terminology a strategic act, thereby providing evidence of recursive awareness of intention. In other words, an animal could disguise its own intentions only to the extent that it knew that the trainer was aware that the animal intended for the trainer to search the selected container. The several 3-year-old chimpanzees tested by Premack led the trainer to select the baited container about 90% of the time. And there was no evidence of any attempts to actively deceive the "bad" trainer. Apparently, recursive awareness of intention is very difficult to demonstrate in chimpanzees, even in those who have been trained in language. The purpose of our study was to examine recursive awareness of intention in human children in a similar situation where strategic acts were advantageous.

One of the most natural and harmless situations for eliciting strategic acts in humans is game playing. Consequently, our procedure involved playing a simple game with the child in which it would be to his or her distinct advantage to engage in certain strategic acts. The participants were 12 boys and 12 girls at each of four age levels: 3, 5, 7, and 9 years. The game was played with a deck of ordinary playing cards from which all the face cards had been removed. The game began with the examiner removing one black and one red card from the deck and placing them face up in front of the child. One player was to keep the deck and turn over one card at a time. After noting the color of each new card, this player was to point to either the black or red card as an indication to the other player who was to guess the color of the new card. After each guess, the new card was to be fully exposed. If the other player guessed the color correctly, then he or she won the new card. However, if the other player guessed incorrectly, the new card was won by the pointing player. The object of the game was to win as many cards as possible. The game was played with each child under two different conditions, one with the child as pointer and one with the child as guesser. Order of condition was counterbalanced within age and sex. In both conditions, the examiner began by playing straight (i.e., guessing the color the child pointed to or pointing to the correct color) but changed to the opposite strategy (i.e., guessing the opposite color the child pointed to or pointing to the incorrect color) if and when the child won four consecutive cards. Then, if the child won four more consecutive cards, the examiner would revert to her original strategy. From then on, the examiner would switch strategy whenever the child won four consecutive cards. In each condition, the game was continued for 30 trials. When the child spontaneously switched strategy, the examiner would probe for the child's reasons asking, for example, "Why did you point to that color?" At the end of the game, the examiner would attempt to get the child to make a general verbal statement about the game by asking, for example, "Did you play in any special way?" All relevant verbalizations made by the child during the game were recorded for later analysis. In order to win consistently in either condition, the child presumably had to strategically disguise his or her intentions by (a) pointing to the incorrect card, (b) guessing the opposite color pointed to by the experimenter, and (c) switching those strategies when appropriate. Such strategic acts would provide evidence that the child was aware that the examiner was aware of the child's intentional state.

Three different indices were used to assess the child's performance in this respect: (a) number of cards won out of 26 (the first 4 trials were ignored since there the examiner played noncompetitively), (b) number of times out of 6 that the criterion of four consecutive wins was achieved, and (c) the sophistication of the child's verbalization about the game. Each of the child's verbalizations during the game was classified according to the following scale: 3—explicit mention of recursion (e.g., "I'm good at tricking you; I know how you're thinking. I know which one you think I'm going to point to"); 2—mention of deception or the need for deception (e.g., "You're tricking me on the colors"); 1—mention of the competitive aspects of the game (e.g., "Now I'll beat you"); and 0—none of the above. Although each of the child's verbalizations was scored separately, the child was awarded only the highest score he or she achieved. Two raters independently scored the verbalizations from five children at each of the four age levels in both conditions. The percentage agreement on these 40 judgments was found to be 92. In addition to these three measures of recursive awareness, the examiner also noted whether or not the child deceptively kept the new card hidden from the examiner when the child was pointing. This would involve hiding an object rather than an intention per se and thus require only a first-level awareness of the other's visual processes (cf. Devries, 1970). The child received a score of 1 if the card was kept hidden and 0 if the card was made visible to the examiner before she guessed about its color. It was evident that each child would characteristically behave one way or the other over the 30 trials of this condition.

Number of wins, number of times criterion was reached, and verbalization score were each subjected to an analysis of variance in which age, sex, and order served as between-subjects factors, and condition served as a within-subjects factor. The analysis of number of wins yielded main effects of age, $F(3, 80) = 57.85, p < 0.001$, and condition, $F(1, 80) = 36.70, p < .001$. There was a steady increase in number of wins with increasing age (means of 2.23, 8.29, 11.46, and 15.90, respectively) with the differences between all three adjacent pairs of means being significant at $p < .05$ according to the Tukey (a) technique (Winer, 1962). There were more wins in the child guessing condition ($\bar{x} = 11.43$) than in the child pointing condition ($\bar{x} = 7.51$).

In the analysis of the number of times criterion was reached, there were main effects for age, $F(3, 80) = 52.48$, $p < .001$, and condition, $F(1, 80) = 19.26$, $p < .001$, as well as an age × condition interaction, $F(3, 80) = 3.32$, $p < .05$. The relevant means for these effects are presented in Table 4.4. Multiple comparisons of these means were made with Tukey's (a) technique for the main effects and with Cicchetti's (1972) extension of this technique for the interaction. There was a steady and significant ($p < .01$) increase in the number of times criterion was reached with each increasing age level. And criterion was reached more often when the child was guesser than when the child was pointer. The age × condition interaction reflects the fact that this condition effect reached statistical significance ($p < .01$) only for the 7-year-olds.

Main effects for age, $F(3, 80) = 16.19$, $p < .001$, and condition, $F(1, 80) = 15.44$, $p < .001$, also emerged in the analysis of verbalization scores. Mean verbalization scores were 0.50 at age 3, 0.94 at age 5, 1.52 at age 7, and 1.92 at age 9, indicating increasingly sophisticated verbalizations with increasing age. Verbalizations were more sophisticated when the child was guesser (1.47) than when the child was pointer (0.97).

The deceptive hiding scores were subjected to an analysis of variance in which age, sex, and order served as between-subjects factors. This analysis yielded a main effect of age, $F(3, 80) = 19.10, p < .001$, indicating an increase in deceptive hiding with increasing age. The mean proportion of deceptive hiders was .29 at age 3, .67 at age 5, .92 at age 7, and 1.00 at age 9. According to

TABLE 4.4
Mean Number of Times Criterion was Reached
in the Study on Recursive Awareness

Age	Condition			
	Child as Pointer		Child as Guesser	Both Conditions
3	0.04	ns^a	0.17	0.10
				s
5	0.79	ns	1.42	1.10
				s
7	1.17	s	2.62	1.90
				s
9	2.83	ns	3.33	3.08
All ages	1.21	s	1.89	

[a]The symbol s between two means indicates that these means differ at $p < .01$. The symbol ns indicates that the two means are not significantly different.

Tukey's (a) technique (Winer, 1962), there was significantly ($p < .01$) more deceptive hiding at ages 5, 7, and 9 than at age 3, and at age 9 than at age 5.

Product–moment correlations among the various dependent measures in this experiment were generally high in both conditions and at all levels. The correlation coefficients collapsed across ages and conditions are presented in table 4.5. The coefficients with the deceptive hiding score may be somewhat lower since they are essentially biserial correlations and because deceptive hiding is the only measure to represent first-, as opposed to second-level, awareness.

The strong age effects on all the recursive measures suggest that recursive awareness of intention was evidenced by children of 5 years and older, but not

TABLE 4.5
Correlations Among the Dependent Variables in the Study on
Recursive Awareness

Variable	Variable			
	1	2	3	4
1. Number of wins	1	.76*	.91*	.56*
2. Number of times criterion reached		1	.79*	.59*
3. Verbalization score			1	.65*
4. Deceptive hiding score				1

*$p < .001$, two-tailed test, $df = 94$.

by 3-year-olds. Number of wins, for example, became substantial only at 5 years and then continued to increase at ages 7 and 9. The 3-year-olds won only about two cards during each game. Also, the criterion of four consecutive wins was reached about once by 5-year-olds, twice by 7-year-olds, and three times by 9-year-olds. This criterion was rarely reached at all by 3-year-olds. Ability to verbalize the underlying strategies appeared to lag behind these behavioral measures, as so often happens in cognitive–developmental research (cf. Brainerd, 1973, 1977). On the average, 5-year-olds were only describing the competitive nature of the game and 9-year-olds were only describing the deceptive elements. Seven-year-olds were about midway between these scale points, and 3-year-olds did not even verbalize the competitive aspects. Explicit mention of the recursive aspects of strategies occurred in only 31 out of the 192 sessions. Thus, although our previously reported studies indicated some accurate first-level awareness of intention in children as young as 3 years, the present findings suggest that recursive awareness of intention may not emerge before about 5 years of age. Recursive knowledge of intention may be relatively advanced not only ontogenetically, but also phylogenetically, as suggested by Premack's (1976) unsuccessful attempts to demonstrate the phenomenon in chimpanzees. It may well be that recursive awareness of intention is one of those few distinctively human characteristics, serving to make our social interactions not only truly interactive but also essentially human.

The other major effect, the tendency for the child to perform better when guessing the color of the card than when pointing to the color, was present on each of the three measures of recursive awareness. One possible explanation for this difference is that it is the pointer who must initiate the deception. Deceptive guessing is more reactive or retaliatory, in that it is not really effective unless the pointer is already behaving deceptively. Because of a power differential between themselves and adults, children may be rather reluctant to initiate a competitive deception of this sort against an adult opponent, although they may be quite willing to retaliate against an adult who has already initiated some deception. Such an account implies that the obtained differences between success in pointing and guessing might diminish if the child played this game against a friend of the same age.

NATURALISTIC OBSERVATIONS ON THE USE OF INTENTION IN MORAL JUDGMENTS

Near the beginning of this paper, the role of intention information in making moral judgments was discussed. Although the moral judgment context may not be especially effective for elucidating many aspects of intention, the relation between the two concepts is certainly an interesting and important topic. It is also a topic which, despite the vast amount of previous and contemporary research on it, has not yet been conclusively exhausted. As stated in the earlier review of this literature, there are now a number of demonstrations that children as young as 5 or 6 years of age can, under certain optimal conditions, use intention information in making moral judgments. But the research presented here indicates that children are well aware of at least some aspects of intentional states at 3 and 4 years of age. Is it posssble that children this young could apply their intentional knowledge to their moral judgments? We have managed to collect a few anecdotal, naturalistic observations that indeed suggest that young children can be quite sophisticated about these matters, at least when it comes to excusing their own moral responsibility for some harm they have caused.

One such case occurred in a prenursery school class when the teacher was asking the children to form a "snake" by joining hands in a single file. As the children were scurrying around attempting to form this snake, one 3-year-old boy happened to elbow a 2-year-old child in the face. The 2-year-old victim naturally started to cry. The teacher promptly went over to the two children and suggested that the 3-year-old apologize to the victim. Apology, of course, is a form of restitution that a person who is acknowledged to be morally responsible for some harm may make to the victim. Interestingly, this child refused to apologize, indignantly claiming that he had not done it "on purpose." Because the action, or at least its consequence, was not intended, he felt very strongly that there was no need to apologize. This was perhaps his way of stating that he was not morally responsible for the harm which he had caused.

Some children, of course, extend this line of argument beyond reasonable bounds. An example we observed was from a 3-year-old girl who was helping to feed her baby brother. After spooning in a few mouthfuls of cereal, she took another spoonful and simply dumped it on the baby's head. Then she turned quickly to her very angry mother and claimed, "I didn't do it on purpose." One of the well-known aspects of the moral judgment literature is that there is often a serious gap between moral judgment and moral behavior, particularly in young children (Grinder, 1964; Medinnus, 1966; Nelson, Grinder, & Biaggio, 1969). This case appears to represent one such gap.

These are just two examples of a number of observations we have collected suggesting that very young children do sometimes use intentional information in making moral judgments. Being essentially anecdotal, these observations are seriously limited in a number of important respects. More systematic and rigorous observational study and experimentation will obviously be necessary to sort out the various alternative interpretations which could easily be offered for these phenomena. Yet these initial observations do suggest a number of interesting possibilities. One is that some sort of naturalistic observational methodology may be an especially effective way to assess the young child's capacity for reasoning about intention and moral judgment. It may be that the traditional interview procedures greatly underestimate what young children actually know about these concepts. Second, these initial observations are consistent with the notion that cognitive structures eventually applied to other people in general originate in the child's early self knowledge of his or her own behaviors and mental states. With time and development, these structures may be gradually extended to the more abstract representations of the hypothetical behaviors and mental states of others. A third suggestion from these observations is that there may be a strong motivational or self-interest component to the emergence of what are often considered to be relatively "cool" cognitive concepts. So far, all of the earliest uses of intention information in moral judgment that we have observed involved excusing oneself from moral responsibility and presumably from the ensuing punishment as well. Eventual applications to judging good or neutral outcomes and to excusing the behaviors of others may derive from these earlier, essentially self-protective notions.

CONCLUSIONS AND DISCUSSION

The principal results of our studies on the child's developing knowledge of intention could perhaps be summarized as follows:

a. By 3 years of age, children are able to distinguish intended actions from a variety of nonintentional behaviors such as mistakes, reflexes, and passive movements.

b. There was also some evidence that children between 3 and 10 years of age treat information on intention just as they treat other sorts of causal information—it is readily assimilated to causal schemes such as that dealing with multiple sufficiency.

c. Three-year-olds also show a clear awareness of the distinction between conditional and nonconditional intentions and are able to identify mistakes with respect to conditional intentions.

d. By age 5 (and possibly even earlier), children can distinguish intending an act from intending a consequence as well as distinguishing intended from not intended acts and consequences. There was some support for the idea that one does not intend what is logically impossible, at least among 9–10-year-olds.

e. Also by age 5, children begin to show evidence of recursive awareness of intention; i.e., they become aware that others are also aware of intentions, in that they are able to disguise their own intentions from others.

f. There is some evidence that children as young as 3 years of age can use intentional information in making moral judgments, at least in situations where it is in their own interest to deny responsibility for harm they themselves have caused.

The foregoing conclusions represent our current best estimates about the young child's emerging capacities to think about intention. They should be regarded as minimal estimates only, because it might well be possible to demonstrate some awareness of intention in even younger children. Certainly, there is some provocative evidence from Piaget (1952) that human infants at least behave intentionally. To what extent infants are aware of these intentional states remains an open question until appropriate methodologies are created. Our own experience is that it is a great advantage working with children who are able to provide verbal responses to verbal questions. Assessing knowledge of intentionality in nonverbal organisms would almost certainly be more challenging; Premack's (1976) efforts with chimpanzees should prove to be inspirational for future researchers in this respect.

One of the more striking outcomes of our research was the absence of any effects of the role of the observer. The three studies dealing with mistakes, reflexive and passive movements, and acts versus consequences each contained an explicit comparison among observers who were themselves agents or observers who were inexperienced or experienced in the behaviors employed. In general, children in all three roles were equally successful in judging intentionality. That is, children could assess the intentions of others as well as they could assess their own, and they were not aided in judging others by previous experience in emitting the precise behaviors to be judged. This should probably not shake our belief in the notion that we have relatively more direct access to our own intentions than to the intentions of others. The philosophical arguments for this (Anscombe, 1957; Hampshire & Hart, 1958) are really quite persuasive. However, the absence of role effects in our experiments certainly raises the question of how children are able to assess the intentions of others so successfully. A number of solutions that could be tested in future research seem possible at this point.

The premise underlying some of our research designs is that the child generalizes his or her own previous self-knowledge to others engaged in familiar behaviors. For example, the child may have had reflexes of his or her own elicited and thus can recognize reflexive behaviors in others. The fact that we did not find self-observation to be superior to observation of others does not actually disconfirm this hypothesis. If this process of generalization occurs early in life, it may be necessary to study children even younger than 3 in order to obtain such a differential effect for self and other. The children in our studies may have been too old for a sensitive test of this formulation.

Another possibility is that the observer could use certain emotional indicators such as facial expressions as cues to inferring the intentions of others. Agents may show disappointment, surprise, or puzzlement when they fail to achieve an intended result and satisfaction when they do achieve what was intended. Furthermore, as suggested by Heider (1958), intention may be inferred when an agent appears to be trying. Although our instructions to agents may have minimized such cues, it is certainly possible that they could be generally useful, particularly in situations where clearly positive or clearly negative outcomes occur, such as in our choose-and-match game.

A related strategy for inferring intentionality in others might be a sort of "positivity rule," wherein the observer assumes that outcomes that are positive for the agent are intended and outcomes that are negative for the agent are not intended. This may be quite similar to the concept of consequentiality, which has been studied by Whiteman et al. (1974). Such a rule could function quite independently of emotional indicators, although some degree of redundancy might be quite common. In our research, a positivity rule would have been applicable to the choose-and-match game, but probably not to tasks that invovled more neutral outcomes such as moving one's leg or arms.

Intentionality could also be judged with a kind of "matching rule," referring to the presence of a match or a mismatch between a stated or inferred intention and an observed result. When the result matches the stated or inferred intention, the observer may conclude that the result was intended. Conversely, when the result does not match the stated or inferred intention, the result may appear *not* to be intended. Perhaps the most clearly applicable case for a matching rule in our research was in the study on intentional versus mistaken behavior where, for example, the agent was trying to point to a particular object or move a particular finger. The matching rule could also have been used in the "elicited wtih instruction to inhibit" condition of the study on intentional versus reflexive or passive behavior. There the resulting movement would not have matched the intention inferred from the examiner's instruction to intend not to move. However, a matching rule would have been less clearly applicable to the standard "elicited" condition of that study where the agent was simply instructed to relax.

Finally, Heider (1958) has argued that intentional action is characterized by equifinality, by which he means that a variety of different means actions all converge on the same end or consequence. Although such a pattern may be somewhat difficult for very young children to discern, it is quite possible that older children would find it useful in certain situations.

It should be clear from this discussion that none of these various possible cues or rules for judging intention in others is infallible and that none of them is applicable in every situation. Future research will be necessary to determine how much reliance observers place on these strategies in particular circumstances.

That young children possess so much knowledge about intentions may come as a surprise to those who believe that people are generally unaware of mental processes and causes of behavior. Nisbett and Wilson (1977), for example, present a good deal of evidence that adults are not very aware of the actual determinants of their behavior. However, our results are not actually inconsistent with this if the distinction between mental processes and mental contents is clearly drawn. Nisbett and Wilson (1977) stress that their evidence concerns only mental processes and not the products or results of those processes, some of which probably do come into awareness. Although people may be well aware of intention, they probably have no idea of the processes by which such intentions are produced nor how such intentions come to generate behavior, if they indeed do generate behavior. Those are matters for psychological researchers to uncover.

ACKNOWLEDGMENTS

This research was supported in part by a grant from the Social Sciences and Humanities Research Council of Canada and conducted with the skillful collaboration of Karen Cloghesy, Daniele Crépeau, Mario Sarda, Frank Shamash, and Diane Wells. Professors James MacDougall, John Macnamara, Morton Mendelson, and Michael Schleifer contributed valuable ideas during the planning stages. The staffs and children of the following daycare centers and schools made the research possible through their generous cooperation: Playskool Day Nursery, McGill Community Family Centre, Concordia University Daycare Centre, CLSC Rivière-des-Prairies, Alfred Joyce, Dunrae Gardens, Notre-Dame-de-La-Paix, Our Lady of Mount Royal, and Riverside.

REFERENCES

Anscombe, G. E. M. *Intention*. London: Blackwell, 1957.
Aquila, R. E. *Intentionality: a study of mental acts*. University Park, Pennsylvania: Pennsylvania State University Press, 1977.
Austin, J. *Lectures on jurisprudence*. London: John Murray, 1873.
Austin, V. D., Ruble, D. N., & Trabasso, T. Recall and order effects as factors in children's moral judgments. *Child Development*, 1977, *48*, 470–474.
Bearison, D. J., & Isaacs, L. Production deficiency in children's moral judgments. *Developmental Psychology*, 1975, *11*, 732–737.
Bentham, J. *An introduction to the principles of morals and legislation*. New York: Hafner, 1948. (Originally published 1789.)
Berg-Cross, L. G. Intentionality, degree of damage, and moral judgments. *Child Development*, 1975, *46*, 970–974.
Berndt, T. J., & Berndt, E. G. Children's use of motives and intentionality in person perception and moral judgment. *Child Development*, 1975, *46*, 904–912.
Bever, T. G. Associations to stimulus-response theories of language. In T. R. Dixon & D. L. Horton (Eds.), *Verbal behavior and general behavior theory*. Englewood Cliffs, N.J.: Prentice Hall, 1968.
Bindra, D. *A theory of intelligent behavior*. New York: Wiley, 1976.
Bindra, D., Clarke, K., & Shultz, T. R. Understanding predictive relations of necessity and sufficiency in formally equivalent "causal" and "logical" problems. *Journal of Experimental Psychology: General*, 1980.
Bloom, L., Lightbown, P., & Hood, L. Structure and variation in child language. *Monographs of the Soceity for Research in Child Development*, 1975, *40*. (2, Serial No. 160.)
Bowerman, M. Semantic factors in the acquisition of rules for word use and sentence construction. In D. M. Morehead & A. E. Morehead (Eds.), *Normal and deficient child language*. Baltimore: University Park Press, 1976.
Braine, M. D. S. On the relation between the natural logic of reasoning and standard logic. *Psychological Review*, 1978, *85*, 1–21.

Brainerd, C. J. Judgments and explanations as criteria for the presence of cognitive structures. *Psychological Bulletin,* 1973, *79,* 172-179.

Brainerd, C. J. Concerning Macnamara's analysis of Piaget's theory of number. *Child Development,* 1976, *47,* 893-896.

Brainerd, C. J. Response criteria in concept development research. *Child Development,* 1977, *48,* 360-366.

Brentano, F. The distinction between mental and physical phenomena. In R. M. Chisholm (Ed.), *Realism and the background of phenomenology.* Glencoe, Ill.: Free Press, 1960.

Brown, R. *A first language: the early stages.* Cambridge, Mass.: Harvard University Press, 1973.

Chandler, M. J., Greenspan, S., & Barenboim, C. Judgments of intentionality in response to videotaped and verbally presented moral dilemmas: The medium is the message. *Child Development,* 1973, *44,* 315-320.

Chomsky, N. Review of verbal behavior. *Language,* 1959, *35,* 26-58.

Cicchetti, D. V. Extension of multiple-range tests to interaction tables in the analysis of variance: A rapid approximate solution. *Psychological Bulletin,* 1972, *77,* 405-408.

D'Arcy, E. *Human acts: An essay in their moral evaluation.* Oxford: Clarendon, 1963.

Davidson, D. Actions, reasons, and causes. *The Journal of Philosophy,* 1963, *60,* 685-700.

Devries, R. The development of role-taking as reflected by behavior of bright, average, and retarded children in a social guessing game. *Child Development,* 1970, *41,* 759-770.

Dunnett, C. W. A multiple comparison procedure for comparing several treatments with a control. *Journal of the American Statistical Association,* 1955, *50,* 1096-1121.

Elkind, D., & Dabek, R. F. Personal injury and property damage in the moral judgments of children. *Child Development,* 1977, *48,* 518-522.

Falmagne, R. J. (Ed.) *Reasoning: Representation and process.* Hillsdale, N.J.: Lawrence Erlbaum Associates, 1975.

Feldman, N. S., Klosson, E. C., Parsons, J. E., Rholes, W. S., & Ruble, D. N. Order of information presentation and children's moral judgments. *Child Development,* 1976, *47,* 556-559.

Flavell, J. H. *The development of role-taking and communication skills in children.* New York: Wiley, 1968.

Gottlieb, D. E., Taylor, S. E. & Ruderman, A. Cognitive bases of children's moral judgments. *Developmental Psychology,* 1977, *13,* 547-556.

Gratch, G. Response alternation in children: A developmental study of orientations to uncertainty. *Vita Humana,* 1964, *7,* 49-60.

Greenwald, A. G. Sensory feedback mechanisms in performance control: with special reference to the ideo-motor mechanism. *Psychological Review,* 1970, *77,* 73-99.

Grinder, R. E. Relations between behavioral and cognitive dimensions of conscience in middle childhood. *Child Development,* 1964, *35,* 881-891.

Gurwitsch, A. Towards a theory of intentionality. *Philosophy and Phenomenological Research,* 1969-70, *30,* 354-367.

Gutkin, D. C. The effect of systematic story changes on intentionality in children's moral judgments. *Child Development,* 1972, *43,* 187-195.

Hampshire, S. *Thought and action.* London: Chatto & Windus, 1965.

Hampshire, S., & Hart, H. L. A. Decision, intention, and certainty. *Mind,* 1958, *67,* 1-12.

Harré, R., & Madden, E. H. *Causal powers: a theory of natural necessity.* Oxford: Blackwell, 1975.

Harré, R., & Secord, P. F. *The explanation of social behavior.* Oxford: Blackwell, 1972.

Heider, F. *The psychology of interpersonal relations.* New York: Wiley, 1958.

Hoffman, M. L. Moral development. In P. H. Mussen (Ed.), *Carmichael's manual of child psychology* (3rd ed., Vol. 2). New York: Wiley, 1970.

Irwin, F. W. *Intentional behavior and motivation: A cognitive theory.* Philadelphia: Lippincott, 1971.

James, W. *The principles of psychology* (Vol. 2). New York: Holt, 1890.

Karniol, R., & Ross, M. The development of causal attributions in social perception. *Journal of Personality and Social Psychology,* 1976, *34,* 455–464.

Keasey, C. B. Young children's attribution of intentionality to themselves and others. *Child Development,* 1977, *48,* 261–264.

Kelley, H. H. *Causal schemata and the attribution process.* New York: General Learning Press, 1972.

Kelley, H. H. The processes of causal attribution. *American Psychologist,* 1973, *28,* 107–128.

Kimble, G. A., & Perlmuter, L. C. The problem of volition. *Psychological Review,* 1970, *77,* 361–384.

Klahr, D., & Wallace, J. G. *Cognitive development: An information-processing view.* Hillsdale, N.J.: Lawrence Erlbaum Associates, 1976.

Leahy, R. L. *The child's conception of mens rea: Information mitigating punishment judgments.* Paper presented at the meeting of Society for Research in Child Development, New Orleans, March, 1977.

Mackie, J. L. *The cement of the universe: A study of causation.* Oxford: Clarendon, 1974.

Macnamara, J. A note on Piaget and number. *Child Development,* 1975, 46, 424–429.

Medinnus, G. R. Behavioral and cognitive measures of conscience development. *Journal of Genetic Psychology,* 1966, *109,* 147–150.

Meiland, J. W. *The nature of intention.* London: Methuen, 1970.

Meldon, A. I. *Free action.* London: Routledge & Kegan Paul, 1961.

Miller, G. A., Galanter, E., & Pribram, K. H. *Plans and the structure of behavior.* New York: Holt, Rinehart, & Winston, 1960.

Mischel, T. (Ed.). *Human action.* New York: Academic Press, 1969.

Nagel, E. *The structure of science: Problems in the logic of scientific explanation.* New York: Harcourt, Brace, & World, 1961.

Nelson, E. A., Grinder, R. E., & Biaggio, A. M. Relationships among behavioral, cognitive–developmental, and self report measures of morality and personality. *Multivariate Behavioral Research,* 1969, *4,* 483–500.

Nisbett, R. E., & Wilson, T. D. Telling more than we can know: Verbal reports on mental processes. *Psychological Review,* 1977, *84,* 231–259.

Nummedal, S. G. & Bass, S. C. Effects of the salience of intention and consequence on children's moral judgments. *Developmental Psychology,* 1976, *12,* 475–476.

Peters, R. S. *The concept of motivation.* New York: Humanities Press, 1958.

Piaget, J. *The moral judgment of the child.* London: Kegan Paul, 1932.

Piaget, J. *The origins of intelligence in children.* New York: International Universities Press, 1952.

Premack, D. Language and intelligence in ape and man. *American Scientist,* 1976, *64,* 674–683.

Schank, R. C., & Abelson, R. P. *Scripts, plans, goals, and understanding: An inquiry into human knowledge structures.* Hillsdale, N.J.: Lawrence Erlbaum Associates, 1977.

Schmidt, C. F. Understanding human action: Recognizing the plans and motives of other persons. In J. S. Carroll & J. W. Payne (Eds.), *Cognition and social behavior.* Hillsdale, N.J.: Lawrence Erlbaum Associates, 1976.

Shultz, T. R. *Rules of causal attribution.* Unpublished manuscript, McGill University, 1979.

Shultz, T. R., & Butkowsky, I. Young children's use of the scheme for multiple sufficient causes in the attribution of real and hypothetical behavior. *Child Development,* 1977, *48,* 464–469.

Shultz, T. R., Butkowsky, I., Pearce, J. W., & Shanfield, H. Development of schemes for the attribution of multiple psychological causes. *Developmental Psycholgoy,* 1975, *11,* 502–510.

Simpson, E. L. Moral development research: A case study of scientific culture bias. *Human Development,* 1974, *17,* 81–106.

Slobin, D. I. Universals of grammatical development in children. In G. B. Flores d'Arcais & W. J. M. Levelt (Eds.), *Advances in psycholinguistics.* New York: American Elsevier, 1970.

Smith, M. C. Children's use of the multiple sufficient cause schema in social perception. *Journal of Personality and Social Psychology,* 1975, *32,* 737–747.

Taylor, C. *The explanation of behavior.* London: Routledge & Kegan Paul, 1964.

Taylor, R. *Action and purpose.* Englewood Cliffs, N.J.: Prentice-Hall, 1966.

Tolman, E. *Purposive behavior in animals and men.* New York: Century, 1932.

Von Wright, G. H. *Explanation and understanding.* London: Routledge & Kegan Paul, 1971.

Wallace, W. A. *Causality and scientific explanation I: Medieval and early classical science.* Ann Arbor, Michigan.: University of Michigan Press, 1972.

Watson, M. W., & Fischer, K. W. A developmental sequence of agent use in late infancy. *Child Development,* 1977, *48,* 828–836.

Wells, D., & Shultz, T. R. *Factors affecting young children's use of the scheme for multiple sufficient causes.* Unpublished manuscript, McGill University, 1978.

Whiteman, M., Brook, J. S., & Gordon, A. S. Children's motivational perception as related to the instrumentality and effect of action. *Developmental Psychology,* 1974, *10,* 929–935.

Williams, G. L. *Criminal Law: The general part.* London: Stevens & Sons, 1953.

Winer, B. J. *Statistical principles in experimental design.* New York: McGraw-Hill, 1962.

5 Social Ecology of the Preschool Peer Group

F. F. Strayer
University of Quebec at Montreal

Ethology is often inappropriately distinguished from other behavioral sciences as the discipline committed to direct observation of naturally occurring behavior. The problem with such a distinction is most readily apparent in the field of child psychology, where a strong emphasis upon the description of natural developmental phenomena has had a long and important history (cf. M. Barker, 1930; R. G. Barker, 1965; Chittenden, 1942; Dawe, 1943; Emmerlich, 1964; Gellert, 1961, 1962; Piaget 1926, 1948, 1951, 1952, 1954; Shirley, 1933; Washburn, 1932). To distinguish between ethologists' and psychologists' approaches to behavior, it is necessary to look beyond their common interest in natural phenomena. The different approaches to descriptive analysis in ethological research and in developmental psychology reflect a basic conceptual difference underlying psychological and ethological investigations. Many biologically oriented researchers actively engaged in the comparative study of behavior have emphasized these conceptual differences (Bateson & Hinde, 1976; Blurton Jones, 1972; Kummer, 1971; Tinbergen, 1963).

AN ETHOLOGICAL APPROACH TO SOCIAL ECOLOGY

Kummer (1971) provides perhaps the most thorough and concise summary of the explanatory network that constitutes the ethological framework for the analysis of behavior. Each type of explanation described by Kummer is associated with a necessary but limited set of specific questions about the nature of behavior.

165

The first set of questions concerns the organization or structure of behavioral phenomena. A common focus in all ethological research is the commitment to providing a sufficiently detailed description of behavioral patterns observed for all members of a given species. Many of the most important advances in child ethology during the past decade have dealt directly with specifying the diversity of behavioral patterns characteristic of young children (e.g., Blurton Jones, 1972; Blurton Jones & Leach, 1972; Brannigan & Humphries, 1972; Grant, 1969; Leach, 1972; McGrew, 1970, 1972; Smith & Connolly, 1972). Although such descriptive studies have not been extended to deal with the analysis of social relationships and group organization, they represent the necessary first step for an ethological analysis of peer-group social ecology. A basic assumption for such an analysis is that qualitative differences in complex social phenomena cannot be understood without a detailed consideration of qualitative differences in the individual action patterns that constitute social exchanges between young children.

Following the derivation of an adequately refined descriptive inventory for behavioral patterns, ethologists turn to questions concerning the immediate causation and immediate function of selected behaviors. Although these analytic problems have dominated traditional psychological research and theory, they play a somewhat different role in ethological investigations. Most importantly, the analysis of immediate antecedants and consequences of behavior allows the ethologist to reorganize the inventory of behavioral patterns into a more meaningful descriptive system; behaviors can be regrouped into larger categories defined in terms of common causal factors (cf. Tinbergen, 1950) or common outcomes (cf. Hinde, 1970). Thus for the ethologist, research on the causation and function of behavior has two quite different benefits. First, such research provides necessary information about factors that influence and control behavioral phenomena. Second, such research facilitates refinement and reorganization of the ethogram for a species by showing either causal or functional similarities in morphologically distinct behavioral units. In addition to emphasizing immediate causation and function, ethology also stresses the historical context of behavior, including the study of ontogenetic and phylogenetic adaptations. Once again, questions about the antecedants and consequences of behavior are at issue, but this time within the larger time-frames necessary for the evolution of species-specific activity and the development of individual differences.

Although Kummer's discussion of the general framework for a biological analysis of behavior suggests a relatively unified conceptual orientation in ethological research, differences in the emphasis has led to considerable diversity within the field. Crook (1970) has argued that there are two quite distinct theoretical approaches in modern ethology. The more traditional approach, classical ethology, focuses directly upon the detailed analysis of behavioral patterns, their immediate causation, and their develpment. The second approach, social ethology or sociobiology, deals more exclusively with patterns of social behavior, the coordination of activity between individuals, and the evolutionary history of social structures. Social ethology emerged as a separate branch of behavioral biology due to a marked increase in field information about social behavior among non-human primates. Given both the complexity and diversity of primate societies and their impact on individual development, the more classic approach to the analysis of individual differences proved inadequate. An adequate account of the contextual influences on social behavior forced primatologists to develop more elaborate methods for the analysis of group organization. According to Crook (1970), the concern in primatology with the social context of individual adaptation directly parallels the more traditional emphasis in classical ethology on the physical environment as the context for both species and individual development. However, social ethologists assume that influences of the physical environment upon the individual are most often mediated by the social ecology of their stable group. In this sense, social ethologists reformulate the traditional organism–enviroment dichotomy in terms of three continually interacting systems: the physical habitat, the social ecology of the group, and, finally, the organism itself. An adequate understanding of individual adaptation to the physical environment requires at least a preliminary analysis of the organization of the social unit in which the individual develops.

Although it was apparent even to the earliest primatologists (e.g., Yerkes, 1928; Zuckerman, 1932) that the integration of individuals into a stable social unit placed important limitations upon their activities, it was less clear how to analyze the patterns of social exchange that comprised the social organization of the primate group. More recently researchers consider that the stability and organization of any social unit depends upon a delicate balance struck between social activities promoting group cohesion and those leading to social dispersion (Wilson, 1975). In this view, group dominance hierarchy formalizes dyadic roles during periods of aggressive conflict, and thus serves as a regulatory system that minimizes dispersive agonistic exchanges between group members. In contrast, activities that promote group cohesion attract individuals to one another and maintain them in a coordinated social unit. Dominance relations have undoubtedly received the majority of research attention in both human and primate social ethology. By comparison, comprehensive studies of cohesive activities have been both fewer in number and more limited in scope. Much of this limitation has resulted from a fragmentation of interest in different forms of cohesive activity. By using only certain behaviors in studies of social attraction, many theorists have provided arguments that are insufficient to account for observed patterns of social cohesion. The theoretical difficulties have involved determining the relative utility of general descriptive concepts such as leadership, control roles, attention structures, attachment bonds, and kinship patterns as necessary and/or sufficient dimensions for the analysis of primate social organization (Chance & Jolly, 1970; DeVore, 1965; Jay, 1968; Jolly, 1972; Kummer, 1971).

In addition to this theoretical confusion, corresponding methodological problems entailed the development of appropriate empirical techniques for the evaluation of these proposed descriptive dimensions for social organization. With the increasing awareness that standardized procedures for assessing primate social relations provided reliable information, but failed to predict social behavior within the group setting (Bernstein, 1970), researchers began to emphasize the descriptive analysis of spontaneously occurring behavior as the most appropriate means of identifying basic dimensions of social ecology for stable groups. This trend toward the use of direct observation culminated in a more systematic approach for the inductive analysis of social relationships and group structures (Hinde, 1976; Hinde and Stevenson-Hinde, 1976). This approach stresses clear distinctions among four levels of social description. The first level entails identification of *social action patterns*. Subsequently, the examination of recurrent sequential combinations of these patterns during the course of social exchange between individuals permits the isolation of characteristic forms of *social interaction* for members of a stable group. The regularity and diversity of such forms of interaction for different dyads suggests larger categories of qualitatively different forms of social exchange that can be used as converging measures of specific dimensions in *social relationships*. Finally, analysis of general principles that summarize the organization of observed relationships provides an empirical basis for the derivation of the *social structures* that constitute the social ecology of the stable group.

ETHOLOGICAL STUDIES OF CHILDREN'S SOCIAL ORGANIZATION

Given the relatively recent formulation of an inductive system for the investigation of social organization, it is not surprising that, in most instances studies in child ethology have not offered detailed information about the social ecology of young children's peer-groups. In fact, most studies have provided more classical analyses of individual behavioral units and the integration of these units into more extended individual action sequences (Blurton Jones & Leach, 1972; McGrew, 1972). The few studies that have dealt more directly with questions about social relationships and group structure have adopted a unidimensional approach to social ecology by emphasizing agonistic interaction and group-dominance hierarchies (Misshakian, 1976; Strayer & Strayer, 1976).

Other researchers have attempted to relate information on social dominance relations to measures of individual differences in rates of social activity. For example, Abramovitch (1976) and Abramovitch and Strayer (1978) reported that dominant group members received more peer attention that subordinate children. However, Vaughn and Waters (1978) found that the distribution of attention among members of their preschool group was more closely related to sociometric popularity than the position within the group status hierarchy. Since the primary objective in each of these studies was to examine individual differences in nonaggressive social behavior as a function of dominance status, the reports provide direct information about the organization of aggressive relations among preschool children, but do not demonstrate the existence of social structures that summarize the organization of attentional or affiliative relations among preschool children. Similarly, research demonstrating differences in sociocognitive abilities and social perception as a function of social dominance (Sluckin & Smith, 1977; Strayer, Chapeskie, & Strayer, 1978) emphasizes the importance of dominance status as an aspect of preschool social ecology, but fails to consider how other dimensions of social organization may provide a better prediction about individual differences in social competence.

Recent research at our own laboratory has emphasized the devleopment of analytic methods that can provide a more complete view of peer-group social ecology. This work involves the concurrent use of observational procedures for the analysis of dispersive, or antisocial, exchanges, as well as cohesive, or positive, social interactions between preschool children during periods of free-play. Our descriptive analyses emphasize the same functional distinction between forms of social behavior that was introduced by McGrew (1972). *Dispersive activities* are defined as those behavioral patterns that are generally followed by a separation of the children involved in interaction, while *cohesive activities* are those behaviors that are more often associated with the maintenance of social proximity, and the continuation of social exchange. Our strategy in the derivation of preschool social structures has been to select a limited set of very specific forms of social exchange from each of these two general classes as primary indices of dyadic relationships and group organization. Questions about the coordination between the resulting relationships and group structures and other types of social behavior entail a second phase of research that presupposes a precise behavioral definition for both social dominance and social cohesion, as well as the elaboration of adequate procedures for their evaluation. The remainder of this chapter provides a summary of our approach to the derivation of dominance and affiliative structures within preschool groups and a preliminary report concerning how such hierarchies and networks are related to the organization of attentional, altruistic, and control activities within the preschool group.

Research Participants, Settings, and Observational Procedures

The following findings are based upon information obtained from observational studies of five different preschool groups. All of the studies were conducted at the preschool centers during the second half of the school year. Thus, all children had at least four months of group experience before we began our analysis of their social relationships. Prior to observations, a minimum of two weeks was spent at each center to guarantee that all children had become accustomed to the presence of our observers. This period permitted observers to become familiar with the name and identifying features of each child. Following this initial phase, systematic observations were conducted during periods which varied from four to eight weeks. Observers used McGrew's (1972) technique of "polite refusal" to minimize social contact with members of the peer-group. Our analyses of social behavior included only those children whose attendance during the observational period was sufficiently frequent to guarantee that they had similar opportunities to participate in social interaction with all other group members. At a practical level, this entailed excluding from our samples children who were absent for more than one quarter of our observational days.

The Langara Preschool Group. Observations at the Langara Preschool Centre in Vancouver, British Columbia, were conducted during the late spring and summer of 1973. The group originally contained 18 children (10 boys and eight girls). Since one girl left the preschool early in the observational period, data are presented for only 17 children who ranged in age from 38 to 65 months (mean age 53 months). Observations were made both indoors and outdoors using portable video equipment. Primary emphasis for video sampling was given to obtaining records of social conflict among group members. This sampling entailed use of a matrix completion method (Altmann, 1974) that maximizes the amount of information available for each dyadic combination of group members.

The Simon Fraser Preschool Group. Observations of children at the Simon Fraser Preschool Center in Vancouver, British Columbia, were conducted during the late spring of 1974. The peer-group originally contained 16 children, but one boy and one girl were both absent for more than 25% of the sampling days. Thus, data are presentd for only 14 children (7 boys and 7 girls) who ranged in age from 38 to 60 months (mean age 48 months). Observations were scheduled daily during a 4-week period. Two 5-min records were obtained for each child on each observational day using a direct focal individual sampling procedure. Observations were tape-recorded and transcribed immediately after each observational period.

The Waterloo Preschool Group.   Observations at the Waterloo Early Education Centre in Waterloo, Ontario, were conducted during a 6-week period from January to March in 1975. The Waterloo group contained 26 regular group members, but seven children were absent for more than 25% of the observational period, and thus were excluded from the final sample. Data are presented for 19 children (10 boys and 9 girls) who ranged in age from 42 to 60 months (mean age 52 months). The Waterloo Centre contained three rooms which were available to the children during free-play periods. The largest central room was equipped with a permanent video system that allowed monitoring of approximately 60% of the space available to the children. Permanent records of social interaction were obtained with this equipment. In addition, direct observation of focal subgroups in the two smaller rooms provided supplementary information on instances of agonistic and affilitative interaction during free-play periods.

La Souritheque Preschool Groups.   Observations were conducted during the spring months of 1978 for two groups of preschool children at La Garderie Souritheque, a French-speaking, community-supported preschool center located in the central urban area of Montreal. Two groups of children were observed at La Souritheque. The Sallopette group contained 16 children (8 boys and 8 girls) who ranged in age from 39 to 56 months (mean age 45 months). The Saltimbanque group contained 15 children (8 boys and 7 girls) who ranged in age from 53 to 72 months (mean age 62 months). Since the parents of a child in each group requested that their children not be included as participants in our research, data are presented for 15 members of the younger group and 14 members of the older group. Observations were conducted for both of these groups during an 8-week period using portable video equipment. The observation schedule required obtaining four 5-min video samples of free-play interaction for each child during each 2-week period of the total observational session.

Records of social exchange in each of the studies were coded using a four-item syntax. For each observational record the initiator, his action, the target, and the target's response were always noted. If one of the necessary elements in the social exchange could not be clearly specified, the exchange was not coded. Reliabilities for the use of the various coding frameworks were evaluated using both correlational procedures and formulas for ratio of agreements to disagreements. Weekly agreement scores were consistently above 80% for direct observation and usually somewhat higher for video coding. Although these measures of reliability were calculated to provide some indication of interobserver consistency in the collection of observational data, they do not reflect the amount of training that was necessary before beginning observations, nor the type of compromises that were necessary for achieving an acceptable level of observer agreement. Needless to say, such compromises generally required abbreviations in the coding frameworks, and the omission of what came to be called ambiguous events. We are currently exploring techniques for assessing the internal validity of observational records as a much needed replacement for standard reliability procedures.

THE ANALYSIS OF SOCIAL DOMINANCE

From a comparative perspective, the resolution of social conflict within a stable group is seldom chaotic, but rather organized in terms of a system of dyadic prerogatives that we call the *social dominance hierarchy*. The concept of social dominance provides perhaps the best illustration of the difference between an ethological and more traditional psychological analysis of preschool social behavior. Social dominance is a descriptive concept that refers to an observable pattern for the resolution of social conflict among members of a stable social group. It is not a property of individuals, but rather a relationship between them. While psychologists have tended to focus upon the frequency of aggressive acts as a measure of an individual disposition, ethologists have more characteristically concerned themselves with patterns of conflict resolution and the implications of such patterns for group stability. From an ethological perspective, the emergence of a stable dominance hierarchy helps to minimize the dispersive effect of social conflict and thus contributes directly to an increase in social cohesion for the group. Given a stable dominance hierarchy, each group member is able to anticipate and avoid the adverse consequences of severe social aggression.

Social dominance essentially involves asymmetrical social relationships. Dyadic dominance refers to the balance of social power between two individuals in a social group, while the group dominance structure refers to the organizational system that summarizes the coordination of all such dyadic relationships. Among most nonhuman primates, the group dominance structure is hierarchically arranged and is governed by a linear transitivity rule. Thus, if individual A is dominant to B, and B is dominant to C, then A should also be dominant to C. Although such transitivity usually prevails among observed dyadic relationships, it is not uncommon to find exceptions where a circular structure better represents the relations between three group members. The appropriateness of the linear dominance model as a summary of the group dominance structure can be evaluated in terms of the proportion of observed relationships that correspond to a linear rule. In primate groups, more than 90% of the observed relations can usually be organized into a linear structure (Strayer, 1976).

The determination of dyadic dominance relationships rests upon the identificiation of specific action patterns that are characteristically used for the initiation and termination of social conflict episodes (Rowell, 1966, 1974).

TABLE 5.1
Frequency and Dyadic Asymmetry
of Observed Social Conflict
at Two Preschools

	Frequency of Exchanges	Asymmetry of Exchanges
Langara (N = 17)		
Aggression	143	92%
Competition	89	91%
Total Conflict	232	88%
Simon Fraser (N = 14)		
Aggression	99	94%
Competition	90	84%
Total Conflict	189	87%

In a recent paper (Strayer & Strayer, 1976), we identified three general categories of social activity that characterize the beginnings of conflict bouts. These categories include *physical attacks, threat gestures,* and *object/position struggles.* The first two categories are comprised of types of behavior that are readily labelled as aggressive, while the third includes competitive activities dealing with the possession of objects and spaces. In addition to these forms of initiated conflict, we described four general categories of responses to conflict. These latter categories included *submissive gestures, object/position loss, help seeking, ignore,* and *counterattacks.* Since only the first four response categories could terminate a conflict bout, there are 12 potential types of social exchange that could terminate an episode of social conflict. Of these twelve possible terminating exchanges, only three were generally asymmetrical across dyadic contexts: (1) *attacks* leading to *submission;* (2) *threats* leading to *submission;* and (3) *struggles* leading to *object/position loss.* Table 5.1 summarizes the level of dyadic asymmetry and the observed frequency of these aggressive and competitive activities observed at two different preschool centers. It is evident from this table that more than four-fifths of these exchanges were unidirectional at the dyadic level. This implies that one member of a dyad generally terminates the conflict episode to his own advantage.

A dyadic representation of aggressive–submissive relations for the Langara group is shown in Fig. 5.1. Since this class of conflict was quite asymmetrical, it was possible to organize the rows and columns in the dyadic matrix to minimize the frequency of observations located below the diagnoal. The resulting serial ordering of individuals reflects social status rankings based upon this class of social exchange. In general, children listed higher in the ordering successfully elicit submission from those ranked lower, although there are two exceptions to this trend that reflect inversions of the linear

LANGARA
Aggression

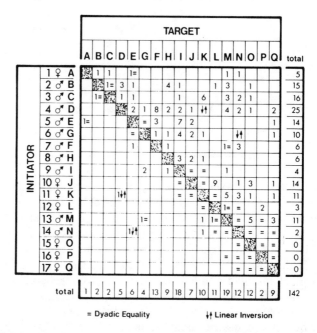

= Dyadic Equality   ⇅ Linear Inversion

FIG. 5.1. Dyadic matrix of aggressive–submissive exchanges for the Langara group.

transitivity rule. Nevertheless, 97% of the observed dyadic dominance relations at Langara conformed to expectations derived from the assumption of a linear status structure for the resolution of preschool social conflict.

Closer inspection of this dyadic matrix emphasizes an important feature of a social-status hierarchy. Position within the final status ranking is not based upon either the absolute frequency of aggressive success or the number of peers who are successfully attacked. Instead, social status is defined in terms of the relative balance of power maintained across dyadic contexts. For example, the first-ranking child in the Langara aggressive matrix was not given the alpha position because she successfully elicited submission more often than other group members or because she dominated a broader range of other children. Her position in the aggressive status hierarchy is based upon the observation that she dominated specific group members who in turn dominated others listed lower in the status structure. This observation emphasizes an important distinction between a hierarchical structure and a simple rank ordering. Although the hierarchy in Fig. 5.1 can be viewed as linear ranking of individuals, its derivation is not tied to a simple individual measure, but rather to an analysis of a network of social relationships that are organized according to specific principles.

Given the level of dyadic asymmetry in observed competitive exchanges, a similar hierarchical analysis was possible for this class of social activity. Figure 5.2 shows the dyadic distribution of this second class of social conflict. Once again the rows and columns in the matrix have been organized to minimize the frequency of observations below the diagnonal, and the resulting order of individuals within the matrix reflects their status ranking based upon competitive exchanges. In general, the properties of this second dyadic matrix are similar to those of the first, although the ordering of individuals is slightly different.

A similar discrepancy between aggressive and competitive status ranking was also evident in our analysis of social conflict at the Simon Fraser Preschool Center. Table 5.2 summarizes the nature of status rankings for

LANGARA
Competition

INITIATOR	B	A	C	I	E	D	G	H	J	K	F	L	M	N	O	P	Q	total
1 ♂ B	▨	1	2	1	↕↑	1	2		1	1	↕↑		1					10
2 ♀ A		▨	1			3	1		1=		4							10
3 ♂ C			▨	=	1	3	1			2	2		2					11
4 ♂ I				▨	=	1	4							↕↑				5
5 ♂ E					▨	1	4		1	1			3	1				12
6 ♂ D	2↕↑	1	2			▨	=	1		1	2	1						10
7 ♂ G			2			=	▨	4	↕↑	1=								7
8 ♂ H								▨	2	1								3
9 ♀ J									▨	=	1							1
10 ♀ K	1=		1						=	▨	1	2			1	1		7
11 ♂ F						2↕↑					▨	=	1	3				6
12 ♀ L											=	▨			1			1
13 ♂ M	1↕↑					1=							▨	1		2		5
14 ♂ N														▨	=	=	=	0
15 ♀ O			1↕↑											=	▨	=	=	1
16 ♀ P														=	=	▨	=	0
17 ♀ Q														=	=	=	▨	0
total	3	3	6	4	2	7	13	8	2	5	7	2	9	11	3	1	3	89

= Dyadic Equality   ↕↑ Linear Inversion

FIG. 5.2.   Dyadic matrix of competitive exchanges for the Langara group.

TABLE 5.2
Comparison of Langara
and Simon Fraser
Status Structures

	Dyads Observed	Linearity of Relations
Langara (N = 17)		
Aggression	41%	97%
Competition	35%	96%
Total Conflict	58%	94%
Simon Fraser (N = 14)		
Aggression	47%	95%
Competition	48%	80%
Total Conflict	73%	88%

each group based upon both classes of social conflict. The vast majority of observed social relationships in both groups could be organized to meet the assumptions of a linear status model. Although aggressive relations corresponded more closely to theoretical predictions about linearity, status rankings based upon each class of conflict were quite similar. Table 5.3 shows the rank-order correlations between each of these initial rankings and a composite dominance hierarchy. All of the correlations are sufficiently high to justify the use of the composite measure as an index of dominance relationships. Perhaps more importantly, the use of both aggressive and competitive exchanges as a general dominance index provides more information for a larger number of dyads in each group and thus permits a more stringent test of predictions from the linear dominance model. Figures 5.3 and 5.4 show the final dominance hierarchies for the groups at Langara and Simon Fraser. Individuals are listed according to their status rank on the

TABLE 5.3
Correlations Between
Agonistic Hierarchies
at Two Preschool Centers

	Aggression	Competition	Dominance
Langara (N = 17)			
Aggression	—		
Competition	.90	—	
Dominance	.98	.90	—
Simon Fraser (N = 14)			
Aggression	—		
Competition	.91	—	
Dominance	.99	.93	—

LANGARA Dominance Hierarchy

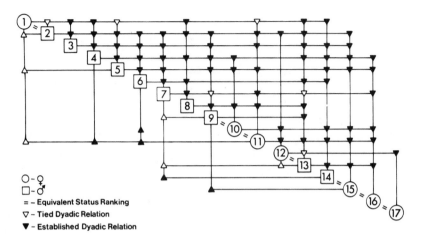

○ – ♀
□ – ♂
= – Equivalent Status Ranking
▽ – Tied Dyadic Relation
▼ – Established Dyadic Relation

FIG. 5.3.   Hierarchical organization of social dominance for the Langara group.

SIMON FRASER Dominance Hierarchy

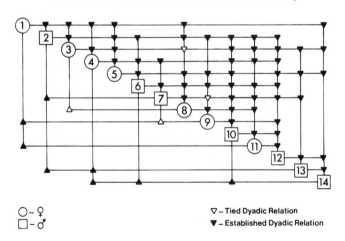

○ – ♀
□ – ♂

▽ – Tied Dyadic Relation
▼ – Established Dyadic Relation

FIG. 5.4.   Hierarchical organization of social dominance for the Simon Fraser group.

diagonal of the figures. The network of lines and arrows show the direction of observed dyadic relationships. In both cases, the linear organization of relationships is reflected by the high density of connectedness above the diagonal, while exceptions to linearity are evident by the degree of connectedness below.

WATERLOO Dominance Hierarchy

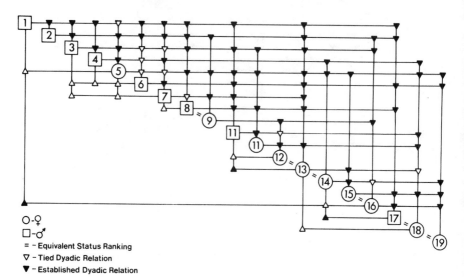

O - ♀
□ - ♂
= – Equivalent Status Ranking
▽ – Tied Dyadic Relation
▼ – Established Dyadic Relation

FIG. 5.5.   Hierarchical organization of social dominance for the Waterloo group.

SALLOPETTE Dominance Hierarchy

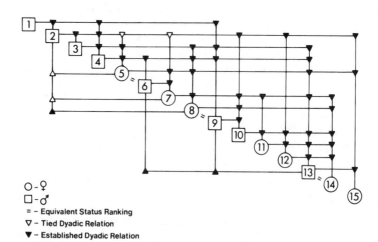

O - ♀
□ - ♂
= – Equivalent Status Ranking
▽ – Tied Dyadic Relation
▼ – Established Dyadic Relation

FIG. 5.6.   Hierarchical organization of social dominance for the Sallopette group.

178

SALTIMBANQUE Dominance Hierarchy

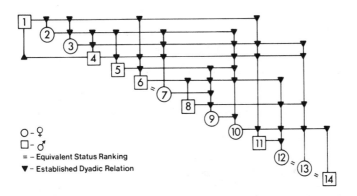

FIG. 5.7. Hierarchical organization of social dominance for the Saltimbanque group.

The results obtained for the first two groups have been replicated in each of our subsequent studies. Social dominance structures for these final groups are shown in Figs. 5.5, 5.6 and 5.7. Table 5.2 summarizes the organization of social dominance for each of these five groups. It is clear that in each case there are exceptions to the rule of linearity. However, in each sample, the vast majority of dyadic exchanges involving submission and loss occurred in an asymmetric fashion across dyadic contexts. Furthermore, the resolution of such dyadic conflict revealed a set of asymmetrical social relationships that consistently conformed to the linear model of social dominance. Finally, in each group, the level of convergence between social rankings based upon component categories of social conflict justified the use of dominance as a general descriptive concept for the regulation of dispersive forms of social exchange within a preschool group. Dominance does not imply only a relationship that is specific to a single type of social exchange, but rather a

TABLE 5.4
Summary of Dominance Relations
at Five Preschool Centers

	Frequency of Exchanges	Asymmetry of Exchanges	Dyads Involved	Linearity of Relations
Langara (N = 17)	232	88%	58%	94%
Simon Fraser (N = 14)	189	87%	73%	88%
Waterloo (N = 19)	134	88%	46%	96%
Sallopette (N = 15)	240	84%	43%	93%
Saltimbanque (N = 14)	82	96%	42%	97%

relationship that is more general across forms of conflict. Thus, the more dominant child had prerogatives involving priority of access, as well as the ability to aggressively intimidate other group members.

THE ANALYSIS OF SOCIAL COHESION

Although a comparative perspective toward preschool social conflict has provided some insight into one structural aspect of peer-group social ecology, corresponding methods for the analysis of cohesive social structures are not well developed. In fact, much of the comparative research on primate social organization, like the research in child social ethology, has placed primary importance upon dominance as an analytic concept. Theoretically, the relative neglect of more positive social bonds is curious, since the analysis of dominance structures assumes that there are more important cohesive factors that make group membership an option for all individuals. Only such cohesive factors would lead to the aggregation of individuals and the need to regulate dispersive social activity with a system of individual prerogatives that we call dominance.

Although elaborate methods for the analysis of naturally occurring cohesive structures have not been developed, considerable theoretical attention has been given to changes in the relative influence of different cohesive factors during the course of individual development (Hinde, 1974). The work of Bowlby (1969, 1973) and Harlow and Harlow (1965) provides an important conceptual framework for the comparative analysis of affectional ties between age-mates. From this perspective, such relationships should involve types of behavioral exchange that are similar in form or function to activities characteristically observed in mother–child attachment. Theoretically, such behaviors should be discriminatively initiated toward specific figures in the stable peer group and have a high probability of being reciprocated by the selected peer.

Our preliminary analyses of cohesive relationships among preschool children entailed regrouping specific behavioral patterns described by classical child ethologists (Blurton Jones, 1972; Smith & Connolly, 1972; McGrew, 1972) into four general categories of attachment behavior. These categories included *proximity behaviors, social orientation, physical contact,* and *postural signals.* Primary emphasis in these initial studies was given to the derivation of a single cohesive network that summarized individual social preferences for each group member. Using sociographic techniques, the obtained cohesive structures appeared as a collection of separate subgroupings, or *social cliques.* Membership in a affiliative clique was based upon each child's strongest social preference. Although such networks accurately reflected stable patterns of social spacing during periods of free play they failed to give sufficient weight to the role of different children as cohesive agents within their respective subgroupings. From more casual observations, it seemed clear that our sociographic cliques corresponded to naturally occurring play groups within the preschool class. Furthermore, the stability of such play groups seemed to depend heavily upon the presence of particular children in each subgrouping who selectively directed affiliative gestures to a wider range of clique members. Thus, a major limitation in these early procedures for the analysis of cohesive structures was the failure to detect multiple affiliative preferences within the preschool group.

Our current approach to the analysis of cohesive social structure entails a more elaborate procedure that permits the identification of multiple preferences for each child. In addition, we have restricted the range of behaviors that form the basis of our assessment of affiliative ties to Proximity and Contact. This more limited set of activities was selected to permit an analysis of cohesive structures that would be methodologically independent from analysis of other social activities, such as attention and control, that have been hypothesized to covary with dominance relationships in stable groups (Chance & Jolly, 1970; Chance & Larsen, 1976).

The dyadic distribution of proximity and contact behaviors between members of the Simon Fraser group are shown in Fig. 5.8, where children are listed according to their position within the group dominance structure. It is clear from even casual inspection of this matrix that the nature of cohesive

SIMON FRASER
Cohesive Activity

INITIATOR	1	2	3	4	5	6	7	8	9	10	11	12	13	14	
♀ 1		5	5	8	16			3	4	2	6	3	7	7	66
♂ 2	1		5	11	5	8	9		8	18	7	12	5	3	92
♀ 3	6	2		11	3	5	9	10	3	8	4	2	5	2	70
♀ 4	3	7	6		10	3	4	10	4	5	20	2	4	11	89
♀ 5	10	5		4		3	1	2	1	10	14	11	3		64
♂ 6	3	11	4	1	7		30	4	13	6	3	29	3	4	118
♂ 7	1	4	2		2	24		7	2	7	1	10		6	66
♀ 8	15	3	11	6	8	2	4		3	2	3	2	2	4	65
♀ 9	6	10	3	4		6	6	3		10	1	15	8	5	77
♂10	4	6	6	3	8	23	2	1	3		8	14	6	2	86
♀11	8	3	1	1	9	3	2	4	2	5		6	3	2	49
♂12	6	11	2	1	12	21	8	4	13	16	5		8	3	110
♂13	6	8	2	4	5	3	7	7	14	9	4	15		1	85
♂14	7	2	7	3	6	1	4	10	3	1	8	3	4		59
	76	77	54	57	91	102	86	65	73	99	84	124	58	50	1096

FIG. 5.8.   Dyadic matrix of affiliative gestures for the Simon Fraser group.

activities in the preschool group differs drastically from forms of social conflict. More than 1,000 affiliative gestures were observed during the same period in which fewer than 200 agonistic episodes were recorded. More importantly, the dyadic distribution of cohesive activity is not similar to that of aggression or competition. The level of dyadic asymmetry in approaches and contacts was only 67%. In general, one of every three affiliative gestures was reciprocated by a social target. The comparatively low level of asymmetry in cohesive behaviors indicates that a hierarchical model cannot adequately represent the organization of affiliative relationships within the preschool group.

However, the distribution of affiliative acts in Fig. 5.8 is not haphazard. Individual tests for each child showed that in all cases group members directed affiliative activity in a significantly non-random fashion ($\chi^2 > 21.03$, df = 12). To determine which group members received more than their expected share of an individual's initiated affiliative activity, frequencies higher than the expected value were examined to determine their contribution to the overall chi square. Instances in which the observed frequency was significantly higher than the expected value ($\chi^2 > 3.85$, df = 1) were selected as reflecting a social preference for the initiating child. The dyadic frequencies in bold print from Fig. 5.8 show the complete set of these significant social choices. It seems interesting to note that social preferences for the Simon Fraser group were equally distributed with respect to the social dominance hierarchy. Half of the observed preferences are located on each side of the diagonal in Fig. 5.8 where children are listed according to status in the dominance structure. This indicates that the direction of dyadic preferences was not systematically related to the direction of dyadic dominance.

The organizational pattern of social preferences at Simon Fraser is shown more clearly in Fig. 5.9, which provides a sociographic representation of individual affiliative choices. This social network shows important differences between individual children in their level of integration within the group's affiliative structure. Half of the children maintained reciprocal affiliative relationships with other group members, and these children appear most central in the cohesive network. Four individuals (3, 4, 8, and 9) preferred specific group members, and were chosen as preferred affiliative targets; but they did not have reciprocal affiliative bonds. Finally three children showed social preferences, but were not chosen by any of their peers. These latter individuals (2, 13, and 14) are the social isolates in the affiliative network in Fig. 5.9.

These same procedures for the derivation of cohesive social structure provided similar results for the Waterloo group. Figure 5.10 shows the affiliative network obtained in this second study. Once again, social preferences were defined as instances where a significant proportion of a child's proximity and contact behaviors were focused upon a particular peer

SIMON FRASER Affiliative Network

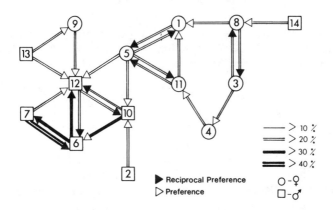

FIG. 5.9. Cohesive network for the Simon Fraser group.

WATERLOO Affiliative Network

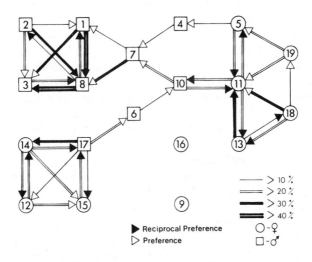

FIG. 5.10. Cohesive network for the Waterloo group.

group member. The Waterloo cohesive network does not have a single central region, but instead is divided into three interconnected subgroups of children. These social cliques are distinguished by a high frequency of internal social bonding, and a lack of reciprocal relationships with nonmembers of the clique. However, even with this clique structure, it was still possible to distinguish different levels of social integration in the group's cohesive network. A large majority of children maintained reciprocal social bonds and appeared as central individuals in their respective subgroups. Other children (4, 6, 7, and 19) did not have reciprocated social preferences and appeard at the periphery of each social clique. Finally, two children (9 and 16) were not discriminative in the distribution of their affiliative behaviors and were not chosen by other members of the peer group. These latter two individuals are not connected to the cohesive structure in Fig. 5.10 and were the social isolates in their group.

Although qualitatively different forms of affiliative connections were evident in each of the two preceding cohesive networks, a more quantitative measure of individual differences in level of social integration involved examining the actual number of affiliative links between each child and other group members. Using this criterion, it was possible to rank members of each group according to their relative contribution to the cohesive structure of the group. Although this measure does not imply that affiliative relationships are organized in a hierarchical fashion, it permits a direct evaluation of the extent to which more dominant children assume central roles in the cohesive network of their social group. The correlation between dominance status and level of affiliative integration was nonsignificant for both the Simon Fraser and Waterloo groups ($\rho = .00$ and $-.01$). These preliminary findings suggested that there are at least two independent dimensions in the organization of the preschool group. Knowledge of a child's position within the social dominance hierarchy does not necessarily predict his role as a cohesive agent in the affiliative structure of the peer group.

Our subsequent analyses of preschool cohesive activity have placed greater emphasis upon affiliative exchanges, rather than merely socially directed affiliative gestures. In these more recent analyses, only proximity and contact behaviors that led to a clear reaction by the social target were included as measures of social preference. In the majority of cases, such reactions included visual orientation, reciprocal approach, or some postural gesture. Our current emphasis upon cohesive exchanges eliminates forms of socially directed behavior that do not lead to the onset of an interaction episode. This more restricted set provides a more stringent definition of cohesive behavior, because it stresses an immediate continuation of social exchange.

The affiliative structures derived from an analysis of cohesive exchanges resembled networks obtained in the two earlier studies. Figure 5.11 shows the affiliative relationships among children in the Sallopette group. This cohesive network contains two social cliques, with internal social bonding and a lack of reciprocal preferences between non-clique members. Similar patterns of cohesive relationships are evident in Fig. 5.12, which shows the affiliative structure for the Saltimbanque group. In both sociograms, the degree of individual integration in the affiliative network can be evaluated from qualitative and quantitative differences in the links between group members.

SALLOPETTE Affiliative Network

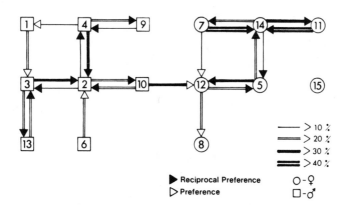

FIG. 5.11.   Cohesive network for the Sallopette group.

SALTIMBANQUE Affiliative Network

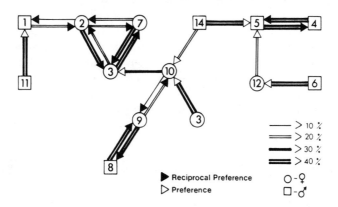

FIG. 5.12.   Cohesive network for the Saltimbanque group.

A comparison of cohesive roles with position in the group dominance hierarchy revealed a positive, but nonsignificant, correlation between the two rankings for the children from the Sallopette (ρ = .25). However, in the Saltimbanque group, the two rankings were highly correlated (ρ = .73). Thus, in the latter group there was a significant tendency for more dominant children to occupy more central affiliative positions in the cohesive structure.

Although the greater correspondence between dominance status and cohesive roles in these latter two groups may be attributable to differences in our social-preference assessment it seems more likely that these findings reflect intergroup variability in the coordination of agonistic and cohesive social structures. We are currently replicating our analysis of affiliative organization using the less stringent procedures that include all forms of socially directed proximity and contact behaviors. It seems that this broader assessment may alter the social preferences of peripheral and isolate children, but that the reciprocal choices that characterize the more central children will remain unchanged. Thus, even with a less stringent criterion of cohesive initiations, we will continue to find at least a modest correlation between dominance position and affiliative roles for some groups. Such intergroup variability in the coordination of different classes of social activity seems intuitively reasonable and may constitute one of the more important differences in the social ecology of stable groups.

DOMINANCE, AFFILIATION, AND OTHER SOCIAL BEHAVIOR

Dominance and affiliation have usually been viewed as primary aspects of social organization among non-human primates. The present findings suggest that these relationships are equally important for the organization of the preschool peer group. In the primate literature, both dominance and affiliative relationships have been discussed as determinants of other forms of social adaptation. For example, both concepts have been related to the distribution of social attention within a stable group (Chance & Jolly, 1970), social learning (Strayer, 1976; Tsumori, 1967), control roles within the social group (Bernstein, 1970; Dolhinow & Bishop, 1972), and group defense (Jolly, 1972). Although the importance of both dominance and cohesive relationships is central at a theoretical level, methods for evaluating the influence of these relationships on other activities remain unclear. Most of the research that has attempted to demonstrate the constraints imposed by dominance or affiliative relations on the organization of other social activity has focused only at the level of individual differences in rates of behavior. Such research has failed to consider how social relationships defined in terms of the stable distribution of these other activities may be coordinated with either dyadic dominance relations or social bonds.

In our most recent research with preschool children, we have begun to explore how knowledge of a child's position within the group dominance hierarchy, or the group affiliative network, can aid in understanding other types of social exchange. The activities that we are currently examining include (1) social attention, (2) social influence, or control and (3) altruistic gestures. Our approach to the analysis of these latter activities parallels our earlier consideration of agonistic and cohesive interaction.

Our description of social attention within each preschool group was based upon information obtained in two different ways. In order to evaluate the relative frequency with which different children served as the *focus of attention* for other group members, instantaneous scan samples were obtained for visual orientation. This sampling procedure did not require that children be engaged in social interaction in order for the receipt of social attention to be coded. Mere regard was sufficient. In addition, the rate of directed *bids for attention* were also coded. Bids included a socially directed gesture not included in the cohesive or agonistic categories that seemed intended to attract the attention of another child.

The description of social control activities included examples of direct and indirect influence directed toward another child. The most *direct influence* consisted of overt intervention by a focal child into the activity of another group member. Such interventions were coded only when they altered or modified the peer's ongoing behavior. More *indirect influence* entailed serving as a model for another group member. Such instances of imitation were coded as *copy* when it was clear that the focal child initiated the mutual activity before the other group member. In cases where it was unclear which child actually began the mutual activity, *join* was coded instead of copy.

Our description of altruistic gestures included two general classes of behavior. Object-related activity included direct *giving* of materials to another child, as well as alternate *sharing* of one or more objects. In addition, unsuccessful efforts to give an object were coded as *offers*. The second class of altruistic activity included giving assistance in the achievement of a common goal. Such assistance occurred both in serious and play contexts and was coded as *helping* behavior. Since records of these social activities were obtained using focal sampling procedures, it was possible to analyze differences in both rates of behavior and social relations for each class of activity.

Our first questions concerned whether position within the affiliative and dominance structures of the preschool group were systematically related to individual differences in the rate of initiated and received social activity. To explore these questions, correlations were computed between rates of social behaviors and position within the two social structures. For the dominance comparisons, children were assigned a numerical value that corresponded to their status in the social hierarchy. For the affiliative comparisons, individuals were rank-ordered according to their position in the affiliative network and the number of significant connections that they had with other group members. Central children were always ranked higher than peripheral group members, who in turn were always ranked higher than social isolates.

Table 5.5 summarizes correlations obtained between positions in the two social structures and rates of initiated social activity. For the younger group of children in the Sallopette, only two forms of initiated social activity were significantly associated with social roles in the peer group. More dominant children initiated more control interactions, while individuals with a central affiliative position initiated more proximity and contact exchanges. Similar,

TABLE 5.5
Correlations Between Dominance
and Affiliative Roles and
Initiation of Social Behaviors

	Sallopette	Saltibanque
Dominance		
Aggression	.29	.60*
Affiliation	.19	.53*
Attention	.12	.24
Control	.46*	.61*
Altruism	.07	.44
Affiliation		
Aggression	.05	.24
Affiliation	.58*	.79*
Attention	.26	.54*
Control	.41	.59*
Altruism	.09	.66*

*$p < .05$.

but stronger correlations were evident in the Saltimbanque group. In addition, both dominance and affiliative roles in the older group were associated with higher rates of initiated aggressive, affiliative, and control exchanges. Finally, more affiliatively central children also initiated more altruistic gestures.

This pattern of significant correlations suggests that social roles within the Saltimbanque group were associated with general individual differences in social participation. High status and affiliatively central children initiated the majority of observed social activity in this group. Analyses of the rates of receiving social activities showed less pervasive differences as a function of social roles (see Table 5.6). Within the younger Sallopette group, dominance status was unrelated to the receipt of social activity. However, children more central in the affilitative structure received significantly more social attention and more affiliative gestures. Again, these same patterns were also evident among the older preschool children. In addition, for the Saltimbanque group dominance status was significantly related to the receipt of both affiliative and altruistic gestures.

The observed correlations between social roles within each group and differential rates of social participation suggest a more pervasive coordination of social activities among members of the older Saltimbanque group. However, it seems important to note that even in the younger Sallopette group, dominance and affiliative roles were systematically related to individual differences in some of the other classes of social activity. Perhaps more importantly, in each cases where roles among the young

TABLE 5.6
Correlations Between Dominance
and Affiliative Roles
and Rate of Received
Social Behaviors

	Sallopette	Saltibanque
Dominance		
Aggression	.39	−.60
Affiliation	−.11	.56*
Attention	−.03	.42
Control	.28	.27
Altruism	.16	.61*
Affiliation		
Aggression	.08	.13
Affiliation	.72*	.81*
Attention	.57*	.65*
Control	.42	.40
Altruism	.28	.42

*$p < .05$.

children were significantly correlated with individual differences in social participation, stronger correlations were evident among members of the older group. Thus, the more pervasive coordination of social activity among the Saltimbanque children may reflect age-related changes in peer group social organization. At both age levels, dominant children tended to initiate more control activities. But among the older children, dominance and the rate of social control was also associated with a corresponding increase in the rate of affiliative gestures. Similarly, affiliative status in each group was positively related to the rate of initiated proximity and contact behaviors. But among the older children, affiliative centrality was also significantly correlated with differential rates in the initiation of other forms of positive social exchange.

The corresponding analyses of receipt of social activity also reveal interesting differences in the social ecology of the two groups. Dominance status among the older children was positivley correlated with the receipt of most forms of social activity. High-status children clearly received significantly more affiliative and altruistic gestures. In addition, there was a nonsignificant tendency for these same individuals to receive more visual attention. The magnitudes of these correlations are quite similar to those reported by other researchers who have investigated the distribution of non-aggressive social behavior in relation to group dominance status (Abramovitch & Strayer, 1978; Strayer, 1978; Vaughn & Waters, 1978). However, the lack of such relationships among the younger children in the Sallopette group suggests that the convergence between social dominance and the receipt of non-agonistic activities may be dependent upon the more general coordination of dominance and affiliative roles in the peer group. In both of the present groups, significantly more attentional behaviors were directed toward affiliatively central children. Perhaps earlier accounts of social attention within the stable peer group have overemphasized the potential cross-species link between status and receipt of social attention. The present results suggest that such a relation may depend upon the convergence of dominance and affiliative roles, and that social attention is more closely coordinated with affiliative ties among group members rather than with asymmetrical power relationships.

Having evaluated individual differences in the rate of social behaviors, our second set of question concerned the coordination of social relations defined by these other forms of social activity. To simplify these comparisons, most preferred targets for attentional, control, and altruistic activities were determined using procedures similar to those that were develped for the identification of affiliative preferences. Table 5.7 shows the extent of agreement between both dominance and affiliative relationships and other social relations defined in terms of attentional, control, and altruistic preferences. Dyadic attention relations were not systematically related to dyadic dominance (see Table 5.7). Instead, there was a slight tendency in both groups for children to select their more preferred affiliative targets as centers of social attention. In contrast, control relations were well coordinated with dyadic dominance in the older group ($\chi^2 = 4.00$, df = 1). Finally, altruistic choices were not directly related to either dyadic dominance or affiliative relations.

The lack of correspondence between dyadic dominance and social attention is shown more clearly in Fig. 5.13 and 5.14. If subordinate children attend more often to higher status group members as predicted by attentional theory (Chance & Jolly, 1970; Chance & Larsen, 1976), we would expect an inverted hierarchical arrangement of attention relationships, with the

TABLE 5.7
Agreement of Affiliative and
Dominance Relations With
Other Social Relationships

	Sallopette		Saltimbanque	
	Dom.	*Aff.*	*Dom.*	*Aff.*
Attention	53%	63%	56%	73%
Control	58%	59%	75%	57%
Altruism	44%	31%	43%	53%

Note: 50% indicates chance agreement.

SALLOPETTE Attention Relations

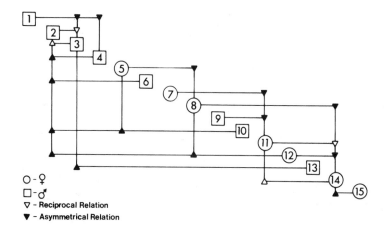

FIG. 5.13.   Attention relations for the Sallopette group.

SALTIMBANQUE Attention Relations

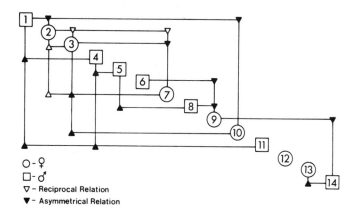

FIG. 5.14.   Attention relations for the Saltimbanque group.

asymmetry in preferences being opposite to that of dyadic dominance. In both groups, nearly half of the observed attentional preferences involved higher status children focusing upon individuals lower in the group dominance hierarchy. These data provide no support for the claim that subordinate group members selectively monitor individuals with higher social status.

SALLOPETTE Control Relations

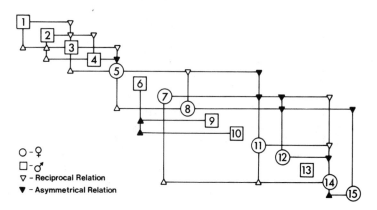

FIG. 5.15.   Control relations for the Sallopette group.

SALTIMBANQUE Control Relations

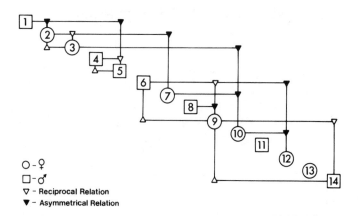

FIG. 5.16.   Control relations for the Saltimbanque group.

A somewhat different pattern was evident in the observed control relations for each group. Figure 5.15 shows the significant targets of social control for members of the Sallopette group. Almost half of these control relations were reciprocal. Among younger children, control activities were often initiated toward group members who also exercised control over the focal child. This was especially the case among the higher ranking boys in the group dominance structure. Figure 5.16 shows that such reciprocal control relations were also evident among some children in the Saltimbanque group. However, in this older group a greater percentage of observed control relations were asymmetrical. More importantly, all such asymmetrical relations corresponded in direction to established dominance relations. This view of dyadic control relations helps clarify the interpretation of the observed correlation between rate of initiated social control and peer-group dominance status. The association of initiated control and status in the Sallopette group is strongly influenced by the network of reciprocal control relations among the highly dominant boys. In contrast, the correlation for the Saltimbanque group reflects both the exercise of social control by dominant to more subordinate group members, as well as occasional reciprocal control relations between highly ranked individuals in the dominance structure. It is only in this latter group that control relations are coordinated with social dominance in a fashion that leads lower ranking group members to be influenced more often by children with higher dominance status.

SUMMARY AND CONCLUSIONS

The present analyses of social behavior demonstrate the importance of clear distinctions between levels of social description in the analysis of naturally occurring behavior. By extending a conceptual approach from comparative social ethology, we were able to provide a naturalistic description of behavioral organization among preschool children that surpassed the traditional analysis of individual differences in rates of selected social activity. Rather, this approach permitted a more sophisticated consideration of social organization that emphasized patterns of dyadic exchange, social relationships, and group structures. A logical extension of the present analytic perspective requires the independent derivation of other social structures based upon noncohesive and nonagonistic social activities. The identification of attentional, altruistic, and/or control structures will require more extensive information on the dyadic distribution of these latter activities. When we have finished our descriptive analysis of all social activity recorded for members of the two Sourithèque groups, we hope to be able to provide a more complete, multidimensional analysis of preschool social ecology. However, the derivation of such additional dimensions for peer-group social organization should not necessarily imply an endless proliferation of social structures. The interesting theoretical questions will involve the number of such dimensions that are necessary for an adequate summary of social relationships among peers. In the present research, both aggressive and competitive conflict were organized in a fashion that justified the identification of a more general dominance hierarchy. It seems likely that other social structures will also be sufficiently interrelated to warrant the derivation of similarly higher order descriptive concepts that summarize the organization of a broader range of social activities. Once we are in a position to determine empirically the number of such higher order constructs that are necessary for the analysis of group structure, we will have made substantial gains in our understanding of both the nature and the development of peer-group social ecology during the preschool years.

For the present, our emphasis upon the derivation of both agonistic and cohesive dimensions led to the demonstration of surprisingly similar social structures in peer groups from heterogeneous cultural, linguistic, and physical backgrounds. More importantly, the derivation of different social structures within the preschool group permitted a stronger test of theoretical speculation about the coordination of social attention and social dominance relations. The present findings fail to support an attentional interpretation of preschool dominance. Instead, our results suggest that social attention is more closely coordinated with cohesive aspects of preschool social organization. The present results also provide preliminary cross-sectional information that indicates that important changes in the organization of social activities within the peer group may occur during the end of the preschool years. The convergence of social roles in the affiliative and dominance structures for the oldest group of children suggests interesting possibilities about changes in peer-group social ecology. Such changes may be related to other, more long-term functions of both cohesive and agonistic activity. Only in this latter group was it possible to distinguish specific individuals who appeared more generally competent on each dimension of our social analysis. In each case, these more competent children were among the older members of the group and seemed to possess individual social skills that exceeded those of more subordinate and peripheral group members. The relatively strong roles they played in both the dominance and cohesive structures corresponds well to our intuitive assessment of their more advanced social competence. The future development of the present techniques for analyzing qualitative differences in social relationships and social roles within the stable peer group could provide a variety of ethologically based social measures that can be explored in relation to more traditional psychological assessments of individual competence. Once again at an intuitive level, psychological measures of social skills and sociocognitive development seem to relate less directly to differential rates of initiated social activities than to differences in the organization of social behavior. Such organization must be examined at the level of coordinated interaction sequences, reciprocal social relationships, and the stability of social roles within the peer group.

REFERENCES

Abramovitch, R. The relation of attention and proximity to rank in preschool children. In M. Chance & R. Larsen (Eds.), *The social structure of attention*. London: Wiley, 1976.

Abramovitch, R., & Strayer, F. F. Preschool social organization: Agonistic, spacing, and attentional behaviors. In P. Pliner, T. Kramer, & T. Alloway (Eds.), *Recent advances in the study of communication and affect*. Vol. 6. New York: Plenum Press, 1978.

Altmann, J. Observational study of behavior: Sampling methods. *Behavior*, 1974, *49*, 227–265.

Barker, M. A technique for studying the social material activities of young children. *Monographs of Society for Research in Child Development*. (No. 3). New York: Columbia University Press, 1930.

Barker, R. G. Explorations in ecological psychology. *American Psychologist*, 1965, *20*, 1–14.

Bateson, P. P. G., & Hinde, R. A. *Growing points in ethology*. Cambridge: Cambridge University Press, 1976.

Bernstein, I. S. Primate status hierarchies. In L. Rosenblum (Ed.), *Primate behavior: Developments in field and laboratory research*. New York: Academic Press, 1970.

Blurton Jones, N. Characteristics of ethological studies of human behavior. In N. Blurton Jones (Ed.), *Ethological studies of child behaviour*. Cambridge: Cambridge University Press, 1972.

Blurton Jones, N., & Leach, G. M. Behaviour of children and their mothers at separation and greeting. In N. Blurton Jones (Ed.), *Ethological studies of child behaviour*. Cambridge: Cambridge University Press, 1972.

Bowlby, J. *Attachment and loss: Volume 1, Attachment*. New York: Basic Books, 1969.

Bowlby, J. *Attachment and loss; Volume II, Separation*, New York: Basic Books, 1973.

Brannigan,C. R., & Humphries, D. A. Human non-verbal behaviour, a means of communication. In N. Blurton Jones (Ed.), *Ethological studies of child behaviour*. Cambridge: Cambridge University Press, 1972.

Chance, M. R., & Jolly, C. J. *Social groups of monkeys and men*. London: Jonathan Cape, 1970.

Chance, M. R. A., & Larsen, R. R. *The social structure of attention*. London: Wiley, 1976.

Chittenden, G. E. An experimental study in measuring and modifying assertive behavior in young children. *Monographs of the Society for Research in Child Development*, 1942, *7*(1).

Crook, J. H. Social organization and the environment: aspects of contemporary social ethology. *Animal Behaviour*, 1970, *18*, 197–209.

Dawe, H. C. Analysis of two hundred quarrels of preschool children. *Child Development*, 1943, *5*, 139–157.

DeVore, I. *Primate behavior: Field studies of monkeys and apes*. New York: Hold, Rinehart and Winston, 1965.

Dolhinow, P., & Bishop. H. The development of motor skills and social relationships among primates. In P. Dolhinow (Ed.), *Primate patterns*. New York: Holt, Rinehart and Winston, 1972.

Emmerlich, W. Continuity and stability in early social development. *Child Development*, 1964, *35*, 311–332.

Gellert, E. Stability and fluctuation in the power relationships of young children. *Journal of Abnormal and Social Psychology*, 1961, *62*, 8–15.

Gellert, E. The effects of change in group composition on the dominant behaviour of young children. *British Journal of Social and Clinical Psychology*, 1962, *1*, 168–181.

Grant, E. C. Human facial expression. *Man*, 1969, *4*, 525–536.

Harlow, H. F., & Harlow, M. K. The affectional systems. In A. Schrier, H. Harlow and F. Stollnitz (Eds.), *Behavior of non-human primates* (Vol. 2). New York: Academic Press, 1965.

Hinde, R. A. *Animal behaviour: A synthesis of ethology and comparative psychology*. (2nd ed.) New York: McGraw-Hill, 1970.

Hinde, R. R. *The biological bases of human social behaviour*. New York: McGraw-Hill, 1974.

Hinde, R. R. Interactions, relationships and social structure. *Man*, 1976, *11*, 1–17.

Hinde, R. A., & Stevenson-Hinde, J. Towards understanding relationships: Dynamic stability. In P. Bateson & R. Hinde (Eds.), *Growing Points in Ethology*. Cambridge: Cambridge University Press, 1976.

Jay, P. C. *Primates: Studies in adaptation and variability*. New York: Holt, Rinehart and Winston, 1968.

Jolly, A. *The evolution of primate behavior*. New York: MacMillan, 1972.

Kummer, H. *Primate societies: Group techniques in ecological adaptation.* Chicago: University of Chicago Press, 1971.

Leach, G. M. A comparison of the social behaviour of some normal and problem children. In N. Blurton Jones (Ed.), *Ethological studies of child behaviour.* Cambridge: Cambridge University Press, 1972.

McGrew, W. C. Glossary of motor patterns of four-year-old nursery school children. In S. Hutt & C. Hutt (Eds.), *Direct observation and measurement of behavior.* Springfield, Ill.: Thomas, 1970.

McGrew, W. C. *An ethological study of children's behavior.* New York: Academic Press, 1972.

Misshakian, E. A. *Aggression and dominance relations in peer groups of children six to forty-five months of age.* Paper presented at the Annual Conference of the Animal Behavior Society, Boulder, Colorado, June, 1976.

Piaget, J. *The language and thought of the child.* London: Routledge and Kegan Paul, 1926.

Piaget, J. *The moral judgement of the child.* New York: Free Press, 1948.

Piaget, J. *Play, dreams and imitation in childhood.* New York: Norton, 1951.

Piaget, J. *The origins of intelligence in children.* New York: International Universities Press, 1952.

Piaget, J. *The construction of reality in the child.* New York: Basic Books, 1954.

Rowell, T. E. Hierarchy in the organization of a captive baboon troop. *Animal Behaviour,* 1966, *14,* 430–443.

Rowell, T. E. The concept of social dominance. *Behavioral Biology,* 1974, *11,* 131–154.

Shirley, M. M. The first two years: a study of twenty-five babies. *Institute of Child Welfare Monograph Series.* No. 7. Minneapolis, Minnesota: University of Minnesota Press, 1933.

Sluckin, A., & Smith, P. Two approaches to the concept of dominance in preschool children. *Child Development,* 1977, *48,* 917–923.

Smith, P., and Connolly, K. Patterns of play and social interaction in preschool children. In N. Blurton Jones (Ed.), *Ethological Studies of Child Behaviour.* Cambridge: Cambridge University Press, 1972.

Strayer, F. F. Learning and imitation as a function of social status in macaque monkeys (*Macaca nemestrina*). *Animal Behaviour,* 1976, *24,* 832–848.

Strayer, F. F. L'organisation sociale chez des enfants d'âge préscolaire. *Sociologie et Société,* 1978, *10*(1), 43–64.

Strayer, F. F., Chapeskie, T. R., & Strayer, J. The perception of preschool social dominance relations. *Aggressive Behavior,* 1978, *4,* 183–192.

Strayer, F. F., & Strayer, J. An ethological analysis of social agonism and dominance relations among preschool children, *Child Development,* 1976, *47,* 980–988.

Tinbergen, N. The hierarchical organization of nervous mechanisms underlying instinctive behaviour. *Symposia of the Society for Experimental Biology,* 1950, *4,* 305–312.

Tinbergen, N. On the aims and methods of ethology. *Zeitschrift für Tierpsychologie* 1963, *20,* 410–433.

Tsumori, A. Newly acquired behavior and social interactions of Japanese monkeys. In S. Altmann (Ed.), *Social communication among primates.* Chicago: University of Chicago Press, 1967.

Vaughn, B., & Waters, E. Social organization among preschooler peers: Dominance, attention and sociometric correlates, In D. Omark, F. Strayer, & D. Freedman, (Eds.), *Peer-group power relations: An ethological perspective on human dominance and submission.* New York: Garland Press, 1978.

Washburn, P. A scheme for grading the reaction of children in a new social situation. *Journal of Genetic Psychology,* 1932, *40,* 84–88.

Wilson, E. O. *Sociobiology: The New Synthesis.* Cambridge, Mass.: Belknap/Harvard University Press, 1975.

Yerkes, R. M. *The great apes.* New Haven, Conn.: Yale University Press, 1928.

Zuckerman, S. *The social life of monkeys and apes.* London: Routledge, 1932.

6

A Developmental Theory of Friendship and Acquaintanceship Processes

John M. Gottman
Jennifer T. Parkhurst
University of Illinois

Brain's recent (1977) anthropological essay concluded that friendship is a universal characteristic of human society. Brain noted that anthropologists have given primary importance to kinship networks, and "having made a ritual obeisance to the importance of emotional ties outside structured kin groups have apparently despaired of describing them in detail [p. 5]." Nonetheless, in many societies the bonds of friendship have powerful rights and obligations that often transcend even kinship bonds. In many societies, best friendships that originate in childhood, including male/female pairs, continue unabated with a special character throughout the lifetime, even after the marriage of both people to others.

The interest in friendship is not limited to anthropologists. There is a general resurgence of interest in friendship among behavioral scientists: Sociologists are compiling ethnographies of naturally occurring friendship groups such as Little League baseball teams (Fine, 1978) and nursery schools (Corsaro, 1978). Ethnologists are studying affiliative as well as dominance networks in schools (see Strayer's chapter, this volume). Sociologists are using stochastic models of sociometric data over time to study the reciprocity of mutual friendship choice (Hallinan & Tuma, 1978); developmental psychologists are beginning to view the interaction of children with their peers, and the processes of friendship and acquaintanceship as important contexts for the study of social development (Lewis & Rosenblum, 1975, 1977).

There is also a growing body of evidence that peer relations are an important factor in a child's social development. There is evidence that sociometric measures of a child's relationships with peers are important predictors of social functioning both in childhood and adulthood (for reviews see Asher, Oden, & Gottman, 1977; Strain, Cooke, & Appoloni, 1976). Research with nonhuman primates also reveals the significance of contact with peers in the early years, particularly for the development of prosocial behavior (Soumi & Harlow, 1975). To some extent it appears that peer-group attachments can compensate for poor family relationships (Freud & Dann, 1951; Sherif & Sherif, 1964). Contrary to the contention that children's peer preferences for specific peers are arbitrary and unstable, there is anecdotal evidence that some very young children form strong and stable attachments to specific peers and express dismay on parting (Hartup, 1975). Also, improved techniques of sociometric measurement demonstrate that young children's peer preferences can be extremely stable (Asher, Singleton, Tinsley, & Hymel, 1977).

Given this renewed interest in peer relationships and friendship, it is remarkable how little basic descriptive research has been conducted to create a data base for generating hypotheses and constructing theories about the processes of friendship and acquaintanceship. Friendship in children and adults has remained a private world. We currently have little knowledge of what friends do together at different ages, what the function of various kinds of behaviors may be, or how children become or fail to become friends when they first become acquainted. It is the major goal of our work to begin the task of description and hypothesis generating.

METHODOLOGICAL ISSUES

Aspects of children's interactions with their peers have been studied in several research traditions. Sociometric measures assess a child's peer preferences within a particular group such as a classroom or school. However, it is important to distinguish studies on the variables that covary with sociometric status from research on children's friendship. The search for predictors of sociometric status is an investigation of *popularity* and not necessarily an investigation of friendship (Hartup, 1975).

Social cognitive research relies on statements by children in response to interviews, problem situations, or story-completion tasks (e.g., Selman, 1976; Youniss, 1975). One general conclusion that appears to be emerging from this research is that children's cognitions about friendship and their understanding of social interactions (e.g., motives and causation) become increasingly complex and differentiated with age. However, this does not rule out the alternative that what develops is vocabulary, the ability to give more abstract answers to questions, or knowledge of normative, cultural expectations about friendship such as sharing and reciprocity. A second problem is that younger children may not understand the questions of the interviewer or what the interviewer wants to know, but may nonetheless behave according to and have awareness of norms about friendship. A charming example of this point can be found in Damon (1977). The interviewed child, Matthew, is 5:10 (5 years, 10 months old); the child's answers are in italics:

> How did you meet Larry? *I saw him and I told him my name and we just became friends.* How do you know Larry likes you? *He plays with me and he gives me toys.* If he didn't give you toys, would he still be your friend? *Yea, I guess so. I didn't ever ask him* [p. 55].

It is clear to Matthew that he and Larry are not friends *because* Larry gives him toys; they are friends *and* Larry gives him toys. The abstract causal question may not receive an articulate answer even though Matthew may understand how you act with your friend. A third problem is inferring that what children say in response to social-cognitive interview procedures is what they think about during social interaction. It may be that people cannot articulate the rules that govern their social interaction. The point was well made by Robinson (1972), a sociolinguist, who wrote:

> If one wishes to find out the rules governing tennis or getting married, one buys a booklet or asks players and experts already conversant with the rules . . . It will be in the regulation of sub-institutional encounters that social psychologists are most interested. Here we may well not be able to ask the players what the rules are; or if we can ask, we should treat replies with skepticism [p. 136].

The regulation of social encounters in a culture is well prescribed, although it may not be as codified or institutionalized as the rules for jury trials and marriage ceremonies. The work of Goffman and others (see, for example, Argyle, 1969) has demonstrated that a great deal of public interaction between strangers is strongly ritualized, even if the participants are unaware of the specific rules. Classic examples are interpersonal distance spacings (the elbow-to-hand distance in our culture) (Hall, 1966), and the interlacing of gaze aversion in strangers passing one another in the street (Schefflen, 1972).

We contend that research on social cognition needs to be supplemented by an observational methodology. However, the observational methodology must meet three specific criteria if it is to be useful. First, the descriptive coding systems employed must be sufficiently rich in detail to describe the interactions of children if it is to be useful for a descriptive, hypothesis-generating function. The point was well expressed by Chevalier-Skolnikoff (1973) in her discussion of the ethological approach to the study of facial expressions in nonhuman primates. She pointed out that in ethological research, the initial stage of investigation is inductive and hypothesis-generating rather than deductive and hypothesis-testing. It is our contention that this important stage of scientific investigation must precede the development of theory. Physics had its Tycho Brahe, who carefully charted the motions of the stars and planets, Johannes Kepler who discovered patterns and phenomena in Brahe's reliable data, and Isaac Newton, who generated theory as an explanation of pattern. In the behavioral sciences we have failed to require clearly described phenomena or patterns in a set of reliable data as a prerequisite for the development of theory.

A second shortcoming of previous observational research in children's social interaction is that it would be essentially impossible for any human to demonstrate high levels of social competence using the coding categories. That is to say, the very choice of the coding categories contains hidden limiting assumptions about what children's capabilities are. As an example, in one coding system of children's social behavior (McGrew, 1972), only one category out of more than 100 categories, called "vocalize," recognizes the fact that preschool children can speak. The data obtained from such coding systems would not be applied to the social behavior of adults, and they place an implicit ceiling on the social competence children can display.

A third shortcoming of most previous observational research is the failure to analyze data sequentially. Most observational data are presented as rates or relative frequencies of specific coding categories, and therefore any sense of sequence and pattern is lost. However, it is precisely in the study of pattern and sequence that we can empirically and quantitatively discover the implicit social rules in a type of interaction.

The recent interest in the observational study of interacting systems, such as the parent-infant system, has led to the development of new techniques for sequential analysis (Bakeman, 1978; Gottman & Bakeman, 1979; Gottman & Notarius, 1978; Sackett, 1977). Much of this work has its roots in ethological approaches, which employ the mathematics of information theory to define a communicative sequence. A communicative sequence occurs when the behavior of one organism reduces uncertainty in the behavior of another organism. Consider the social behavior of an organism for which we have no a priori knowledge of which behaviors have communicative significance. For example, suppose we were studying spider crabs (Hazlett & Estabrook, 1974). We would notice that these crabs do not move very often; in fact, the unconditional base rate of crab B moving is about .03. To understand the communicative significance of a single chilepid raise of crab A, we may look at the conditional probability of crab B moving on those occasions following crab A's single chilepid raise. We find it is .03. The single chilepid raise of crab A has resulted in no reduction of uncertainty in crab B's behavior. But when we look at the forward chilepid extension of crab A, we find that the conditional probability of crab B's movement is .65. The forward chilepid extension has definite communicative value. Furthermore, we note that 35% of the time that crab B does not move after A's forward chilepid extension, there is a fight. There are thus two likely patterns, one of which results in a fight. Longer chains are constructed in a similar way using a method called lag sequential analysis developed by Sackett (1977).

Historical Roots of Methodological Issues

Some of the problems we have discussed in the Spartan design of observational coding systems can be traced to the influence of Piaget's (1930) *The Language and Thought of the Child,* because it argued strongly that most of the speech of preschool children is not conversation at all, but the solitary narration of play in the presence of another child, a phenomenon Piaget called *collective monologue.* Piaget studied the conversations of a group of children in a Montessori preschool, an education program not known for its encouragement of children's social interaction with peers.

Piaget reported the following conversation among children drawing at the same table:

1. Pie: But the trams that are hooked on behind don't have any flags
2. Pie: They don't have any carriages hooked on
3. Pie: (to Bea) 'T'sa tram that hasn't got no carriages
4. Pie: (to Hei) This tram hasn't got no carriages, Hei, look, it isn't red, d'you see
5. Pie: A funny gentleman
6. Pie: A funny gentleman . . . I'm leaving the tram white
7. Ez::   I'm doing it yellow
8. Pie: No, you mustn't do it all yellow. I'm doing the stair case, look.
9. Bea: I can't come this afternoon, I've got a Eurythmic class
10. Pie: What did you say?
11. Bea: I can't come this afternoon, I've got a Eurythmic class
12. Pie: What did you say?
13. Bea: (No answer)
14. Pie: (to Bea) Leave him alone
         [teacher interrupts]

When analyzing this conversation, Piaget concluded that in Pie's first several lines:

> He is not speaking to anyone. He is thinking aloud over his own drawing, just as the people of the working classes mutter to themselves over their work . . . He cares very little who is listening to him . . . He does not care whether the person he addresses has really heard him or not [p. 3].

An alternative interpretation of these first few lines is that Pie's intent is to get *someone's* attention, and that is why he continues to rephrase his initial statement, and address it to different people. Piaget refers to the sequence as an illustration of collective monologue. Bea's answer to Pie in line 9 certainly does seem "devoid of any connection with what he has just been saying [Piaget, 1930, p. 30]," but, on the other hand, it is hard to agree with Piaget that "it is obvious that he [Pie] does not seek to understand" since lines 10 and 12 are requests by Pie for some kind of elaboration of repetition.

Furthermore, it is interesting that Piaget considers lines 5 to 8 as additional examples of collective monologue. Pie's line "I'm leaving the tram white" followed by Ez's line "I'm doing it yellow" is not different from a sequence we might overhear in the faculty lounge, "I got a $2,000 raise," "I got an $800 raise." We would probably consider both a low form of dialogue, but dialogue nonetheless. There must have been a great deal of confusion between Piaget's adapted information code and collective monologue. The sequence "I'm coloring mine white"/"I'm coloring mine green" would be considered collective monologue while the sequence "I shall have one tomorrow"/"I shall have mine this afternoon" would be considered adapted information. Thus Piaget's own examples would lead one to suspect his method of coding a sequence as collective monologue, and this therefore leaves unanswered the question of how connected preschool children's speech is.

In Piaget's discussion of questions and answers we see dramatically the problem with ignoring sequence. The mere presentation of percentages of questions and answers is of far less interest to the egocentrism argument than the conditional probability of answering a non-rhetorical question rather than ignoring it.

Piaget was primarily interested in whether children's questions were of a causal nature, and he excluded from this requests for "psychological explanation, 'intentions' as we shall call them [p. 52]." An example of these psychological requests was "Why was he crying?" and a reexamination of one of Piaget's tables [p. 54] shows that 56% of children's questions concerned such questions (intentions or actions, e.g., "Why has he gone away?"). This is, in fact, the most striking feature of this table, but it passes without comment. However, clearly for the children in Piaget's sample, questions about psychological explanations are highly salient. Piaget uses the infrequency of nonsocial causal questions as evidence that the children are not functioning cognitively at a high level. Since throughout his monograph he assumes low-level cognitive functioning to be equivalent to socially nonadapted functioning, he ends by using the children's social orientation as a negation of its own existence. On the contrary, children's questions about the psychological motivation of others demonstrate that children are aware of the distinction between the I and the not-I.

The problem with coding a child's utterance as "egocentric" can be illustrated dramatically with children's repetitions. Piaget considers all repetitions examples of egocentric speech. This position has recently been aptly criticized by Keenan (1977), who noted that two-year-old children used repetition for a host of communicative functions and distinguished among these functions by varying their tone of voice. For example, repetition can be used to query ("Turn it around"/"Turn it around?"/"No, the other way"/"Other way?") or to agree enthusiastically ("And we're going to have hot dogs"/"Hot dogs!") or to comply ("Aren't I a good cook? Say 'yes, the greatest'"/"Yes, the greatest" [softly]/"That's right"/"The greatest!" [loudly]). Repetition can be clearly an important aspect of early discourse and is not to be automatically discarded as "egocentric."

Piaget's conclusion about egocentrism in children's speech is partly a result of his failure to distinguish children's activity-based talk narrating play, which may be connected, from collective monologue. A separate analysis of connected activity talk and collective monologue and careful redefinition would seem necessary before we could confidently accept Piaget's high estimates for the proportion of speech that is collective monologue.

Connectedness in Children's Communication

Mueller (1972) videotape-recorded the play of 24 pairs of unacquainted preschool children and coded the social consequences of each utterance as either a "success" or a "failure," depending on whether or not the listener clearly responded to the utterance verbally or nonverbally. Another group of coders independently coded various potential causes for success or failure, including the clarity of the utterance, its grammatical completeness, the degree of its social adaptation in terms of specifying referents, and its use of attention-getting devices. Sixty-two percent of all utterances were success, while only 15% were clearly failures; 23% fell into a partial failure category in which the listener attended to the speaker visually but did not reply. Having the listener's attention and using commands or questions were highly predictive of success. Mueller's children were totally unacquainted, in contrast to the children in Piaget's sample. We might expect communicative failure to be different among unacquainted children, although it is difficult to predict the direction of the difference. Children who are friends may feel more comfortable than strangers and be more likely to ignore one another, much as a husband and wife who comfortably go about their separate activities in the same room. Or, on the other hand, because they are familiar they may be more likely to have developed patterns of play and have a greater variety of methods of achieving and maintaining rapport.

A year later, Garvey and Hogan (1973) studied 18 dyads of nursery school children in the same age range as the children in Mueller's (1972) study. The dyads were from the same nursery school and presumably were more acquainted than the children in Mueller's study. The dyads were also videotaped. The utterance rates reported by Garvey and Hogan were twice that reported by Meuller, and they attribute this difference to the fact that the children in their study were "previously acquainted whereas Mueller's subjects were strangers [p. 564]." Furthermore, the dyads were judged to be connected, or "in focus," an average of 66% of the time, somewhat higher than Mueller's 62% of the time, although the two variables used to assess connectedness were not identical across the two studies.

Taken together, these two studies certainly challenge Piaget's conclusions about the lack of connectedness in the speech of preschool children. Recent research on connectedness in children's speech has further weakened the conception of young children as egocentric (see, for example, Ervin-Tripp & Mitchell-Kernan, 1977) or as incapable of appropriately modifying messages as a function of the special needs of a listener (see, for example, Shatz & Gelman, 1973). Nonetheless, the extent to which and the conditions in which young children are egocentric are still lively research questions.

The Garvey and Hogan (1973) study was more important for an additional reason: It introduced sociolinguistic considerations into the developmental literature on children's interactions. Two immediate contributions can be noted. The first is that Garvey and Hogan presented the first examples from the speech of the children that represent clear evidence of the fact that the speech of these children is connected. The second immediate contribution was that it focused attention on *patterns* of exchange, such as Schegloff's (1968) *summons-answer routine*. This pattern is a sequence found in conversational openings. It is of the following form: (1) Speaker A summons speaker B (Example: "Hey, you know what?"); (2) Speaker B answers (Example: "No, what?"); (3) Speaker A responds (Example: "Sometime you can come to my house."). Garvey and Hogan found 23 examples of this routine, but the examples were complex and displayed considerable variety, including jokes ("Hey, you know what?" "What?" "You're a nut.") and the "rhetorical gambit." The identification of these patterns was not based on sequential analyses of quantitative data; only anecdotal data were presented about these complex patterns. Nonetheless, they indicated the remarkable richness in children's discourse.

The Sociolinguistic Approach

Speech communities establish implicit social rules, and sociolinguistics is concerned with the discovery of these rules through an analysis of the community's language. For example, both alternative forms of address (Ervin-Tripp, 1969) and alternative forms of a directive may be used for different kinds of relationships (Ervin-Tripp, 1977).

Garvey (1974), applying sociolinguistic methods to the study of children's social play, catalogued recurring patterns of interaction. She concluded that: The structure of the interpersonal behaviors can be described in terms of the rules governing alternation of participation (turns), the substantive and formal relations of the alternating behaviors, and the manner in which sequences are built up (rounds) [p. 166]. Unfortunately, although frequencies of specific patterns are presented in sociolinguistic research, statistical data are often omitted; consequently, it is difficult to have any confidence in conclusions about differences between groups. The major contributions of the approach are descriptive, taxonomic, and hypothesis-generating; and, indeed, the reported examples bring the data vividly to life.

To detect patterns among a stream of linguistic coding categories, however, it is first necessary to rule out the rival hypothesis that no patterns exist in the data. In any random stream we can detect *examples* of a particular pairing of codes (such as AB), but this does not in itself demonstrate that the pairs have not arisen by chance alone. While no one would argue that language is random, the simple counting of pairs (or triples, or N-tuples) is inadequate for the study of the rules and sequences sociolinguists are interested in. In the ethological approach to the empirical identification of interaction sequences using information theory just discussed, the comparison of conditional to unconditional probabilities is a basic procedure. Statistical tests for this comparison have been presented in Bakeman (1978), Gottman (1979a,b), Gottman and Bakeman (1979), Gottman and Notarius (1978), and Sackett (1977). It will be important in our subsequent discussion to point out that a high frequency of the pair of codes AB does not, by itself, imply an AB sequence. The code B may be a frequent code, and *to establish an AB sequence we would have to demonstrate that its occurrence given that A has preceded it $(p(B/A))$ is greater than its occurrence unconditionally $(p(B))$.*

There are several theoretical implications of this methodological point. First, an empirically based method for detecting sequences would avoid the problem of isolating only some speech patterns for study and ignoring others whose social functions may be equally important. An empirical approach to sequence analysis may detect sequences that are important, but more pedestrian. Furthermore, such an analysis would make it possible to determine which codes do not have social communicative value.

A second issue concerns the analysis of social competence. Garvey (1974) discussed the abilities that underlie social play "to account for the structures of play described above" [p. 169]. Here again, we must question whether one or several compelling *examples* of a sequence are adequate to rule out the hypothesis that the sample is drawn from a random generator. Even if we ignore this problem, we must distinguish between the compelling examples and anecdotes that may convince us that the children probably have a set of competencies and the study of patterns designed to *characterize* the interaction.

A number of interesting questions about interactions may be addressed: If we are interested in friendship and its development, we may wish to distinguish the interaction (and social rules) of friends from those of strangers as a function of age. For these analyses, we need to discover the common or frequent *sequences* that characterize a particular group. One or two (or even 20) interesting instances will not suffice for this purpose. We must compare linkages between specific codes across groups. We can also assess the degree of predictability in a sequence, which would be one way of quantifying the concept of the "structure" of a sequence. This will make it possible to compare quantitatively how ritualized a sequence is and the relative predictability of sequences across groups. We can also detect where sequences end, if we mean by this a return to baseline levels of uncertainty in prediction. By searching for asymmetry in predictability between the two interacting people, we can determine who, if anyone, is controlling the interaction. By studying dyadic interaction in different social situations, we can determine to what extent a child modifies sequences as a function of context. We can quantify the degree of connection among the children's behaviors by examining the likelihood that certain specific code sequences will occur, such as clarification in response to a request for clarification (e.g., "What wheel?"/"The one for the tractor"), and how this changes as a function of age, or other contextual variables.

To summarize, the use of quantitative methods of sequence analysis has advantages over the nonstatistical techniques currently used by sociolinguists; among these are that it becomes possible (a) to rule out the hypothesis that examples of code pairs are random pairings; (b) to empirically identify patterns of interest that might otherwise go unnoticed; (c) to *characterize* the interaction by identifying common sequences; (d) to search for variables that control the emergence of specific patterns (e.g., age, acquaintanceship, setting); (e) to determine where sequences end; (f) to assess the degree of predictability in a sequence, or how ritualized a sequence is; (g) to determine if one member of the dyad is controlling the interaction; and (h) to determine which codes do *not* have social communicative value.

It is important to note that it makes a great deal of difference whether one is primarily a linguist studying social interaction as a context for analyzing language use in discourse, or primarily a developmental social psychologist who uses language to characterize interaction. While sharp distinctions are oversimplifications, the distinction is crucial in designing research and it is also crucial in reviewing research by others. Consider several examples that might distinguish the linguist from the social psychologist. The following two statements are both examples of the *tag question,* which is a question that asks for some form of agreement: (1) "He's coming home, isn't he?" and (2) "He's coming home, right?" The first statement represents a higher level of linguistic competence than the second, because it involves a *specific* transformation on the stem "He's coming home" rather than employing a universal tag such as "Right?" This distinction on a dimension of linguistic competence would be of more interest to the linguist than to the social psychologist, who would see in both forms a request for agreement.

In some cases, however, the social psychologist would make distinctions that the linguist would ignore. A linguistic interest would lead a sociolinguist to be interested in child discourse in part as a context for the study of the mastery of specific forms, such as the summons-answer sequence studied by Garvey and Hogan (1973). This sequence could take the following forms: (a) "Hey, you know what?"/"What?"/"I'm going to give you this to keep"; (b) "Hey, you know what?"/"What?"/ "I'm smashing up your parrot cage, you baby"; or (c) "Hey, you know what?"/"What?"/"You're a pickle, that's what." Although these examples all display competence with the same basic form, their social psychological meanings are different and would be considered different sequences for that reason.

We now turn to a discussion of the elements of the quantitative observational methodology for which we have been arguing.

OBSERVATIONAL METHODOLOGY: THE CODING AND ANALYSIS OF INTERACTIONS

Any scientific investigation that includes quantification, even when it is as primitive as counting events, must develop a classification or "coding" system. The coding system is always a simplification of nature: It considers some events salient and other events outside its domain; it rules that diverse events are in the same category and, hence, some information is inevitably lost; it also decides that some events are inherently distinct. Implicit in the design of a coding system are the choice of a meaningful unit and the psychometric requirements of reliable measurement. We discuss recent developments in the general theory of reliable measurement, particularly the following three: (1) Cohen's kappa (Hollenbeck, 1978); (2) generalizability theory (Cronbach, Gleser, Nanda, & Rajaratnam, 1972); and (3) the special requirements of sequential analysis of observational data.

Before we begin this discussion of modern reliability theory, we should acknowledge that the results of scientific investigations are limited by the codes we employ. Any coding system is arbitrary to some degree, due to the practical decisions that must be made in its design. One may arrive at different results with a different coding system that illuminates a different facet of the data. At best, we can hope for some convergence toward the truth by the convergence of several coding systems, each of which highlights a different issue of importance. This approach was taken in the research reported in this chapter.

It is also the case that a coding system can be modified as more is learned about the functions of the codes from research experience. These modifications encompass a range of theoretical issues that can be summarized in the two practical questions, "When should categories be lumped together?" and "When should categories be split?"

Lumping and Splitting

Obviously, the choice of coding categories is determined by the questions of interest to an investigator. In our case we are interested in friendship, and we therefore want to examine those aspects of conversation that have the most implications for friendship. In this regard, one approach to the practical questions of lumping and splitting is to deal with them in terms of the "social function" of codes. The information-theory perspective implies that if two codes have similar social consequences (in the sense of the sequential connection just discussed), then they can be lumped; if not, they can be split. This is by no means the only possible criterion for lumping and splitting. For example, we might decide to lump two relatively infrequent codes that are conceptually similar and often confused by coders, so that the combined code will have more acceptable levels of reliability than its subcodes. If there are several forms of what was originally chosen as one code, we can decide to split the code if we can find different forms that have different consequences, or if the use of the different forms varies systematically with another variable of importance. For example, Ervin-Tripp (1977) distinguished several forms of making demands: need statements ("I wanna", "I have to"); imperatives ("Gimme"); embedded imperatives ("Could you give me?"); permission directives ("Is it okay if I have?"); question directives (that leave the action implied); and hints.

In this chapter we report a study of alternative forms of several codes to assess whether these different linguistic forms have different frequencies as a function of age, levels of acquaintanceship, and whether the speaker is the guest or the host, and whether they have different social consequences. The decision to lump codes according to social function reveals our interest in social interaction per se. Such lumping may obscure other important differences, of course. For example, a code may subsume statements that imply different cognitive processes, although they affect the social interaction in the same way. An investigator who decides to split on the basis of cognitive process must be careful not to assume that the two codes function differently socially. Piaget's categorization of the utterances *"I'm leaving the tram white"/"I'm doing it yellow"* as collective monologue and the utterances *"I shall have one tomorrow"/"I shall have mine this afternoon"* as adapted information ignores the fact in both cases the children are comparing what they are doing or will be doing.

The Coding Unit

A wide variety of units have been used in previous research on conversation. The three most common units are the utterance, which is any speech separated by pauses; the phrase, which is separated by punctuation; and the sentence. Each unit has its shortcomings. People do not always express ideas without pausing, as in "I'm going to make mine [pause] green." It does not seem sensible to make this two units. People do not always complete their sentence, as in the following samples:

1. "Something's broken. Right here! This is my rocking chair. My daddy for! Wanh! Going underwater! Going Brah! Under there! Going bells!" [ringing bell]
2. "Oh, a lion, Gaah!"
3. "A...a elephant"/"No. Winnie the Pooh and Smokey the Bear."
4. "Toosh, tooksh, shooh"/"Goochen, goochen, goo."

The sentence unit would likely drive an English teacher beserk; verbs are often discarded, fragments repeated, and ideas intrude parenthetically during speech.

In research on the conversation of married couples, Gottman and his associates (e.g., Gottman, Markman, & Notarius, 1977) have used a unit called the "thought unit," which is one expressed idea or fragment. This unit can sometimes be one utterance or several, and it can be either a phrase or a sentence. In coding a sequence of thought units, Gottman employed Weiss, Hops, and Patterson's (1973) concept of a behavior unit, which is defined by shifts in code categories. This makes it possible to use a flexible unit depending on the "meaning" of a set of utterances defined by the coding system itself. From the point of view of the conversation, this is a data-reduction technique; for example, a series of utterances that give instructions could be considered one code even though they are interrupted by pauses (e.g., "First you put this on this (pause) then you snap this on (pause) when you're finished...") or two utterances that give reassurance could be considered as one sympathy code (e.g., "Don't cry [pause] your daddy'll be back soon."). The thought unit also makes it possible to code as a function of context; for example, if a child says "Here's mine [pause] here's yours," the thought unit involves assigning roles to both children, or sharing, whereas the utterances coded separately might be coded as two commands. On the other hand, this scheme has definite weaknesses. For example, the behavioral unit does not allow one to detect a sequence of similar codes within the same child. Clearly the choice of a unit is an important issue, and it is not independent of the design of the coding system.

Sequences and the Coding Unit.   In coding any speech unit, it is necessary to deal with the fact that it is embedded in a particular context. Nonetheless, there are two broad approaches to context; one is empirical and the other is logical. Suppose we have a code called "activity talk," denoted AT, which is a child's narration of his play (e.g., "I'm coloring mine green"). If we have observed a sequence "I'm coloring mine green"/"I'm coloring mine yellow," in the empirical approach we code this as AT/AT, symbolizing activity talk by both children. An obtained sequence could then be interpreted as a comparison sequence. In the logical approach, the second AT is not regarded as activity talk at all, but comparison. Either approach is defensible, but notice that the logical approach is faced with the problem of a *sliding unit;* no code can be defined except by its function in a context. The empirical approach derives the various functions of a code by the sequences obtained instead of making this judgment during the coding process. The functions of a code arise from the structure in the empirical approach, in the sense that structure is defined by elements that are connected predictably in a sequence analysis.

Reliability. Three issues of interobserver reliability must be addressed. The first of these is the inadequacy of ratios of agreement to agreement-plus-disagreement, or percentage agreement. Hartmann (1977) pointed out that there are several serious problems with this measure: It has no measurement scale; it is dependent on marginal probabilities in the summary table between two observers; it does not provide any index of chance levels of agreement; it provides no information about sources of measurement error; it is dependent on the size of the interval used to define coding blocks; and, finally, it is a statistic with no metric properties or known distribution statistics. An alternative statistic is Cohen's kappa, which does control for agreement by chance alone and the distributional properties of which are well known (see Hollenbeck, 1978).

A second issue is that the index of interobserver agreement used should depend on the generalizability claim the investigator makes for the coding system. The contribution of the theory of generalizability of Cronbach et al. (1972) is that there is no one single index of reliability; each index of reliability involves some universe to which an investigator wishes to generalize, such as occasions of measurement or a set of coders. The index is a function of the variance accounted for by a relevant experimental variable and the irrelevant variable across which the experimenter wishes to generalize. It is thus necessary for the investigator to design and conduct an *appropriate* generalizability study for each coding system used. The assessment of reliability thus is not an automatic calculation of some universally agreed-upon statistic.

A third issue is that the choice of an index of reliability depends on the dependent variables in the investigation. For example, if the dependent variables are percentages of a set of codes across a set of transcripts, simple correlations between two observers are adequate. These correlations should be computed on percentages and not frequencies. However, this statistic is not adequate if one is describing *sequences* within transcripts. Observer 1 may have recorded Code A 50 times and Observer 2 may also have recorded Code A 50 times in the same transcript, but they may never have agreed on when it occurred within a transcript. The invocation is that the criterion selected for reliability assessments must fit the variables under study. Sequential analysis requires agreement to be tied to the smallest specific coding unit and not to be tallied over blocks of coding units (see also Johnson & Bolstad, 1973).

The Mathematics of Sequential Analysis. We now turn to a brief conceptual review of sequential analysis. For elaboration, the reader is referred to Attneave (1959), Bakeman and Dabbs (1976), Gottman and Bakeman (1979), Gottman and Notarius (1978), Gottman (1979), and Sackett (1977). Sequential analysis had its origin in a classic paper by Shannon and Weaver (1949) on information theory. Suppose we begin with a corpus of codes, such as BWBBWWBWBWWWW...For example, they may be a person's attempt to stimulate random selections of successive black or white balls that fill an infinite urn (Attneave, 1959). We want to discover whether the sequence is random, or whether there is some guessing pattern.

To detect pattern we proceed in a series of steps. First, are the codes equally likely, or is there an asymmetry in their relative frequencies? Second, is there a *digram structure;* that is, by knowing that one code just occurred, do we gain any ability to predict the occurrence of the subsequent code? In English, for example, not all letters occur with equal frequency; for example, the letter A occurs more frequently than the letter Z. Also, there is a digram structure; for example, the letter U is more likely to follow the letter Q than is the letter P.

Next we ask if there is a trigram structure to the series of codes. Note that in each case we search for asymmetry in some frequency; at first we search for asymmetry in the frequencies of B and W; next we search for asymmetry in the frequencies of the pairs BB, BW, WB, WW. But note also that we must detect asymmetry at each step that provides new information. For example, if there were many more BB and WW pairs, this would create an asymmetry in the triples we select. But we are interested in trigram structure that is independent of, or provides new information over and above, what we already know from our knowledge about the digram structure. Shannon and Weaver's information statistic provides this information, in addition to having other useful mathematical properties.

Note that our example consisted of only two codes, B and W. If we have a complex coding system with 50 codes, our diagram matrix would have 50 × 50, or 2,500 cells. Our trigram matrix would have 125,000 cells. To have confidence that our corpus is large enough so that our trigram frequencies in each cell are representative, we might require twelve million observations. Also, much of our asymmetry would be trivial to us because some sets of code combinations might logically never follow. For example, in studying monkeys, it would not be too interesting to know that a mother's running hardly ever follows feeding her infant.

An alternative approach is to consider each code as a binary time series. A *time series* is a set of observations that are ordered along some dimension, usually called "time"; a binary series assumes one of two values, such as zero or one. The codes BWBBWW would be represented as two time series, one for B, which is 101100, and one for W, which is 010011. Note that in this presentation both B and W can occur at the same time by both being equal to one. Gottman (1979b) showed that the mathematics of time series analysis (see, for example, Box & Jenkins, 1970; Glass, Willson, & Gottman, 1975; Gottman & Glass, 1978) applied to the problem of attempting to predict one time series from the past of the other time series (with varying lags) can be well approximated by the z-score statistic proposed by Sackett (1977). Sackett's suggestion was to use the z-score approximation of the normal distribution to the binomial distribution in comparing conditional to unconditional probabilites. The z-score is

$$z = (X\text{-}NP)/(NPQ)^{1/2}$$

where X is the observed joint frequency of the two codes, NP is the predicted (unconditional) frequency assuming independence of the two codes, and NPQ is the variance of the difference between predicted and observed frequencies (where $Q = 1\text{-}P$). If the z-score is an adequate approximation to the normal distribution, which it is if N is large enough (greater than 25) and NPQ is at least 9 (Siegel, 1956), then if $z > 1.96$, the difference between conditional and unconditional probabilities can be considered significant at $p < .05$. Sackett suggested that the z-score can be calculated as a function of lags within one series, called "autolags," or as a function of lags scross two series, called "crosslags."

Under some stationarity assumptions, the two methods are identical, but the extent to which these assumptions are met in experience and the consequences of their violation have yet to be explored. The advantages of Sackett's method are many. Probably the most important is that investigators are usually not interested in overall questions such as "Is there a digram structure in my data?" They are more typically concerned with the predictability between specific codes as a function of lag, because evidence of a particular sequential connection will provide a measure of a construct of interest (such as reciprocity).

An important practical problem arises in applying this method to the study of dyadic social interaction. Ideally, each dyad should be studied separately, and analysis of variance technique applied to some scaled statistic, such as the z-score, to compare groups on some measure of sequential connection. However, there usually is not enough data for each dyad to make this a realistic possibility. This is true because, all too often, the most interesting codes are not those of highest frequency. Our alternative has been to pool data across dyads within groups. This method should be used conservatively, Gottman (1979a), in a series of investigations of marital interaction, recommended replication of results; and in the marital research in which the approach was used, results replicated remarkably well across studies. To combine two data streams, use a series of dummy codes longer than the maximum lag in the analysis, then discard all instances of the dummy code and transitions to and from dummy codes for the computations. This computational device avoids the problem of joining the tail and head of two independent data streams. It does not avoid potential problems of nonstationarity. To compare sequential connections between groups throughout the present research, we utilize the fact that for large N (instances of the criterion code) and for $NPQ > 9$ (P = conditional probability, $Q = 1-P$), the z-score is nearly normally distributed with zero mean and unit variance. We are thus in the position of comparing scores that are in normal standard deviation units. The following decision rule will be employed: *If z-scores between groups are at least 1.96 units (e.g., 1.96 deviations) apart, we will refer to this as a significant difference between groups; if z-scores between groups are between 1.00 and 1.96 units apart, we will refer to this as a marginally significant difference between groups.*

DESCRIPTION OF THE PROJECT

In this chapter we will report the results of the first study in a series of investigations on the development of children's friendship and on how children become acquainted with strangers. Each study in the series involved collecting audiotape-recording of two children, transcribing these tapes, and coding them using both the transcripts and the tapes.

The first study involved 13 host children ranging in age from 2:11 to 6:1 (mean age 4:8.2, s.d. = 10.7 months) with their best friends or with a stranger, each within a year of the host in age. The mean difference in age between friends was 8 months; the difference was between the strangers, 7 months. Of the 26 dyads studied, 13 were female-female pairs, nine were female-male pairs, and four were male-male pairs. All children were tape-recorded in the home of the host child, playing with a stranger or with a child that the parents said was the child's best friend. Home recording was chosen on the basis of a pilot comparison of the interaction of one dyad in the home and in the Psychology Department playroom. In the playroom, the children were initially far more likely to ignore one another, to fight over territory and new toys, and to avoid fantasy play than they were in the home, although these differences declined considerably after two 2-hour visits to the playroom.

The second study was an 8-month longitudinal study of one 4-year-old best friend dyad; 11 tapes were obtained during this period. Although we will refer to this study, we will not systematically present the results here. Each dyad was audiotaped, using a casette tape recorder and a 90-min cassette. The parents of the host subject did the recording and made all arrangements for the other children to visit. Parents were asked to arrange that other children not be present and to leave the children alone as much as possible. Sections of the transcripts taken with mothers present were not coded. The recorder was placed where it was visible to the children; and the parents were asked to habituate their child before the first play session to the presence of the recorder. The children played in the room where the host usually played with friends in that household, and they had available to them whatever toys were normally present.

Tapes were transcribed by at least two transcribers; the second transcriber checked and corrected the transcripts. The approximately 56 hrs of tape took about 900 hrs to transcribe and approximately 2800 hrs to code with all three systems that we present in this chapter.

SIX SOCIAL PROCESSES

The research reported in this chapter is designed to explore the role of six related social processes in children's friendship. These processes have been discussed in disparate areas of social and developmental psychology, but they have rarely been described in the same exploratory study. Taken together, these processes may have considerable power in describing the children's interaction. In the present investigation they are studied as a function of age, acquaintanceship of the children, and the role of the child (guest or host). The processes are: (1) the connectedness of the interaction; (2) the clarity of the communication; (3) social comparison; (4) control; (5) conflict and its resolution; and (6) fantasy. Each process, the methods used to investigate each process, and results are discussed in this chapter.

Connectedness

We have reviewed research on the issue of connectedness in children's speech and Piaget's hypothesis that young children's speech is egocentric, characterized by collective monologue. To study the role of connectedness in children's friendship, we designed a system of four codes: (1) collective monologue; (2) activity-based talk; (3) fantasy; and (4) conversation. Each line of the transcript was numbered; a line represented a turn in talking.

Coders were trained with a coding manual and sample transcripts. They were instructed to describe the sequence of activities and topics in children's interaction by dividing the transcript into blocks of unbroken talk that was unified by its content. They used brief notes to summarize the themes of each block of transcript. The basic division made in the code manual was between connected and unconnected speech. The manual stated that "Speech is unconnected when the children are talking independently on separate tracks and not responding to one another. This is called collective monologue." The four codes are defined as follows:

1. *Collective monologue (CM):* A block of collective monologue is an unbroken stretch during which the children are talking about different things, and during which statements are neither responses to previous statements by the other, nor are they responded to. A CM block may be only one line long. Note that to be connected to a previous utterance by the other child, only part of a unified sequence of talk need relate. Thus, for example, in the following *all* of B would be connected: A: "This one is too hard."/ B: "Well here's an easy one we can do. You do this part and I'll do her clothes. I'm gonna make them pink. Pink's my favorite color."

2. *Activity-based talk (AT):* This kind of block may include argument, negotiation, discussion, comparison, explanation, and/or commentary related to the children's present activities or surroundings. This code does not apply to discussions of abstract or general topics, past or future events, or things and people who are absent, but has its focus on the concrete and immediate. It does not include fantasy play.

3. *Fantasy:* This consists of negotiations, directions, narrative, and role-playing related to the development of a fantasy or role-play. Some examples are: playing house; pretending to be robots and constructing a sequence in which they replace each other's batteries; talking for a skeleton and a dinosaur (little figures) who are holding a conversation; pretending to be babies; pretending that "Mr. Nobody" has caused something to happen; enacting a sequence in which the children are playing themselves "Let's play Eric and Naomi and I come over to visit and ring your doorbell and you answer the door"; playing that some dolls (given roles) are taking a boat trip.

4. *Conversation:* This is coded for conversations whose focus is on events, things, or people outside of the present situation or on abstract or general concerns. Conversations that focus on something (activity, plan, person, or thing) in the present situation are coded activity-based talk (AT).

Coders were blind to the ages or degree of acquaintanceship of the children.

Results From First Coding System.   The proportion of each of the four codes was calculated for each transcript. For each transcript, a second coder independently coded eight pages of transcript, and the correlations between the two coders' proportions for the sample was computed. The reliability correlations were: collective monologue, .62; activity talk, .92; fantasy, .94; and conversation, .81. All correlations were significantly different from zero,

TABLE 6.1
Mean Portions of Speech Types

	Mean Portions				
	Acquaintanceship		Age		
Variable	Friend	Stranger	Young	Old	Grand Mean
Collective monologue	.036	.093	.074	.050	.065
Activity-based talk	.610	.657	.554	.762	.634
Fantasy	.296	.127	.294	.164	.231
Conversation	.056	.086	.077	.062	.070

with the most frequent code confusions occurring between collective monologue and activity talk.

Tapes were divided into two groups, those for which the host was under 5:0 (16 tapes) and those for which the host was 5:0 or older (10 tapes). Data were analyzed using four univariate 2 × 2 repeated measures analyses of variance, with acquaintanceship (friend or stranger) as the repeated-measure factor, age as the between-subject factor, and the four codes as dependent variables. Table 6.1 shows a summary of these results.[1] The central result, contrary to Piaget's hypothesis, is that there is not a significant developmental effect in the collective monologue variable, $F(1, 11) = 2.03$, $p > .05$. Furthermore, only 6.5% of the children's speech was coded as collective monologue. To examine the possibility that the division of the groups at the host's age of 5:0 years was arbitrary and produced a weak test of the developmental hypothesis, correlations were computed between the host's age and the proportion of collective monologue separately for friends and strangers. For friends, the correlation with age was –.21, and for strangers it was .09. Neither correlation was significant.

The results do show that collective monologue is much more likely among strangers (9.3%) than among friends (3.6%), $F(1, 11) = 8.01$, $p < .05$. Also, fantasy was much more likely for friends (29.6%) than for strangers (12.7%), $F(1,11) = 7.81$, $p < .05$. It is important that there were no significant interaction effects between age and acquaintanceship, all $Fs < 1.00$. The fact that fantasy play is much more characteristic of close relationships regardless of age will be further investigated by sequential analyses of the same data with a more detailed coding system.

Contrary to Piaget's characterization of the conversations of young children, activity talk increases with age, $F(1, 11) = 5.58$, $p < .05$. Fantasy

---

[1]All results in this chapter remain unchanged when analyzed by the arcsine $\sqrt{x}$ transformation that is customary for proportional data.

decreases with age, although the F-ratio is only marginally significant $F(1, 11) = 3.62, p < .10$. Older children may be much more likely to continue with activities than to engage in fantasy play. Conversation does not increase with age, $F < 1.00$, or as a function of acquaintanceship, $F(1, 11) = 1.71, p > .10$.

The summary of these children's conversations that is provided by this coding system adds weight against a view of young children as egocentric. It also suggests the importance of controlling the degree of acquaintanceship of the children in developmental investigations. However, in terms of its ability to describe the conversations of children, these results are, at best, provocative. Why are younger children less likely to engage in activity talk than older children? Why is fantasy more likely among friends than strangers, and why does it seem to decline with age? To answer these questions, we designed other coding systems.

Second Coding System. The coding system described first is inadequate with respect to both describing the children's interaction and investigating the remaining five social processes mentioned earlier in this section. A second coding system was designed that was sufficiently detailed for the application of sequential analytic techniques, and a coding manual and a manual for training coders have been prepared. This subsection of the chapter will summarize the 16 codes, the four double codes, and present generalizability study results separately for each coding category. Categories were created to describe the children's conversation exhaustively as well as to study the social processes we thought relevant to friendship. Abbreviated definitions of these categories follow. In our work extensive manuals are necessary to define the codes. These include numerous examples that make fine distinctions.

1. *Coding units.* The coder divides the transcript into thought units as he or she codes with slash marks as follows:
   That's Pooh/ Give him to me/
   A study to assess the reliability between two people of the slash marks produced nearly perfect agreement on the location of the slash marks. Coding units are defined by a code transition, so that coding and unitizing are not independent.
2. *Double codes.* There are four double codes that can co-occur and occur with the other codes. They are:
   a. *F/: Fantasy* is coded whenever a child is speaking in role within a framework of a fantasy, for example, "Up, up, and away!" Note that this fantasy code is more restricted than its use in the first coding system.
   b. *Q/: Question* is coded whenever a statement is made to sound like a question, for example, "Is that mine?"

c. *J/: Joke* is coded whenever an utterance is accompanied by laughter, silliness, or joking. Examples include jokes, bathroom humor, silliness, giggling, laughter, and exuberance.

d. *S/: Squabble* is coded for angry, annoyed, disgusted, or other squabbling, which includes insults, yelling, whining, sarcasm, verbal or physical aggression, threats, retaliation, or tattling.

3. *Content codes.* There are sixteen codes:

a. *DE: Demand* is coded whenever the speaker demands attention or a response (e.g., "Look at me!").

b. *ME: Me* is coded whenever the speaker is talking about himself or herself, referring to the speaker's activities, plans, accomplishments, attributes, possessions, or abilities (e.g., "I'm making mine orange").

c. *FE: Feelings* is coded for statements that have to do with the speaker's wants, feelings, opinions, likes, dislikes, and needs (e.g., "I gotta go potty"; "I wanna play house"; "I have to close this").

d. *MR: Mindreading* is coded when a feeling, motive, attitude, personality trait, experience, or opinion is attributed to the other person (e.g., "You hate Jason").

e. *IF: Infers feeling* is coded for an attribution of feeling or opinion that has come out of the situation; in other words, the attribution is a reasonable inference for the circumstances (e.g., one child pretends to eat ice cream and says "Ah" and the other child says "That's good, isn't it?" This last statement would be coded IF.).

f. *SY: Sympathy and comfort* is coded when there is an attempt to console, protect, defend, or ease distress (e.g., "Don't worry, we'll be back soon").

g. *OF: Offers* is coded when help, thoughtfulness, or generosity is offered (e.g., "Here, I'll fix it" or "I made this for you").

h. *AH: Asks Help* is coded when a speaker requests help or assistance (e.g., "Will you tie my shoes?").

i. *YM: You and Me* is coded when the speaker is working for closeness or unity between himself and the other child by emphasizing cooperation, common interest, common experience, concerted action, or shared experiences from which others are shut out (e.g., "Let's play pirates" or "I'm five too").

j. *RU: Rule* is coded when a rule or principle with general usefulness for behaving is invoked or created (e.g., "We can take turns").

k. *IN: Information Exchange* is coded whenever simple information is asked for or given (e.g., "My mommy's getting a new baby sitter"). Note that for IN to follow a QIN, it must always be relevant to the question, or it is coded NCM.

l. *IN*: Information About Other* is coded if the information is a narration of other persons's activity (e.g., "You're painting it blue").

m. *CM: Clarifies Message* is coded if the speaker clarifies a statement, restates it with some alteration, or gives an explanation or reason (e.g., "The one up there./ The gray one with red on it./ " The last statement would be coded CM.).

n. *NCM: Failure to Clarify Message* is coded when the speaker fails to adjust a message in response to the other's confusion (e.g., in the sequence "Where's your dumb straw?" "What's a dumb straw?" "*Your* dumb straw" the last statement would be coded NCM.).

o. *AG: Agreement* is coded for statements having to do with agreement, compliance, or pleasure with the other, what he does, has, or wants (e.g., "Yeah that's right").

p. *DG: Disagreement* is coded for noncooperation or disapproval directed toward the other child, the other's statements, possessions, or behavior (e.g., "I am not!").

There is a great need for empirically-based data reduction since logically the number of codes possible is $2 \times 2 \times 2 \times 2 \times 16 = 256$, or 512 codes for both children. For the simplest sequential analysis this would produce a 512×512 matrix or 262, 144 conditional probabilities at each lag. Obviously, the task of data analysis would be considerably reduced if some code combinations did not co-occur; thus, our first task was to create a reduced set of codes based on frequencies of occurrence and co-occurrence. On the basis of the first 20 tapes we keypunched, we calculated the frequency of occurrence and co-occurrence of the double codes. Table 6.2 suggests that, except for the question double code, the double codes are relatively independent. We decided to create four additional content codes with the question double code: Question for information (QIN) ("What time is it?"), Question for clarification of message (QCM) ("What's a dumb straw?"), Question for agreement (QAG) ("The dolly's going to sleep, right?"; "Right?" is a QAG), and Question about feelings (QFE) ("What do you want to do?"). The QAG is the tag question. For this analysis, the other three double codes were coded as Squabble (S), Joke (J), and Fantasy (F), regardless of which content code they occurred with. Also, a hierarchy was established so that in the rare co-occurrence of double codes, Squabble took precedence over Jokes, which took precedence over Fantasy. This was a decision based on our impressions of how the double codes functioned in the rare instances of their co-occurrence. Also, because mindreading (MR) and infers feeling (IF) occurred so infrequently, and because they had similar consequences, they were lumped together into a code called Feelings Inferred (FI).

TABLE 6.2
Co-occurrence of Double Codes for Host Child for
Twenty Tapes (Frequencies are Nearly Identical for
Guest Child).

Double Code(s)	Frequency
None	4,014
Squabbles (S)	92
Jokes (J)	215
JS	0
Question (Q)	1,117
QS	3
QJ	16
JQS	0
Fantasy (F)	694
FS	5
FJ	12
JFS	0
FQ	129
FQS	0
FQJ	1
FQJS	0

A generalizability study, addressing the issues raised by Cronbach et al. (1972) was conducted for this system. Reliability in the context of the present investigation involves the claim that, of the total variance occurrences of a particular code across codes and subject, most of the variance is accounted for by subject variance and not coder variance or coder-by-subject interaction (see also Wiggins, 1973, Chapter 7). This approach to reliability assessment was first applied to observational data by Jones, Reid, and Patterson (1975). They calculated total frequencies of a particular code for observer and independent reliability checker over subjects. The design is within-subjects analysis of variance, repeated over coders. However, this analysis is appropriate only if the data are not analyzed sequentially, because high reliability can be obtained in the analysis if both coders observe a similar number of a particular code, regardless of where in a transcript these occurrences are observed. Observers may thus not agree at all on specific utterances and this analysis will yield a high coefficient of generalizability.

A more stringent procedure that is appropriate for sequential analysis is to tie agreement to specific utterances. A matrix of agreements and disagreements can be tallied for the two coders by proceeding through the transcript unit by unit. Suppose that there are three codes, A, B, and C, and the matrix for a particular transcript is as displayed in Table 6.3. Diagonal entries represent agreement on particular utterances. For Code A, we can calculate two numbers, the total number of diagonal entries (five in this case)

TABLE 6.3
Matrix for Reliability Assessment for Sequential Analysis
for One Particular Transcript

		Coder 2		
		A	*B*	*C*
	A	+++	//	/
Coder 1	B	/	+++ /	/
	C		/	+++ /

and the total number of diagonal plus off-diagonal entries. These two numbers form the entries in the repeated-measures design illustrated in Table 6.4. Perfect agreement is obtained if all the 0_i are zero, and this agreement represents agreement tied to specific units of transcript. In the perfect agreement case, total variance is entirely accounted for by variance across subjects as in the Jones et al. (1975) analysis, but agreement is localized at particular utterances. There are three relevant generalizability claims: (1) coders agree with the reliability checker; (2) agreement is independent of the length of the transcript segment sampled; (3) high reliabilities are obtained for each coding (and double coding) category. Table 6.5 is a summary of the results of the generalizability study. Eight transcripts were checked for two pages, and nine other transcripts were checked for four pages. Generalizability coefficients in Table 6.5 are remarkably high for every code with the possible exception of the Infers Feeling code, for the two page sample, in which only one occurrence was detected by only one observer.

The coding system behaves the way a good measuring instrument should; reliabilities generally increase with segment length of the transcript sampled; and reliabilities are high for each code, regardless of coder. This coding system therefore has potential for use in detailed sequential analysis of coding categories, without excessively lumping coding categories to obtain acceptable levels of reliability.

TABLE 6.4
Method of Reliability Assessment for Sequential Analysis
Using Generalizability Theory for One Code.

Transcript #	Diagonal	Diag. + off-Diagonal
1	d_1	$d_1 + o_1$
2	d_2	$d_2 + o_2$
N	d_N	$d_n + o_N$

TABLE 6.5
Coefficients of Generalizability as a Function of Segment Length Sampled by the
Reliability Checker

Code	Two Pages	Frequency of code	Four Pages	Frequency of code
Demand	.989	111	.968	370
Me	.919	203	.973	334
Feeling	.852	84	.958	194
Mindreading	1.000	2	.786	3
Infers Feeling	.016	1	1.000	2
Sympathy	1.000	2	.956	11
Offers	1.000	4	.827	31
Asks Help	1.000	2	1.000	12
You and Me	.892	71	.966	62
Rule	1.000	2	.997	34
Information	.860	319	.987	842
Information about Other	—	0	.792	7
Clarifies Message	.969	96	.949	181
Fails to Clarify Message	.793	21	.970	63
Agrees	.982	109	.978	230
Disagrees	.878	39	.946	109
Double Codes				
Fantasy	.981	35	.999	374
Question	.997	183	.999	514
Jokes	.975	26	.992	38
Squabbles*	1.000	2	.621	15

*Over four generalizability studies, alpha for squabbles averaged .905.

An additional generalizability study that is not reported here showed that there was no reliability decay over time, using the procedure of a reliability checker coding a sample of every tape and discussing discrepancies and code confusions (using a table such as Table 6.3) with each coder. Coders also took turns as reliability checker to avoid problems of reliability drift. Cohen's kappas were always significantly above chance levels of agreement.

Communication Clarity

The clarity of communication in social interaction has been considered important in many fields. For example, a comprehensive review by Jacob (1975) concluded that the clarity of communication was the most consistent discriminator between interaction in normal families and families with a schizophrenic member. In our data, lowest interobserver correlations in the first coding system were obtained for the collective monologue code. In the normal stream of conversation, it was often difficult for observers to agree on whether the speech was or was not connected. Research on referential communication in children, that is, a speaker's ability to specify to a listener to what it is that he is referring to, has faced a similar problem. Asher (1978) wrote:

> One way that referential communication might be studied would be to observe people in their everyday environment as they go about the task of describing, explaining, giving directions, and so on. A serious obstacle to this sort of method is the fact that it is not usually possible to determine from observation exactly what a speaker is intending to communicate [p. 1].

In fact, research on referential communication in children has largely abandoned naturalistic observation in favor of experimental tasks that make it possible to program a speaker's intent and to assess the listener's reception of the message. The decision may have been made at great cost, becuase it is not at all clear to what extent performance on these laboratory tasks can be generalized to social interaction (see Asher, 1978). Asher (1978) pointed out that an advantage of structured laboratory tasks is that they make it possible to examine component processes in referential communication, but he added: "Still, it could be that highly unfamiliar laboratory tasks are creating an exaggerated picture of childhood incompetence [msp. 42]."

Asher argued that a different picture of children's competence in referential communication might arise from a study of their everyday transactions. Asher suggested that in adult-child interactions, adults may compensate for child's lack of clarity by modifying their messages, and he added that children often use pointing to specify a referrent (Wellman & Lempers, 1977). In peer interaction, it would be valuable to study what we are calling communication clarity in situ.

We propose that a solution to the problem of using observational methods is to study specific sequences in which a speaker's intent is known, and we suggest that these sequences are provided in a speaker's request for clarification or information from the listener. Garvey (1977) brought these speech events to our attention in her suggestion that the "contingent query" is a basic "modular component of discourse" [p. 64]. She was not interested in the same issue we are addressing, but in the use of the contingent query in the regulation of speech. We propose that an alternative to using laboratory tasks to assess the extent to which children communicate clearly, and how this varies with age and other contextual variables, is to perform sequential analyses of children's response to requests for information and clarification from their peers.

The argument is, that we will know that children fail to communicate clearly to the extent that we can detect predictable sequences between a request for clarification by one child and a failure to clarify by the other child

(QCM → NCM, in our notation), and to the extent that a request for information by one child is not followed by relevant information by the other child (QIN → NCM).

Unfortunately, when we examine the data, we discover that there is a problem with the proposed solution—namely, that we must detect a relatively infrequent event. Recall that sequential analysis requires the comparison of conditional to unconditional probabilities such as is provided by z-scores (Bakeman, 1978; Gottman, 1979a,b; Sackett, 1977), and for the z-score to be a valid approximation to the normal distribution a sufficient number of occurrences of these questions must be obtained. An examination of the relative frequencies of questions for information and questions for clarification show that, across age and acquaintanceship, guests are much more likely to ask questions than hosts. Therefore, we will present the sequential analyses only for questions asked by guests.[2]

Table 6.6 presents the z-scores and the conditional probabilities that requests for information and requests for clarification will not be responded to adequately. Examine the request-for-information column. We observe the surprising result that the communication of friends differs across age in the following way: Older hosts are *more* likely to display a communicative failure (12.5%) than younger hosts (7.2%). Among strangers, the pattern is reversed for information requests: Older hosts are *less* likely to display a communicative failure (11.7%) than younger hosts (13.8%). These last two conditional probabilities may not be reliably different; however, their z-score are more than 1.96 units apart (which was our decision rule for comparing groups). This is an example of the importance of replication in connection with conclusions from sequential analyses (see our section in this chapter on the limitations of the work presented here).

Examine the request for clarification column in Table 6.6. In response to requests for clarification by the guest, once again we observe that among both friends and strangers older children are more likely to display a communicative failure than younger children.

In general, younger children are more responsive to their friends and less responsive to strangers than older children. One rival hypothesis about developmental effects we obtained on the failure to clarify messages (the NCM code) is that for older friends what *adult* coders independently code as an NCM is really quite clear to the children. We can eliminate this hypothesis by employing lag sequential anaysis on the NCM code. If a common third element of a QCM → NCM chain is another question, independent of age, then the NCM is also confusing for the child, who must ask another question. This was indeed the case. For example, for a chain initiated by the host, for

---

[2]With more subjects or longer speech samples, this limitation would not be necessary.

TABLE 6.6
Failures to Respond Adequately to the Guest's
Request for Information or Clarification (z-scores
Given; Conditional Probabilities in Parentheses)

Group	Request for Information	Request for Clarification
Friends		
Young	14.55 (.072)	7.98 (.121)
Old	19.39 (.125)	13.20 (.333)
Strangers		
Young	17.20 (.138)	14.01 (.500)
Old	15.03 (.117)	26.50 (.514)

young friends the most likely question following a QCM → NCM chain was a question for information QIN ($p = .122$, $= 2.26$); for older friends the most likely question was a question about feelings, QFE ($p = .100$, $z = 6.22$).

If these developmental results about the interaction of friends were *reversed,* we would probably be tempted to conclude glibly that we had found further evidence that communicative competence improves with age. It is interesting that we are reluctant to conclude that anything positive declines with age. Nonetheless, we must admit that these data fly in the face of our intuitions about children's communicative competence. It is probably the case that these results do not represent a complete picture of social development, of course. Is it possible that there is something about friendship in young children that makes communication clarity vital? We are reminded of the result Piaget overlooked in his own data, that young children are extremely concerned about psychological explanations of people's behavior. Both results may be tapping a process that is important to children at a particular stage of social development.

Social Comparison

The formation of a friendship may in part be based on two children learning, as they converse, that they are similar. Conversely, one possible function of friendship is that it provides an opportunity for social comparison. Hence, it is reasonable that social comparison is likely to play a role in the interaction of friends and in the acquaintanceship process.

In the area of mate selection, it can be argued that stable, close relationships are formed by a sequential filtering process. There is evidence to suggest that dating couples who are more similar on a variety of dimensions are more likely to marry than those that are less similar (see, for example, Huston & Levinger, 1978). On the other hand, Levinger and his colleagues found some evidence that over a long period of time, "pairs with high value consensus were less likely to progress than those with low consensus [Huston & Levinger, 1978, p. 141]."

Perhaps some dissimilarity in the context of a previously established major similarity is attractive as relationships continue. In terms of social interaction and the ontogeny of relationships, this implies that it is first important to establish common ground before defining differences and "separate territory," which suggests some kind of sequential filter of similarity → dissimilarity (see also Fromkin, 1972). In the context of conversation, this suggests that both the exploration of common ground and the expression of differences could in some way be important processes in friendship and acquaintanceship.

We propose that three sequences are indicative of different social comparison activities in conversation. These are *Me → You-and-Me* (ME → YM) sequences such as "I'm doing mine green"/"Me too"; *Me → Me* sequences such as "I'm doing mine green"/"I'm doing mine yellow"; and *Questions about Feelings* (QFE → FE) such as "Do you like coffee?"/"I hate it." The ME → YM sequence is an expression of building common ground, or *solidarity* social comparison. The ME → ME sequence is an expression of *contrast* or an expression of differences. The QFE → FE sequence is an *exploration* of opinion of feeling. As opposed to the ME → ME sequence, the question about feelings (QFE) does not commit the speaker. Table 6.7 presents the z-scores and conditional probabilities.

Young friends engage in all three activities, with the guest more responsive to the host than vice versa. Older friends do not predictably (i.e., with z-scores > 1.96) engage in much social comparison activity, but of all three activities, older friends are most likely to engage in contrast activity. With strangers, both young and old children engage primarily in contrast activities, but a marginal result is that older children do more exploration than younger children. Thus, exploration of feelings and establishment of solidarity or common ground was more characteristic of younger than older friends in our sample. Older friends did not characteristically engage in our three types of social comparison (all z-scores for older friends were less than 1.96); but when they did, they were most likely to engage in social contrast. Young friendship may thus be similar to the first stage of the sequential-filtering process we mentioned earlier; that is, young friends may emphasize establishing common ground, or a "me too" type of social comparison. Older friends seem less involved with social comparison; they most characteristically emphasized individuation or contrast, much as in the second stage of the sequential filter process.

However, these patterns were less pronounced in interactions between strangers. Young children engage in all three kinds of social comparison with friends, but engage only in contrast activities with strangers. Perhaps younger children are less skillful or mor shy with strangers than older children.

TABLE 6.7
Sequence Indicative of Three Different Social Comparison Activities

Process Initiated By		Solidarity Me → You and Me	Contrast Me → Me	Exploration Question Feeling → Feeling
Friends				
Young	Host	3.47 (.048)	2.52 (.099)	5.02 (.147)
	Guest	1.49 (.033)	3.35 (.111)	-.26 (.020)
Old	Host	-1.45 (.015)	1.39 (.099)	.46 (.040)
	Guest	.07 (.033)	1.67 (.117)	.09 (.030)
Strangers				
Young	Host	1.00 (.020)	2.50 (.100)	1.12 (.048)
	Guest	.03 (.020)	3.45 (.163)	.00 (.000)
Old	Host	.63 (.020)	3.29 (.111)	1.38 (.069)
	Guest	-.44 (.024)	2.95 (.127)	1.31 (.065)

Control

An important aspect of social interaction is mutual influence, or control. The forms that people use to influence others in conversation are probably the most widely studied aspect of sociolinguistics (for example, see Ervin-Tripp, 1977). We explore the effectiveness of four alternative forms of influence attempts: (1) imperatives or demands, DE (i.e., "Gimme that!"); (2) expressions of needs, wants and feelings, FE (i.e., "I need that"); (3) expression of a plan that involves both, YM (i.e., "Let's take a car ride"); and, (4) a polite suggestion QFE (i.e., "Do you wanna play Superman and Wonder Woman?"). The effectiveness of each form of exercising control can be assessed empirically by the likelihood of each form in eliciting subsequent compliance or agreement (AG) from the other child. The four forms differ in the following ways: Imperatives ("Gimme") and the expression of needs or desires ("I wanna") are less polite forms than a plan for both and a polite suggestion. They also involve statements only about "I" ("I want," "I need," or "Give me") rather than statements about "We" or questions about "You" ("Let's" and "Do you wanna?"). Furthermore, imperatives and the expression of needs differ in the amount of inference necessary by the listener. The statement of need may not contain a clear requirement for a specific action or compliance (i.e., "I need to cut this" as opposed to "Gimme those scissors"). (See also Ervin-Tripp, 1977.)

In our sample, young friends were more likely to respond to a wide range of control attempts than older friends, who were somewhat less responsive to imperatives and the expression of needs. Among strangers, however, older children were more likely than younger children to respond to a variety of control attempts, particularly imperative and expressed needs. Older strangers are much like younger friends in the pattern of their compliance.

These results for friends are consistent with the "climate of agreement" finding among young friends that emerged from our analysis of social comparison activity. Once again, young children are more agreeable to their friends than they are to strangers, but older children seemed to have learned the importance of being agreeable to strangers. Older children behave in a manner that is reminiscent of the consistent finding that married adults are much more polite and agreeable in interaction with strangers than with their spouses (Birchler, Weiss, & Vincent, 1975; Ryder, 1968; Winter, Ferreira, & Bowers, 1973). Younger children do demand the use of polite *forms* from strangers; this is particularly true of younger guests, who will virtually fail to respond to any other control attempt from their unfamiliar hosts. But clearly younger children were less agreeable to a wide range of control attempts from strangers than they were to those same attempts by their friends.

In analyzing the relative effectiveness of specific control attempts across age and levels of acquaintanceship, polite suggestions stated as questions

TABLE 6.8
The Effectiveness of Four Alternative Forms of Control in Eliciting Agreement

Control Attempt Initiated By		Imperatives ("Gimme") (DE)	Express Needs ("I wanna") FE	Plan for Both ("Let's") (YM)	Polite Suggestion ("Do you wanna?") (QFE)
Friends					
Young	Host	4.06 (.099)	3.02 (.104)	2.14 (.093)	5.78 (.265)
	Guest	2.55 (.077)	3.37 (.110)	2.28 (.091)	3.89 (.163)
Old	Host	.55 (.050)	1.51 (.070)	5.25 (.136)	2.00 (.120)
	Guest	3.22 (.084)	-.21 (.038)	5.66 (.154)	6.66 (.273)
Strangers					
Young	Host	1.57 (.060)	-.68 (.027)	.38 (.048)	7.85 (.205)
	Guest	3.98 (.097)	.40 (.043)	1.32 (.071)	3.57 (.167)
Old	Host	2.01 (.060)	3.56 (.099)	1.47 (.062)	3.99 (.172)
	Guest	4.05 (.094)	1.99 (.070)	2.07 (.085)	4.81 (.194)

emerge as the most effective control tactic. Polite suggestions worked best for hosts in younger children and best for guests in older children. The tactic we have labeled Plan for Both was not as effective among strangers as it was among friends, and it was always more effective for older than for younger children.

The two impolite forms differ in the amount of inference necessary for compliance by the listener. Thus, we might expect imperative to be more successful among younger children than among older children. This was generally true among friends, but among strangers there were no major differences across age (i.e., z-scores and conditional probabilities were comparable). The major difference for the effectiveness of imperatives was that, among older friends, guests were not as likely to comply with the host's imperatives as among younger friends. Once again, this is consistent with the hypothesis that creating a climate of agreement characterizes the interactions of young friends.

Because of the additional inference required, we would expect younger children to be less compliant to the expression of needs than to imperatives. This was true of their interaction with strangers, but not true of their interaction with friends. Perhaps the inference is easier for young children with familiar peers than with strangers. This is consistent with the fact that older children were as responsive to both forms with strangers.

Conflict and Its Resolution

Disagreement and conflict are pervasive characteristics of social intercourse and have been studied in developmental psychology under various headings such as "aggression" or "assertion" (see, for example, Hartup, 1970; Patterson, Littman, & Bricker, 1967). Recently, Brenneis, and Lein (1977) studied elementary-school children playing roles in four verbal disputes. They did not report to the extent to which the children in the study were acquainted. The authors were aware of the possibility that the role plays might not be representative of everyday interaction, but they presumed that the primary differences were that everyday interaction is more hostile. They wrote, "Children's disputes may end in tussles or grabbing matches which we did not allow... However, by-and-large, the techniques used in role played disputes also occur in everyday interactions" [p. 50]. This conclusion may be correct but it raises the question of to what extent the escalating nature of the verbal duals they described *characterize* the interactions of children. Unfortunately, they did not present quantitative analyses of their data. Their role plays involve the resolution of situations such as one child having snatched a ball from the other, or the children being instructed to have a dispute about who is smartest. This may represent a set of limited situations in which no motive may exist for avoiding or resolving conflict.

To investigate conflict and its resolution we selected the two codes designed for the purpose, Disagreement (DG) and Squabbles (S). Squabbles is a code that always involves the paralinguistic features of anger, annoyance, disgust, yelling, whining, sarcasm and/or insults, threats, physical aggression, retaliation, or tattling. Squabbles is thus a code that represents an escalated form of conflict. Whereas Squabbles are clear emotional expressions of conflict, disagreements may have many functions. It is conceivable that people in a relationship that permits disagreement may be more competent socially. Sequences including disagreement could represent important prosocial activities of negotiation and compromise, as opposed to unresolved conflict.

It is generally acknowledged that as children develop they become more cooperative and less likely to squabble (see, for example, Hartup, 1970); but is less well known how, specifically, children go about being more cooperative. It is also generally acknowledged that children's knowledge of and use of social rules increases with age, particularly the rule of sharing (see Damon, 1977), but is less well known to what extent children actually use rules to resolve conflict. The roles of humor, fantasy, and the expression of support or empathy in resolving conflict have not been studied, yet it was our impression from listening to tapes of our participants' conversations that they might play an important role in conflict resolution.

Lag Sequential Analysis

To examine the role of all these tactics, we employed a method of exploratory data analysis devised by Sackett (1977) called *lag sequential analysis*. In this approach, a code of interest is designated the "criterion" code, and the conditional probabilities and z-scores of all the other codes at various lags beyond the criterion are computed. This results in a *probability profile* that can be used to identify potential likely sequences. Gottman and Bakeman (1979) discussed the advantages of lag sequences analysis over Markovian methods and information theory from the standpoint of requiring less data for analysis. They also discussed the cautions necessary in interpreting results.

Bakeman and Dabbs (1976) pointed out that the method has the advantage, over other sequential techniques such as Markovian methods, that it permits the identification of sequences with indefinite elements. Such a sequence begins with the criterion code but it may, at some specific lag, be impossible to predict the intervening code; for example, the sequence Disagrees-Something Unpredictable-Jokes-Agrees may be inferred from a probability profile. Unfortunately, in the present investigation there are too few instances of conflict to go beyond two lags. It is interesting in itself that in particular Squabbling was an infrequent code in the interactions of all groups, averaging only .43% of the interaction (with a standard deviation of

.19%). The only significant difference in these proportions was that older hosts squabbled with their friends less frequently than younger hosts - $t(11) = 3.16$, $p < .01$; younger mean = .8%; older mean = .2%.

Perhaps the greatest problem in lag sequence analysis is reporting the results. For two lags, if z-scores and conditional probabilities were to be reported for the consequences of the two criterion codes of disagreement and squabbles by both host and guest for all other codes, we would have to present 704 numbers, most of them nonsignificant. Furthermore, the number of potential comparisons becomes astronomical. As an alternative, we propose to present only those codes at each lag for which z exceeded 1.96 (see Sackett, 1977), and for which the conditional probability exceeds .070.[3] These criteria will considerably reduce the results presented. We will also present those two-lag z-scores that are greater than 1.96 and the respective conditional probabilities that the conflict continues (or escalates to squabbling when disagreement is the criterion code.)

Resolving Disagreements. Table 6.9 presents the consequences of disagreement by the host. The most striking result is that it is overwhelmingly likely that the host will give a rationale (CM) clarifying the disagreement. (A CM code following disagreement always meant that a reason was given for the disagreement.) This was more likely for younger than older children. Furthermore, for young children it was more likely among friends than among strangers, while for older children it was more likely to occur among strangers than among friends. Once again we observe the phenomenon that young children are more responsive to their friends than to strangers, whereas the opposite is true for older children (examine the conditional probabilities of message clarification following disagreement in Table 6.9).

In terms of the success of the techniques used to inhibit subsequent continued disagreement by the host and elicit agreement from the guest, young children are more successful with both friends and strangers than older children. Examining the z-scores and conditional probabilities of continued disagreement by lag 2, we find that both groups of children are less successful with strangers than with friends. Among strangers the younger guest is also more agreeable than the older guest, since Guest Agrees did not have a z-score greater than 1.96 for older strangers. The older guest among strangers is not

---

[3]For two codes this can be considered significant at $p < .05$ under assumptions that the binomial distribution approximates the normal. For many codes we do not yet know what the nominal alpha would be. Gottman (1979a, b) showed that it varies with autocorrelations. We do not know what extent it is affected by the nonindependence of the codes. The .070 figure is arbitrary.

TABLE 6.9
Consequences of Disagreement by the Host

	z-score	Conditional Probability
Young Friends		
Host Clarifies Message[a]	22.77	.352
Guest Disagrees	3.89	.077
Guest Agrees (Lag 2)	2.76	.092
Host Continues to Disagree (Lag 2)	.59	.041
Old Friends		
Host Clarifies Message	12.23	.203
Guest Disagrees	2.09	.070
Guest Agrees	2.04	.078
Host Continues to Disagree (Lag 2)	2.06	.063
Young Strangers		
Host Clarifies Message	15.45	.300
Host Makes Demand (DE form)	2.28	.144
Guest Agrees (Lag 2)	2.55	.089
Host Continues to Disagree (Lag 2)	4.40	.100
Old Strangers		
Host Clarifies Message	11.75	.281
Guest Asks Question for Information	2.37	.124
Guest Asks Tag Question	7.37	.107
Host Continues to Disagree (Lag 2)	7.36	.140

[a]If not indicated as such a code is at lag 1 from the criterion, i.e., disagreement by the host.

inactive, however, but uses both questions for information and tag question (e.g., "Right?"), which is the type of question most likely to elicit agreement. For older strangers, the probability of agreement following a guest's tag question was .149, $z = 5.28$.

Table 6.10 presents the results of the consequences of a guest's disagreement. Comparing Tables 6.9 and 6.10, note first that there is a slight tendency that the host is more likely to reciprocate a disagreement by the guest with another disagreement than conversely. This slight tendency toward asymmetry may be a reflection of the fact that both children are aware that they are in the host's territory. The host is not as ready as the guest to comply.

Asymmetry in the predictability of behavior in dyadic interaction was suggested by Gottman (1979a,b) as an operational definition of dominance in social interaction. The idea is that the subordinate's behavior should be more predictable from the dominant person's behavior than vice versa. This definition is consistent with patterns of dominance observed in a variety of research applications (Gottman, 1979a). Gottman (1979b) showed that this definition of dominance can be operationalized using cross-spectral time

TABLE 6.10
Consequences of Disagreement by the Guest

	z-score	Conditional Probability
Young Friends		
Host Disagrees (Lag 2)	4.48	.095
Guest Makes Demand (DE)	2.88	.131
Guest Talks in Fantasy Role (F)	22.32	.351
Guest Continues to Disagree (Lag 2)	−.37	.024
Old Friends		
Host Disagrees	3.02	.076
Guest Talks in Fantasy Role (F)	11.55	.153
Guest Continues to Disagree (Lag 2)	.45	.042
Young Strangers		
Guest Talks in Fantasy Role (F)	8.44	.145
Guest Agrees (Lag 2)	2.15	.087
Guest Continues to Disagree (Lag 2)	.53	.029
Old Strangers		
Host Disagrees	3.56	.101
Host Disagrees (Lag 2)	3.61	.101
Guest Talks in Fantasy Role	13.06	2.75
Guest Continues to Disagree (Lag 2)	2.72	.058

series analysis, using the slope of the phase spectrum.[4] The importance of this definition is evident once one realizes that in many social interactions dominance patterns, once established, do not need to be continually re-established. Indeed, part of the function of a dominance relation is that it minimizes conflict (Wilson, 1975). Hence, in continuously interacting groups that have a social history, it is difficult to observe dominance patterning using naturalistic observation. It is not feasible to deprive children of water for 22 hours and to observe who drinks first at a dripping faucet, which is a useful technique with monkeys in captivity (Stephenson, personal communication). Furthermore, specific behaviors that establish dominance are likely to be extremely rare, brief, telegraphed versions of their former selves; and each interacting group may have established dominance dialects (see Gottman, 1979a). The asymmetry-in-predictability measure should overcome these

---

[4]Although we do not present the results here, our analysis of the phase spectra of our data shows that, when there is a dominance patterning among friends, hosts are significantly more dominant than guests, and that this is true across age. The host's dominance with a friend is negatively correlated with his dominance with a stranger ($r = -.39$), independent of age. We mention these results only to underscore the potential application of time-series methods for the study of social interaction.

problems, since it is a construct that spans a range of behaviors, searching for sequential asymmetry rather than a specific sequence that indicates dominance.

Note the striking absence of message clarification by the guest, and instead the use of speaking within a fantasy role. This strategy is used across age and acquaintanceship, though it is more likely for young children with their friends and more likely for older children with strangers. For this strategy to be appropriate, it must mean either that guests tend to restrict their disagreement largely to fantasy play, when they can quickly follow their disagreement by speaking as a character in the fantasy play, or that the guest quickly shifts to a brief speech within a fantasy role. This is marked constraint on the guest, and young friends are more likely to display it than older friends. However, once again we see a reversal of this developmental effect with strangers: Among strangers, older guests are more likely to use this tactic than younger guests.

In terms of effectiveness in inhibiting subsequent disagreement, older guests are less effective than younger guests, which is contrary to the prediction that younger children are more likely than older children to engage in escalating bouts of disagreement with their peers.

To summarize, the major tactics for inhibiting continued disagreement are similar across age and acquaintanceship. However, *younger* children use these tactics more effectively than older children with both friends and strangers. This result is surprising, and it is inconsistent with a common finding in the developmental literature (e.g., Hartup, 1970), that children become more cooperative with peers as they develop. The pattern of results is, however, similar to those for communication clarity (see Table 6.6). One possible explanation of the results for disagreement is that continued disagreement among younger children has more serious negative consequences than it does among older children, and therefore younger children are less tolerant of continued disagreement than older children.

To test this hypothesis, it would be necessary to show first that disagreement could lead predictably to squabbling, and, second, that younger children were less effective than older children at de-escalating squabbling. We examined whether continued disagreements led to squabbles and whether these probabilities differ across age by computing the 16 conditional probabilities and z-scores with disagreement as the criterion and squabbles by either child as the consequent code after five lags, which was as far as it was reasonable to examine the data sequentially. There were no consistent differences across age either for friends or for strangers. Therefore, we could not find evidence that continued disagreements had more severe consequences for younger children than for older children, at least in terms of the probability of transitions to squabbling. We turn next to an analysis of how (and how well) children cope with squabbles when they *do* arise.

Resolving Squabbles.   The results of the consequences of squabbling are now presented. In general, once they begin, squabbles tend to persist with high z-scores for as long as we have data to compute. In Markovian terms, this means that squabbles are "absorbing states" than once entered are difficult to leave. We suspect that they "burn" themselves out. Figure 6.1 is a summary of our exploratory lag sequential analyses of squabbles codes for friends. The ordinate presents the maximum z-score at each lag, that is, the z-score the child (guest or host) with the highest z-score. These data are tentative because squabbles was an infrequent code. Nonetheless, they do suggest that squabbles among friends may burn out faster in older children.

Figure 6.2 is a summary of the equivalent analyses among strangers. Note that with strangers, across age, children find it most difficult to de-escalate squabbling, particularly when it is initiated by the guest.

To study what tactics children use to keep squabbles from continuing, we can examine the immediate first and second lag consequences of squabbling. Tabe 5.11 presents the consequences of the hosts squabbling. Note the striking absence of the invocation of rules among friends. In friend pairs, young guests use sympathy and offers of help and hosts use jokes, but with low probability. It may be that among young friends, host-initiated squabbles simply burn out rather than being resolved by anything the hosts or guests do. Among older friends, however, guests respond to squabbles by asking a question about the host's feelings; and they do this relatively often. Therefore,

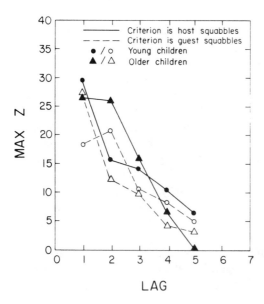

FIG. 6.1.   Autolags and crosslags of squabbling among friends.

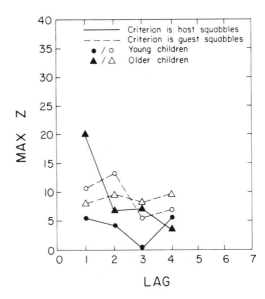

FIG. 6.2.   Autolags and crosslags
of squabbling among strangers.

it may be that older children are more effective at resolving squabbles initiated by the host than younger children. *Note that, for both age groups, the response to squabbles always directly acknowledges and attends to the hosts's feelings.*

TABLE 6.11
Consequences of the Host Squabbling

	z-score	Conditional Probability
Young Friends		
Host Jokes	2.87	.043
Guest Expresses Sympathy (Lag 2)	4.35	.021
Guest Offers (Lag 2)	3.21	.043
Old Friends		
Guest Asks Question about Host's Feelings	3.21	.100
Young Strangers		
Host Talks Within Fantasy Role	2.55	.154
Host Invokes Rule	3.83	.077
Host Jokes (Lag 2)	2.24	.077
Guest Disagrees	3.44	.154
Old Strangers		
Host Talks Within Fantasy Role	2.34	.056
Guest Expresses Feeling Or Opinion	3.65	.167
Guest Disagrees	3.16	.111

Only among young strangers do we see rules used to resolve conflict. Our impression of the data is that these rules are almost invariably rules of territoriality or sharing. They are used by the host, who also used joking and talking within a fantasy role. Older strangers also talk within a fantasy role and express a feeling or opinion, but they do not use rules predictably.

The consequences of the guest's squabbling are presented in Table 6.12. Recall that the techniques used by older friends for resolving host-initiated squabbles were more effective than those used by younger friends (see Figs. 6.1 and 6.2), and they tended to be questions by the guest about the host's feelings, rather than rule invocation. Similarly, although young friends do use rules to cope with guests' squabbling, the conditional probabilities are quite low. The emphasis in social-cognitive literature on children's use of rules such as sharing and other reciprocity norms (i.e., taking turns) may be exaggerated, particularly for the purposes of conflict resolution. What should be explored, instead are children's use of the exploration of feelings, sympathy, offers of assistance, jokes, and fantasy to cope with conflict.

We were surprised that in our data squabbles and disagreement were relatively rare occurrences, given the great amount of attention that has been devoted to the study of aggression in children. The anomaly may be a function of the fact that we are studying children at home and not at school. Furthermore, perhaps the incompetence of young children to de-escalate squabbles with friends or strangers and the incompetence of both groups to

TABLE 6.12
Consequences of the Guest Squabbling

	z-score	Conditional Probability
Young Friends		
Guest Expresses Feeling or Opinion	2.54	.083
Guest Jokes (Lag 2)	3.30	.056
Guest Invokes Rule (Lag 2)	2.37	.028
Old Friends		
Host Speaks Within Fantasy Role	2.58	.133
Host Expresses Sympathy (Lag 2)	8.18	.067
Guest Offers (Lag 2)	4.06	.067
Guest Asks Question About		
Host's Feelings	2.50	.067
Young Strangers		
Host You and Me Code (Lag 2)	2.08	.111
Guest Asks Question for Information	2.20	.222
Old Strangers		
Host Speaks Within Fantasy Role	2.74	.071
Host Disagrees	4.15	.214

de-escalate squabbles with strangers accounts for the great amount of attention devoted to this issue in the developmental literature. In other contexts the base rate of squabbling might increase dramatically. In fact, we compared the amount of squabbling of two 4-year-old best friends in two sessions in a laboratory playroom with the amount of squabbling at home. We found that the relative frequency of squabbling at home was much lower than it was in the laboratory playroom. Context differences may relate to the clarity of territorial rules implicit in the context.

If we focus on the de-escalation of squabbling among friends, in which all children were relatively competent, but in which older children were more competent than younger children, we can conclude that among friends rules are less effective devices for de-escalating conflict than the expression of sympathy and asking questions about feelings. Although the research on children's sympathy is scant, Murphy's (1937) classic observational study in young children detected the expression of sympathy in response to hurt or distress expressed by a peer. It is an impressive social skill to be able to express sympathy in response to interpersonal conflict as opposed to intrapersonal distress, and it is not surprising that we find the tactic primarily with older friends. In the de-escalation of squabbling among friends, older children clearly display greater competence than younger children. Perhaps it is this very same incompetence of younger children at de-escalating squabbles that leads them to avoid prolonged disagreements.

Fantasy

Earlier in this chapter we reported that the proportion of fantasy is greater with increasing age as activity talk increases. The second coding system defined fantasy in a more restricted way as talking within the role of a character in the fantasy. In the second coding system, for fantasy by the host there was a significant developmental main effect, $F(1, 10) = 19.75, p < .005$ (younger average proportion = .039, older average proportion = .018), a significant acquaintanceship effect, $F(1, 10) = 8.57, p < .025$ (friends average = .043, strangers average = .017), and no significant interaction effect, $F(1, 10) = .12$, n.s. A similar pattern was obtained for fantasy by the guest, with a marginally significant development effect $F(1, 10) = 4.38$, $p < .10$, a marginally significant acquaintanceship effect, $F(1, 10) = 3.67$, $p < .10$, and a marginally significant interaction effect (young friends average = .035; old friends average = .022; young strangers average = .018; old strangers average = .023).

These results are quite consistent with those obtained with the first coding system. However, the results do not describe the extent to which the children are engaged with one another for an extended continuous period, as opposed to frequent brief periods of fantasy play. To explore this question, each fantasy was coded in terms of its extension as either:

1. initiated—one child suggests a fantasy or speaks in role, but the other child ignores or refuses to continue the fantasy;

2. brief—the other child agrees or responds briefly to the initiation of a fantasy but it never goes beyond three lines;

3. developed—the fantasy is developed or continued for a period of time; or

4. extended—the fantasy goes on for more than a page and a half of dialogue. For this coding scheme, the initiation of a fantasy was considered to be assignment or invention of roles, or characters, suggestion of a particular situation, scene, or action, or speaking within a role.

Pretense or activity consistent with the fantasy, as well as fantasy-related negotiation, beyond the point of initiation, were included in judging the length of the fantasy.

Each fantasy was weighted using a point system: 1 for an initiated fantasy, 2 for a brief fantasy, 3 for a developed fantasy, and 4 for an extended fantasy. There was a significant developmental effect, $F(1, 10) = 6.54, p < .05$, with the fantasies of younger children more extended; a highly significant acquaintanceship effect, $F(1, 10) = 21.06, p < .001$, with the fantasies of friends more extended; and no significant interaction effect, $F(1, 10) = 1.62$, n.s.

In addition to our earlier analyses of fantasy, the thematic content of each fantasy was coded as either Domestic or Adventure. The domestic category included fantasies with the following themes: (1) doctor; (2) house; (3) food preparation; (4) baby; (5) making a phone call; (6) hairdresser; (7) boy and girl friend; (8) family trip; (9) pets; (10) other domestic (includes being at the beach and playing school). The Adventure category included fantasies with the following themes: (1) monsters; (2) super heroes; (3) cops and robbers; (4) T.V. characters; (5) other adventures (e.g., fairy tales). Table 6.13 presents the proportion of domestic or adventure fantasies that were developed or extended. The extension of domestic fantasies appears to be a better

TABLE 6.13
Proportion of Domestic or Adventure Fantasies That
Were Developed or Extended

Group	Proportion	
	Domestic	Adventure
Young Friends	1.00	.40
Old Friends	.70	.50
Young Strangers	.50	.38
Old Strangers	.29	.29

discriminator developmentally and between friends and strangers than the extension of adventure fantasies. Domestic fantasies were coded for extension as described above. The developmental effect for age was significant $F(1, 10) = 4.97, p < .05$. Neither the acquaintanceship effect, $F(1, 10) = 2.56$, nor the interaction, $F(1, 10) = .26$, were significant, although acquaintanceship means were in the predicted direction.

One interesting fact is that some strangers, particularly young strangers, got along so well that they asked to (and in one case did) continue seeing one another. Our impression was that young strangers either hit it off extremely well and acted as friends, or they did not get along at all, whereas older strangers seemed to strike a middle ground. Younger children did not seem to have as developed a sense that there is a different way to act with strangers. All the young strangers who seemed to hit it off engaged in extended or developed domestic fantasies, whereas those who got along less well did not have developed or extended domestic fantasies. The one young child whose domestic fantasies with a stranger were as developed as with a friend asked to see the other child again; the one young child whose domestic fantasies with a stranger were *more* developed than with a friend did, in fact, see the stranger again and the two later became friends.

Summary of Major Findings

What did we find in comparing young children's friendships to older children's friendships? The friendships of younger children were characterized by more fantasy, more talking in fantasy roles, more extended fantasies, less activity-based talk, greater communication clarity, more social comparison activity (particularly emphasizing solidarity), compliance to a wider range of control attempts, greater likelihood of explaining disagreement and avoiding continued disagreement, and less ability to de-escalate squabbles than the friendships of older children. We suggested that many of these findings supported the hypothesis that younger friendships create a "climate of agreement," whereas older friends appear more able to tolerate disagreement.

For several social processes, patterns were more characteristic of younger than older children across acquaintanceship levels. This was true of the likelihood of activity-based talk, fantasy, communication clarity, and the host's explanation for his disagreement. For a number of other social processes, we discovered patterns that were more characteristic of young friends than of older friends, but also more characteristic of older strangers than young strangers. This was the case for exploration-of-feeling social comparison, for the effectiveness of control attempts using imperatives and the expression of wants and needs, and for the use of speaking in a fantasy role as a tactic by the guest to de-escalate the guest's disagreement.

A DEVELOPMENTAL THEORY
OF FRIENDSHIP AND
ACQUAINTANCESHIP PROCESSES

We use the results that discriminated friends from strangers as a heuristic for hypothesizing about the dynamics of the acquaintanceship process. These hypotheses about the transition of some children from strangers to friends are thus used as a device for organizing our results.

We propose that it is possible to predict which young children who are strangers will eventually become friends. More specifically, we are currently testing the theory that there is a specific hierarchy of interactional events that tends to take place as young children become friends. The lower events in the hierarchy, if successfully completed by the application of specific social skills, make it possible to proceed to other events that create greater intimacy. While it is possible for children to stop at any level of the hierarchy, the degree of intimacy in their relationship will be related to the level they attain. The relationship will not continue if children cannot manage the first three levels.

The Process Hierarchy.   Table 6.14 is a summary of our theory of the acquaintanceship process in young children. We suggest that two strangers will be likely to become close friends to the extent that they are able to move down the flowchart. First we describe the prototypical progression through the hierarchy, and then we discuss exceptions.

We propose that obtaining agreement from a stranger is very important to young children and determines, to a large extent, their progression toward friendship. The young host initially tries to interest the stranger in something, usually in a show and tell fashion, showing the guest around and describing his possessions and attributes ("I got these books for Christmas"; "I can read the words in this one").

The skills that come into play in this level of the hierarchy of events are the connectedness of the conversation and the clarity of the communication. The following excerpt is an example from the interaction of two young strangers who did not get along very well. The host (B) had tried to show his guest (D) several things he thought were very interesting, and this is yet another attempt:

B: I just got this guitar from my grandmother and ... well, I have to sing it ... to pick a song. Bum, bum, bear went swimming e non no [sings]. This is a Spanish song. Quass quiss dass dose nass, quass, quiss quass quiss quass quiss, ose nass quiss, qua, que, no no nwa wa qui qua qua qua qua qui [sung].

D: Where's ...

B: Old McDonald had a farm [sung].

D: Where's your dumb straw?

B: What?

TABLE 6.14
Theoretical Flowchart of the Acquaintanceship Process in Children Aged 2 to 5

Likelihood of a Friendship[a]	Interactional Event	Salient Social Skills
1	Host tries to interest guest: Show and tell is likely	1. Connected Discourse 2. Communication Clarity
2	Social Comparison Activity	1. Establishing Solidarity before Contrast (Common Ground) 2. Offers
3	Activity Talk with Subsequent Control Attempts	1. Guest's compliance to host's polite suggestions 2. Guest's eventual compliance to host's Imperatives
4	Disagreements Arise	Disagreements are resolved: 1. Host gives rationale for disagreement 2. Guest talks in fantasy role Squabbles burn out
5	Stereotyped Fantasy Initiated	
6	Stereotyped Fantasy is Developed or Extended	
7	Stereotype of Fantasy Decreases	
8	Less Stereotyped Fantasy	1. Expression of Important Feelings with subsequent support and solidarity by other child 2. Resolution of Conflict

[a]These numbers illustrate the increasing likelihood that the children will become friends.

D: Where's your dumb straw?
B: What's a dumb straw?
D: *Your* dumb straw.
B: That's a trouble shooter (very irritated).

In this example D never explained what he meant by a "dumb straw" in response to B's request for clarification. The first step in acquaintanceship for young children is connected conversation in which messages are clarified in response to a request, in which the guest participates in a connected fashion, usually by asking questions for information of the host, and in which these questions for information are appropriately responded to.

The show and tell process leads naturally to social comparison, usually of possessions, but also of attributes (age, place of residence, number of siblings, etc.). We propose that exploration of feeling (QFE → FE) and solidarity (ME → YM) social comparisons that bring out and establish common ground are important at this stage, as opposed to contrasts (ME → ME). Contrasts, on the other hand are positive events once an activity has been agreed upon, which follows naturally from the show and tell, and when most of the conversation is activity talk. In other words, once common ground is established, revealed differences are interesting. Once a friendship is established, the content of interactional events such as social comparison may change. For example, as two friends, Jonathan (4:8) and Genevieve (4:8), engaged in Activity talk, their similarity social comparison concerned what they wanted to be when they grew up:

73. G: ...know how many things I am?
74. J: How many?
75. G: A studier, and a ordinary dancer, and an Indian, and a dinosaur trainer. How you think that is?
76. J: Ah, when, when I grow up I'm going to be all the things. I'm going to be a fireman, a policeman, and a rocketship man, and a dinosaur person.

Among strangers, during social comparison, an offer by the host ("You can play with this") will lead naturally into an activity play interaction. Activity talk may also be introduced by suggestions or other means. Continued social comparison often takes place during such an activity talk period. During activity talk periods (i.e., coloring, glueing and pasting, dump trucks—these are not fantasy play periods), the number of control attempts increase, and it is important that the guest comply, particularly to polite suggestions by the host (QFE → AG). A measure of increased interpersonal comfort (or intimacy) is the compliance to imperatives, or direct demands (DE → AG), and the more subtle expressed need (FE → AG).

In these control attempts, conflict and disagreement are natural, and the ability to resolve disagreements (note we are not saying squabbles, but perhaps we should add the likelihood that squabbles will burn out quickly) is important. We have noted two tactics that children use following their own disagreement, namely the host's giving a rationale for the disagreement and the guest's switching to a fantasy role after a disagreement. Fantasy appears to function here to dissolve the confrontation in the disagreement.

The next level in the hierarchy is the success of the fantasy play. By the juxtaposition of 4 and 5 in Table 6.14, we do not mean to imply that fantasies are commonly begun by a response to the guest's disagreement. In fact, this is an unlikely way for fantasies to begin. Fantasies differ in the amount of role-assignment, plot-elaboration, and hence the amount of continual renegotiation they require or permit. For example, doctor requires more invention and negotiation than preparing food or making a phone call, which are less demanding. Fantasies also differ in how clearly prescribed the roles are. In playing monsters, the roles are less well defined than the roles when playing well-known T.V. characters. We suggest that the ability to have extended fantasies is the next step, and that the less stereotyped the fantasy the children are able to sustain, the closer their relationship will be.

Our longitudinal study of the fantasy themes of one particular pair of 4-year-old best friends (Eric and Naomi) led us to believe the ability to provide mutual support and the ability to resolve conflict in unstereotyped fantasies is essential in establishing and maintaining intimacy among young friends. We were amazed at the level of emotional expressiveness, sympathy, and support and also by both the anguish caused by intense conflict and the complexity of the solutions these children used in coping with conflict. We will present several excerpts from transcripts that illustrate this later stage of the hierarchy we have proposed.

The first two excerpts are from Eric and Naomi, and illustrate the amount of emotional support provided by one friend during nonstereotyped fantasy play.

Excerpt 1:
282. N. No, it's time for our birthday. We better clean up quickly.
283. E. Well, I'd rather play with my skeleton. Hold on there everyone. Snappers. I am the skeleton.
284. E. I'm the skeleton. Ooh, hee.. Hugh, ha, ha. You're hiding.
285. N. Hey, in the top drawer, there's the ...
286. E. I am, the skeleton, whoa.
287. N. There's the feet [clattering].
288. E. [Screams] A skeleton, Everyone a skeleton.
289. N. I'm your friend. The dinosaur.
290. E. Oh, hi dinosaur. You know, no one likes me.
291. N. But I like you. I'm your friend.
292. E. But none of my other friends like me. They don't like my new suit. They don't like my skeleton suit. It's really just me. They think I'm a dumb-dumb.
293. N. I know what. He's a good skeleton.
294. E. I am not a dumb-dumb, and that's so.
295. N. I'm not calling you a dumb-dumb. I'm calling you a friendly skeleton.

Excerpt 2:
N: Agh, this is nice. Wow, where are you going? We're going back to our house.
E: This is my house, remember?
N: Where are your parents, remember?
E: My parents? I don't have any parents. My Mommy and Daddy went, they didn't like me anymore.
N: So they went someplace else?

E: I live here all alone. Hey, you can live with me.

N: Yes, and keep you company. I'll cook the food.

E: Okay, that's a great idea. You can make my bells. My ding-a-ling bells.

N: And we all can go to bed too.

E: Yeah, I'm going to bed. It's past my bedtime right now. My nap.

N: You better get in.

Both these excerpts illustrate the social support and solidarity that the nonstereotyped fantasy play of young friends can provide.

Another type of episode we have found illustrates a form of solidarity that we will call "shared deviance." In shared deviance children either plot or carry out actions they know to be forbidden. An example we observed were two 5-year olds who planned to poison the host's mother.

Not all children start at the beginning of this hierarchy. Young children will adopt a high-risk strategy in which they begin with fantasy. This strategy is either highly successful or disastrous. Children will either become friends instantly, or their interaction will end in fury and adult intervention.

We now turn to a consideration of the developmental aspects of this theory.

Developmental Considerations

The acquaintanceship process among older children, that is, children over 5, is more difficult to specify. One reason for this is that older children have acquired the adult way of interacting with strangers. With respect to the social process we have studied in this chapter, young children appear to act as if they believed you have to be "good" to your friends and try your best to make friends with strangers, which is either very successful or not successful at all. Older children appear to have chosen a middle ground. Their interaction is characterized with both friends and strangers by more activity talk and less fantasy than is the case -for younger children. With strangers, younger children are more likely to fail to provide appropriate information in response to a guest's questions for information than older children, but the reverse is true for friends; and, younger children are much less likely to leave their messages unclarified with both friends and strangers than older children. Younger children are much more likely than older children to engage in social comparisons that establish common ground with their friends. This difference did not exist for strangers (see Table 7). It is as if younger children were more concerned with establishing a climate of agreeing with their friends, a "me too" kind of social comparison, than older children. Young friends are more predictably likely to comply with almost any control attempt by their friends than older children , but this was not the case for younger children's interaction with strangers (see Table 6.8). In fact, older children were more responsive to a wide range of control attempts by strangers than younger children.

Clearly, in our data, younger hosts are worse at resolving squabbles with strangers than older children. This is not the case for disagreements because of the great concern younger hosts have for giving a reason for their disagreement. Perhaps older children are more capable of tolerating and more interested in disagreement. This may reflect a process of increasing individuation in development. The fact that older children seem less concerned about continued disagreement with strangers provides further support for the concept that younger children attempt to create a "climate of agreement" in their interaction with peers.

We are led to propose the over-arching hypothesis that close friendship is more important to children before the age of 5 than it is later. This may be a critical developmental period in establishing close relationships with friends. Thereafter, children may be both less responsive to friends and less interested in making friends with strangers. Older children are in many ways more skillful with strangers than younger children, but it appears that their goals have changed. They may have learned how to get along with strangers better at the cost of less intimacy with fewer friends.

Furthermore, young children pursue a high risk strategy in acquaintanceship; they will attempt to engage their peers in activities that have a high potential for intimacy but also a high risk of unclear communication, continued disagreement or squabbling, which are disasterous. Older children pursue a more conservative course with strangers; they pursue a low-risk, low-intimacy strategy, and are thus more likely to continue in an activity-talk modality rather than attempting fantasy.

Limitation and Current Directions

There are several limitations of the investigation we presented in this chapter that have led us to design carefully controlled replications and extensions of our work. These include the need for replication because of the small subject sample size, the need to sample from same-sex as well as cross-sex friendships, the need to address a wider age range, the need for an adult friendship comparison group, the need to determine whether effects obtained are independent of procedural artifacts such as the mother's having gathered the tapes, her uncontrolled intrusions into the play sessions, and the need for control for the length of the friendship, independent of the age of the children. We have completed five studies to address these and other methodological issues and are planning to publish our findings when all studies are completed.

Replication is essential in this work because many sequential connections and comparisons may capitalize on chance. We have attempted to deal with this problem in our work by selecting only specific patterns to examine. Nonetheless, our next study is a replication study, sampling from male-male, female-female, and male-female best friend dyads at two age groups, 2–5 and 6–9. Taping is done by a female experimenter and tapes are obtained controlling the mother's presence or absence in the host child's room. Quantitative information on the closeness of the frienship is obtained from a child sociometric and a mother questionnaire.

An additional context for describing peer interaction is mother-child interaction during the taping, and specially gathered mother-child conversation. The reason for this latter sampling is the following. One observation of "motherese" is that adults present a simplified version of their language to children (Bates, 1975), presumably for educational pruposes. On our tapes, we have observed that children also present a simplified version of *their* language to parents, compared to the language they use with peers. We thus think the simplified linguistic code hypothesis may be an artifact of the nature of parent-child discourse, which is usually brief, designed for such purposes as to instruct, to warn, to ask for something, to give something, or to exchange information economically.

In the course of pilot testing the procedures of this replication study, we discovered the fact that cross-sex friendships are extremely rare in the 6–9 age group. In fact, we canvassed five neighborhoods in Champaign-Urbana, door-to-door, to fill this cell of the study. We also noticed in the study presented in this chapter that cross-sex friendships among young children had the most extended, emotionally disclosing, and responsive fantasies; in short, we felt that they were the most intimate friendships. We will be exploring the reasons for the decline of cross-sex friendships once children reach school age. In an unpublished study, Benson and Gottman (1976) observed a sharp drop in cross-sex interaction after kindergarten, so the effect may be quite general. These interactional results clearly parallel the eventual developmental sociometric split by sex, which is even more marked than racial splits (Singleton & Asher, 1977).

A second study was designed to replicate and extend the work on acquaintanceship, once again sampling from same and cross-sex pairings and from the large age range previously described. In this study, however, the children knew that they would play together three times. We designed the study in this way so that we could observe children's progress toward (or away from) friendship over time in relation to the hierarchy we proposed. The other two child studies are longitudinal studies of best friendship.

The adult friendship study (with Dorothy Ginsberg) compares the conversations of same-sex roommates who are close friends with those who are not close. We developed and validated a measure of the closeness of friendship among college students in two pilot studies, one using a within-subjects and the other using a between-subjects design. These data are currently being coded with essentially the same coding system as we used with the child data, except that we had to add categories such as a large category for gossip. The study with Ginsberg of adults and another study (with Gwendolyn Mettetal) of children 7–14 will examine the roles of gossip, self-disclosure, and shared problem-solving in friendship, and the patterns of their development in children's interaction with age.

One limitation of our methods is that we code nonverbal behavior only in the vocal, paralinguistic channel. We should note that this is an extremely rich channel of nonverbal data in children's interaction with peers. Videotapes would make it possible to code facial and body cues as well. It is much easier to bring a video camera into a child's home than to obtain natural interaction in front of a camera. We have not yet solved the problems of the obtrusiveness of videotape equipment with children, although we have solved these problems with adult friends, siblings, and married couples. Corsaro (personal communication) had success videotaping two friends in a home, so we believe it possible. We are currently pilot testing procedures for obtaining useable videotapes of young friends at home and in the laboratory. The evidence on young children's extensive use of gestural forms of communication (see Mueller, 1972) suggests to us that the additional information provided by videotapes would, if anything, increase the picture of the communicative competency of young children; that is, our results probably *underestimate* the age differences we obtained in favor of young friends.

A final issue we wish to address concerns the inadequacy of all of our coding systems taken together. We are constructing a qualitative category system to sample episodes of importance in children's conversation. To explore children's *conceptions* of friendship, we are coding children's spontaneous verbalizations about friendship. Developmental psychologists interested in social cognition have studied children's changing conceptions of friendship (Selman, 1976); the spontaneous talk of acquaintances can clarify the role of processes such as the use of rules (such as cleaning up) in the formation of friendships. This is illustrated in the following excerpt from two 4-year-old strangers:

N: Well, I want you to be my friend.

J: What?

N: I want you to be my friend. Well, I love playing with you [pause] you should help to clean up my room after we have played. Don't you know. You can't just play without cleaning up. You'll have to stay here.

The following excerpt illustrates the role of sharing and giving gifts in the affirmation of friendship:

E: Hey, can I have this tugboat too? You want this tugboat?
N: Yea.
E: Here's the tugboat. Naomi, I wish this tugboat was mine.
N: You can keep it if you want to.
E: For ever and ever?
N: If you like, I will... I will lend you...
E: Can I keep it?
N: Yes, and I'll... I'll live with you.
E: You won't live with me?
N: I would.
E: You won't live with me if I have this little tug? And you'll still live with me if I don't have it?
N: Yes.

We are also exploring specific uses of rules, the role of humor, and other methods for establishing closeness such as private referrents to previous events, confiding and advice giving, understanding adults' motives, society's rules, and conversations figuring out the world, such as the processes of birth, growing up, and death.

We wish to convey to readers that we feel as if we have stumbled into a vast world provided by the context of the conversations of friends; and as strangers we are only beginning to become acquainted with this world and the opportunities it provides for studying children's social development.

Several things are clear: Social relationships are an intense concern to very young children, their competence is great, and their abilities are complex. We hope to have made a contribution toward challenging the implicit assumption in developmental psychology that development is simply a linear process with increasing trend, and that all children continue, by successive approximations and with varying degrees of success, to develop into the "mature, competent adult," namely us. It is quite possible that young children are more competent at some things than older children (or adults), and one of these things may be friendship. If that is true, even to some degree, then we may have something very important to learn from young children, something that we may have forgotten in growing up.

REFERENCES

Argyle, M. *Social interaction.* Chicago: Aldine, 1969.

Asher, S. R. Referential communication. In G. J. Whitehurst & B. J. Zimmerman (Eds.), *The functions of language and cognition.* New York: Academic Press, 1978.

Asher, S. R., Oden, S. L., & Gottman, J. M. Children's friendships in school settings. In L. G. Katz (Ed.), *Current topics in early childhood education (Vol. 1)*. Hillsdale, N.J.: Ablex, 1977.

Asher, S. R., Singleton, L. C., Tinsley, B., & Hymel, S. *The reliability of young children's sociometric ratings*. Unpublished manuscript, University of Illiniois, 1977. (Department of Educational Psychology, Champaign, IL. 61820.)

Attneave, F. *Applications of information theory to psychology*. N.Y.: Holt, 1959.

Bakeman, R. Untangling streams of behavior: Sequential analysis of observational data. In G. P. Sackett (Ed.), *Observing behavior, Vol. II: Data collection and analysis methods*. Baltimore: University Park Press, 1978.

Bakeman, R., & Dabbs, J. M., Jr. Social interaction observed: Some approaches to the analysis of behavior streams. *Personality and Social Psychology Bulletin*, 1976, *2*, 335–345.

Bates, E. Peer relations and the acquisition of knowledge. In M. Lewis & L. A. Rosenblum (Eds.), *Friendship and peer relations*. New York: Wiley, 1975.

Benson, C., & Gottman, J. M. *Popularity, social structure, and social interaction in children*. Unpublished manuscript, 1976.

Birchler, G., Weiss, R., & Vincent, J. Multimethod analysis of social reinforcement exchange between maritally distressed and nondistressed spouse and stranger dyads. *Journal of Personality and Social Psychology*, 1975, *31*, 349–360.

Box, G. E. P., & Jenkins, G. M. *Time-series analysis: Forecasting and control*. San Francisco: Holden-Day, 1970.

Brain, R. *Friends and lovers*. New York: Pocket Books, 1977.

Brenneis, D., & Lein, L. "You fruithead": A sociolinguistic approach to children's dispute settlement. In S. Ervin-Tripp & C. Mitchell-Kernan (Eds.), *Child discourse*. New York: Academic Press, 1977.

Chevalier-Skolnikoff, S. Facial expression of emotion in nonhuman primates. In P. Ekman (Ed.), *Darwin and facial expression*. New York: Academic Press, 1973.

Corsaro, W. A. *Friendship in the nursery school: Social organization in a peer environment*. Paper presented at an SRCD study group on the development of friendships, University of Illinois, Champaign, 1978.

Cronbach, L. J., Gleser, G. C., Nanda, H., & Rajaratnam, N. *The dependability of behavioral measurements: Theory of generalizability for scores and profiles*. New York: Wiley, 1972.

Damon, W. *The social world of the child*. San Francisco: Jossey-Bass, 1977.

Ervin-Tripp, S. M. Sociolinguistics. In L. Berkowitz (Ed.), *Advances in experimental social psychology (Vol. 4)*. New York: Academic Press, 1969.

Ervin-Tripp, S. Wait for me, roller skate. In S. Ervin-Tripp & C. Mitchell-Kernan (Eds.), *Child discourse*. New York: Academic Press, 1977.

Ervin-Tripp, S., & Mitchell-Kernan, C. (Eds.) *Child discourse*. New York: Academic Press, 1977.

Fine, G. A. *Impression management and preadolescent behavior: Friends as socializers*. Paper presented at an SRCD study group on the development of friendships, University of Illinois, Champaign, 1978.

Freud, A., & Dann, S. An experiment in group upbringing. In R. Eissler, A. Freud, H. Hartmann, & E. Kris (Eds.), *The psychoanalytic study of the children (Vol. 6)*. New York: International Universities Press, 1951.

Fromkin, H. L. Feelings of interpersonal undistinctiveness: An unpleasant affective status. *Journal of Experimental Research in Personality*, 1972, *6*, 178–185.

Garvey, C. Some properties of social play. *Merrill-Palmer Quarterly*, 1974, *20*, 163–180.

Garvey, C. The contingent query: A dependent act in conversation. In M. Lewis & L. A. Rosenblum (Eds.), *Interaction, conversation and the development of language*. New York: Wiley, 1977.

Garvey, C. & Hogan, R. Social speech and social interaction: Egocentrism revisited. *Child Development*, 1973, *44*, 562–568.

Glass, G. V., Willson, V. L., & Gottman, J. M. *Design and analysis of time-series experiments.* Boulder, Col.: Colorado University Associated Press, 1975.

Gottman, J. M. *Marital interaction: Experimental investigations.* New York: Academic Press, in press. (a)

Gottman, J. M. Detecting cyclicity in social interaction. *Psychological Bulletin,* in press. (b)

Gottman, J. M., & Bakeman, R. The sequential analysis of observational data. In M. Lamb, S. Soumi, & G. Stephenson (Eds.), *Methodological problems in the study of social interaction.* Madison, Wis.: University of Wisconsin Press, 1979.

Gottman, J. M., & Glass, G. V. Analysis of interrupted time-series experiments. In T. Kratochwill (Ed.), *Strategies to evaluate change in single subject research.* New York: Academic Press, 1978.

Gottman, J., Markman, H., & Notarius, C. The topography of marital conflict: A sequential analysis of verbal and nonverbal behavior. *Journal of Marriage and the Family,* 1977, *39,* 461–477.

Gottman, J., & Notarius, C. Sequential analysis of observational data using markov chains. In T. Kratochwill (Ed.), *Strategies to evaluate change in single subject research.* New York: Academic Press, 1978.

Hall, E. T. *The hidden dimension.* New York: Doubleday, 1966.

Hallinan, M. T., & Tuma, N. B. *Differential effects of classroom characteristics on black and white friendships.* Paper presented at an SRCD study group on the development of friendships, University of Illinois, Champaign, 1978.

Hartmann, D. P. Considerations in the choice of interobserver reliability estimates. *Journal of Applied Behavior Analysis,* 1977, *10,* 103–116.

Hartup, W. W. Peer social organization. In P. Mussen (Ed.), *Manual of child psychology (Vol. 2).* New York: Wiley, 1970.

Hartup, W. W. The origins of friendships. In M. Lewis & L. A. Rosenblum (Eds.), *Friendship and peer relations.* New York: Wiley, 1975.

Hazlett, B. A., & Estabrook, G. F. Examination of agonistic behavior by character analysis. I. The spider crab (*Microphrys bicornutus*). *Behaviour,* 1974, *48,* 131–144.

Hollenbeck, A. R. Problems of reliability in observational research. In G. P. Sackett (Ed.), *Observing behavior (Vol. II).* Baltimore, Md.: University Park Press, 1978.

Huston, T. L., & Levinger, G. Interpersonal attraction and relationships. *Annual Review of Psychology,* 1978, *29,* 115–156.

Jacob, T. Family interaction in disturbed and normal families: A methodological and substantive review. *Psychological Bulletin,* 1975, *82,* 33–65.

Johnson, S. M., & Bolstad, O. D. Methodological issues in naturalistic observation: Some problems and solutions for field research. In L. A. Hammerlynch, L. C. Handy, & E. J. Mash (Eds.), *Behavior change.* Champaign, Ill.: Research Press, 1973.

Jones, R. R., Reid, J. B., & Patterson, G. R. Naturalistic observation in clinical assessment. In P. McReynolds (Ed.), *Advances in psychological assessment (Vol. 3).* San Francisco, Cali.: Jossey-Bass, 1975.

Keenan, E. O. Making it last: Repetition in children's discourse. In S. Ervin-Tripp & C. Mitchell-Kernan (Eds.), *Child discourse.* New York: Academic Press, 1977.

Lewis, M., & Rosenblum, L. A. (Eds.) *Friendship and peer relations.* New York: Wiley, 1975.

Lewis, M., & Rosenblum, L. A. (Eds.). *Interaction, conversation, and the development of language.* New York: Wiley, 1977.

McGrew, W. C. *An ethological study of children's behavior.* New York: Academic Press, 1972.

Meuller, E. The maintenance of verbal exchanges between young children. *Child Development,* 1972, *43,* 930–938.

Murphy, L. B. *Social behavior and child personality.* New York: Columbia University Press, 1937.

Patterson, G. R., Littman, R. A., & Bricker, W. Assertive behavior in children: A step toward a theory of aggression. *Monographs of the Society for Research in Child Development,* 1967, *32,* (5, Serial No. 113).

Piaget, J. *The language and thought of the child.* Cleveland: World Publishing, 1930.

Robinson, W. P. *Language and social behavior.* Harmondsworth, Middlesex, Eng.: Penguin, 1972.

Ryder, R. G. Husband-wife dyads versus married strangers. *Family Process,* 1968, *7,* 233–238.

Sackett, G. P. The lag sequential analysis of contingency and cyclicity in behavioral interaction research. In J.Osofsky (Ed.), *Handbook of infant development.* New York: Wiley, 1977.

Schefflen, A. E. *Body language and social order.* Englewood Cliffs, N.J.: Prentice Hall, 1972.

Schegloff, E. A. Sequencing in conversational openings. *American Anthropologist,* 1968, *70,* 1075–1095.

Selman, R. The development of interpersonal reasoning. In A. Pick (Ed.), *Minnesota symposia on child psychology (Vol. 10).* Minneapolis, Minn.: University of Minnesota Press, 1976.

Shannon, C. E., & Weaver, W. *The mathematical theory of communcation.* Urbana, Ill.: University of Illinois Press, 1949.

Shatz, M., & Gelman, R. The development of communication skills: Modifications in the speech of young children as a function of listener. *SRCD Monographs,* 1973, *38,* (5, Serial No. 152).

Sherif, M., & Sherif, C. W. *Reference groups.* New York: Harper & Row, 1964.

Siegel, S. *Nonparametric statistics for the behavioral sciences.* New York: McGraw-Hill, 1956.

Singleton, L. C., & Asher, S. R. Peer preferences and social interaction among third-grade children in an integrated school district. *Journal of Educational Psychology,* 1977, *69,* 330–336.

Soumi, S. J., & Harlow, H. F. The role and reason of peer relationships in rhesus monkeys. In M. Lewis & L. A. Rosenblum (Eds.), *Friendship and peer relations.* New York: Wiley, 1975.

Stephenson, G. R. Testing for group specific communication patterns in Japanese Macaques. *Symposia of the Fourth International Congress of Primatology,* 1973, *1,* 1–75.

Strain, P. S., Cooke, T. P., & Appoloni, T. *Teaching exceptional children.* New York: Academic Press, 1976.

Weiss, R. L., Hops, H., & Patterson, G. R. A framework for conceptualizing marital conflict: a technology for altering, some data for evaluating it. In L. A. Hammerlynck, L. C. Handy, & E. J. Mash (Eds.), *Behavior change: The fourth Banff conference on behavior modification.* Champaign, Ill.: Research Press, 1973.

Wellman, H. M., & Lempers, J. D. The naturalistic communication abilities of two-year-olds. *Child Development,* 1977, *48,* 1052–1057.

Wiggins, J. S. *Personality and prediction.* Reading, Mass.: Addison-Wesley, 1973.

Wilson, E. O. *Sociobiology: The new synthesis.* Cambridge, Mass.: Harvard University Press, 1975.

Winter, E., Ferreira, A., & Bowers, N. Decision-making in married and unrelated couples. *Family Process,* 1973, *12,* 83–94.

Youniss, J. Another perspective on social cognition. In A. Pick (Ed.), *Minnesota symposia on child psychology (Vol. 9).* Minneapolis, Minn.: University of Minnesota Press, 1975.

7

Commentary

Carroll E. Izard
University of Delaware

Richard A. Shweder
University of Chicago

Willard W. Hartup
University of Minnesota

TRENDS IN RESEARCH ON EMOTIONAL DEVELOPMENT

The speakers and the Institute of Child Development faculty who participated in the 1978 Symposium helped consolidate several trends and highlight various issues in the study of emotions in human development. The observations that will be discussed here represent the interactions of the new knowledge provided by the speakers, questioners, and commentators, and the concepts and feelings (affective-cognitive structures) that I brought with me. The issues range from the earthy matter of getting wider agreement on the names of the things we are studying to measurement problems brought about in part by the currently inadequate differentiation of different levels or classes of emotion concepts.

How Do We Label the Concepts or Constructs in the Emotion Domain?

The problem of terminology is basic to good research. The name or label that we give to a phenomenon serves as part of the conceptual framework for establishing the operations by which we measure it. Kagan (1978) has discussed the problem of terminology in some detail and has considered it one of the major problems confronting us. Some investigators have difficulty deciding whether they are studying emotions or affects, whether these terms are interchangeable, or whether they have different meanings. Some constructs are now called affects that were once called traits or attitudes.

I have suggested that we consider affect as a broad term that encompasses emotions and physiological need states and that we consider as fundamental emotions those that are universally recognized by a distinct pattern of facial behavior. Recent evidence suggests that most of these emotions are identifiable in early infancy—the first 9 months of life. Accepting this definition of fundamental emotions would not restrict us to a small range of concepts, because there is virtually an infinite number of patterns or combinations of fundamental emotions, each having different motivational impact on cognition and behavior. If we take the view that certain emotions are basic by virtue of their universality and are identifiable in early infancy, we can then examine ways in which each of these emotions functions in relation to other developmental processes in the cognitive, social, and motor domains. This approach to naming things makes the assumption that there is heuristic value in a separate nomenclature for emotion, cognitive, and social processes. While holding tightly to this assumption, it is further assumed that there is interdependence and continual interaction between emotion, cognitive, social, and motor processes.

But my approach to naming is not offered as *the* solution. Rather, it is mentioned briefly here for illustrative purposes. I recognize that the problems of terminology will be solved as empirical research demonstrates functional relationships between operationally defined and labeled emotion concepts and concepts in other domains of the personality.

The Ontogeny of Emotions or Emotion Expressions

In deference to the terminological issue just discussed, it seems wise in the discussion of the ontogeny of emotions to restrict ourselves to the concept of emotion expression. We may or may not assume that emotion expressions or emotional behavior is concomitant with an emotion state or felt emotion in consciousness, but in the prelingual infant we have no method of determining precisely the existence or nature of qualities of consciousness.

Knowledge of the ontogeny of emotion expressions is critical. We cannot say much about the relationships between emotional and cognitive development until we know when a particular emotion expression becomes functional in the life of the infant. There are a number of important questions that cannot be answered without such knowledge. What is the frequency of occurrence of the different emotion expressions in daily life? Are there stages in emotional development that relate to the emergence of different emotion expressions and the consequent increase in complexity of the emotion system?

I belive there is a very special problem involved in the study of the ontogeny of emotion expressions. This is the question of whether the emotion of interest can be identified in terms of expressive behavior. Some of us assume that some emotion is present in consciousness at some level of intensity all the time. We recognize that evidence in favor of this assumption relies heavily on our ability to identify the emotion of interest behaviorally.

Systematic study of the ontogeny of emotion expressions is now underway in several laboratories (e.g., Izard, Huebner, Risser, McGinnes, & Dougherty, 1978; Parisi & Izard, 1977; Hiatt, Campos, & Emde, 1977). Investigators in two of these laboratories are also studying the perceived ontogeny of emotion expressions. That is, they are determining when mothers report the emergence of the various expressions in their infants (e.g., Buechler, Izard, & Huebner, 1978; Emde, this volume). The perceived ontogeny is highly important since it is the parent or caregiver's perception and interpretation of the infant's emotion expression that influences parent-infant interactions and relationships.

Emotion–Cognition Relationships

It is rather widely recognized that there is such a thing as attachment or an emotional bond between infant and parent, as well as between lovers and friends. The possibility of relationships or bonds between emotions and symbols is less widely recognized and less discussed and researched. This is not a new issue. Katz and Stotland (1959) defined attitude in such a way as to include an emotion–cognition relationship. Tomkins (1962) discussed idio-affective organizations. Kagan's (1972) definition of motive implies an affective and cognitive component. Building on all of these notions, I have discussed the concept of affective–cognitive structures and the role of such structures in motivation and personality development (Izard, 1977; 1978).

Research such as that reported by Weiner, Kun, and Benesh-Weiner at this Symposium offers the possibility of bridging the increasingly strong area of research in social cognition with research on the development of affective–cognitive structures. Weiner et al. are looking at the emergence of understanding of different emotion concepts. Progress in this line of research could lead to fruitful research on the role of emotion concepts and emotional understanding in social behavior.

The emotions which Weiner et al. have found to be best understood by young children are among those which I have designated as fundamental emotions (e.g., surprise, anger, shame), and those that are least well understood are those I have designated as affective–cognitive structures (e.g., pride). Many of us would probably agree that expressions of anger can be identified in young infants, while the identification of pride must await certain cognitive developments including the development of the concept of self and the ability to make social comparisons.

Developmental Continuity in the Emotion Domain

Kagan and his colleagues (e.g., Kagan, Kearsley, & Zelazo, 1978) have summarized two decades of search for developmental continuities from infancy to adulthood; and they have concluded that the weight of the evidence shows that there are no such phenomena in the cognitive domain. Search for continuities in the emotion domain during this same time span took place largely in terms of the difficult-to-define concept of temperament, a concept which has always been considered to include emotion components. The findings of investigators in this area (e.g., Thomas & Chess, 1977) have been a bit more favorable to the notion of developmental continuities, but the findings from this area have been subject to a number of criticisms and not widely accepted. A recent increase in wider acceptance of temperament research has been brought about in part by improvements in methods of measurement (McDevitt, 1976; Rothbart, 1977).

The work of Scarr and Salapatek (1970) suggested some continuity in emotion thresholds from 6 to 18 months. The work of Ainsworth (1978) demonstrated the existence of apparently important emotion-related behaviors in the first year of life. In particular, she has shown that the one-year-old infant's behavior in the Ainsworth strange situation provides evidence for the reliable classification of infants' attachments to the caregiver as secure, anxious, or avoidant. The 10-year longitudinal study reported by Jeanne and Jack Block at this Symposium suggests continuity in emotion-related variables from 3 to 10 years of age. These new findings on temperament, attachment, adaptiveness, and emotion traits—all emotion-related concepts or variables—suggest that there will be an increasing number of investigators in the search for continuities in the emotion domain.

Emotions and Social Development

Since young infants cannot communicate linguistically, their contacts and interactions with caregivers and other persons is solely dependent on expressive behavior. Such expressive behavior is widely acknowledged to be largely, if not entirely, a function of affect. Thus it appears that the most fundamental of all social relationships (the infant–caregiver attachment) develops as a function of affect expression. The functional importance of expressive behavior or emotion communication is evident in the development of the infant–caregiver attachment. The infant's behavior in the Ainsworth strange situation makes it possible to classify the infant in terms of type of attachment and the type of attachment in turn predicts adaptiveness in the second and third year of life (Sroufe & Waters, 1977; Waters, 1978).

The research reported at this Symposium by Gottman suggests that emotions and affect expressions play a role in the development and continuation of friendship. Although he has not yet worked with specific emotion variables, he sees friendship as defined in part by an affective bond and as serving a number of functions, including therapeutic ones. He sees *reciprocal* kidding and teasing—behaviors that certainly include the expression and eliciting of emotion—as serving a bonding function in developing and maintaining friendship. Perhaps these beginnings in research on emotions and social behavior are not sufficient to predict an increasing trend of activity in this area, but they point clearly to the possibilities of emotion variables increasing our knowledge and understanding of such important phenomena as attachment and friendship.

The Measurement of Emotions in Infants and Children

The future of the trends and the resolutions of the issues discussed in the foregoing pages depend ultimately on the success with which we measure the relevant concepts and variables. First, there is the problem of sorting out the concepts and determining their complexity and their relationships one to the other. It seems to me that emotions and emotion-related phenomena are currently being measured in three different areas, and in each domain measurement is being done at different conceptual levels and with different operations.

Measurements of Variables in the Emotion Area. It is becoming more and more widely accepted that measurement must be focused on one of emotion's three components—the neurophysiological functions, the expressive behavior, or the subjective experience that defines the emotion as a quality of consciousness. For each of these components there are micromeasures and macromeasures. A good example of measurement in the neurophysiological realm is the studies of Schwartz and his colleagues (e.g., Schwartz, Fair, Salt, Mandel, & Klerman, 1976), who have shown predictable relationships between patterns of electromyographic changes in facial muscles and the type of self-induced emotion imagery. They have also shown that the profiles of normals and depressives imagining a typical day are significantly different, with the former looking more like profiles of people imagining a happy situation and the profiles of the latter looking like the profiles of people imagining a sad situation. A good example of a micromeasure of the expressive component of emotion is the application of Ekman and Friesen's *FACS* as reported by Oster and Ekman at this Symposium in 1976 and by Izard at the Second National Conference on Body Language (Izard, Huebner, Risser, McGinnes, & Dougherty, 1978). A good example of a macromeasure of the expressive signals of emotion is the ethological method reported by Strayer at this Symposium and in a recent paper by Charlesworth (1978). While these methods have not yet incorporated a highly differentiated set of emotion variables, the prospect of movement in this direction is highly promising. The contribution of human ethology to the study of emotional development may depend in part, however, on our ability to adapt micromeasures of expression to field research or to come up with entirely new measurement techniques.

The use of systematic self-report measures of emotion states and processes in consciousness was well demonstrated in this Symposium in the paper by Emde. His use of the Differential Emotions Scale to measure changes in moods and emotion states in mothers and in babies as perceived by mothers promises to complement and extend the current research on the development of temperament and the mother–infant relationship.

The Measurement of Emotion-Related Social behaviors. The approaches of Strayer and Charlesworth and other human ethologists are also relevant to this area. Ethologists measure behaviors in natural settings, and a large proportion of such behavior has been demonstrated to be social (Charlesworth, 1978). Ethological observations are often made in the framework of concepts such as aggression or agonistic behavior on the one hand, or withdrawal or escape behavior on the other. These are surely emotion-related social behaviors, but a finer understanding of them and their role in the econiche would surely be facilitated by more highly differentiated emotion concepts.

The seminal work of Ainsworth is an outstanding example of research on emotion-related social behavior, and as already noted, the recent research of Sroufe, Waters, and others has shown that the type of attachment that characterizes the infant's relationship to the caregiver is an important predictor of adaptive behavior from one to three years of life. I consider Gottman's work on friendship another example of a study of emotion-related social behaviors that might be significantly facilitated by the introduction of more discrete measures of emotion concepts.

Emotion-cognition Interactions and Relationships. There are several research beginnings in this area. The approach of Weiner et al. in using social cognition as an index of emotional understanding is one example. Their findings also illustrate a need for finer discriminations among levels of emotion and emotion-related concepts. The previously discussed distinction between anger as a fundamental emotion and pride as an affective–cognitive structure or a function of emotion–cognition interactions illustrates this need. The Blocks successful demonstration of continuities of trait-like phenomena that could be considered as emotion traits or affective–cognitive structures is another example of the measurement of emotion–cognition relations.

Two other types of research represent developments in this area. The first is the use of emotion expressions as indexes of cognitive development. This has been exemplified by Ramsay and Campos (1978), who showed that the smile was the best of several possible indicators of Piaget's stage 4 of the development of the object concept. Charlesworth's work (1969) on emotion response to the misexpected suggests the possibility that reliable indexes of the intensification of interest (or possibly surprise) when expectation is violated might provide a useful benchmark for cognitive development over a wide age range. Indexes of intensification of interest or possibly of surprise at increasingly complex expectancy violations should correlate with increasing cognitive complexity or cognitive growth.

Emotions and Personality Develpment

Due in part to criticisms of the current concepts of traits, in part to a vigorous defense of situational determinants in cognitive psychology, and in part to other sources, personality theory and research has languished for more than a decade. It seems reasonable to expect that personality research and, in particular, research on the development of the self-concept and on personality development will show renewed vigor by virtue of the research reported here, particularly that which shows developmental continuity of indices of emotions, emotion-related traits, and emotion-related adaptive behavior.

Carroll E. Izard

REFERENCES

Ainsworth, M. D. *Patterns of attachment.* Hillsdale, N.J.: Lawrence Erlbaum Associates, 1978.

Buechler, S., Izard, C. E., & Huebner, R. *Mothers' responses to their infants' emotion expressions.* Unpublished manuscript, 1978.

Charlesworth, W. R. The role of surprise in cognitive development. In D. Elkind & J. Flavell (Eds.), *Studies in cognitive development.* London: Oxford University Press, 1969.

Charlesworth, W. R. Ethology: Understanding the other half of intelligence. *Social Science Information,* 1978, *17* (2), 231–277.

Hiatt, S., Campos, J. J., & Emde, R. N. *Fear, surprise, and happiness: The patterning of facial expression in infants.* Paper presented at the Meeting of the Society for Research in Child Development, New Orleans, March 1977.

Izard, C. E. *Human emotions.* New York: Plenum Press, 1977.

Izard, C. E. On the development of emotions and emotion–cognition relationships in infancy. In M. Lewis & L. A. Rosenblum (Eds.), *The development of affect.* New York: Plenum Press, 1978.

Izard, C. E., Huebner, R., Risser, D., McGinnis, G., & Dougherty, L. *The repetory of emotion expressions in infants one-nine months old.* Paper presented at the Conference on Body Language, City University of New York, October 1978.

Kagan, J. Motives and development. *Journal of Personality and Social Psychology,* 1972, *22,* 51–66.

Kagan, J. On emotion and its development: A working paper. In M. Lewis & L. A. Rosenblum (Eds.), *The development of affect.* New York: Plenum Press, 1978.

Kagan, J., Kearsley, R. B., & Zelazo, P. R. *Infancy: Its place in human development.* Cambridge: Harvard University Press, 1978.

Katz, D., & Stotland, E. A preliminary statement to a theory of attitude structure and change. In S. Koch (Ed.), *Psychology: A study of a science* (Vol. 3). New York: McGraw-Hill, 1959.

McDevitt, S. C. *A longitudinal assessment of continuity and stability in temperamental characteristics from infancy to early childhood.* Unpublished thesis, Temple University, 1976.

Parisi, S., & Izard, C. E. *Five-, seven-, and nine-month-old infants' facial responses to twenty stimulus situations.* Unpublished manuscript, 1977.

Ramsay, D. C., & Campos, J. J. The onset of representation and entry into stage 6 of object permanence development. *Developmental Psychology,* 1978, *14,* 79–86.

Rothbart, M. K. *Development of a caretaker report temperament scale for use with 3-, 6-, 9-, and 12-month-old infants.* Paper presented at the Meeting of the Society for Research in Child Development, New Orleans, March 1977.

Scarr, S., & Salapatek, P. Patterns of fear development during infancy. *Merrill-Palmer Quarterly,* 1970, *16,* 53–90.

Schwartz, G. E., Fair, P. L., Salt, P., Mandel, M. R., & Klerman, J. L. Facial muscle patterning to affective imagery in depressed and non-depressed subjects. *Science,* 1976, *192,* 489–491.

Sroufe, L., & Waters, E. Attachment as an organizational construct. *Child Development,* 1977, *48,* 1184–1199.

Thomas, A., & Chess, S. *Temperament and development.* New York: Bruner/Mazel, 1977.

Tomkins, S. S. *Affect, imagery, consciousness* (Vol. 1). *The positive affects.* New York: Springer, 1962.

Waters, E. The reliability and stability of individual differences in infant–mother attachment. *Child Development,* 1978, *49* (2), 483–494.

SCIENTIFIC THOUGHT AND SOCIAL COGNITION

There has been a tendency in the psychological literature to assimilate social cognition to the schemata of science. In this essay I provide a brief and partial corrective by sketching a few of the ways social cognition is more than or other than science.

The image of man as "scientist" ("logician" or "statistician") has an important place in the study of social cognition. In some areas of our lives, both adults and children engage in applied science. When scientific goals are pursued, we evaluate evidence, draw inductive and deductive inferences, make predictions, estimate likelihoods, and construct explanations for what goes with what and what causes what in our social and nonsocial experiences.

The image of man as scientist is not only important; it has certain appealing advantages. Science makes available to us relatively explicit and powerful normative schemata (e.g., J. S. Mill's principles of agreement and difference, the canons of experimental design, Bayes' rules for statistical inference, the canons of propositional calculus, and so forth) that can be applied, and tinkered with, as descriptive models of experimental, statistical, and deductive reasoning in everyday life. Thus, research on man as scientist has flourished, and one can point with satisfaction to progress in our understanding of how ordinary folk evaluate evidence, estimate likelihoods, draw inferences, and so forth. (See, for example, Braine, 1978; D'Andrade, 1974; Estes, 1976; Inhelder & Piaget, 1958; Jones, 1972; Kelley, 1967; Nisbett, Borgida, Crandall & Reed, 1976; & Rosch, 1975, 1978; Ross, 1977; Shweder, 1977; Tversky & Kahneman, 1974; Wason & Johnson-Laird, 1972; also see the chapter by Weiner, Kun, & Weiner this volume.)

Science is not all there is to social cognition, however. The goals, methods, and modes of reasoning of the ordinary social thinker are not typically those of the scientist, and the conceptual schemes of everyday life are not typically designed to serve the needs of man as scientist. To the extent that investigations of social cognition are dominated by the image of man as scientist, much that ought to concern us will be overlooked. To the extent that social cognition is equated with science, much to which we do direct our attention will be misconstrued. The man-as-scientist scheme can be stretched only so far. Some distinctions are called for.

Social Categorization: Prescriptive or Descriptive?

By a category I mean a collection of things that are treated as if they were equivalent (or mutually substituted) for the sake of a particular intellectual enterprise or project (e.g., science, law, aesthetics, etc.). Knowledge is, in part, an understanding of these enterprises, an understanding worth having because it provides us with the criteria we need to distinguish apt categories ("full professors," "tax-exempt income," "uncles," "the letter E") from inept categories ("botanists whose fathers had beards," "Americans living in Colorado who were born with the umbilical cord draped around their necks").

Categories (e.g., "red things") do not have truth-value; they are neither true nor false. A category label or description merely picks out and gathers together certain things for equal treatment in one intellectual enterprise or another, although *one* of these enterprises, namely science, judges the aptness of its categories by their ability to lead to the discovery of truths.

The intellectual enterprise we call science presupposes that the world is "a scene of recurrent kinds of events and changes which exemplify certain regular connexions [Hart, 1961, p. 184]." In keeping with this presupposition, the primary goal of scientific categorization is to collect things together about which one can make inductive generalizations ("things that are hot" are "things that hurt"; "children weaned abruptly from their mother's breast" will become "adults with oral anxieties"). In other words, categorization, from a scientific viewpoint, is a tool for summarizing the regularities of nature (Gilmour, 1937, 1951; Rosch, 1975, 1978).

It follows that a fundamental criterion for judging the aptness of a *scientific* classification is that it be "founded on attributes which have a number of other attributes correlated with them" or alternatively, as Gilmour (1937) proposed, a scientific classification becomes more apt (and less inept) "the more propositions there are regarding its constituent classes [p. 1040]." Thus, as Gilmour notes, "a classification of mankind on the basis of nationality is more natural [apt] than one based on the initial letter of surnames, because more [apt] propositions can be made regarding an Englishman (e.g., that he probably speaks English, knows "God Save the King," has a white skin, etc.) than about a man whose name begins with E [p. 1040]." It seems to me that contemporary theories of category formation, which argue that categories are basically encodings of "real world" correlational structures (e.g., Rosch, 1975; Rosch & Mervis, 1975; Rosch, Mervis, Gray, Johnson, & Boyes-Braem, 1976), have taken the scientific intellectual enterprise as the prototype of all intellectual enterprises, with the attendant risk that scientific thinking may be a poor model of social cognition in general.

Most social categories are not inductive in their intent, nor do they serve the needs of man as scientist. A primary goal of social categorization is to tell the world how it *ought* to behave. Man as rule-maker, legislator, judge, and moralist (in contrast to man as scientist) constructs categories of things the behavior of which, and to which, can be regulated or governed by prescriptions, recommendations, and taboos. What is a "daughter?" Among other things, that's a potentially sexy person with whom one should not have sex. What is a "relative," "wife," "friend," or "employee?" Each is a category defined in large part by sanctionable conduct and obligations. They are prescriptive, not descriptive, in intent; they provide "models for reality," not "models of reality" (Mischel, 1964; Geertz, 1973). For the most part, mapping correlational structure is not what social categorization is about.

There is probably no single criterion for judging the aptness (versus ineptness) of a social category, although the variety of critera that are relevant do not typically seem to involve correlated attributes or propositional power.

The social world is eminently prescriptive. As one enters the world of norms, recommendations, and taboos, one is confronted with diverse forms of conventional, customary, legal, and moral practice and evaluation (e.g., Much & Shweder, 1978; Turiel, 1978a, 1978b) for which the man-as-scientist metaphor seems strikingly inappropriate. The aptness of most social categories seems to have more to do with consensus, tradition, law and moral conviction than with the search for truth. In some cases, a social category, like the categorical inscriptions in our alphabet (e.g., "the letter E"), becomes apt simply because people agree to honor it. It's the done thing.

There is a message in all this for developmentalists concerned with social cognition. Most developmental theorists (e.g., Kohlberg, 1969, 1971; Piaget 1967) assume that earlier forms of understanding become obsolete as they are replaced by newer and more adequate forms of understanding. Pre-Copernican astronomy is replaced by post-Copernican astronomy. Pre-operational thinking is replaced by concrete operational thinking. The image is one of progress and advance.

This developmental image seems most suited to scientific thinking. A criterion such as inductive validity (or propositional richness) can be readily converted into a universal yardstick for comparing various forms of understanding and judging their relative worth. Formal operational thinking can do everything that concrete operational thinking can do, plus more.

The developmental image, however, begins to break down as one moves away from purely scientific thinking. Plato was not replaced by Aristotle, and after 2000 years Platonist and Aristotelian philosophers are still fighting; no resolution is in sight. The same can be said for the various "schools" of social theory currently available. Behaviorists and psychoanalysts have read Piaget; neither group is about to pack up its tent. As Gallie (1968) remarks, there is something "essentially contestable" about social concepts, which is another indication, I believe, that "science" is not what social thought is primarily about. A corollary view is that there is no universal standard of comparative adequacy for judging social concepts (e.g., friendship, kinship, etc.), and that older forms of understanding are not necessarily deficient. Thus, I am not surprised that Gottman and Parkhurst (this volume) expressed some doubt that our adult concepts of "friendship" are any better or more advanced than the "friendship" concepts of young children. Social concepts are characteristically value-laden, and determinations of what should be valued are characteristically dispute-ridden.

Models of change in developmental psychology have been drawn primarily from the world of science, where images of progress and advance dominate. Perhaps models of change for social cognition should be drawn as well from the worlds of fashion, aesthetics, and philology, in which change is incessant yet rarely directional and questions of progress do not typically arise. In the world of fashion, older forms become obsolete only to be renewed. In the world of aesthetics, older forms don't become obsolete. The old (e.g., da Vinci) and the new (e.g., Picasso) co-exist as equally valid forms of representation (see Goodman, 1978). In the world of words and their meanings, older usages do disappear, but the new terms and usages that replace them are just different, not better. The evolution of theories in science may be a Procrustean metaphor for the ontogeny of social understandings.

Social Description:
Main Effects or
Interaction Effects?

Many social scientists aspire to the kinds of knowledge possessed by physicists and chemists; they aspire to reduce social conduct to a small set of universally valid generalizations or laws. The aspiration is a dubious one, and it has produced its fair share of despair (e.g., see Cronbach, 1975). When social thinkers leave their prescriptive enterprises behind and attempt to understand and summarize the regularities of social life, what they discover is a world of complex, context-dependent interaction effects and multiple necessary conditions, not neat main effects or broadly valid generalizations (e.g., see Campbell, 1972).

Of course, all knowledge of regularities, cause and effect relationships, etc., is conditional. This is true for the physicist as well as for the social scientist. The physicist, however, can feel relatively secure that (a) the conditions (e.g., the existence of the sun, the motion of the planets) that interact with particular empirical generalizations in physics change very slowly, if at all, and thus can be safely ignored; and (b) empirical generalizations can be discovered (e.g., the laws of gravitational attraction) which hold across a wide variety of ordinary conditions (see Hart & Honoré, 1973, p. 42). Where the physicist is secure, the social thinker *qua* scientist must wring his hands.

Social conduct does not readily lend itself to description in terms of a small set of universally valid empirical generalizations. We seem to live in a social world in which interaction effects predominate (see e.g., Cronbach, 1975; Geertz, 1973; Mischel, 1968, 1973; Moos, 1968, 1969; Raush, Dittman & Taylor, 1959). In the personality domain, for example, it has been discovered that different situations affect different persons differentially, and the differential effects vary by response mode. The child who seeks attention more than others when adults are absent does not seek attention more than others when adults are present, and the particular reversals that take place for "seeking attention" are not the ones that take place for "seeking help." In the educational domain aptitude per se does not predict response to instructional treatment, and the various aptitude-by-instructional-treatment interaction effects are themselves modified by the sex of the student, and so forth. As Cronbach (1975) remarks,

> Once we attend to interactions, we enter a hall of mirrors that extends to infinity. However far we carry our analysis—to third order or fifth order or any other—untested interactions of still higher order can be envisioned [p. 119].

Moreover, many of these potential higher order interactions (time, place, person, sex, culture, historical epoch, etc.) seem to matter.

Social conduct is the result of multiple necessary conditions of restricted scope. Thus, the generalizations of the social thinker *qua* scientist must be narrowly context-dependent. Moreover, many of the multiple necessary conditions for social conduct are matters of "meaning" (e.g., the actor's interpretation of the situation), which are notoriously subject to fluctuation and rapid change. Thus, "generalizations decay" (Cronbach, 1975). The social world is a world of "meanings," and like the meaning of a word, it won't sit still.

What all this suggests is that it is concrete thinking rather than abstract thinking that has an elevated place in social life; to adequately understand social conduct, one must engage in the unparsimonious proliferation of context-dependent insights. Small differences (in situation, person, sex, time, etc.) make a difference and cannot be overlooked. That is the conclusion demanded by all the evidence on interaction effects, and it is the conclusion drawn by Cronbach (1975): "Though enduring systematic theories about man in society are not likely to be achieved ... one reasonable aspiration is to assess local events accurately [p. 126]," which is of course what clinicians, historians, ethnographers, and ordinary folk living in society have been up to for some time.

The social knowledge of ordinary folk living in society is terribly mundane; like clinical, historical, and ethnographic understanding, it usually involves knowing a lot about the past workings of a person, a setting, or an institution. The organization of this social knowledge is inelegant and complex, and requires, at best, quite low-level inferencing processes. Some of this knowledge is episodic; ordinary folk know what follows what in time. Some of this knowledge is repetitive and context-specific; ordinary folk know how so-an-so behaved last time under such-and-such circumstances. Early work in anthropology and linguistics on "event-structures" (e.g., Pike, 1954) and recent work in social psychology on "scripts" (Schank & Abelson, 1977) is, in part, a recognition that the schemata of social knowledge have little in common with the nomological schemata of the physicist or chemist.

There are two ways professional social scientists have managed to underestimate the context-dependent nature of ordinary social knowledge. One way has been to engage in aggregated actuarial prediction without regard to what happens in any one context or another (see the chapter by Block & Block in this volume). For example, as Cronbach (1975) pointed out:

> A total score on a religious attitude questionnaire turns out to be a fine predictor of response in real life, when the criterion is an average over 100 kinds of relevant activity, saying grace, voicing conscientious objection, etc..... The trait measure, however, has negligible power to forecast what the high scorer is likely to do in any one situation [p. 120].

(For more of this aspect, see Mischel, 1968.)

A second way to underestimate the context-dependent nature of social knowledge has been to focus deliberately on universal concepts, concepts such as intention, justice, cause, etc. Attention to such universal concepts is characteristic of cognitive–developmental researchers (see the chapter by Shultz in this volume). It is an attractive strategy for anyone searching for general laws of social conduct. The strategy is based on the assumptions that (a) behavior is the product of "internal" dispositions and "external" pressures; and (b) if there are universal properties of people (e.g., the intuitive concept of "fairness") and universal properties of the environment, then there will be universal properties of behavior (see Sears, 1961). The difficulty with this strategy is that to identify universal concepts, one must empty them of all specific content (intention to do what? fairness with respect to what?). This is a difficulty because it is precisely the specific content of a concept that interacts with its universal content to produce a behavior. Focusing on universal concepts is like searching for the "real" artichoke by divesting it of its leaves (Wittgenstein, 1958, paragraph 164). Having divested universal concepts of any specific content, the researcher can say very little about social conduct.

Consider, for example, the concept of justice (fairness or equity). This is a concept that has received much attention in the moral development literature. Stated abstractly ("treat like cases alike and different cases differently;" Hart, 1961, p. 155), "justice" may well be a universal principle, along with such concepts as cause, intention, time, space, number, etc. Notice, however, as Hart remarks, that the concept of justice is incomplete. It "cannot afford any determinate guide to conduct. . . . This is so because any set of human beings will resemble each other in some respects and differ from each other in others and, until it is established what resemblances and differences are relevant, 'treat like cases alike' must remain an empty form [p. 155]." To most Americans, for example, there is nothing unjust about denying a 7-year-old the right to vote, enter into contracts, etc. The exclusion of 7-year-olds from the electoral process does not violate our concept of justice. It merely indicates that we subscribe to certain beliefs that in certain relevant respects children are not like adults (e.g., children but not adults lack the information needed to make an informed decision). Historically and cross-culturally, there have been many places in the world where, given received wisdom and without relinquishing a concept of justice, the difference between a man and a woman, one ethnic group and another, has seemed as obvious as the difference between an adult and a child seems to us.

In short, the concept of justice must be formulated at a very general level to count as a universal. However, once it is formulated in such general terms, it can not help us predict how persons or peoples will behave with one another, at least not until we learn all about a person or people's quite special notions of how things are alike and different. To know this, we must examine social cognition (and its development) in context (and in history). We must do what has rarely been done, even by ethnographers: We must learn how to investigate the content-rich, mundane, tacit messages incessantly transmitted in everyday life. Social discourse (see Austin, 1961; Goffman, 1976; Scott & Lyman, 1968; Searle, 1974) may not be the royal road to social cognition, but it is a fine road too little traveled.

Causal Attribution in the Social Arena: Laboratory or Courtroom?

I have argued that *social* cognition is not primarily scientific in intent, and that to the extent that it *is* scientific in intent, the organization of social knowledge is mundane, context-dependent, and concrete, and has little in common with the abstract, law-like formulations of the physicist or chemist. One implication of this view is that ordinarily people satisfy their need for prediction and control by simply knowing a lot about how relevant people have behaved in the past in relevant situations. A second implication is that in ordinary life "the demands of the situation in which we ask for the cause of what has happened, and that in which we are concerned to predict are very different [Hart & Honoré, 1973, p. 43]." Typically in everyday life, as Hart and Honoré note

The "effect" has happened [e.g., a child's leg is broken]: it is a particularly puzzling or unusual occurrence, or divergence from the standard state or performance of something.... When we look for the cause of this we are looking for something, usually earlier in time, which is abnormal or an interference in the sense that it is not present when things are as usual [e.g., a sudden blow with a stick] [p. 43].

Sometimes our search for causes is guided as well by a desire to assign blame, in which case some abnormal occurrences (e.g., the blow) are more relevant than others (e.g., the child was visiting a new friend). The main point, however, is that in everyday life, identifying a cause for an effect may have little to do with prediction. As Hart and Honoré (1973) point out

> We identify a "blow" as the cause of a child's broken leg without caring or knowing what conditions must also be satisfied, if a blow of just that force is always followed by such an injury. When we learn later that the blow would be sufficient only if the bone structure was, as in the chld's case, of less than a certain thickness, nothing is added to the initial statement that this blow caused the injury...[p. 42].

The goal was not to predict or post-dict the effect of a blow of such-and-such intensity. It was to conduct an inquest, in the service of goals other than prediction and control. But what goals? I look forward to the day when attribution theorists move out of the laboratory, relinquish the standardized questionnaire, abandon the context-free hypothetical, and undertake investigations of causal reasoning (including reasons for engaging in it) in everyday life.

Conclusion: Social Understanding as a Distinctive Mode of Thought

What one thinks about has some influence on how one thinks. The interpretive schemata appropriate to the physical world are different from those appropriate to the biological or the social worlds and vice versa. In our own culture, the physical sciences seem to have an elevated position (it is quite the opposite in certain traditional non-Western societies; see Horton, 1967); thus it is perhaps to be expected that the organization of knowledge in physics and chemistry is often adopted wholesale as the ideal for social understanding. Perhaps it was also to be expected that this inappropriate and unrealistic ideal would lead to despair (Cronbach, 1975) and self-denigration (Horton, 1968). Horton, for example, feels disturbingly "on target" when he asks, "Just how far have psychoanalysis, behaviorism, structural-functionalism, and other basic Western theories of higher human behavior really advanced our understanding of ourselves?" He suggests that the social knowledge and understandings of "traditional" peoples "have a surprising amount to say to the psychologist and sociologist [p. 60]." (Also see Peters, 1958, on social knowledge and ordinary language analysis.)

I am not one to romanticize the understandings of everyday life (see

Shweder, 1975, 1977, 1978). However, I do suspect that we not only have much to learn about the prescriptive, concrete, context-dependent, script-like, and inquisitional schemata of mundane social cognition; we also have something to learn from ordinary social thought. Given our scientific respect for rigorous and systematic observation, we may one day even be able to surpass it.

Richard A. Shweder

REFERENCES

Austin, J. L. A plea for excuses. J. Austin (ed.), In *Philosophical papers*. London: Oxford University Press, 1961.

Braine, M. D. S. On the relation between the natural logic of reasoning and standard logic. *Psychological Review*, 1978, *85*, 1–21.

Campbell, D. T., Herskovits, Cultural relativism and metascience. In F. Herskovits (Ed.), *Cultural relativism*. New York: Random House, 1972.

Cronbach, L. J. Beyond the two disciplines of scientific psychology. *American Psychologist*, 1975, *30*, 116–127.

D'Andrade, R. G. Memory and the assessment of behavior. In T. Blalock (Ed.), *Measurement in the social sciences*. Chicago: Aldine-Atherton, 1974.

Estes, W. K. The cognitive side of probability learning. *Psychological Review*, 1976, *83*, 37–64.

Gallie, W. B. Essentially contested concepts. In *Philosophy and historical understanding*. New York: Schocken Books, 1968.

Geertz, C. *The interpretation of cultures*. New York: Basic Books, 1973.

Gilmour, J. S. L. A taxonomic problem. *Nature*, 1937, *139*, 1040–1042.

Gilmour, J. S. L. The development of taxonomic theory since 1851. *Nature*, 1951, *168*, 400–402.

Goffman, E. Replies and responses. *Language in Society*, 1976, *5*, 257–313.

Goodman, N. *Ways of worldmaking*. Indianapolis: Hackett Publishing Co., 1978.

Hart, H. L. A. *The concept of law*. London: Oxford University Press, 1961.

Hart, H. L. A., & Honoré, A. M. *Causation in the law*. London: Oxford University Press, 1973.

Horton, R. African traditional thought and Western science. *Africa*, 1967, *37*, 50–71, 159–187.

Horton, R. Neo-Tylorianism: Sound sense or sinister prejudice, *Man*, 1968, *3*, 625–634.

Inhelder, B., & Piaget, J. *The growth of logical thinking from childhood to adolescence*. New York: Basic Books, 1958.

Jones, E. E. *Attribution: Perceiving the causes of behavior*. Morristown, N.J.: General Learning Press, 1972.

Kelley, H. H. Attribution theory in social psychology. In D. Levine (Ed.), *Nebraska Symposium on Motivation* (Vol. 15). Lincoln: University of Nebraska Press, 1967.

Kohlberg, L. Stage and sequence: The cognitive–developmental approach to socialization. In D. A. Goslin (Ed.), *Handbook of socialization theory and research*. New York: Rand McNally, 1969.

Kohlberg, L. From is to ought: How to commit the naturalistic fallacy and get away with it in the study of moral development. In T. Mischel (Ed.), *Cognitive development and epistemology*. New York: Academic Press, 1971.

Mischel, W. *Personality and assessment*. New York: Wiley, 1968.

Mischel, W. Towards a cognitive social learning reconceptualization of personality. *Psychological Review*, 1973, *80*, 252–283.

Moos, R. H. Situational analysis of a therapeutic community millieu. *Journal of Abnormal Psychology*, 1968, *73*, 48–61.

Moos, R. H. Sources of variance in responses to questionnaires and in behavior. *Journal of Abnormal Psychology,* 1969, *74,* 405–412.

Much, N. C., & Shweder, R. A. Speaking of rules: The analysis of culture in breach. In W. Damon (Ed.), *New directions for child development: Moral development.* San Francisco: Jossey-Bass, 1978.

Nisbett, R. E., Borgida, E., Crandell, R., & Reed, H. Popular induction: Information is not necessarily informative. In J. S. Carroll & J. W. Payne (Eds.), *Cognition and social behavior.* New York: Halsted, 1976.

Peters, R. S. *The concept of motivation.* New York: Humanities Press, 1958.

Piaget, J. *Six psychological studies.* New York: Random House, 1967.

Pike, K. L. *Language in relation to a unified theory of the structure of human behavior, Part 1.* Glendale, Calif.: Summer Institute of Linguistics, 1954.

Raush, H. L., Dittman, A. T., & Taylor, T. J. Person, setting, and change in social interaction. *Human Relations,* 1959, *12,* 361–377.

Rosch, E. Universals and cultural specifics in human categorization. In R. W. Brislin, S. Bochner, & W. J. Lonner (Eds.), *Cross-cultural perspectives on learning.* New York: Wiley, 1975.

Rosch, E. Principles of categorization, In E. Rosch & B. B. Lloyd (Eds.), *Cognition and categorization.* Potomac, Md.: Lawrence Erlbaum Associates, 1978.

Rosch, E., & Mervis, C. B. Family resemblances: Studies in the internal structure of categories. *Cognitive Psychology,* 1975, *7,* 573–605.

Rosch, E., Mervis, C. B., Gray, W. D., Johnson, D. M., & Boyes-Braem, P. Basic objects in natural categories. *Cognitive Psychology,* 1976, *8,* 382–439.

Ross, L. The intuitive psychologist and his shortcomings: Distortions in the attribution process. In L. Berkowitz (Ed.), *Advances in experimental social psychology* (Vol. 10). New York: Academic Press, 1977.

Schank, R., & Abelson, R. *Scripts, plans, goals, and understanding.* Hillsdale, N.J.: Lawrence Erlbaum Associates, 1977.

Scott, M., & Lyman, S. Accounts. *American Sociological Review,* 1968, *33,* 46–62.

Searle, J. R. *Speech acts.* London: Cambridge University Press, 1974.

Sears, R. Transcultural variables and conceptual equivalence, In B. Kaplan (Ed.), *Studying personality cross-culturally.* New York: Harper and Row, 1961.

Shweder, R. A. How relevant is an individual difference theory of personality? *Journal of Personaltiy,* 1975, *43,* 455–484.

Shweder, R. A. Likeness and likelihood in everyday thought: Magical thinking in judgments about personality. *Current Anthropology,* 1977, *18,* 637–648. Reprinted in P. N. Johnson & P. C. Wason (Eds.), *Thinking: Readings in cognitive science.* London: Cambridge University Press, 1978.

Turiel, E. The development of concepts of social structure: Social convention. In J. Glick & A. Clarke-Stewart (Eds.), *Personality and social development* (Vol. 1). New York: Gardner Press, 1978. (a)

Turiel, E. Social regulations and domains of social concepts. In W. Damon (Ed.), *New directions for child development: Social cognition.* San Francisco: Jossey-Bass, 1978. (b)

Tversky, A., & Kahneman, D. Judgment under uncertainty: Heuristics and biases. *Science,* 1974, *185,* 1124–1131.

Wason, P. C., & Johnson-Laird, P. N. *Psychology of reasoning.* London: B. T. Batsford, 1972.

Wittgenstein, L. *Philosophical investigations.* New York: Macmillan, 1958.

TOWARD A SOCIAL PSYCHOLOGY
OF CHILDHOOD
TRENDS AND ISSUES

Early investigators conceived the essence of socialization to be the assimilation of an asocial infant/child into a complex society. Children themselves were not assigned a central role in this process, nor were children viewed as socializing creatures as well as creatures to be socialized (Rheingold, 1969). "Miniature theories of social action" (Sears, 1959) were the wellsprings of this early research, by means of which an accounting was made for the inculcation of such generalized traits as aggression, dependency, and achievement.

The individual's integration into society is currently conceived in somewhat different terms, i.e., the ensuring that genetic material survives through equilibrative interaction with the social environment. Socialization consists of the interaction between a changing child and a changing world and involves both assimilation and accommodation. An active, rather than a passive, organism is its basis. Such views require that research workers be alert for "built in" features of the social repertoire and for evidence that the child exerts an influence on other individuals in addition to being influenced by them.

Every childhood social action must be examined as an element in social interaction, and social relations must be examined in terms of *reciprocal causalities* (cf., Klein, Jorgensen, & Miller, 1978)—either *linear* (as when A causes some change in B), *synchronous* (as when A and B simultaneously produce some change in each other), or *cyclic* (as when causal cycles recur through time). To study socialization it is necessary to examine children's motivations to maintain contact with other individuals as well as the complementary motivations of the individuals with whom they interact. The great need in contemporary socialization research is for "miniature theories of social *inter*action" rather than for "miniature theories of social action."

Systems Issues

Everyone recognizes that the social world of the child consists of many worlds—e.g., family system, peer system, and the school. The child's earliest social experiences involve the family—a complex unit whose composition varies widely according to ecological and cultural circumstance (Feiring & Lewis, 1978). The intricate interrelations existing within this social network are becoming much clearer as a consequence of observational studies in infancy and early childhood (cf. Emde, this volume), particularly since contemporary investigators are concerned with the manner in which these interrelations play themselves out over time rather than with their structure at a single point. Intro-familial relations, of course, have been examined in many longitudinal studies, including the long-term investigations conducted at the Fels Research Institute and the University of California, Berkeley. But those studies do not seem to have been originally conceived in terms of social reciprocities cycling through time. Post hoc analyses have revealed relatively stable "central orientations" that suggest such a view of the child's socialization (cf. Bronson, 1969), but the effects of family social structures on child development have been otherwise difficult to detect.

Peer relations and social institutions (e.g., schools) become significant socialization contexts early in childhood, and remain so. These milieus contribute much more extensively to the growth of various social competencies than was appreciated in earlier decades. In fact, it is difficult now to understand how the child can achieve full maturity in social awareness and communication, affect regulation, and the maintenance of enduring social relations in the absence of commerce with individuals outside the nuclear family. Social engagements within the family are not likely to be egalitarian; but at the same time, egalitarian experiences seem to be necessary for the advancement of certain basic social and cognitive skills (Piaget, 1932; Sullivan, 1953). Strayer's research (this volume) illustrates how various hierarchies, especially linear hierarchies based on observation of dominance behaviors among nursery school children, mark the peer system. Considerable variation exists from group to group in the symmetry and stability of these structures, but their vestiges are built into peer relations from very early in childhood. Affective and cognitive correlates of social structuring, as well as developmental changes, have been examined. Such studies elucidate the organizational complexities of the peer system, setting the stage for investigations to determine the role of peer relations in the behavioral development of the individual child.

The interdependencies existing among the family system, the peer system, and the school as a social system are not well understood. Does the nature of the social adaptation in the infant-mother dyad determine the effectiveness of the child's adaptation in the peer culture? Does the attainment of "trust" in early family relations determine the outcomes of aggressive socialization in later peer relations? Does the self-esteem generated in the child's interactions with the mother determine either the quantity or the quality of social interaction with other social agents? Such questions have been asked repeatedly by child development researchers, but are asked now with a new urgency. Sooner or later, Emde's work should tell us more about these conjunctions, especially the linkage between early family relations and early peer relations. Studies of individual differences in ego-resiliency and ego-control by the Blocks (this volume) also stress continuities in the coping mechanisms employed by the child across social systems.

Ecological Views

Earlier methodologies in socialization research (e.g., retrospective maternal interviews and laboratory "analog" experiments) have been criticized for their lack of ecological validity. The issues involved in these controversies are complex and have been debated extensively. Two central issues are: (a) the weakness of the current data base for making generalizations to socialization in the naturalistic context; and (b) the lack of a data base which illuminates the manner in which social activity is adapted to the situation in which it occurs. More writing has been devoted to the first issue than the second, even though the two issues are interrelated.

The studies contained in this volume reflect an ecological concern in different ways. Strayer, for example, has obtained an excellent naturalistic account of one social system of which the child is a member—the same-age peer group. The methodology involved was direct observation; the categorization and coding strategies were meticulous and extensive. Sample size was small, however, a factor that should not be overlooked, because hierarchical variations were extensive from group to group. Gottman's work illustrates a more indirect concern with the problem of ecological validity. The very fact that the investigator listened to the conversations taking place between friends, rather than asking the children about them, is a step toward a clearer conception of friendships and their role in child development. Obtaining representative naturalistic samples of conversations between friends, however, is a difficult task; consequently, the constraints of the laboratory have not been removed entirely from this work.

The other studies included in this volume provide even more indirect indications of concern with ecological issues. The Blocks, for example, have sampled the child's behavior in an enormous number of testing and observational situations, illustrating their commitment to divergent rather than converging measurement strategies. Many of their "situational" tests, however, are highly contrived. The experiments by Shultz and by Weiner Kun, and Benesh-Weiner were aimed at encouraging the child to reveal what he/she knows about the social world through direct discourse, but with probes into the child's social understanding that were uncontaminated by the immediate situational context.

This volume contains relatively little research directed at the second ecological issue just mentioned—the manner in which the behavior of the individual child is adapted to the situational context. Yet the microenvironment needs to be studied systematically in order to understand the manner in which physical setting, task demands, and the actors involved affect the course of social development. Interaction with fathers is different from interaction with mothers; interaction with agemates is different from interaction with non-agemates; certain interactions occur differently in small and large spaces; and social organization is not the same in play and in "work." These situational vicissitudes are themselves central issues when socialization is conceived as an adaptive process.

One can also contend that the cultural context—i.e., the macro-environment—should be studied as an ecological niche. Patterns of social interaction need evaluation in terms of their adaptational significance in the cultural milieu, as well as within the microenvironment. Again, cross-cultural comparisons are needed not merely to establish the outer limits on the generalizations that can be made from empirical work, but rather to understand the intricate processes by which social activity combines with elements of the "ecosystem" to determine the survival of the genetic material. The volume at hand provides no examples of this kind of thinking or data-gathering, but these remain relatively rare in the literature as a whole.

Developmental Issues

Childhood socialization must be studied in developmental terms. What does this mean? To be concerned with development suggests, first, attention to continuities and discontinuities in various social activities (e.g., harm-doing, nurturance-giving, and achievement-striving) during the years before maturity. A developmental view, however, suggests more than an examination of individual differences in the frequency of certain behaviors at different times in the lives of infants, children, and adolescents. Attention must be paid to changes across the life-span in the morphology and functioning of the various behavior systems, the organization and reorganization of various cognitive and "not-so-cognitive" structures as these constrain social activity (cf. Block & Block, this volume), and the role of social experience in the development of normative attitudes toward oneself and others. Although thousands of studies have been devoted to the interrelations between parent characteristics and characteristics of their children (and additional thousands of investigations devoted to the conditions that mediate behavior maintenance and change), a surprisingly small number deal with socialization within a true developmental perspective.

Early changes toward a developmental social psychology could be detected several years ago in research on the origins of social relations in infancy. Not only was attachment reassessed as a developmental phenomenon (even though Freud had pioneered in this direction decades previously), but research workers established basic norms with respect to the behavioral repertoire involved in early attachment relations—e.g., smiling, vocalizing, crying, following, visual preferences, auditory discrimination of social stimuli, and stranger fear. These norms greatly enlarged our understanding of the manner in which the social repertoire originates and becomes organized in the service of adaptive objectives. Emde's work (this volume) continues in this tradition and contributes importantly to it.

Other work in this volume elaborates on the notion that socialization may be constrained by cognitive and language development as well as by social vicissitudes. Although cause-and-effect linkages between general cognitive development and social/cognitive development are virtually impossible to establish, these studies reveal that: (a) language usage is related to both social relations and developmental status (Gottman, this volume); (b) the child's conceptions of intentionality depend on both context and developmental status (Shultz); and (c) children's use of attributions relating to achievement striving are similarly sensitive (Weiner, Kun, Benesh-Weiner).

To elaborate: In most previous investigations, the relations between children and their friends have been studied within a nondevelopmental framework. Although certain continuities were discovered across early, middle, and late childhood in the correlates of social attraction (cf. Hartup, 1970), the interrelations among cognitive, affective, and social factors in children's interactions with their associates have received little attention. How does the development of communicative skills constrain children's interaction with their friends? How do children utilize social information at various ages in relation to friendship status? Is friendship status involved in affect regulation and how does this linkage change over time? How do social expectations alter social attraction as children grow older?

Gottman's work (this volume) is a rare example of research on children's interactions with their friends within a developmental framework. The results show that complexities and nuances in children's communications with their friends appear to be greater among older children than among younger children but, in other instances, communications seem to become more inefficient, more telescoped, and less elaborate as children grow older. Indeed, this work could serve as a prototype because it extends normative knowledge about a significant social network involved in childhood socialization and also suggests certain ways that cognitive development may be linked to it. This volume contains, too, an elegant accounting by Shultz of the manner in which developmental status constrains children's understanding of intentionality. Since intentional attributions play an important role in social interaction among adults, the significance of this information about origins can hardly be overestimated.

Historical Issues

The social worlds of children are in constant flux. Social environments are unstable, in some degree, from day to day and month to month, but they also change historically (Baltes, Cornelius, & Nesselroade, 1978). Since social adaptation refers explicitly to the fitness of behavior within a specific environmental context, childhood socialization must be conceived in relation to changing rather than to static environments. The study of childhood socialization thus becomes a complex enterprise focussed on changing individuals in changing worlds.

Students who are interested in socialization processes, as distinguished from substantive elements, may find historical analysis to be of little interest. But every substantive datum dealing with socialization is the product of a particular time and a particular place, and is thus constrained. Long-cited literature in our field needs reevaluation, across epochs, to test its current applicability. In addition, historical analysis needs to be used to test certain notions about cause-and-effect—e.g., the relation between family structure and sex-role development. Significantly, none of the contributors to this volume has dealt effectively with the changing individual in relation to long-term changes in the world. Could the editor have located such a contributor? It is doubtful. But maybe such a contributor can be found for the 20th volume in this series.

Toward a Synthesis

Research on social, cognitive, and affective development has become more "integrative" in many laboratories, both in the United States and abroad. Earlier studies of the processes of socialization have been augmented to include thorough examination of the connections between social behavior and intellective processes—including the child's understanding of social phenomena and the role of cognitive processes as mediators in social and affective development. Impetus for this synthesis comes from many quarters: the rediscovery of Piaget's theorizing about the relation between social experience and cognitive development, the application of information-processing models of cognitive functions to the individual's reactions to social events, and contemporary trends in ego psychology. Affective variables have reentered research on socialization after a long hiatus; the new look in much socialization research bears more than a superficial resemblance to the likes of Freud, Sullivan, and Erikson.

The participants in the 1978 Minnesota Symposium clearly possess interests in these "connections" and a willingness to break away from the classical divisions such as socialization, cognitive development, and emotional functions. There is a strong indication that our ultimate objective is not to understand the child as social cognizer, social learner, social perceiver, or social actor, but rather, to understand the development of "persons." This goal does not consist of a vague intuitive understanding of some essence of the "whole child" but involves a clear articulation of those interdependencies among actions and among individuals that will make better predictions possible about the course of the "persons" growth and development.

A new synthesis cannot actually be found in the present volume—either in the individual contributions or in the collection as a whole. But a new synthesis in the social psychology of childhood seems imminent, nevertheless.

Willard W. Hartup

REFERENCES

Baltes, P., Cornelius, S., & Nesselroade, J. Cohort effects in behavioral development: Theoretical and methodological perspectives. In W. A. Collins (Ed.), *Minnesota symposia on child psychology Vol. 11.* Hillsdale, N.J.: Lawrence Erlbaum Associates, 1978.

Bronson, W. C. Stable patterns of behavior: The significance of enduring orientations for personality development. In J. P. Hill (Ed.), *Minnesota symposia on child psychology* (Vol. 2). Minneapolis: University of Minnesota Press, 1969.

Feiring, C., & Lewis, M. The child as a member of the family system. *Behavioral Science,* 1978, *23,* 225–233.

Hartup, W. W. Peer relations and social organization. In P. H. Mussen (Ed.), *Carmichael's manual of child psychology* (Vol. 2). New York: Wiley, 1970.

Klein, D. M., Jorgensen, S. R., & Miller, B. C. Research methods and developmental reciprocity in families. In R. M. Lerner & G. B. Spanier (Eds.), *Child influences on marital and family interaction.* New York: Academic Press, 1978.

Piaget, J. *The moral judgement of the child.* Glencoe, Ill.: Free Press, 1932.

Rheingold, H. L. The social and socializing infant. In D. A. Goslin (Ed.), *Handbook of socialization theory and research.* Chicago: Rand McNally, 1969.

Sears, R. R. Personality theory: The next forty years. In B. R. McCandless (Ed.), Iowa Child Welfare Research Station, State University of Iowa: The fortieth anniversary. *Monographs of the Society for Research in Child Development,* 1959, *24,* (3, Whole No. 74).

Sullivan, H. S. *The interpersonal theory of psychiatry.* New York: Norton, 1953.

Contributors

Jeanne Block and *Jack Block* hold doctorates in psychology from Stanford University, where they began their long-term involvement in research on personality and its development. Both are now at the University of California, Berkeley, where Jeanne Block is Research Psychologist in the Institute of Human Development and Jack Block is Professor of Psychology.

Robert N. Emde, M. D., is a graduate of the Columbia University College of Physicians and Surgeons and the Denver Institute of Psychoanalysis. He is currently Professor of Psychiatry, University of Colorado Medical Center.

John M. Gottman earned his doctorate in clinical psychology at the University of Wisconsin and is now Associate Professor of Psychology at the University of Illinois. *Jennifer Parkhurst* completed her undergraduate education at the University of Colorado and is now pursuing doctoral studies in psychology at Illinois.

Thomas R. Shultz, who holds a doctorate from Yale University, is Associate Professor of Psychology at McGill University. During 1978 and 1979, he was a visiting scholar at the University of Oxford, England.

F. F. Strayer earned his doctorate at Simon Fraser University and formerly taught at York University. He is now Professor of Psychology at the Université du Québec à Montréal.

Bernard Weiner, Professor of Psychology at the University of California, Los Angeles, earned his doctorate at the University of Michigan and spent 1970 and 1971 as a Guggenheim Fellow at Ruhr University, Bochum, Germany. Before UCLA, he was a member of the psychology faculty at the

University of Minnesota. *Anna Kun* received her doctorate at UCLA and is now Assistant Professor of Psychology at the University of California, Santa Barbara. *Marijana Benish-Weiner* holds a doctorate from UCLA, where she is engaged in research on moral development from an attributional perspective.

Author Index

Subject Index